JavaServer Faces

A Practical Approach
for Beginners

B.M. Harwani

Managing Director
Microchip Computer Education (MCE)
Ajmer

PHI Learning Private Limited

New Delhi-110001
2009

Rs. 325.00

JAVASERVER FACES—A Practical Approach for Beginners
B.M. Harwani

© 2009 by PHI Learning Private Limited, New Delhi. All rights reserved. No part of this book may be reproduced in any form, by mimeograph or any other means, without permission in writing from the publisher.

Trademarks
Java, J2EE, and JCP are trademarks or registered trademarks of Sun Microsystems, Inc. in the United States and other countries.
NetBeans, Sun, Sun Microsystems, the Sun logo, Java and Solaris are trademarks or registered trademarks of Sun Microsystems, Inc. in the United States and other countries.
MySQL is a registered trademark of MySQL AB in Sweden and other countries. MySQL is a trademark in the United States and other countries.
"Apache Tomcat" and "Tomcat" are trademarks of the Apache Software Foundation.
The Eclipse Foundation and Eclipse projects have created a number of trademarks and logos to identify the Eclipse community and individual Eclipse projects. In addition to the 'Eclipse' trademark, the Eclipse Foundation has introduced seven trademarks and logos:
Eclipse Foundation Member,
EclipseCon,
Eclipse Summit,
Built on Eclipse,
Eclipse Ready,
Eclipse Incubation and
Eclipse Proposals.
RED HAT and JBOSS are registered trademarks of Red Hat, Inc. and its subsidiaries in the United States and other countries. Other company, product and service names may be trademarks or service marks of others.

Screenshots are provided under Apache License.

ISBN-978-81-203-3709-1

The export rights of this book are vested solely with the publisher.

Published by Asoke K. Ghosh, PHI Learning Private Limited, M-97, Connaught Circus, New Delhi-110001 and Printed by Mudrak, 30-A, Patparganj, Delhi-110091.

To my Mother
Nita Harwani
*Whatever I am today is just
because of moral values taught by her*

*To all scientists
who participated in
successful launch of Chandrayaan-I*

Contents

Preface

JavaServer Faces is a new exciting technology emerged for developing web applications based on Java technologies. Developed by Java Community Process (JCP), JSF is strongly supported by all major vendors.

Since JSF supports RAD (Rapid Application Development) style of application development, web developers can quickly develop powerful applications using drag and drop technology. Also JSF provides standard APIs and tag libraries required to build web-based user interfaces. Besides this, JSF also has a rich API which can be used to build custom User Interface (UI) components, custom validation classes (validators), and server-side event listeners. JSP provides a large collection of pre-built UI components which a developer can use directly to make web applications.

To add more, JSF uses Model View Controller (MVC) design pattern to develop the applications which are easier to maintain.

Through this book, I have tried to explain how to use major UI components practically with complete running examples. Step by step approach is used for making custom converters, validators and components with screen shots and explanation of statements used at each step. Also explained how to make JSF based applications using NetBeans IDE. The idea behind writing this book is to provide a professional, developer and a trainer a step by step practical approach to understand the basic controls of JSF and how to use them in real life applications.

Chapter 1 introduces JSF architecture, its life cycle and its main components, and also covers a brief introduction of JSF tag libraries. Chapter 2 explains the installation steps of the softwares required to run and implement JSF. It includes the steps to create and run a simple JSF application, and also how to create Managed Bean and set the navigation rules to move from one web page to another. It also covers how to write properties file and use in JSF. Chapter 3 includes expression language and its use, to access Managed Bean attributes. Chapter 4 presents a practical usage of different components like text field, text area, image, command button, menu, listbox, checkbox, radio button, panelgrid, panelgroup, datatable, selectmany checkbox, etc. Every component is explained with a running program as they act as a building block for any web application. Chapter 5 deals with the use of standard converters in JSF. It also covers the usage of DateTime converter, Number converter and the step by step creation of custom converters. Chapter 6 provides the use of validation in web applications and the application of some validations to a web page. It explains in depth how to create custom validators by creating custom validators like phone number validator, email id validator and so on. Chapter 7 explores event objects in JSF and demonstrates with running example how the action methods and event listeners are applied in web applications. Chapter 8 describes different navigation rules and the application of static and dynamic navigation to a web application. Chapter 9 discusses the features of NetBeans IDE, and explains how the simple controls like Drop down control, Listbox, Radio button group, Checkbox group are used in NetBeans. It also explains how to create Managed Bean and how to apply navigation rules to an application via NetBeans. Finally it covers the usage of validation and converters with NetBeans and how to make custom validator and to use data time converter. Chapter 10 includes all the steps required in creating custom components. Two custom components: label component and email components are created and explained. It also explains the registration of the custom UI component in faces-config.xml file. Chapter 11 elaborates the installation of JBoss tools, eclipse and different jar files to apply Ajax to JSF application. The creation and deployment of RichFaces and Ajax4Jsf application are also explained step by step.

Any suggestions of improving this book will be highly appreciated. I am accessible at bmharwani@yahoo.com

B.M. HARWANI

1

JavaServer Faces: An Overview

LEARNING OBJECTIVES

In this chapter, we will learn:

- What JSF is
- How JSF is better than Struts
- What the architecture of JSF is
- How JSF works and what its life cycle is
- About the main components of JSF
- About the JSF tag libraries

JavaServer Faces (JSF) has emerged as a latest technology for developing web applications. So, it is time to understand what JSF is and what its different components are. Also, we will see how these components play their role in the execution of web applications.

INTRODUCTION

JavaServer Faces (JSF) is a new exciting technology for developing web applications based on Java technologies. It was developed by Java Community Process (JCP), a community of web application experts from different groups like Jakarta Struts, Oracle, Sun, IBM, ATG, etc. The objective was to create a standard framework for developing web applications with rich user interfaces.

The JSF specification was developed under JCP as JSR 127, which released JSF 1.0 and 1.1, and JSR 252 which released JSF 1.2.

JSF is a server-side technology used for building Java-based web applications that run on the server side, and render the user interface back to the client. This technology provides web application life cycle management through a controller servlet. Users can even create their own custom user interface components in this technology.

The JavaServer Faces (JSF) technology provides:

- A rich API that we can use to build custom User Interface (UI) components, custom validation classes (validators), and server-side event listeners.
- A set of JSP tags that generate HTML form elements that can be bound to JavaBean properties.

Comparing JSF to Apache Struts

JSF has become the first choice of web developers because of the flexibility that it provides. JSF is able to accomplish everything Struts can, plus more.

Advantages of Struts

Some of the advantages of Struts are as follows:

- It is a mature and proven framework deployed successfully on many projects.
- Uses the front controller and command patterns and can handle sophisticated controller logic.
- Supports declarative exception handling and internationalization.
- Availability of lots of documentation and reference materials.
- Large developer base.
- Broad tool and IDE support.
- Open source.

Disadvantages of Struts

Some of the disadvantages of Struts are as follows:

- Struts is very JSP-centric.
- Struts does not hide details of the Java language to web developers.
- Action forms are linked programmatically to the Struts framework.

JSF is an evolution of a few frameworks, including Struts. It is better than Struts in various ways.

Advantages of JSF

Some advantages of JSF are as follow:

- JSF is a specification from Sun. All major vendors provide strong support for JSF.
- JSF uses the page controller pattern and therefore, aids in page rich applications.
- JSF has a well-defined request life cycle. We can build our own render toolkit. Separating the rendering portion from the controller portion of the framework allows extensibility.

- Because JSF has a rich component model, it favours a RAD (Rapid Application Development) style of development. We can now build web pages using **drag and drop** technology.

Disadvantages of JSF

The disadvantages of JSF are as follows:

- JSF is still quite new and evolving.
- The goal of JSF is more oriented to RAD, through which powerful applications **can be** built using a set of reusable components.
- Struts navigation is more flexible and can support more complex **controller logic.**

JSF ARCHITECTURE

JSF uses Model-View-Controller (MVC) design pattern to develop the applications **which are** easier to maintain.

MVC

In MVC design, a client (browser) sends a request to the server. The web server **receives the** request, populates the request object with the various parameter values from the **client and sends** it to the servlet. The servlet which acts as a controller, analyzes the request, **then will interact** with the model (JavaBeans) that executes the various application business **logic and then** chooses which view to be shown to the Client. The MVC design pattern splits **an application** design into three separate parts: Model, View and Controller.

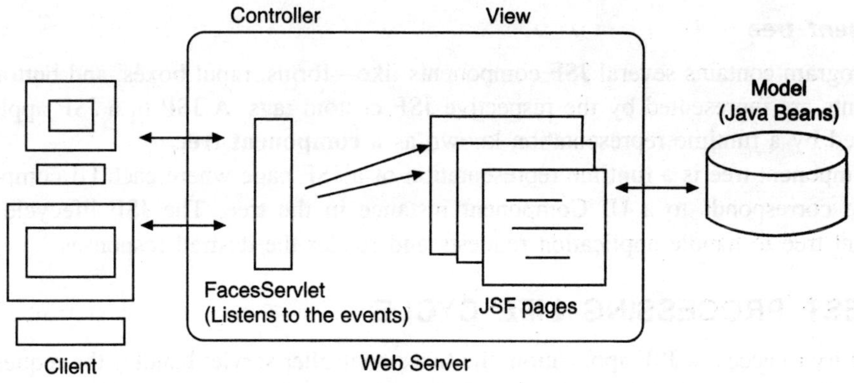

Figure 1.1 A MVC design.

Model represents data and handles business operations. The **view** handles output. It accesses the model to retrieve data for display. The **controller** handles input and manipulates the model or changes the view accordingly in response to user input.

How JSF Works

A JSF application consists of several things like—JavaServer Pages (JSP), JavaBean, deployment descriptor file, application configuration file, etc.

Event handling in JSF is managed by a special servlet called the FacesServlet. That is, when an event like clicking a button or pressing an Enter key occurs, the event notification is sent to the server. On the server is a web container that contains this special servlet: FacesServlet to handle the event.

FacesServlet

The FacesServlet acts as the front controller and handles all JSF-related requests. It works as an engine for all JSF applications. Its does the following jobs:

- Handles all JSF related requests.
- Builds component tree of the JSP whose control fires an event.
- Accesses all JSP pages in the application.
- Creates an event object and passes it to a registered listener.

The servlet FacesServlet manages the request processing life cycle in JSF applications. It creates an object called *FacesContext*, which contains the information necessary for request processing. When a JSF page is first requested, JSF builds a new, empty component tree (runtime representation of a JSF page) and saves it in the FacesContext instance.

Since, all requests must be directed to this servlet, this job of passing all requests to this servlet is done with the help of deployment descriptor file: web.xml (explained in detail in Chapter 2). For the time being it is enough to understand that the deployment descriptor file has a servlet-mapping element in it which is used to map a particular URL pattern to the FacesServlet.

Component tree

A JSP program contains several JSF components like—forms, input boxes, and buttons. These components are represented by the respective JSF custom tags. A JSP in a JSF application is represented by a runtime representation known as a **component tree.**

A component tree is a runtime representation of a JSF page where each UI component tag in a page corresponds to a UI Component instance in the tree. The JSF lifecycle uses the component tree to handle application requests and render the desired responses.

REQUEST PROCESSING LIFE CYCLE

When we try to access a JSF application, the faces controller servlet handles the request by first preparing the object called FacesContext that holds all application data. The controller then routes the user to the requested page. The page usually renders application data from the JSF context using a simple Expression Language (EL). Upon subsequent requests, the controller updates the model data according to the input.

During processing, FacesContext is the object that is modified. The series of actions necessary for JSF request processing by the life cycle object is referred to as the request processing life cycle (Figure 1.2).

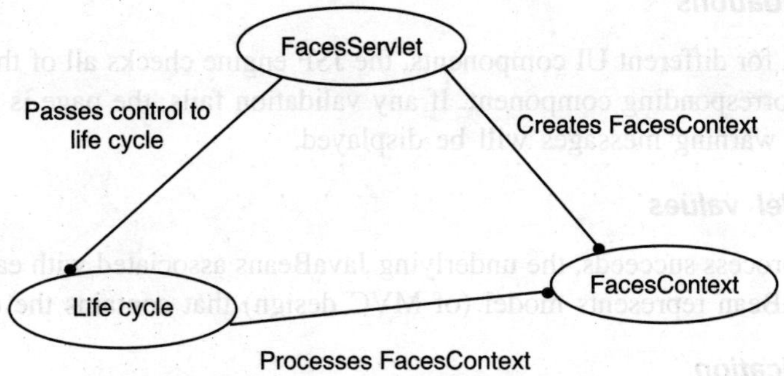

Figure 1.2 Request Processing Life Cycle.

JSF LIFE CYCLE

When a request is sent to the JSF engine, it creates a tree containing a set of *components*. This component tree is used to process the request, and an appropriate response is generated for the user. The FacesServlet accomplishes this in six steps (Figure 1.3).

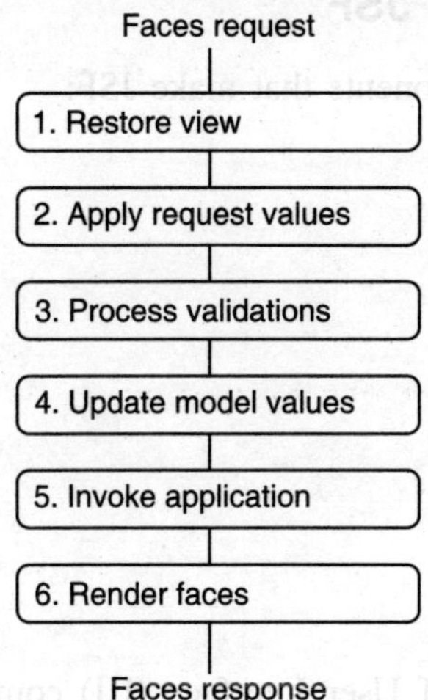

Figure 1.3 JSF Life Cycle.

1. Restore view

The restore view phase is where the JSF engine produces the component tree, which is a runtime representation of a JSF page where each UI component tag in a page corresponds to a UI component instance in the tree. This tree is used for all of the subsequent processing stages.

2. Apply request values

In this phase, client is provided a view where he/she feeds data to be assigned to corresponding UI components.

3. Process validations

On receiving data for different UI components, the JSF engine checks all of the input validators associated with corresponding component. If any validation fails, the page is rendered with the original data and warning messages will be displayed.

4. Update model values

If the validation process succeeds, the underlying JavaBeans associated with each UI component are updated. JavaBean represents model (of MVC design) that contains the data.

5. Invoke application

After the model has been updated, the JSF engine invokes any business logic actions requested by the user.

6. Render response

In this phase, the response is sent back to the client application. The FacesContext object is updated before rendering the response to the client.

MAIN COMPONENTS OF JSF

The following are the main components that make JSF:

- UI components
- Renderer
- Validator
- Backing beans
- Converter
- Events and event listeners
- Messages
- Navigation

UI Components

JSP provides a large collection of User Interface (UI) components that are used to get user response and to make web applications. UI components are a stateful objects built as JavaBeans which live on the server side (not on the client) and they have properties, methods, and have event handling mechanism. The thing to remember is that the UI components cannot render by itself, they need renderers to represent themselves. There are several renderers associated with every UI component, as a result JSF UI components render according to the capability of the client, i.e., depending on the client type, suitable version of UI component is rendered.

Note: A component cannot render itself, it just represents the properties and the behaviour of the control. It is the responsibility of the renderer to display the component. The rendering is handled separately by renderer components in JSF in the form of renderer kits. Sun's JSF implementation comes with the standard HTML rendering kit.

Renderers

A component cannot render itself. It is the responsibility of the renderer to display the component and translate the user input values into the values that the component can understand. The JSF component architecture is designed in such a way that the component classes maintain a component's state. A component can work with many renderers. The JavaServer Faces implementation includes a standard renderKit for rendering to an HTML client. Renderers create a visual representation for the client.

Validators

Validators are used for confirming that the data entered by the user is correct or not. JavaServer Faces technology supports a mechanism for validating a component's local data during the process validations phase, before model object data (JavaBean attribute) is updated. Model object data is updated only in case the data entered is valid.

JSF supports several Validator classes that are used for validating data of different types. The list of Validator classes is as follows:

Table 1.1 Validator Classes and its Description

Validator Class	Description
`DoubleRangeValidator`	Validates that an input field provides a value that may be converted to a double
`LengthValidator`	Validates that an input field provides a string (or a value that may be converted to a string) and that its length is within the supplied maximum and minimum values
`LongRangeValidator`	Validates that an input field provides a string that may be converted to a long and that it is within the supplied maximum and minimum values
`RequiredValidator`	Validates that an input field has a value that is not null. If the value is set to a string, the length of that string must be one character or more.
`StringRangeValidator`	Validates that an input field provides a string and that it is within the supplied maximum and minimum values.

Backing Beans

A backing bean defines UI component properties. A typical JavaServer Faces application includes one or more backing beans, which are server-side objects associated with UI components used in the page. Backing beans are basically JavaBeans which contain logic and properties of the UI components. It also defines methods that perform functions associated with a component, which include validation, event handling, and navigation processing. We use a JSF EL expression to bind the value of a UI component with a specific backing bean property.

Example:

```
<h:inputText id="Roll" value="#{UserBean.userRoll}" />
```

In this example, UI Component is a text box with id: Roll. UserBean is the backing bean and the data entered by the user in the text box will update the UserBean's attribute: userRoll. In other words, this JSF EL expression binds the Roll component's value to the UserBean. userRoll backing bean attribute.

Typically we have one backing bean per JSF page. For a backing bean to be available when the application starts, *we register it as a managed bean* with a name and scope in application configuration file: `faces-config.xml`.

Managed bean

The backing beans of a JSF application when defined in the application configuration file (`faces-config.xml`) is known as *managed bean*. They are defined in `faces-config.xml` file using the managed-bean element type, within which the name of the bean, the fully qualified class name of the bean along with some descriptive information can be declared. A configuration file can contain any number of managed beans.

Managed beans are standard Java classes that are used to represent the user inputs. They may even act as listeners and can handle the appropriate actions. Each managed-bean element registers a JavaBean that JSF will instantiate and store in the specified scope. The scope defines how long this bean object is valid. Possible values for scope are **session, request** and **application**.

Brief description of different scopes.

Application: It means the JavaBean object is valid for the whole application i.e. it will exist until the application terminates and can be used by all the users of the application.

Request: It means the JavaBean object is accessible by all web pages processing the same request.

Session: It means the JavaBean object is available only for the current session. The moment browser is closed or session is timed out or is destroyed the JavaBean object becomes unavailable.

The managed-bean element is defined in Figure 1.4.

The managed-bean-name specifies the name that will be used to refer to the JavaBean throughout the application.

The managed-bean-class element contains the fully qualified class name for the JavaBean.

The managed-bean-scope element defines the scope of the JavaBean. The possible values for this element are application, session, request, or none.

For example, consider this bean configuration:

```
UserBean in faces-config.xml
<managed-bean>
<managed-bean-name>UserBean</managed-bean-name>
<managed-bean-class> User</managed-bean-class>
<managed-bean-scope>session</managed-bean-scope>
. . .
</managed-bean>
```

In above managed bean, the class name is User class which will be referred in application by name UserBean.

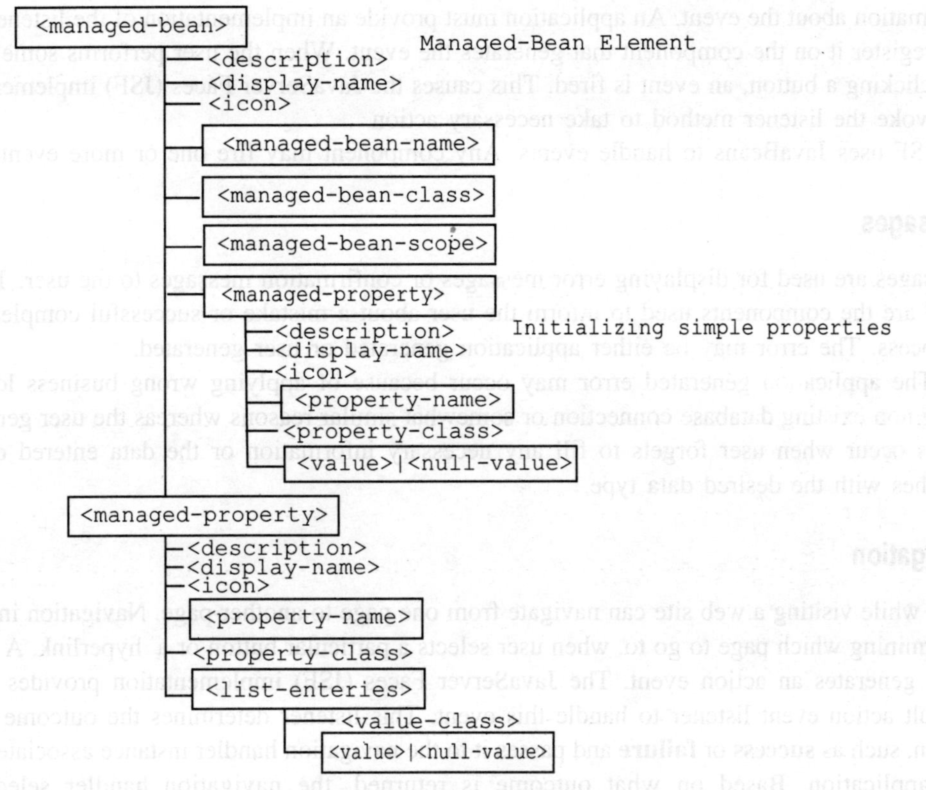

Figure 1.4 Managed-Bean elements.

Converters

Every request that is passed from the client to the server is interpreted as a string value only. The string object has to be manually converted to the appropriate data type before being processed. JSF provides converters for common types like dates, boolean or numbers, etc. Moreover, user can develop additional custom converters to suit his needs.

Example:

```
<h:outputText value="#{UserBean.dateBirth}" >
<f:convertDateTime pattern="MMM-dd-yyyy"/>
</h:outputText>
```

As we can see in the above example that the *dateBirth* before being displayed is first converted in *MMM-dd-yyyy* format. For example: Jan-15-2009.

Events and Event Listeners

JavaServer Faces technology defines listener and event classes for handling events generated by UI components. An Event object identifies the component that generates the event and stores information about the event. An application must provide an implementation of the listener class and register it on the component that generates the event. When the user performs some action like clicking a button, an event is fired. This causes the JavaServer Faces (JSF) implementation to invoke the listener method to take necessary action.

JSF uses JavaBeans to handle events. Any component may fire one or more events.

Messages

Messages are used for displaying error messages or confirmation messages to the user. That is, these are the components used to inform the user about a mistake or successful completion of a process. The error may be either application generated or user generated.

The application generated error may occur because of applying wrong business logic or using non existing database connection or somewhat similar reasons whereas the user generated errors occur when user forgets to fill any necessary information or the data entered doesn't matches with the desired data type.

Navigation

User while visiting a web site can navigate from one page to another page. Navigation involves determining which page to go to, when user selects a particular button or a hyperlink. A button click generates an action event. The JavaServer Faces (JSF) implementation provides a new default action event listener to handle this event. This listener determines the outcome of the action, such as **success** or **failure** and passes it to the navigation handler instance associated with the application. Based on what outcome is returned, the navigation handler selects the appropriate page by consulting the application configuration file.

In other words, it is the navigation handler which is responsible for deciding which page to load depending on the outcome of an action method.

Navigation rule

Each navigation rule defines how to get from one page to the other pages of the application. The navigation rule elements can contain any number of navigation-case elements, each of which defines the page to open next on the basis of outcome.

Example:

```
<navigation-rule>
   <from-view-id>/index.jsp</from-view-id>
      <navigation-case>
         <from-outcome>login</from-outcome>
         <to-view-id>/login.jsp</to-view-id>
      </navigation-case>
      <navigation-case>
         <from-outcome>newuser</from-outcome>
         <to-view-id>/newuser.jsp</to-view-id>
      </navigation-case>
</navigation-rule>
```

This code states that if the outcome is *login* from the `index.jsp file`, then navigate to `login.jsp file` and if the outcome is `newuser`, then navigate to `newuser.jsp file`.

The outcome can be defined by the action attribute of the UI command component that submits the form:

Example:

```
<h:command_button id="submit" action="login" label="Login" />
```

In above example, we can see that the UI command component is a button with id: "submit" and when we click this button, it will return an outcome: "login".

The from-view-id element is the identifier of the page of origin.

The navigation-case element represents a possible target. A navigation-rule element can have zero or several `navigation-case` sub-elements. Each navigation-case element specifies the target page for a particular outcome. An outcome can come from the action attribute of the UI command component in the from-view-id element.

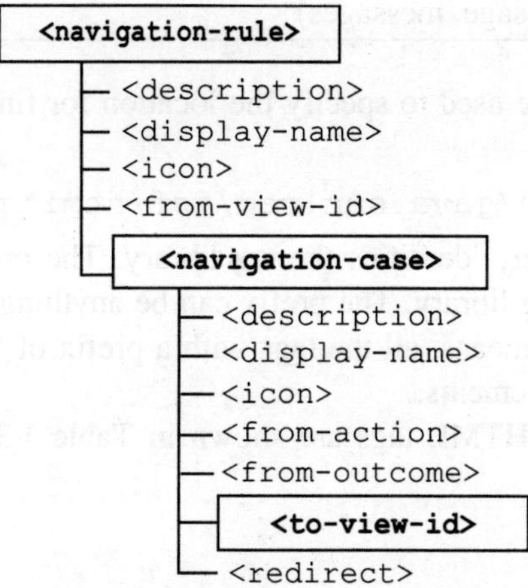

Figure 1.5   Navigation rule hierarchy.

The to-view-id element specifies the target page. The from-outcome value is the outcome of processing the page of origin i.e. the page defined in from-view-id element.

A JSP page consists of a collection of tags.

What are TAGS

Tags in JSP represents a task or an action that we want to perform in a page.
For example:

```
<h:form>
```

This tag creates an input form to receive data from the user and sends it to the server

```
<h:outputText>
```

This tag displays a line of text

A set of tags represent a tag library. In JSF, two categories of tag libraries are available:

JSF HTML Tag Library

The html tag library defines tags for representing common HTML user interface components. The HTML components are like text fields, buttons, form, etc. HTML tags can be divided into different categories (Table 1.2).

Table 1.2 Categories of HTML tags

Inputs	(inputText, inputTextarea)
Outputs	(outputText, outputLabel)
Commands	(commandButton)
Selections	(selectOneRadio, selectOneListbox, selectOneMenu for radio buttons, list boxes, menu, etc.)
Layouts	(panelGrid)
Data tables	(dataTable)
Errors and messages	(message, messages)

In JSF, the taglib directive used to specify the location for finding the JSF HTML tags that define HTML elements is:

```
<%@ taglib uri="http://java.sun.com/jsf/html" prefix="h" %>
```

The uri attribute value uniquely identifies the tag library. The prefix attribute value is used to distinguish tags from other tag library. The prefix can be anything like 'h' or anything else. But in case, we use prefix: 'h', it means, all the tags with a prefix of 'h' are considered as JSF tags that represent HTML form elements.

The list of standard JSF HTML tags are shown in Table 1.3.

JSF Core Tag Library

The core tag library provide tags which are responsible for categorizing the various UI elements in the form, to provide validation and conversion, to manage event listeners for a particular UI component and so on. The tags in jsf core library are independent of any rendering technology and can therefore be used with any render kit.

Recall, that a component cannot render itself. It is the responsibility of the Renderer to display it on the client. A render kit defines how component classes map to component tags appropriate for a particular client. The JavaServer Faces implementation includes a standard render kit for rendering to an HTML client.

In JSF, the taglib directive used to specify the location of the JSF core tag library is shown as:

```
<%@ taglib uri="http://java.sun.com/jsf/core" prefix="f" %>
```

Again, the uri attribute value uniquely identifies the tag library. The prefix can be anything like "f" or anything else. If we use prefix: "f", it means, all the tags with a prefix of "f" are considered as JSF core tags.

Table 1.3 Standard JSF HTML tags

Component Tag	Description
h:column	Configures template columns for an <h:dataTable> component.
h:commandButton	Creates a UI button to submit a form to the application.
h:commandLink	Creates a link to another page or another location on the page.
h:dataTable	Creates a data table on the page.
h:form	Creates an input form. The inner tags of the form receive the data that will be submitted with the form.
h:graphicImage	Displays an image on the page
h:inputHidden	Creates a field invisible to the user, typically used to pass variables from page to page.
h:inputSecret	Creates a password input field.
h:inputText	Creates a simple user input text field.
h:inputTextarea	Creates a user input text area for multiple lines of text.
h:message	Receives the first message for the component.
h:messages	Receives all queued messages for the component.
h:outputFormat	Displays a localized message.
h:outputLabel	Displays a nested component as a label for a specified input field.
h:outputLink	Links to another page or location on a page without generating an action event.
h:outputText	Displays a line of text.
h:panelGrid	Creates container table for other components.
h:panelGroup	Creates a container to group a set of components under one parent.
h:selectBooleanCheckbox	Creates a simple yes/no user checkbox.
h:selectManyCheckbox	Creates a set of checkboxes from which the user can select multiple values.
h:selectManyListbox	Creates a set of items, all displayed at once, from which a user can select multiple items.
h:selectManyMenu	Creates a set of items from which a user can select multiple items.
h:selectOneListbox	Creates a set of items, all displayed at once, from which a user can select one item.
h:selectOneMenu	Creates a set of items from which a user can select one item.
h:selectOneRadio	Creates a set of radio buttons from which the user can select one value.

The list of JSF core tags are shown in Table 1.4.

Table 1.4   JSF core tags

f:view	Creates the top-level view
f:subview	Creates a subview of a view
f:attribute	Adds an attribute to a component
f:param	Constructs a parameter component
f:converter	Adds an arbitrary converter to a component
f:converterDateTime	Adds a datetime converter to a component
f:converterNumber	Adds a number converter to a component
f:actionListener	Adds an action listener to a component
f:valueChangeListener	Adds a valuechange listener to a component
f:validator	Adds a validator to a component
f:validateDoubleRange	Validates a double range for a component's value
f:validateLength	Validates the length of a component's value
f:validateLongRange	Validates a long range for a component's value
f:facet	Adds a facet to a component
f:loadBundle	Loads a resource bundle, stores properties as a Map
f:selectitems	Specifies items for a select one or select many component
f:selectitem	Specifies an item for a select one or select many component
f:verbatim	Adds markup to a JSF page

These tags are practically used and explained through running programs in coming chapters.

SUMMARY

So, now we know what are the components in JSF and how they effect a web application development.

In this chapter we have learnt:

- Introduction of JSF
- JSF architecture and its life cycle
- Main components of JSF and their role
- About JSF tag libraries

Now that we've learned how JSF internally works, we can now go ahead with installation of JSF and get wet by making and executing small web applications.

REVIEW QUESTIONS

1.1   What is the role of FacesServlet in JSF?

1.2   What are backing beans?

1.3   What do you mean by navigation in JSF?

1.4   What do you mean by MVC design?

2

Setting Up JSF

In this chapter, we will learn:

- About Installing JSF
- About creating and running first JSF web application
- About creating managed bean
- How Servlet mapping is done in deployment descriptor file: web.xml to invoke FacesServlet
- To specify page navigation rules and managed bean in application configuration file: faces-config.xml
- How properties file can be used in a web application

A deep understanding of these initial starters will make it easier for us to make larger web applications using JSF HTML tags and JSF expression language explained in forthcoming chapters.

BEFORE BEGINNING WITH JSF INSTALLATION

Before beginning with installation of JSF, we must have JDK (Java Development Kit) installed on our computer. So, first of all install JDK1.5 or any higher version available. Just download its setup file from the net and double click on it and JDK will be automatically installed on our machine. Also set the Environment variable JAVA_HOME to specify the location where JDK is installed. To do so, select MyComputer->View system information->Advanced ->Environment Variables->New and enter the location of the folder where JDK is installed as shown in Figure 2.1.

Figure 2.1   Setting Java_Home Environment variable.

INSTALLING JSF

For successful JSF installation, following steps are necessary:

1. Installing JSF compliant web container (also called web server), like Apache Tomcat, IBM WebSphere, etc. We are using Tomcat for our examples.
2. Downloading JSF Reference Implementation.
3. Copying JSTL library in web container's lib directory.
4. Setting up classpath for library files.

Installing Tomcat

Tomcat is a web container where our JSP pages and servlets are deployed (stored). The job of the web container is to handle execution of the JSP pages and servlets and provide necessary services that are required for running a web application like: threading, resource pooling, security, authentication etc.

When a client needs to access a JSP page, it makes a request to the web container via browser and the web container executes the desired JSP page and responds back to the client by sending HTML code to its browser.

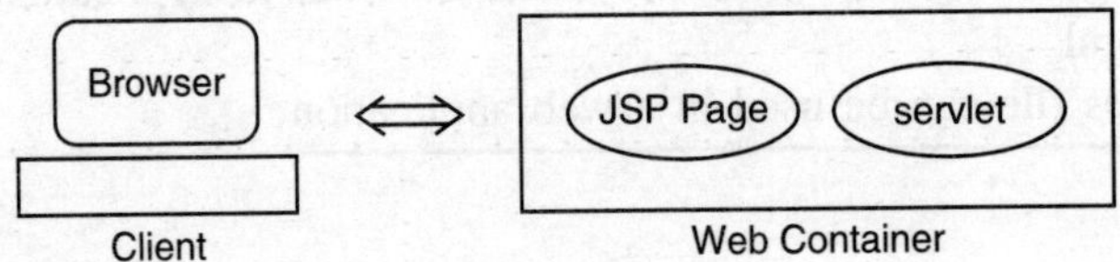

We are going to install Tomcat in this section.

Steps for installing Tomcat are as follows:

1. Go to `http://tomcat.apache.org` and download the latest version of tomcat. I have downloaded `tomcat apache-tomcat-6.0.14.zip` file for developing and testing the examples in this book.
2. Unzip the downloaded file to a folder say `C:\apache-tomcat-6.0.14` (it can be any folder).
3. Go to bin sub folder of the folder where tomcat is unzipped and type 'catalina run' and press Enter key. This should generate the output shown in Figure 2.2.

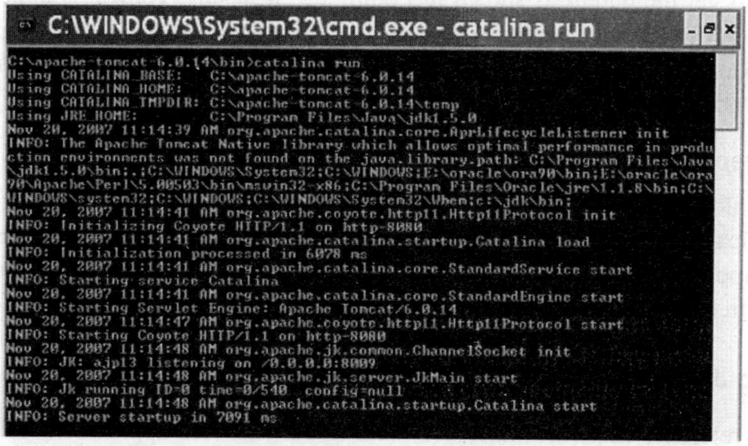

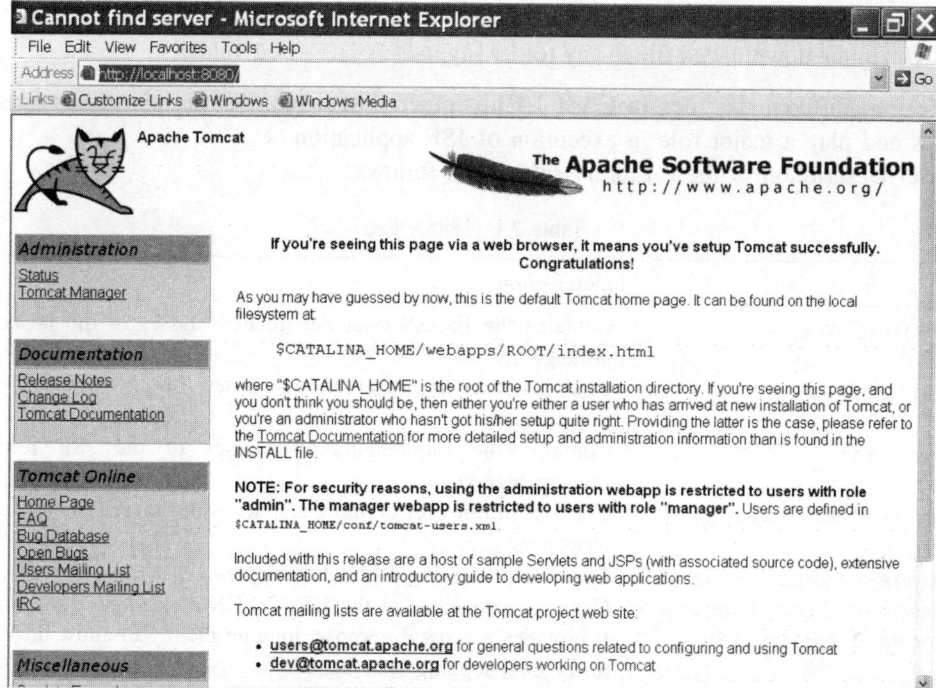

Figure 2.2 Tomcat starting up.

If we get the output as shown in Figure 2.2, it means Tomcat is successfully started and is in running mode.

4. Now to test whether Tomcat server is up and is working, open the browser and point it at following address `http://localhost:8080/`, the browser should display the Tomcat server home page as shown in Figure 2.3.

Figure 2.3 Display of Tomcat Server Home Page.

If we don't get the output as shown in Figure 2.3, it means, Tomcat is either not installed properly or is not in running mode. In that case, again download the Tomcat zip file from net and assure yourself that its files are properly unzipped in the given folder. Check it again by giving command: `catalina run` in the bin sub folder.

What just happened?

We have downloaded and installed Tomcat — a web container, we will be using for deploying our web applications. We can even use other servers like Oracle Application Server or IBM WebSphere Application Server, etc. I have preferred Tomcat server as it is open source and is available for free. It supports multiple platforms and is easy to install.

Downloading JSF Reference Implementation

We need JSF reference implementation for running our JSF web applications as it contains the tag libraries. The reference implementation consists of compiled java code (that we will be requiring for using different UI (user interface) components and event listeners also known as JSF libraries) which are in the form of jar files. The java class files are stored in compressed form in jar files.

To install reference implementations, the steps are as follows:

1. Go to `https://javaserverfaces.dev.java.net/` and download the reference implementation of `JSF 1.1` or higher version. We have used JSF1.1 reference implementation in this book.
2. Unzip the downloaded file to any folder say in `C:\jsf-1.1` folder.

We find different jar files in C:\jsf-1.1\lib folder. These jar files are also known as JSF libraries and play a major role in execution of JSF application.

Brief Description of these Library Files is as follows.

Table 2.1 Library files

Library File	Description
`jsf-api.jar`	Contains the FacesServlet and related classes in the javax.faces package
`jsf-impl.jar`	Contains the implementation classes of the JSF reference implementation
`jsf-ri.jar`	Contains the implementation classes of the JSF reference implementation
`commons-beanutils.jar`	Contains utilities for defining and accessing JavaBeans component properties
`commons-digester.jar`	Used for processing XML documents
`commons-collections.jar`	Contains extensions of the Java 2 SDK collections framework
`commons-logging.jar`	It provides a general purpose, logging facility to allow developers to try their logging statements

Directory Structure of Our Web Application

To make any web application in Tomcat, we usually make a directory in its webapps folder. Suppose, we want to make a web application by name "trial". So, we create a directory by name trial in C:\apache-tomcat-6.0.14\webapps folder.

In the trial directory, we create a sub directory by name: WEB-INF. In WEB-INF directory, we create two sub directories by name: classes and lib.

The structure of our web application may appear as:

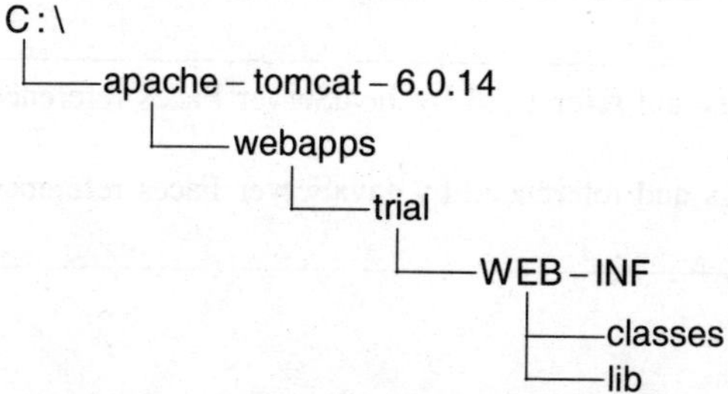

Each directory is meant for some purpose like :

trial– it is for storing all jsp programs

WEB-INF– it is for storing application configuration file: faces-config.xml and deployment descriptor file : web.xml

classes– it is for storing JavaBean files

lib– it is for storing JSF libraries (jar files)

Copy all the JSF library files (jsf-api.jar, jsf-impl.jar, commons-beanutils.jar, commons-collections.jar, commons-digester.jar and commons-logging.jar) from C:\jsf-1.1\lib folder into lib folder of our trial application i.e. in C:\apache-tomcat-6.0.14\webapps\trial\WEB-INF\lib folder.

Note: Copy two jar files: jsf-api.jar and jsf-impl.jar from C:\jsf-1.1\lib folder into lib folder of our tomcat server i.e. into C:\apache-tomcat-6.0.14\lib folder.

OTHER JAR FILES

Beside above jar files, JSF framework uses the JavaServer Pages Standard Tag Library (JSTL) also to implement custom actions and it is assumed that the web container we use provides the necessary JAR files for JSTL. In other words the Tomcat server must provide these jar files: `jstl.jar` and `standard.jar`. We need to copy these jar files in our web application's lib directory.

Copying JSTL Library Files in Web Application's Lib Directory

1. Download the files from Internet if not provided by Tomcat server.
2. Copy JSTL library comprising `standard.jar` and `jstl.jar` files from `C:\apache-tomcat-6.0.14\webapps\examples\WEB-INF\lib` folder

(if tomcat server provides) into "`apache tomcat 6.0.13\webapps\trial\WEB-INF\lib`" directory trial is a directory of our web application.

We have copied the `jstl.jar` and `standard.jar` files into our web application folder as the tags defined in these jar file are used in a JSF applications. JSTL supports common tasks such as iteration, conditional processing, parsing, internationalization and database access.

Description of JSTL library files is shown in Table 2.2.

Table 2.2   JSTL library files

Library File	Description
`jstl.jar`	Required to use JSTL tags and referenced by JavaServer Faces reference implementation classes
`standard.jar`	Required to use JSTL tags and referenced by JavaServer Faces reference implementation classes

Setting the Classpath for Jar Files

To set up classpath for the jar files copied, following steps are followed:

1. We select `My Computer->View system information->Advanced tab->Environment Variables->New`.

2. Create an environment variable Classpath with following contents:

   `C:\apache-tomcat-6.0.14\lib\servlet-api.jar;C:\apache-tomcat-6.0.14\lib\jsf-impl.jar;`

   `C:\apache-tomcat-6.0.14\lib\jsf-api.jar;` see Figure 2.4.

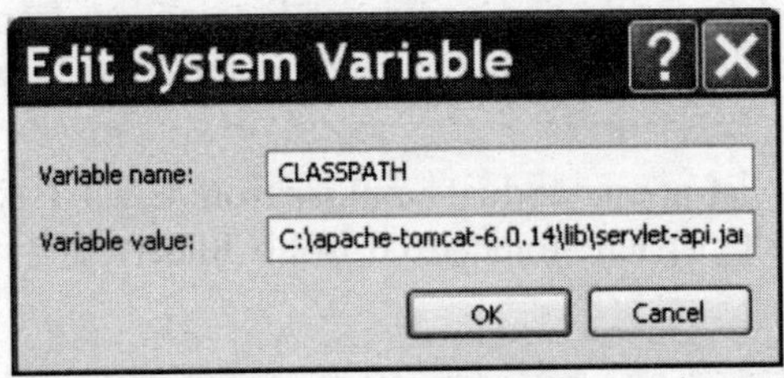

Figure 2.4   Enter the required path and press OK.

Note: The servlet-api.jar file is used for compiling our JavaBean class files. So, we have to include it in the CLASSPATH along with JSF reference implementation jar files.

Now, since JSF is successfully installed, we can jump right away creating our first web application.

CREATING A 'BLANK SLATE' FOR OUR APPLICATION

All web applications use a standard directory structure. We can deploy a Web application as a collection of files that use this directory structure, known as exploded directory format, or as an archived file called a WAR file.

This directory structure contains a directory called WEB-INF which contains the deployment descriptors and two subdirectories for storing compiled Java classes and library JAR files. These subdirectories are respectively named classes and lib. Let's make a blank slate of a directory structure and deployment descriptors which will be required in all web application that we will be making soon.

Setting up Folders

1. Create a directory "`trial`" under "`apache-tomcat-6.0.14\webapps`" folder. We can create directory by any other name also.
2. Create `WEB-INF` directory under "`apache-tomcat-6.0.14\webapps\trial`" folder.
3. Create classes and lib directories under "`apache-tomcat-6.0.14\webapps\trial\WEB-INF`" folder.
4. In all, the structure of our trial application will be as shown in Figure 2.5.

```
trial
        index.jsp
    WEB-INF
            faces-config.xml
            web.xml

        classes
        lib
                commons-beanutils.jar
                commons-collections.jar
                commons-digester.jar
                commons-logging.jar
                jsf-api.jar
                jsf-impl.jar
                jstl.jar
                standard.jar
```

Figure 2.5 Structure of trial application.

So far we have only the folders—so we will have to add the files in a minute.

We created a folder called trial, which is to be the name of our web app. When it's done, users will access it using `http://servername/trial`.

The `WEB-INF` folder designates the root for all internal application files. This folder contains the application deployment descriptor (`web.xml`) file, application configuration file (`faces-config.xml`) and sub folders for other resources like java class files, libraries, etc.

The reason why we need to create `WEB-INF` folder is that JSF applications are the standard Java web applications in which all pieces like user interface files, class files, libraries, etc. must be packaged in a directory structure and then deployed as a `WAR` (Web Application Archive) file in a web container. A web container is used for providing runtime environment to Java web applications. We have used Apache Tomcat as a web container for our applications.

Note: `WEB-INF` folder is created in uppercase and is inaccessible to the browser.

Within that, we will use the classes folder used to store the JavaBean and its class files. JavaBeans are used for holding the data entered by user and also for performing certain processing on the basis of user actions.

The lib folder is to store Java Archive (JAR) files which are required for all JSF applications. JAR files are nothing but the compressed form of Java class files.

Next, we need to create those XML files that go in our WEB-INF folder.

Creating `web.xml`

1. Create a deployment descriptor (web.xml) file in the WEB-INF folder.
2. Enter the following content and save the file:

```xml
<?xml version='1.0' encoding='UTF-8'?>
<!DOCTYPE web-app PUBLIC
"-//Sun Microsystems, Inc.//DTD Web Application 2.3//EN"
"http://java.sun.com/dtd/web-app_2_3.dtd">

<web-app>
<!-- Faces Servlet -->
  <servlet>
    <servlet-name>Faces Servlet</servlet-name>
    <servlet-class>javax.faces.webapp.FacesServlet
    </servlet-class>
    <load-on-startup> 1 </load-on-startup>
</servlet>

<!-- Faces Servlet Mapping -->
  <servlet-mapping>
    <servlet-name>Faces Servlet</servlet-name>
    <url-pattern>/faces/*</url-pattern>
  </servlet-mapping>
</web-app>
```

Recall from the first chapter that all the event handling is handled by FacesServlet and to direct all requests to this servlet we take the help of deployment descriptor file. There are two sections in the deployment descriptor file. `<servlet>` element is used to map the `"javax.faces.webapp.FacesServlet"` servlet class to a symbolic name, i.e., FacesServlet is an alias for `"javax.faces.webapp.FacesServlet"` servlet. The `<servlet-mapping>` element states that any request containing the pattern `/faces/` in the URL must be passed to the FacesServlet.

The load-on-startup element has a value of **true** or which indicates that the FacesServlet should be loaded when the application starts up.

Creating `faces-config.xml`

1. In the same folder as `web.xml`, create a file called `faces-config.xml`.
2. Enter the following code:

```
<?xml version='1.0' encoding='UTF-8'?>
<!DOCTYPE faces-config PUBLIC
"-//Sun Microsystems, Inc.//DTD JavaServer Faces Config
1.1//EN"
"http://java.sun.com/dtd/web-facesconfig_1_1.dtd">
<faces-config>
</faces-config>
```

3. Save the file

What just happened?

`faces-config.xml` is an application configuration file which can be used to configure many aspects of the application like bean management, page navigation, custom UI components, custom validators, etc. But we can even make a small web application which may not require any bean or navigation to another page, in that case we may leave this file.

CREATING OUR FIRST JSF APPLICATION

Since in our application (trial), application deployment descriptor (`web.xml`) file, application configuration file (`faces-config.xml`) and library files are already copied in their respective folder, we only need a jsp file for interacting with the user.

Create User Interface (JSP File)

The program that we are going to first make just displays a welcome message to the user. The steps are as follows:

1. Create `index.jsp` file into "`apache-tomcat-6.0.14\webapps\trial\`" directory
2. Enter following code in that file:

```
<!DOCTYPE HTML PUBLIC "-//W3C//DTD HTML 4.01 Transitional//EN">
<%@taglib uri="http://java.sun.com/jsf/html" prefix="h"%>
<%@taglib uri="http://java.sun.com/jsf/core" prefix="f"%>
<html>
  <body>
    <f:view>
      <h:outputText value="Welcome to our Shopping Mall"/>
    </f:view>
  </body>
</html>
```

Explanation of Code

The first two lines are the directives which specify the location to find the JSF HTML tags and JSF core tags respectively.

JSF HTML tags:

```
<%@ taglib uri="http://java.sun.com/jsf/html" prefix="h" %>
```

JSF Core tags:

```
<%@ taglib uri="http://java.sun.com/jsf/core" prefix="f" %>
```

Recall from the first chapter that JSF provides two custom tag libraries to help us rapidly write web applications. In order to include the tags specified in above tag libraries in our web application, we have included both of them in our program. The JSF HTML tag library defines tags that represent UI components. The JSF core tag library defines core actions for registering event handlers, using validators with components, and so on.

<f:view> tag: <f:view> tag which is defined in the `JSF core` library specifies the start of the JSF component tree. We know that a JavaServer Faces page is internally represented by a tree of components. At the root of the tree is the `UIViewRoot` component and <f:view> represents this component on the page. That is, this tag acts as a container of all the rest of components in the web page.

```
<f:view>
... other faces tags
</f:view>
```

<h:outputText>:   <h:outputText tag is defined in the JSF HTML tag library and is used for creating component for displaying formatted output on the screen. So, in above program, the tag `<h:outputText value=" Welcome to our Shopping Mall "/>` generates "Welcome to our Shopping Mall" on the browser.

3. Test the application:

To test application, run Tomcat and then type `http://localhost:8080/trial/ faces/index.jsp` in the browser. The browser should display "Welcome to our Shopping Mall" message as shown in Figure 2.6.

Figure 2.6   Display of formatted output text.

In the <f:view> tag, we can define one more tag: <h:form> tag, which defines an input form. This form is submitted to the server when a button is clicked. The tags representing the form components like textfields and buttons (<h:commandButton>), etc. must be nested inside the form tag. We can even write simple HTML tags in it.

So, let's include <h:form> tag in above `index.jsp` file.

Including Form Tag

To do so, modify the contents of index.jsp page as follows:

```
<%@ taglib uri="http://java.sun.com/jsf/html" prefix="h" %>
```

```
<%@ taglib uri="http://java.sun.com/jsf/core" prefix="f" %>
<body>
  <f:view>
    <h:form>
      <h1>Believe in God</h1>
    </h:form>
  </f:view>
</body>
```

In the above program, we have first written the taglib directives for including jsf html tag and jsf core tag libraries respectively. Then, we are using a view tag (root of the component tree) and in it we have included a form tag. In the form tag, we have used a simple HTML tag to display a message.

Test the Application

To test application, run Tomcat and then type `http://localhost:8080/trial/faces/index.jsp` in the browser. The browser should display the output as shown in Figure 2.7.

Address   http://localhost:8080/trial/faces/index.jsp

Believe in God

Figure 2.7   Display of Form Tag.

MODIFYING JSP PAGE TO ACCEPT USER NAME

In the following example, we are going to modify the jsp page so that it prompts the user to enter his/her name and then displays a welcome message. There are following steps to make a JSF web application:

- Create user interface (JSP files)
- Create managed bean
- Write navigation rules
- Compile the application
- Deploy and test the application

Application that Asks Users to Type their Name

For this application, we need to create two jsp pages:

One is `index.jsp` page which prompts the user to enter his/her name and another is `welcome.jsp` page to display a welcome message.

`index.jsp` page prompts the user to enter his name and the name entered in the page will be binded with UserBean (JavaBean) attribute. The name entered by user is then displayed through `welcome.jsp` page along with the welcome message.

Note: Through `index.jsp` page we set the attribute (name) of UserBean class (model) and through `welcome.jsp` page, we get the attribute (name) of UserBean class.

1. Modify the contents of index JSP as follows:

```
<%@ taglib uri="http://java.sun.com/jsf/html" prefix="h" %>
<%@ taglib uri="http://java.sun.com/jsf/core" prefix="f" %>
<html>
<head>
  <title> </title>
</head>
<body>
  <f:view>
    <h1>
      <h:outputText value=" Welcome to our Shopping Mall "/>
    </h1>
    <h:form id="LoginForm">
      <h:outputText value="Enter Your Name:"/>
      <h:inputText value="#{UserBean.userName}" />
      <h:commandButton action="welcome" value="Submit" />
    </h:form>
  </f:view>
</body>
</html>
```

2. Save the above file in "`webapps\trial`" directory.

Explanation

The code that generates forms and buttons:

```
1. <h:form id="LoginForm">
2. <h:outputText value="Enter Your Name:"/>
3. <h:inputText value="#{UserBean.userName}" />
4. <h:commandButton action="welcome" value="Submit" />
5. </h:form>
```

Line 1:   Generates HTML code for the form.

Line 2:   Prints the message "`Enter Your Name`" on the screen.

Line 3:   `<h:inputText value="#{UserBean.userName}" />`

It creates HTML text input element, where user can enter his name. The name entered by the user is assigned to the userName attribute of the managed bean: UserBean. "`#{UserBean.userName}`" is an expression which binds the textfield with the managed bean attribute "`userName`". The bean and its attributes are explained in coming steps.

Line 4:   Creates HTML submit button with the text "`Submit`" on it.

`action="welcome"` specifies that the outcome of processing this file (i.e. the value that comes from the action property of the UI command component-button) will be "welcome". This value will be used in "from-outcome" of-faces-config.xml file for navigating to the desired page: welcome.jsp

Line 5:   Creates HTML forms end tag </form>

Next file is welcome.jsp, which displays the welcome message to the user.

Creating the Welcome Message

1. The contents of welcome.jsp are:

```
<%@ taglib uri="http://java.sun.com/jsf/html" prefix="h" %>
<%@ taglib uri="http://java.sun.com/jsf/core" prefix="f" %>
<html>
    <head>
        <title> </title>
    </head>
<body>
    <f:view>
        <h3>
            <h:outputText value="Welcome" />,
            <h:outputText value="#{UserBean.userName}" /> to our
                Shopping Mall
        </h3>
        </f:view>
</body>
</html>
```

2. Save above jsp page in "webapps\trial" directory.

Explanation

Above program is for displaying welcome message along with the name of the user. The code `<h:outputText value="#{UserBean.userName}" />` is for retrieving the contents of the userName attribute stored in JavaBean: UserBean.

Create Managed Bean

Now we will create a JavaBean that will hold the data sent by the form (name of the user). The JSF managed bean is a JavaBean component whose attributes and methods are used by JSF components. Our managed bean is created by name User.java.

1. Create a java file: User.java with following contents:

```
public class User {
    String userName;
    public String getUserName() {
    return userName;
```

```
  }
  public void setUserName(String name) {
    userName = name;
  }
}
```

2. Save `User.java` into "`webapps\trial\WEB-INF\classes` directory.

Explanation

This class is a simple JavaBean with one attribute and setter/getter methods. The bean simply captures the name entered by a user after the user clicks the submit button. This way the bean provides a bridge between the JSP page and the application logic.

Note: The statement `<h:inputText value="#{UserBean.userName}" />` invokes following method of the JavaBean—UserBean:

```
public void setUserName(String name) {
    userName = name;
}
```

This method sets the value of the attribute: userName equal to the name entered by the user. Similarly, the statement `<h:outputText value="#{UserBean.userName}" />` invokes following method of the JavaBean—UserBean:

```
public String getUserName() {
    return userName;
}
```

This method displays the contents of the value stored in userName attribute of the JavaBean: UserBean

Registering the bean: The JavaBean:UserBean will not work until and unless it is registered in application configuration file: `faces-config.xml` file.

Register the Bean in `faces-config.xml`

We register the JavaBean in the "`faces-config.xml`" using the following code:

```
<managed-bean>
    <managed-bean-name>UserBean</managed-bean-name>
    <managed-bean-class>User</managed-bean-class>
    <managed-bean-scope>request</managed-bean-scope>
</managed-bean>
```

Explanation

Above code specifies that the class name of the managed bean is `User.class` and is referred to in the application as **UserBean**.

For JavaBean management, we use the managed-bean element in the `faces-config.xml` application configuration file. The managed-bean element includes details of the bean:

The managed-bean-name   specifies the name that will be used to refer to the JavaBean throughout the application.

The managed-bean-class   contains the fully qualified class name for the JavaBean.

The managed-bean-scope   defines the scope of the JavaBean. The possible values for this element are application, session, request, or none.

Specifying the navigation rule: Through the navigation rule, we can specify which next page to open on what action.

Write Navigation Rules

Through navigation rules, the application comes to know which jsp page to jump at on occurrence of a particular event. Open the `faces-config.xml` and add the following code to define the navigation rule:

```
<navigation-rule>
   <from-view-id>/index.jsp</from-view-id>
   <navigation-case>
      <from-outcome>welcome</from-outcome>
      <to-view-id>/welcome.jsp</to-view-id>
   </navigation-case>
</navigation-rule>
```

Explanation

Above code specifies that if in `index.jsp` file, the outcome of an event (i.e., the value of the action property of the UI command component: button) is "`welcome`", then navigate to the `welcome.jsp` page.

The `from-view-id` element is the identifier of the page of origin. To describe the navigation rule for a JSP page called `index.jsp`, the following is the value of the from-view-id sub element:

```
<from-view-id>/index.jsp</from-view-id>
```

The `navigation-case` element represents a possible target. A `navigation-rule` element can have zero or several navigation-case sub elements. Each navigation-case element specifies the target page for a particular outcome of the `from-view-id` processing. An outcome can come from the action attribute of the UI command component in the `from-view-id` element.

Example:

```
<navigation-case>
<from-outcome>welcome</from-outcome>
<to-view-id>/welcome.jsp</to-view-id>
</navigation-case>
```

The `to-view-id` element specifies the target page. The from-outcome value is the outcome of processing of the file specified in the `from-view-id`. This value comes from the action property of the UI command component that triggered the Action Event in the file specified in `from-view-id`.

The overall contents of `faces-config.xml` is:

```xml
<?xml version='1.0' encoding='UTF-8'?>
<!DOCTYPE faces-config PUBLIC
"-//Sun Microsystems, Inc.//DTD JavaServer Faces Config 1.1//EN"
"http://java.sun.com/dtd/web-facesconfig_1_1.dtd">
<faces-config>
<navigation-rule>
        <from-view-id>/index.jsp</from-view-id>
        <navigation-case>
            <from-outcome>welcome</from-outcome>
            <to-view-id>/welcome.jsp</to-view-id>
        </navigation-case>
</navigation-rule>
<managed-bean>
        <managed-bean-name>UserBean</managed-bean-name>
        <managed-bean-class>User</managed-bean-class>
        <managed-bean-scope>request</managed-bean-scope>
</managed-bean>
</faces-config>
```

No need to make any changes in the deployment descriptor `file: web.xml`. Same file can be used for this application too.

Compile and Run Your Application

Its time to compile the JavaBean file. Recall that we have made our JavaBean in classes folder with the name User.java and are using it in our web application by name UserBean. Open the command prompt and go to the classes folder of our application (trial) and give following command:

```
C:\apache-tomcat-6.0.14\webapps\trial\WEB-INF\classes>  javac
User.java
```

To test the application run tomcat and in the browser type:
`http://localhost:8080/trial/faces/index.jsp`. The browser displays the input screen as shown in Figure 2.8.

Figure 2.8   Enter a name and press submit Button.

We will enter a name and select `Submit` button. The welcome screen should look like as shown in Figure 2.9.

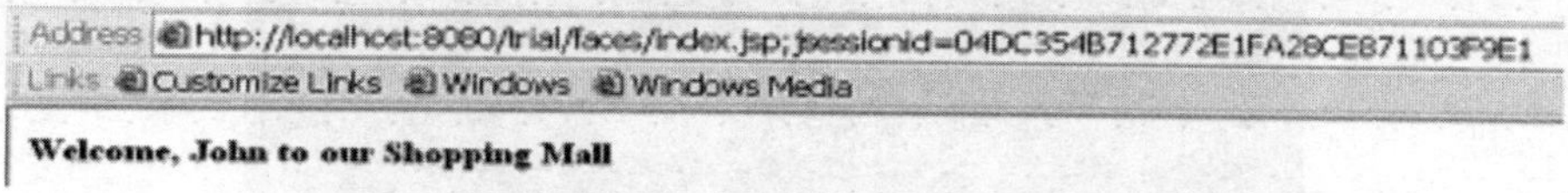

Address http://localhost:8080/trial/faces/index.jsp;jsessionid=04DC354B712772E1FA28CE871103F9E1
Links Customize Links Windows Windows Media
Welcome, John to our Shopping Mall

Figure 2.9 Display of welcome screen.

Explanation

To understand what actually happened, please refer to the index.jsp program. The name entered by user is assigned to `userName` attribute of UserBean. That is, `setUserName()` method of UserBean (`User.java` file) is executed to assign the name entered by the user to `userName` attribute.

Remember that the statement `<h:inputText value="#{UserBean.userName}"/>` invokes `setUserName()` method and `<h:outputText value="#{UserBean.userName}"/>` invokes `getUserName()` method of JavaBean.

After feeding the name (in `index.jsp` page), when user selects `Submit` button, an outcome: "welcome" is generated. Using navigation rule specified in application configuration file: `faces-config.xml`, the application will come to know that if the outcome of an event (i.e., the value of the action property of the UI command component which triggers the ActionEvent) is "welcome" then navigate to the `welcome.jsp` page. So, `welcome.jsp` page is executed which displays the user name along with the welcome message on the screen.

PROPERTIES FILE

A properties file is a file where we can store all the messages of our web application. Messages means the prompts, text strings, etc. we use in our web application while asking some input from the user or while displaying some information. The advantage of keeping the messages separate from the JSP page is that we can quickly modify the messages when desired without editing the JSP page. A properties file is a file containing param=value pairs.

To try it practically, let's modify our application:

Create a Properties File

To handle all the messages of our application, we create a properties file by name **messages.properties** in the classes folder of our trial application.

Put this text in the properties file:

messages.properties

```
inputname_header=Welcome to our Shopping Mall
prompt=Enter your name:
greeting_text=Welcome
button_text=Submit
```

The overall structure of our trial application is given in Figure 2.10.

```
trial
    welcome.jsp
    index.jsp

    WEB-INF
        faces-config.xml
        web.xml

        classes
            messages.properties
            User.class
            User.java

        lib
            commons-beanutils.jar
            commons-collections.jar
            commons-digester.jar
            commons-logging.jar
            jsf-api.jar
            jsf-impl.jar
            jstl.jar
            standard.jar
```

Figure 2.10   Structure of trial application.

We can see that one file is extra: message.properties file is included in classes sub folder.

Modify `index.jsp` file

After creating a properties file, we need to modify the `index.jsp` file.
1. Modify the contents of `index.jsp` file as:

```jsp
<%@ taglib uri="http://java.sun.com/jsf/html" prefix="h" %>
<%@ taglib uri="http://java.sun.com/jsf/core" prefix="f" %>
<f:loadBundle basename="messages" var="msg"/>

<html>
    <head>
        <title> </title>
    </head>
    <body>
     <f:view>
        <h1>
            <h:outputText value="#{msg.inputname_header}"/>
        </h1>
         <h:form id="LoginForm">
            <h:outputText value="#{msg.prompt}"/>
            <h:inputText value="#{UserBean.userName}" />
            <h:commandButton action="welcome"
            value="#{msg.button_text}" />
            </h:form>
        </f:view>
        </body>
    </html>
```

Explanation

```
<f:loadBundle basename="messages" var="msg"/>
```

Above statement loads our properties file: messages.properties (also called resource bundle) that holds our messages. This properties file will be referred to in the application by name: **msg**

```
<h:outputText value="#{msg.inputname_header}"/>
```

This tag simply tells JSF to look in the resource bundle defined at the top of the page and in it look up for the value of inputname_header property and print its value here.

```
1. <h:form id="LoginForm">
2. <h:outputText value="#{msg.prompt}"/>
3. <h:inputText id="name" value="#{UserBean.userName}" />
4. <h:commandButton action="welcome"
   value="#{msg.button_text}" />
5. </h:form>
```

Line 1: Creates an HTML form using JSF tags.

Line 2: Prints a message from the properties file. The value of prompt property is displayed i.e. Enter your name: text is displayed on the screen.

Line 3: Creates an HTML input text box. The id is used internally to identify the input text box. In the value attribute we connect (bind) the input textbox to the managed bean attribute: userName of UserBean.

Line 4: Creates the HTML form's submit button. The button's value is being retrieved from the properties file. So, on the button, the text: Submit appears. While the button's action attribute is set to "welcome" which creates the navigation-outcome and will be used for navigation in faces-config.xml file.

After index.jsp file, we need to modify welcome.jsp file.

Modify `welcome.jsp` file

1. Modify the contents of welcome.jsp file as shown:

```
<%@ taglib uri="http://java.sun.com/jsf/html" prefix="h" %>
<%@ taglib uri="http://java.sun.com/jsf/core" prefix="f" %>
<f:loadBundle basename="messages" var="msg"/>

<html>
    <head>
        <title></title>
    </head>
    <body>
        <f:view>
            <h:outputText value="#{msg.greeting_text}" />,
            <h:outputText value="#{UserBean.userName}" />
        </f:view>
    </body>
</html>
```

Explanation

The value of the `greeting_text` from properties file is retrieved and is displayed along with the value of userName attribute of UserBean JavaBean. That is, the welcome message is displayed along with value in UserName attribute.

The JavaBean: `User.java` is same as the earlier example. No need of modifying its contents. It contains the usual setter and getter methods for the userName attribute.

The contents of `faces-config.xml` in `WEB-INF` folder will be same and no need of modifying it as the navigation rules and the managed bean are same as that of earlier applications. Similarly, the deployment descriptor file: web.xml file is also left unchanged. No need of compiling the JavaBean.

Test the Application

Now, we can run our application, just restart Tomcat and launch the application by opening the browser and type: http://localhost:8080/trial/faces/index.jsp as shown in Figure 2.11.

Figure 2.11   Enter a name and press submit Button.

Enter your name and select `Submit` button. The name fed in above web page sets the attribute (userName) of managed bean: UserBean. The contents of attribute: userBean are retrieved through `welcome.jsp` page as shown in Figure 2.12.

Welcome , john

Figure 2.12   Name is set as attribute and then retrieved on the screen.

SUMMARY

We learned in this chapter about how to write simple web applications and how to configure application configuration and deployment descriptor files to run them

Specifically, we covered:

- Installation of JSF.
- Creating and running simple web applications.
- Creation of managed bean and using it for storing and retrieving information fed by user.
- Mapping of servlet in deployment descriptor file: `web.xml` to invoke FacesServlet.
- How page navigation rules and managed bean are specified in application configuration file: `faces-config.xml`.
- Using properties files in a web application.

Since we have learnt how to write simple web applications, we can now dwell deep for writing larger applications.

REVIEW QUESTIONS

2.1 Write a JSF program to display your name, address and phone number on the screen.

2.2 Write a JSF program to enter a numerical value and display its square value.

2.3 Write a JSF program to enter a name and display it in upper case along with a welcome message.

2.4 Write the above program using properties file.

3

Expression Language

┤ LEARNING OBJECTIVE ├

In this chapter, we will learn:

- What expression language is

THE EXPRESSION LANGUAGE

The expression language (EL) provides not only a better way of writing expressions, but also an easy method of binding JavaBean attributes to application data. For example, to access name attribute from a JavaBean say UserBean, we can write expressions: "`${UserBean.name}`" in JSP or "`#{UserBean.name}`" in JSF.

There is a lot of difference in expression languages of JSP and JSF because of the difference in evaluation technique used in each of them.

Limitations of JSP expression language

- In JSP, the expressions are evaluated *immediately*, that is, they are immediately parsed and response is generated, whereas we want deferred evaluation in case of JSF because, the expression has to be evaluated at different phases of life cycle rather than immediately. It is so because, when the user enters values into the UI components and submits the page, those values are converted, validated, and propagated to server-side data objects in the respective phases of life cycle.
- Another problem with the immediate evaluation of expressions is that it is done in read-only mode. Whereas in Java Server Faces, we may need to update server side objects, so read only mode will not serve the purpose.

- Another problem is that JSF components need to invoke methods during various stages of the life cycle in order to validate data and handle different events. JSP functions can only be used to call static methods and cannot be used to dynamically.

For all these reasons, a more powerful expression language called *unified expression language* was created which is a union of JSP and JSF expression languages. The unified EL has the following new features:

- Deferred expressions, which can be evaluated at different stages of the page life cycle.
- Expressions that can set data of external objects as well as get that data (allows updation).
- Method expressions, which can invoke methods that perform event handling, validation, and other functions for the JavaServer Faces UI components.

Unified Expression Language

By the name only, we can guess that the Unified Expression Language supports the expression languages of both JSP as well as that of JSF, named as JavaServer Pages Standard Tag Library (JSTL).

JavaServer Faces EL Expression Syntax

JSF EL can be used to bind JavaBeans to component properties to simplify how the components access data from various sources. JSF EL expressions use the syntax: **#{expr};**

A JavaServer Faces expression can be a value-binding expression (for binding UI components) or a method-binding expression (for referencing backing bean methods).

The following example shows a JSF inputText tag, which represents a text field component into which a user enters a value. The inputText tag's value attribute references an expression that points to the name attribute of the UserBean bean.

```
<h:inputText id="name" value="#{UserBean.name}"/>
```

Method expressions

A JSF component tag uses method expressions to invoke methods that perform some processing for the component that the tag is representing on the page.

```
<h:inputText id="roll" value="#{UserBean.roll}"
    validator="#{UserBean.validateRoll}"/>
```

The validator attribute of the inputText component tag references a method called validateRoll in the bean called UserBean. The validateRoll method is invoked during the process validation phase of the life cycle.

Different Literals, Operators and Reserved words used in Unified Expression Language are as follows:

Literals: The expression language defines the following literals:

Boolean: True and false

Integer: As in Java

Floating point: As in Java

String:	With single and double quotes; `"is escaped as \"`, `'is escaped as \'`, and `\` is escaped as `\\`.
Null:	Null

Operators: Expression language provides the following operators:

Arithmetic:	+, - (binary), *, /, div, %, mod, - (unary)
Logical:	and, &&, or, ǁ, not, !
Relational:	==, eq, !=, ne, <, lt, >, gt, <=, ge, >=, i.e., comparisons can be made against other values, or against boolean, string, integer, or floating point literals.
Empty:	The empty operator is a prefix operation that can be used to determine whether a value is null or empty.
Conditional:	A ? B : C. Evaluate B or C, depending on the result of the evaluation of A.

Reserved words

The following words are reserved for the expression language and must not be used as identifiers:

and	false	le	not
div	ge	lt	null
empty	gt	mod	or
eq	instanceof	ne	true

SUMMARY

The summary of this chapter can be expressed in following points:

- Expression language is used to access data stored in JavaBeans
- The expression in JSF are evaluated at different phases of life cycle
- Unified expression language is better than JSP EL as it is the union of JSP and JSF expression languages
- The JSF EL syntax of binding component to JavaBeans is #{expr}

REVIEW QUESTIONS

3.1 What are the limitations of JSP expression language?

3.2 What is unified expression language and how it is better than JSP EL?

4

JSF HTML Tags

In this chapter, we will learn:

- How input text fields and text areas can be used to fetch data from the user
- How image is displayed in a web page
- How checkboxes can be binded with JavaBean component
- How h:selectOnemenu (dropdown control) is used for displaying different options
- How h:selectOneRadio (radio button) works in JSF
- How h:selectOneListbox (list box) accepts a single response from the user
- How information can be organized in panel grid
- How to use styles to uniformly format the page
- How to use panel groups to group related data
- How to display information in data table
- How h:selectManyCheckbox is used to accept more than one choice from the user

The html tag library contains a list of tags heavily required for user interface which includes text fields, buttons, form, etc. The HTML tags are grouped in different categories on the basis of their functions:

- Input text fields and text areas
- Displaying text and images
- Command buttons and links
- Selections tags (checkbox, listbox, menu, radio)
- Layouts (panelgrid)

- Data table (datatable);
- Errors and messages (message, messages)

Let's start with the first category to understand these HTML tags practically.

INPUT TEXT FIELDS AND TEXT AREAS

Input controls are used for feeding data and also for updating the attributes of the associated JavaBean. Remember that whatever data we enter in a web page has to be attached to some attribute of the JavaBean (which is later used for displaying, retrieving information) via outputText tags. The input family members generate `<input>` element which is rendered with type "`text`". JSF supports three varieties of inputs represented by the tags as shown in Table 4.1.

Table 4.1   Three Input Tags

Tags	Usage
• `h:inputText`	used for feeding single line text
• `h:inputSecret`	used for feeding passwords
• `h:inputTextarea`	used for feeding multiline text

All three tags have these attributes in common: immediate, required, value and valueChangeListener (Table 4.2).

Table 4.2   Various Attributes of the Three Input Tags

Attributes	Description
immediate	It performs validation early in the life cycle
redisplay	Used only with `h:inputSecret`. If its value is true, the value in the input field is redisplayed when the web page is reloaded. The value is discarded and is not redisplayed if its value is false.
required	It means the component requires input when the form is submitted
valueChangeListener	If any change in the value occurs, the specified listener is invoked
cols	For `h:inputTextarea` only—specifies the number of columns
rows	For `h:inputTextarea` only—specifies the number of rows
size	This attribute specifies the number of visible characters in a text field. It is not precise as fonts have different width.
maxlength	This attribute specifies the maximum number of characters a text field will display. That attribute is precise.

Examples:

- `<h:inputText value=''#{UserBean.userName}'' />`

  It displays an input text box and the text entered in it is assigned to userName attribute of the JavaBean: UserBean. The text entered in the text box will be echoed on the screen and will be visible to others.

- ```
<h:inputSecret value=''#{UserBean.userPass}'' />
```

  It displays an input text box and the text entered in it is assigned to userPass attribute (for storing passwords) of the JavaBean: UserBean. The text entered in the text box will not be echoed on the screen. Only few dots will appear corresponding to the characters typed by the user and nobody can seen what text has been typed in.

The h:inputTextarea has cols and rows attributes to specify the number of columns and rows, respectively, in the text area. To place text in separate lines, they can be separated by inserting new line characters ('\n') in between.

*Examples:*

- ```
<h:inputTextarea rows="3" cols="40"/>
```

  It displays a blank text area of 3 rows and 40 columns wide. If data entered is of more than 3 rows, scroll bars will appear.

- ```
<h:inputTextarea value="Believe in God\n Life is Great"
rows="3" cols="20"/>
```

  It displays a text area of 3 rows and 20 columns wide with two lines of text in it. That is, the two lines : Believe in God and Life is Great appears in the text area in two separate lines.

- ```
<h:inputTextarea id="Address" value="#{UserBean.address}"
rows="4" cols="40"/><br/>
```

  It displays a text area of 4 rows and 40 columns wide and whatever data is entered by the user is assigned to **address** attribute of **UserBean** JavaBean.

DISPLAYING TEXT AND IMAGES

JSF applications use the following tags to display text and images:

- h:outputText
- h:outputFormat
- h:graphicImage

h:outputText

This tag is used for displaying plain text and if we need to apply styles to it uniformly, we may attach CSS styles with it. When we specify the style or styleClass attributes, h:outputText generates the HTML **span** element. Also, h:outputText and h:outputFormat have one attribute called: **escape**. By default, the escape attribute is false, but if we set it to true, the characters like: > < & are converted to < > and & respectively.

Note: When > and < are converted to < and > respectively, they no more act as HTML tags and hence don't perform any action, but are just displayed as such

Example:

```
<h:outputText value="Welcome to our <b>Shopping Mall </b>" />
```

Output on Browser: Welcome to our <b>Shopping Mall </b>

Since escape attribute is not used, and its default value being true, the tag: <b> will be converted to <b> hence Browser won't be able to recognize it as HTML tag and instead of making the matter bold, it will be displayed as such.

```
<h:outputText value="Welcome to our <b>Shopping Mall </b>"
escape="false"/>
```

Output on Browser: Welcome to our **Shopping Mall**

We can see that when escape is false, the meaning of < and > remains the same and are not converted into < and > respectively. Hence, browser recognizes them as HTML tags and takes the corresponding action i.e. makes the enclosed matter bold.

h:outputFormat

This tag is used for displaying parameterized text. That is, the component can insert values at specified places in the string.

Example:

```
<h:outputFormat value="Hello {0}. Welcome to our {1}">
<f:param value="#{UserBean.userName}"/>
<f:param value="Shopping Mall"/>
```

Output on Browser: Hello John. Welcome to our Shopping Mall (assuming that the value of the userName attribute of the JavaBean: UserBean is "John").

We can see that parameters start with value zero: {0}, {1}, {2}....The first parameter value is substituted wherever {0} appears in the text. Similarly, the second parameter value is substituted wherever {1} appears in the text. That is why the text: "Shopping Mall" appears at the place of {1}.

The tag h:outputFormat can also be used for repeating variables in a single string of text.

Example:

```
<h:outputFormat value="Hello {0}. Welcome to our {1}. {0}, you
can now start shopping">
<f:param value="#{UserBean.userName}"/>
<f:param value="Shopping Mall"/>
```

Output on Browser: Hello John. Welcome to our Shopping Mall. John, you can now start shopping.

In the above example, we can see that {0} appears twice in the string, so John is displayed twice without having to repeat value-binding expression: #{UserBean.userName}.

h:graphicImage

This tag is used for displaying images. It displays an <img> element whose **src** attribute is set to **url** property of the component.

Example:

```
<h:graphicImage value="/toy.jpg" />
```
It displays a image by name toy.jpg

```
<h:graphicImage url="/images/camera1.jpg" alt="Camera Model No
C2001" width="75" height="100" />
```

It displays an image `camera1.jpg` from images folder resized to the given width and height. The alternate text (the text that appears when mouse is over the image) displays the text: "Camera Model No C2001".

COMMAND BUTTONS AND LINKS

JSF applications use the following tags to create events and to invoke the respective event handlers:

- h:outputLink
- h:commandButton
- h:commandLink

h:outputLink

The h:outputLink tag generates an HTML anchor <a> element that points to a target which may be an image or a web page(hyperlink) we want to navigate at. The value property of this tag represents the **url** of the target web page. Clicking on the generated link takes us to the destination web page.

Example:

```
<h:outputLink value="courses.jsp">
      <h:outputText value="Courses offered" />
</h:outputLink>
```

Output on Browser: *Courses offered*

If we click the link: "Courses offered", we will be taken to the web page: courses.jsp. We can see in above example that the component's value (courses.jsp) maps to href value of the hyperlink and the text within the hyperlink appears from the nested h:outputText component.

The h:commandButton and h:commandLink both invoke actions when a button or link is activated.

h:commandButton

The h:commandButton tag generates an HTML input element whose type is button, image, submit, or reset, depending on the attributes we specify.

Examples:

```
<h:commandButton image="/images/book.jpg"/>
<h:commandButton value="submit" type="submit"/>
<h:commandButton value="reset" type="reset"/>
<h:commandButton action="submit" value="Submit" />
```

In all the examples given above, if we click the command button(even it is in the form of image), it will lead to some action like invoking a method or navigating to some web page, etc.

Common usages of the command button are:

- Validating the contents of the fields
- Navigating to some other web page for either processing the data entered or for storing it into Model

h:commandLink

This tag displays a command link, but acts similarly as command button, i.e., this tag generates an HTML anchor element that acts like a form submit button.

The following application demonstrates the use of h:graphicImage, h:inputTextarea, h:selectBooleanCheckbox and h:commandButton tags. h:selectBooleanCheckbox displays a checkbox and user has the option to check or uncheck it. If it is checked (selected), it sets the value "true" to the binded JavaBean attribute else sets the value "false" to it. For this application, we are going to develop two pages index11.jsp and response.jsp. The index11.jsp displays an image and prompts the user to enter his address. The address entered in the page is binded with **UserBean** (JavaBean) attribute:**address**. Also, user is asked to select a checkbox, if he wants to pay by credit card (no need of selecting the checkbox if he pays in cash). The checkbox selected in the page is binded with UserBean (JavaBean) attribute:**paybycard**. The address fed by user is then displayed through response.jsp page along with the message that user wants to pay by credit card or by cash.

Note: Through index11.jsp page, we set the attributes: **address** and **paybycard** of UserBean class (model) and through response.jsp page, we get the values stored in these attributes. Make a file index11.jsp with the below given contents in "webapps\trial" directory.

index11.jsp

```
<%@ taglib uri="http://java.sun.com/jsf/html" prefix="h" %>
<%@ taglib uri="http://java.sun.com/jsf/core" prefix="f" %>

<html>
    <head>
```

```
            <title> </title>
        </head>
        <body>
            <f:view>
                <h:form >
                    <h:graphicImage value="/toy.jpg" /><br/><br/>
                    <h:outputText value="Enter Your Address:"/>
                    <h:inputTextarea id="Address"
                        value="#{UserBean.address}" rows="4"
                        cols="40"/><br/>
                    <h:outputText value="Payment though credit card :"/>
                    <h:selectBooleanCheckbox
                        value="#{UserBean.paybycard}" /><br/>
                    <h:commandButton action="submit" value="Submit" />
                </h:form>
            </f:view>
        </body>
</html>
```

Also make another file `response.jsp` with the below given contents in "webapps\trial" directory.

response.jsp

```
<%@ taglib uri="http://java.sun.com/jsf/html" prefix="h" %>
<%@ taglib uri="http://java.sun.com/jsf/core" prefix="f" %>

<html>
    <head>
        <title> </title>
    </head>
    <body>
        <f:view>
            <h:outputText value="The information supplied is"/>
            <br/>
            <h:outputText value="Address :" />
            <h:outputText value="#{UserBean.address}" /> <br/>
            <h:outputText value="Payment will be done by card : "/>
            <h:outputText value="#{UserBean.paybycard}" /> <br/>
        </f:view>
    </body>
</html>
```

Now we will create a bean that will hold the data sent by the form: address and paybycard. We know that JSF managed bean is a JavaBean component whose property and methods are used by JSF components. It is a class file having attributes and their respective setter and getter methods. Make a file `User.java` in "webapps\trial\WEB-INF\classes directory with the below given contents. The bean simply captures the address and paybycard entered by the user when be clicks the submit button. Here is the code of our managed bean (User.java):

User.java

```java
public class User {
    String address;
    boolean paybycard;
    public String getAddress() {
        return address;
    }
    public void setAddress(String add) {
        address = add;
    }
    public boolean getPaybycard() {
        return paybycard;
    }
    public void setPaybycard(boolean card) {
        paybycard =card;
    }
}
```

Compile the JavaBean application

Open the command prompt and go to the classes folder of our application (trial) and give following command:

```
C:\apache-tomcat-6.0.14\webapps\trial\WEB-INF\classes>  javac
User.java
```

Let us create an application configuration file: `faces-config.xml` in WEB-INF folder of our application to specify the name our JavaBean and also the condition of navigating to `response.jsp` page from `index11.jsp` page. The contents of the `faces-config.xml` file are as follows:

faces-config.xml

```xml
<?xml version='1.0' encoding='UTF-8'?>
<!DOCTYPE faces-config PUBLIC
"-//Sun Microsystems, Inc.//DTD JavaServer Faces Config 1.1//EN"
"http://java.sun.com/dtd/web-facesconfig_1_1.dtd">
<faces-config>
    <navigation-rule>
        <from-view-id>/index11.jsp</from-view-id>
        <navigation-case>
        <from-outcome>submit</from-outcome>
        <to-view-id>/response.jsp</to-view-id>
        </navigation-case>
```

```
    </navigation-rule>
    <managed-bean>
        <managed-bean-name>UserBean</managed-bean-name>
        <managed-bean-class>User</managed-bean-class>
        <managed-bean-scope>request</managed-bean-scope>
    </managed-bean>
</faces-config>
```

Above code specifies that the class name of the managed bean is **User.class** and is referred to in the application as **UserBean**. It also specifies that if in `index11.jsp` file, the outcome of an event is "submit", then navigate to the `response.jsp` page.

Note: The `to-view-id` element specifies the target page. The from-outcome value is the outcome of processing of the file specified in the `from-view-id`.

Also make a deployment descriptor file `web.xml` in WEB-INF folder of our application to register the FacesServlet (the engine of all JSF applications). Also, through <servlet-mapping> element we need to state that any request containing the pattern /faces/ in the URL must be passed to the FacesServlet. Also, we set the "load-on-startup" element to true, so that the FacesServlet should be loaded when the application starts up.

The contents of web.xml are:

web.xml

```
<?xml version='1.0' encoding='UTF-8'?>
<!DOCTYPE web-app PUBLIC
"-//Sun Microsystems, Inc.//DTD Web Application 2.3//EN"
"http://java.sun.com/dtd/web-app_2_3.dtd">
<web-app>
    <!-- Faces Servlet -->
    <servlet>
        <servlet-name>Faces Servlet</servlet-name>
    <servlet-class>javax.faces.webapp.FacesServlet
    </servlet-class>
        <load-on-startup> 1 </load-on-startup>
    </servlet>
    <!-- Faces Servlet Mapping -->
    <servlet-mapping>
        <servlet-name>Faces Servlet</servlet-name>
        <url-pattern>/faces/*</url-pattern>
    </servlet-mapping>
</web-app>
```

To run the application, run Tomcat and in the browser type: `http://localhost:8080/trial/faces/index11.jsp`. The browser displays an image and asks to enter address and whether we are going to pay by credit card or not. After filling in the information, select `Submit` button (Figure 4.1).

Figure 4.1 Provide the required information and press Submit button.

We get following output (Figure 4.2):

Figure 4.2 Information is displayed as output.

SELECTION TAGS

Usually in every web form, we want certain information from the visitor like his areas of interest, his choices, his requirements, etc. What else can be a better way to get information from the visitor other than providing him a couple of checkboxes, combo boxes, radio buttons, etc. and asking him to choose whatever suits him the best.

JavaServer Faces has seven tags for making selections:

- `h:selectBooleanCheckbox`
- `h:selectManyCheckbox`
- `h:selectOneRadio`
- `h:selectOneListbox`
- `h:selectManyListbox`
- `h:selectOneMenu`
- `h:selectManyMenu`

Tags which begin with selectOne lets us select one item from a set of options and it includes radio buttons, single-select menus, or listboxes.

The selectMany tags allows the user to select more than one item from a set of options and it includes checkboxes, multiselect menus, or listboxes.

h:selectBooleanCheckbox

The h:selectBooleanCheckbox tag as the name suggests render a checkbox which can be binded to a boolean bean property. If it is selected (checked), assigns value **true** to the binded bean attribute else assigns **false** to it.

h:selectManyCheckbox

The h:selectManyCheckbox displays several checkboxes in the form of a table and user can select any number of them. Since the display format is in the form of a table, this tag maps to an HTML <table> element with several <input> elements of type "checkbox".

h:selectOneRadio

The h:selectOneRadio displays several radio buttons in the form of a table and the user can select one item at a time. This tag is rendered as a <table> element (as it is displayed in the form of a table) with several <input> elements of type "radio". The radio buttons are laid vertically if the layout property is: "PAGEDIRECTION" or horizontally if the layout property is: "LINEDIRECTION".

Attributes unique to the two tags: h:selectOneRadio and h:selectManyCheckbox are:

- border
- enabledClass and disabledClass
- layout

Table 4.3 Attributes unique to two Selection Tags

Attributes	Description
border	It specifies the width of the border.
enabledClass and disabledClass	Specify CSS classes used when the checkboxes or radio buttons are enabled or disabled, respectively.
layout	This attribute can be either LINEDIRECTION (horizontal) or PAGEDIRECTION (vertical). LINEDIRECTION is the default.

h:selectOneListbox

h:selectOneListbox tag as the name suggests allows the user to select a single option from a list of choices. It renders the component as an HTML <select> element with the name attribute set to the component's ID and the size attribute set to the value of the component's size property.

h:selectManyListbox

h:selectManyListbox tag displays several options to the user allowing him to select more than one option of them. The child items within a listbox control are displayed as a <select> element.

h:selectOneMenu

h:selectOneMenu tag displays its child items in a listbox and the number of items displayed is always one. It renders the component as an HTML <select> element with the size attribute set to 1. All of its items configured by child UISelectItem or UISelectItems components are rendered as <option> elements.

Example:

```
<h:selectOneMenu id="food" value="#{FoodBean.foodName}">
    <f:selectItem itemValue="pizza" itemLabel="Pizza" />
    <f:selectItem itemValue="burgar" itemLabel="Burgar" />
    <f:selectItem itemValue="chowmein" itemLabel="Chowmein" />
    <f:selectItem itemValue="hotdog" itemLabel="Hot Dog" />
</h:selectOneMenu>
```

We can see that user is provided four items to choose from (all the items referenced by component <f:selectItem> are rendered as <option> elements). The selected option is assigned to **foodName** attribute of **FoodBean** JavaBean.

Example:

```
<h:selectOneMenu id="food" value="#{FoodBean.foodName}"
    required="true">
    <f:selectItems value="#{FoodBean.foodNames}" />
</h:selectOneMenu>
```

In this example, the options are retrieved from the foodNames array of FoodBean JavaBean. As said earlier, items referenced by <f:selectItems> or <f:selectItem> component are rendered as <option> elements.

We can see in above examples that we use f:selectItem or f:selectItems to specify the items.

The list of different attributes used with Components are given in Table 4.4.

Table 4.4   Attributes and its Description

Attribute	Description
id	It refers the component ID
itemDescription	It is the description of the item that doesn't appears on the screen
itemDisabled	It makes the item appear as disabled (if set to true)
itemLabel	It is the text that appears as option on the screen
itemValue	It is the value, which is passed to the server
value	It is the value binding expression that binds the selected option to the given JavaBean attribute.

h:selectManyMenu

h:selectManyMenu tag displays its child items in the form of a listbox. It renders the component as an HTML <select> element and all the child items are rendered as <option> elements. It allows the user to select more than one item from the set of options.

The following application demonstrates the use of h:selectOneMenu tag. For this application, we are going to develop two pages index5.jsp and bill.jsp. The index5.jsp displays four items of fast food and prompts the user to select one of them. The food selected in the page is binded with FoodBean (JavaBean) attribute: foodName. The food selected by the user is then displayed through bill.jsp page along with the bill amount.

Note: Through index5.jsp page, we set the attribute: foodName of FoodBean class and through bill.jsp page, we get the value stored in this attribute. Make a file index5.jsp with the below given contents in "webapps\trial" directory.

index5.jsp

```jsp
<%@ taglib uri="http://java.sun.com/jsf/html" prefix="h" %>
<%@ taglib uri="http://java.sun.com/jsf/core" prefix="f" %>

<html>
<head>
    <title> </title>
</head>
<body>
    <f:view>
      <h:form id="FastFood">
      <h:outputText value="Select your food "/>
      <h:selectOneMenu id="food" value="#{FoodBean.foodName}">
         <f:selectItem itemValue="pizza" itemLabel="Pizza" />
         <f:selectItem itemValue="burgar" itemLabel="Burgar" />
         <f:selectItem itemValue="chowmein" itemLabel="Chowmein"/>
         <f:selectItem itemValue="hotdog" itemLabel="Hot Dog" />
      </h:selectOneMenu>
      <h:commandButton action="submit" value="Submit" />
      </h:form>
    </f:view>
</body>
</html>
```

With the help of h:selectOneMenu tag, we display four items. All of its items are specified with the help of <f:selectItem> elements.

Also make another file bill.jsp with the below given contents in "webapps\trial" directory. This file will display the name of the fast food selected by the user and also the bill amount.

bill.jsp

```
<%@ taglib uri="http://java.sun.com/jsf/html" prefix="h" %>
<%@ taglib uri="http://java.sun.com/jsf/core" prefix="f" %>
<html>
<head>
    <title> </title>
</head>
<body>
    <f:view>
    <h3>
        <h:outputText value="You have selected" />
        <h:outputText value="#{FoodBean.foodName}" /> <br/>
        <h:outputText value="and your bill is " />
        <h:outputText value="#{FoodBean.billAmt}" /> <br/>
    </h3>
    </f:view>
</body>
</html>
```

The statement `<h:outputText value="#{FoodBean.billAmt}" />` invokes `getBillAmt()` method of the JavaBean: FoodBean.

Now we will create a JavaBean that will hold the type of food selected by the user and also computes the bill amount. Let us make a file `Food.java` in `webapps\trial\WEB-INF\classes` directory with the below given contents.

Food.java

```
public class Food {
    private String foodName;
    private Integer billAmt=null;

    public String getFoodName() {
        return foodName;
    }
    public void setFoodName(String name) {
        foodName = name;
    }
    public Integer getBillAmt() {
        calc();
        return billAmt;
    }
    public void calc()
    {
        if(foodName.equals("pizza"))setBillAmt(80);
```

```
            if(foodName.equals("burgar"))setBillAmt(30);
            if(foodName.equals("chowmein"))setBillAmt(40);
            if(foodName.equals("hotdog"))setBillAmt(25);
        }
    public void setBillAmt(Integer amt) {
        billAmt = amt;
        }
}
```

We can see in the above code that the method `getBillAmt()` invokes `calc()` method. `calc()` method checks the value assigned to `foodName` attribute (through `index5.jsp` page) and accordingly sets the value of `billAmt` attribute. The value assigned to `billAmt` attribute is then returned.

Compile the JavaBean Application

Open the command prompt and go to the classes folder of our application (trial) and give following command:

```
C:\apache-tomcat-6.0.14\webapps\trial\WEB-INF\classes>  javac
Food.java
```

Let us create an application configuration file: `faces-config.xml` in `WEB-INF` folder of our application to specify the name our JavaBean and also the condition of navigating to `bill.jsp` page from `index5.jsp` page. The contents of the `faces-config.xml` file are as follows:

faces-config.xml

```
<?xml version='1.0' encoding='UTF-8'?>
<!DOCTYPE faces-config PUBLIC
"-//Sun Microsystems, Inc.//DTD JavaServer Faces Config 1.1//EN"
"http://java.sun.com/dtd/web-facesconfig_1_1.dtd">
<faces-config>
<navigation-rule>
    <from-view-id>/index5.jsp</from-view-id>
    <navigation-case>
        <from-outcome>submit</from-outcome>
        <to-view-id>/bill.jsp</to-view-id>
    </navigation-case>
</navigation-rule>
<managed-bean>
    <managed-bean-name>FoodBean</managed-bean-name>
    <managed-bean-class>Food</managed-bean-class>
    <managed-bean-scope>request</managed-bean-scope>
</managed-bean>
</faces-config>
```

Code on previous page specifies that the class name of the managed bean is `Food.class` and is referred to in the application as `FoodBean`. It also specifies that if in `index5.jsp` file, the outcome of an event fired by the UI command component is "submit", then navigate to the `bill.jsp page`.

We use the same deployment descriptor file: `web.xml` (in `WEB-INF` folder) that we have made in earlier application.

To run the application, run Tomcat and in the browser type: `http://localhost:8080/trial/faces/index5.jsp`. The browser displays a list of fast food available and asks the user to select one. After selecting a food, user can select `Submit` button (Figure 4.3).

Figure 4.3   Selection of an item from the List and press Submit button.

The output that we get is as follows:

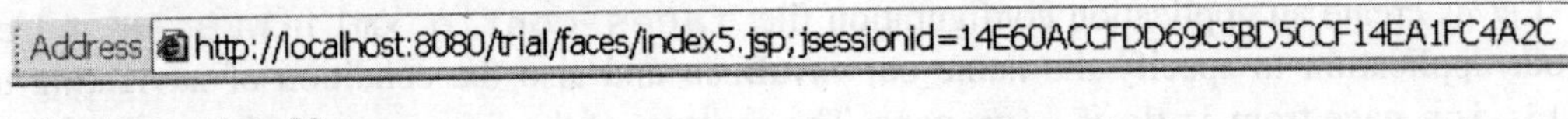

**You have selected burgar
and your bill is 30**

Figure 4.4   Output Displayed with the Bill.

Accessing the Choices from the Backing Bean

As, we can see in above example that all the select tag choices: `Pizza`, `Burgar`, `Chowmein`, `HotDog` are published in the page (`index5.jsp`). But suppose, we want all the choices to be hidden inside backing bean, then we can use `<f:selectItems>` element to display all the choiccs as used in the below given application.

For this application, we are going to develop two pages `index10.jsp` and `bill.jsp`. The `index10.jsp` displays four items of fast food and prompts the user to select one of them. Instead of `<f:selectItem>` element, in this program we use `<f:selectItems>` element to display all the options. The food selected in the page is binded with `FoodBean` (JavaBean) attribute: `foodName`. The food selected by the user is then displayed through `bill.jsp` page along with the bill amount.

index10.jsp

```
<%@ taglib uri="http://java.sun.com/jsf/html" prefix="h" %>
<%@ taglib uri="http://java.sun.com/jsf/core" prefix="f" %>

<html>
```

```
    <head>
      <title> </title>
    </head>
    <body>
      <f:view>
        <h:form id="FastFood">
        <h:outputText value="Select your food "/>
        <h:selectOneMenu id="food" value="#{FoodBean.foodName}"
          required="true">
          <f:selectItems value="#{FoodBean.foodNames}" />
        </h:selectOneMenu>
        <h:commandButton action="submit" value="Submit" />
        </h:form>
      </f:view>
    </body>
</html>
```

From the above code we can see, the choices are not displayed in the page, but instead they are accessed with the help of array (**foodNames**) defined in the backing bean using `<f:selectItems>` element. Selected value is assigned to string attribute: **foodName**. In the backing bean: FoodName, we have to define the elements for foodNames array so that they can display as selection tag.

JavaBean, BackingBean and ManagedBean all refer to the same thing.

The file `bill.jsp` is same as of earlier application. This file will display the name of the fast food selected by the user and also the bill amount.

bill.jsp

```
<%@ taglib uri="http://java.sun.com/jsf/html" prefix="h" %>
<%@ taglib uri="http://java.sun.com/jsf/core" prefix="f" %>
<html>
    <head>
      <title> </title>
    </head>
    <body>
      <f:view>
      <h3>
        <h:outputText value="You have selected" />
        <h:outputText value="#{FoodBean.foodName}" /> <br/>
        <h:outputText value="and your bill is" />
        <h:outputText value="#{FoodBean.billAmt}" /> <br/>
      </h3>
      </f:view>
    </body>
</html>
```

The statement `<h:outputText value="#{FoodBean.billAmt}" />` invokes `getBillAmt()` method of the JavaBean: **FoodBean** to display the bill amount.

Now we will create a JavaBean to define an array: foodNames of type `SelectItem` in which we specify all the fast food options that we want to display: pizza, burgar, chowmein, hotdog, etc. We also define two attributes: `foodName` and `billAmt` that will hold the type of food selected by the user and computes the bill amount respectively. This JavaBean is created by name `Food.java` in "webapps\trial\WEB-INF\classes directory with the given contents:

Food.java

```java
import javax.faces.model.SelectItem;
public class Food {
    private String foodName;
    private Integer billAmt=null;
    private static SelectItem[] foodNames={
        new SelectItem("pizza"),
        new SelectItem("burgar"),
        new SelectItem("chowmein"),
        new SelectItem("hotdog"),
    };
    public String getFoodName() {
        return foodName;
    }
    public void setFoodName(String name) {
        foodName = name;
    }
    public SelectItem[] getFoodNames()
    {
        return foodNames;
    }
    public Integer getBillAmt() {
        calc();
        return billAmt;
    }
    public void calc()
    {
        if(foodName.equals("pizza"))setBillAmt(80);
        if(foodName.equals("burgar"))setBillAmt(30);
        if(foodName.equals("chowmein"))setBillAmt(40);
        if(foodName.equals("hotdog"))setBillAmt(25);
    }
    public void setBillAmt(Integer amt) {
        billAmt = amt;
    }
}
```

We are defining a string array foodNames with four strings: pizza, burgar, chowmein, hotdog. These strings will be displayed as choices to the user.

Compile the JavaBean Application

Open the command prompt and go to the classes folder of our application (trial) and give following command:

```
C:\apache-tomcat-6.0.14\webapps\trial\WEB-INF\classes>   javac
Food.java
```

Let us create an application configuration file: faces-config.xml in WEB-INF folder of our application to specify the name of JavaBean and also the condition of navigating to bill.jsp page from index10.jsp page. The contents of the faces-config.xml file are as follows:

faces-config.xml

```
<?xml version='1.0' encoding='UTF-8'?>
<!DOCTYPE faces-config PUBLIC
"-//Sun Microsystems, Inc.//DTD JavaServer Faces Config 1.1//EN"
"http://java.sun.com/dtd/web-facesconfig_1_1.dtd">
<faces-config>
<navigation-rule>
      <from-view-id>/index10.jsp</from-view-id>
      <navigation-case>
            <from-outcome>submit</from-outcome>
            <to-view-id>/bill.jsp</to-view-id>
      </navigation-case>
</navigation-rule>
<managed-bean>
      <managed-bean-name>FoodBean</managed-bean-name>
      <managed-bean-class>Food</managed-bean-class>
      <managed-bean-scope>request</managed-bean-scope>
</managed-bean>
</faces-config>
```

Above code specifies that the class name of the managed bean is Food.class and is referred to in the application as FoodBean. It also specifies that if in index10.jsp file, the outcome of an event fired by the UI command component is "submit", then navigate to the bill.jsp page.

We use the same deployment discriptor file: web.xml that we created earlier.

To run the application, run Tomcat and in the browser type: http://localhost: 8080/trial/faces/index10.jsp. The browser displays a list of fast foods available and asks user to select one. After selecting a food, select Submit button:

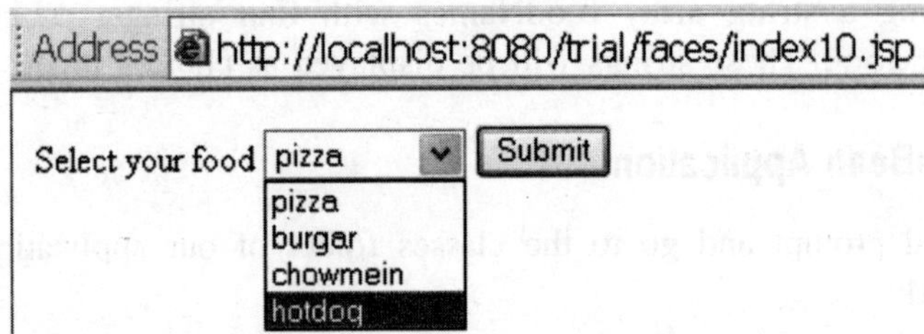

Figure 4.5   Select an item from the List & press Submit button.

We get the output as shown below in Figure 4.6.

Figure 4.6   Output displayed.

Demonstrating RadioButton and ListBox

The following application demonstrates the use of `h:selectOneRadio` and `h:selectOneListbox` tags. For this application, we are going to develop two pages `index6.jsp` and `bill.jsp`. The `index6.jsp` displays four items of fast food and prompts the user to select one of them as is done in the earlier applications. The only difference is that the earlier application was made with the help of `h:selectOneMenu` tag and this application is made with the help of `h:selectOneListbox` tag. The difference between these two tags is that the number of items displayed in case of `h:selectOneMenu` tag is always one so it appears as a combo box, whereas in case of `h:selectOneListbox` tag, we can define the size of component, hence, the number of visible options can be more. The **food** selected in the page is binded with **FoodBean** (JavaBean) attribute: **foodName**. Beside selection of food, we also prompt user to select his/her sex which is binded with FoodBean (JavaBean) attribute: **sex**. The food selected by the user and the sex is then displayed through `bill.jsp` page along with the bill amount. Let us first make a file index6.jsp with the below given contents in "`webapps\trial`" directory.

index6.jsp

```
<%@ taglib uri="http://java.sun.com/jsf/html" prefix="h" %>
<%@ taglib uri="http://java.sun.com/jsf/core" prefix="f" %>

<html>
    <head>
      <title> </title>
    </head>
    <body>
      <f:view>
```

```
    <h:form>
      <h:outputText value="Sex:"/>
      <h:selectOneRadio value="#{FoodBean.sex}"
      layout="pageDirection" >
      <f:selectItem itemValue="Male" itemLabel="Male" />
      <f:selectItem itemValue="Female" itemLabel="Female"/>
  </h:selectOneRadio>
      <br/>
      <h:outputText value="Select your Fast Food:"/><br/>
      <h:selectOneListbox id="food" value=
                                    "#{FoodBean.foodName}"
        size="3">
        <f:selectItem itemValue="pizza" itemLabel="Pizza"/>
        <f:selectItem itemValue="burgar" itemLabel="Burgar" />
        <f:selectItem itemValue="chowmein"
          itemLabel="Chowmein"/>
        <f:selectItem itemValue="hotdog" itemLabel="Hot Dog" />
      </h:selectOneListbox> <br/>
      <h:commandButton action="submit" value="Submit" />
    </h:form>
  </f:view>
  </body>
</html>
```

With the help of `h:selectOneRadio` tag, we display two options: Male and Female specified with the help of `<f:selectItem>` elements. The option selected by the user will be assigned to **sex** attribute of the JavaBean: **FoodBean**. Similarly, by the help of `h:selectOneListbox` tag, we display four items of fast food. Since size of the tag is set to **"3"**, so three options will be visible at a time and user can use scroll bars to see the invisible options. The selected food will be assigned to **foodName** attribute of JavaBean: **FoodBean**.

Also make another file `bill.jsp` with the below given contents in "webapps\trial" directory. This file will display the sex of the user and name of the fast food selected along with the bill amount.

bill.jsp

```
<%@ taglib uri="http://java.sun.com/jsf/html" prefix="h" %>
<%@ taglib uri="http://java.sun.com/jsf/core" prefix="f" %>
<html>
    <head>
      <title> </title>
    </head>
    <body>
      <f:view>
        <h3>
```

```
            <h:outputText value="You are a" />
            <h:outputText value="#{FoodBean.sex}" /> <br/>
            <h:outputText value="You have selected" />
            <h:outputText value="#{FoodBean.foodName}" /> <br/>
            <h:outputText value="and your bill is" />
            <h:outputText value="#{FoodBean.billAmt}" /> <br/>
        </h3>
      </f:view>
    </body>
</html>
```

The statement `<h:outputText value="#{FoodBean.sex}" />` invokes `getSex ()` method of the JavaBean: **FoodBean** and displays the value assigned to **sex** attribute by index6.jsp page. Similarly, `<h:outputText value="#{FoodBean.foodName}" />` invokes `getFoodName ()` method of the JavaBean: **FoodBean** to display the food selected (and assigned to **foodName** attribute of the FoodBean) by the user in index6.jsp page. Also, `<h:outputText value="#{FoodBean.billAmt}" />` invokes `getBillAmt ()` method of the JavaBean: FoodBean to display the bill amount.

Now we will create a JavaBean that will hold the type of food selected by the user and also computes the bill amount. Let us make a file `Food.java` in "`webapps\trial\WEB-INF\classes` directory with the below given contents:

Food.java

```
public class Food {
    private String foodName;
    private String sex;
    private Integer billAmt=null;

    public String getFoodName () {
        return foodName;
    }
    public void setFoodName (String name) {
        foodName = name;
    }
    public String getSex () {
        return sex;
    }
    public void setSex (String sx) {
        sex = sx;
    }
    public Integer getBillAmt () {
        calc ();
        return billAmt;
    }
```

```
    public void calc()
    {
        if(foodName.equals("pizza"))setBillAmt(80);
        if(foodName.equals("burgar"))setBillAmt(30);
        if(foodName.equals("chowmein"))setBillAmt(40);
        if(foodName.equals("hotdog"))setBillAmt(25);
    }
    public void setBillAmt(Integer amt) {
        billAmt = amt;
    }
}
```

As usual, the above given JavaBean also consists of setter and getter methods of their respective attributes: `foodName, sex, billAmt`. The method `getBillAmt()` invokes `calc()` method. The `calc()` method checks the value assigned to `foodName` attribute (through `index6.jsp` page) and accordingly sets the value of `billAmt` attribute. The value assigned to `billAmt` attribute is then returned.

Compile the JavaBean Application

Open the command prompt and go to the classes folder of our application (trial) and give following command:

```
C:\apache-tomcat-6.0.14\webapps\trial\WEB-INF\classes>   javac
Food.java
```

Lets create an application configuration file: `faces-config.xml` in WEB-INF folder of our application to specify the name our JavaBean and also the condition of navigating to `bill.jsp` page from `index6.jsp` page. The contents of the `faces-config.xml` file are as follows:

faces-config.xml

```
<?xml version='1.0' encoding='UTF-8'?>
<!DOCTYPE faces-config PUBLIC
"-//Sun Microsystems, Inc.//DTD JavaServer Faces Config 1.1//EN"
"http://java.sun.com/dtd/web-facesconfig_1_1.dtd">
<faces-config>
<navigation-rule>
    <from-view-id>/index6.jsp</from-view-id>
    <navigation-case>
        <from-outcome>submit</from-outcome>
        <to-view-id>/bill.jsp</to-view-id>
    </navigation-case>
</navigation-rule>
<managed-bean>
```

```
    <managed-bean-name>FoodBean</managed-bean-name>
    <managed-bean-class>Food</managed-bean-class>
    <managed-bean-scope>request</managed-bean-scope>
</managed-bean>
</faces-config>
```

Above code specifies that the class name of the managed bean is `Food.class` and is referred to in the application as FoodBean. It also specifies that if in `index6.jsp` file, the outcome of an event fired by the UI command component is `"submit"`, then navigate to the `bill.jsp` page

We use the same deployment descriptor file: `web.xml` (in WEB-INF folder that we made in earlier application).

To run the application, run Tomcat and in the browser type: `http://localhost:8080/trial/faces/index6.jsp`. The application asks the user to specify his/her sex and displays a list of Fast Food available out of which one has to be selected. After selecting a food, select `Submit` button (Figure 4.7).

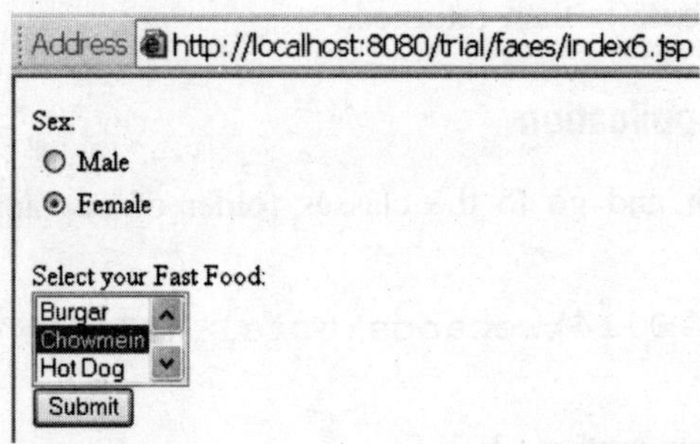

Figure 4.7   Select your sex & food and press Submit button

We get the output as shown in Figure 4.8.

Figure 4.8   Output displayed.

h:panelGrid

The `h:panelGrid` tag is for generating the HTML table element that is usually used for either proper alignment of the components or for displaying tabular data. The components in the panelgrid are placed in columns from left to right and from top to bottom. The number of columns in the table are specified with the help of columns attribute (the default value is 1). Different attributes that can be used with `h:panelGrid` tag are shown in Table 4.5.

Table 4.5 Attributes for `h:panelGrid`

Attributes	Description
bgcolor	To specify the background color for the table
border	To specify the width of the table's border
cellpadding	To specify the padding around table cells
cellspacing	To specify the spacing between table cells
columnClasses	It is list of CSS classes for applying styles to columns separated by comma.
columns	To specify the number of columns in the table
footerClass	It is the CSS class for the table footer
frame	It is specifying the sides of the frame surrounding the table. Valid values are: none, above, below, hsides, vsides, lhs, rhs, box, border
headerClass	It is the CSS class for the table header
rowClasses	It is list of CSS classes for applying styles to rows separated by comma
rules	To draw lines between cells. Valid values are: groups, rows, columns, all

The following application demonstrates the use of `h:panelGrid` tag. For this application, we are going to develop one page `index12.jsp`. This page displays two student records where each record consists of RollNo, Name and Marks. In this application we don't need any JavaBean. Let's first make a file `index12.jsp` with the below given contents in "webapps\trial" directory.

index12.jsp

```
<%@ taglib uri="http://java.sun.com/jsf/html" prefix="h" %>
<%@ taglib uri="http://java.sun.com/jsf/core" prefix="f" %>

<html>
   <head>
     <title> </title>
   </head>
   <body>
     <f:view>
       <h:form>
             <h:panelGrid columns="3" cellpadding="1" border="1"
               width="40%">
             <f:facet name="header">
               <h:outputText value="Details of students"/>
             </f:facet>
             <h:outputText value="Roll No"/>
             <h:outputText value="Name"/>
             <h:outputText value="Marks"/>
             <h:outputText value="101"/>
             <h:outputText value="Johny"/>
             <h:outputText value="85"/>
```

```
        <h:outputText value="102"/>
        <h:outputText value="Peter"/>
        <h:outputText value="95"/>
      </h:panelGrid>
    </h:form>
  </f:view>
 </body>
</html>
```

As, we can see in above code that by using <f:facet> tag, we can display and configure header of the table. We can configure both header as well as footer for the HTML table element generated by h:panelGrid using facets which in turn map to <thead> and <tfoot> table sub elements. The header is displayed as a single row spanning all columns and is styled with the CSS class specified by the **headerClass** attribute. Similarly, footer also spans all columns and is styled with the CSS class specified by the **footerClass** attribute.

To run the application, run Tomcat and in the browser type: `http://localhost:8080/trial/faces/index12.jsp`. The application displays a table containing two student records as shown in Figure 4.9.

Address http://localhost:8080/trial/faces/index12.jsp

Details of students		
Roll No	Name	Marks
101	Johny	85
102	Peter	95

Figure 4.9   Application displaying few records using h:panelGrid tag.

USING STYLES

To make our components more attractive, we can use CSS styles. CSS styles can be either inline that is written within the tag (style) or externally written in a separate file with extension CSS and referred in the current tag using: styleClass.

Example:

```
<h:outputText value="#{UserBean.roll}" style="border: thin solid blue"/>
```

We can see that we have used inline style in above example and hence, the roll number will appear in blue color with a thin border.

Instead of using a hardwired style, we can also write styles in a separate stylesheet. Define a CSS style such as:

```
.prompts {
    color:red;
}
```

Place preceding code in a stylesheet, say by name: `styles.css`. Add a link element inside the head element in the JSF page as shown here:

```
<link href="styles.css" rel="stylesheet" type="text/css"/>
```

Then apply styles by using the `styleClass` attribute in the component's tag.

```
<h:outputText value="Enter your name" styleClass="prompts"/>
```

By using the stylesheet, not only the styles can be applied uniformly to several components but also the maintenance is easy, meaning we can easily update the styles.

The table that we displayed using panel grid can be made more attractive by using styles. Consider a file `style.css` with following contents:

styles.css

```
body {
    background: Yellow;
}
.hdclass {
    background: Red;
}
.evenRows {
    font-style: italic;
}
.oddRows {
    font-size: 1.5em;
}
```

After making the stylesheet, we add a link element inside the head element in the JSF page and then use the `styleClass` attribute in `<h:panelGrid>`. To demonstrate this, let's make a file `index13.jsp` with the below given contents in "webapps\trial" directory.

index13.jsp

```
<%@ taglib uri="http://java.sun.com/jsf/html" prefix="h" %>
<%@ taglib uri="http://java.sun.com/jsf/core" prefix="f" %>

<html>
   <head>
     <title> </title>
   </head>
   <link href="styles.css" rel="stylesheet" type="text/css"/>
   <body>
     <f:view>
       <h:form>
       <h:panelGrid columns="3" headerClass="hdclass"
         rowClasses="oddRows,evenRows" cellpadding="1"
         border="1" width="40%">
```

```
        <f:facet name="header">
          <h:outputText value="Details of students"/>
        </f:facet>
        <h:outputText value="Roll No"/>
        <h:outputText value="Name"/>
        <h:outputText value="Marks"/>
        <h:outputText value="101"/>
        <h:outputText value="Johny"/>
        <h:outputText value="85"/>
        <h:outputText value="102"/>
        <h:outputText value="Peter"/>
        <h:outputText value="95"/>
      </h:panelGrid>
    </h:form>
   </f:view>
  </body>
</html>
```

We can see that different colors are applied at the body background and the header (which is displayed as a single row spanning all columns) with the help of CSS class specified by the `headerClass` attribute. Also different style is applied at the odd number of rows and even number of rows as specified by `rowClasses` attribute.

To run the application, run Tomcat and in the browser type: `http://localhost:8080/trial/faces/index13.jsp`. The application displays a table containing two student records with styles applied in the background, headers and rows as shown in Figure 4.10.

Details of students		
Roll No	Name	Marks
101	*Johny*	*85*
102	Peter	95

Figure 4.10   Display of students record with styles applied.

h:panelGroup

`h:panelGrid` is often used in conjunction with `h:panelGroup`, which groups two or more components so they are treated as one. For example, we might group an input field and it's error message, like this:

```
<h:panelGrid columns="2">
   ...
```

```
<h:panelGroup>
    <h:inputText id="name"value="#{UserBean.userName}">
    <h:message for="name"/>
</h:panelGroup>
...
</h:panelGrid>
```

Grouping the text field and error message puts them in the same table cell. Without that grouping, the error message component would occupy its own cell. In the absence of an error message, the error message component produces no output, and leads to an empty cell.

The following application consists of a form that asks for the user's name and address. We have added a **required validator** with `h:inputText`'s **required** attribute to the name text box and used an `h:message` tag to display the corresponding error when that constraint is violated (i.e., error message will be displayed if the name text box is left blank). Similarly, we have placed a constraint on address text box that it cannot be of less than 2 characters and cannot be more than 50 characters. If the address text box is not within the given range, error message will be displayed with the help of `h:message` tag. Let's make a file `index14.jsp` with the below given contents in "webapps\trial" directory.

index14.jsp

```
<%@ taglib uri="http://java.sun.com/jsf/html" prefix="h" %>
<%@ taglib uri="http://java.sun.com/jsf/core" prefix="f" %>

<html>
   <head>
     <title> </title>
   </head>
   <body>
     <f:view>
       <h:form >
         <h:panelGrid columns="2" cellpadding="1" border="1"
           width="40%">
           <f:facet name="header">
             <h:outputText value="Enter your details"/>
           </f:facet>
           <h:outputText value="Enter Your Name:"/>
           <h:panelGroup>
             <h:inputText id="name" value="#{UserBean.userName}"
               required="true"/>
             <h:message for="name" />
           </h:panelGroup>
           <h:outputText value="Enter Your Address:"/>
           <h:panelGroup>
             <h:inputText id="address"
```

```
            value="#{UserBean.address}" required="true">
            <f:validateLength minimum="2" maximum="50"/>
            <h:message for="address" />
         </h:inputText>
       </h:panelGroup>
     </h:panelGrid>
    <h:commandButton action="response" value="Submit" />
  </h:form>
 </f:view>
</body>
</html>
```

We can see in above code that the input text box and the error message are grouped into one cell with the help of panelGroup tag. Now in case an error occurs, the error message will not occupy another cell but will be displayed in the same cell where input text box is kept.

Now we will create a bean that will hold the name and address supplied by the user. Let us make a file User.java in webapps\trial\WEB-INF\classes directory with the below given contents.

User.java

```
public class User {
    String userName;
    String address;

    public String getUserName() {
        return userName;
    }
    public void setUserName(String name) {
        userName = name;
    }
    public String getAddress() {
        return address;
    }
    public void setAddress(String add) {
        address = add;
    }
}
```

As usual, the above given JavaBean consists of setter and getter methods of the respective attributes: **userName** and **address**.

Compile the JavaBean application

Open the command prompt and go to the classes folder of our application (trial) and give following command:

```
C:\apache-tomcat-6.0.14\webapps\trial\WEB-INF\classes> javac
User.java
```

To run the application, run Tomcat and in the browser type: `http://localhost:8080/trial/faces/index14.jsp`. The application prompts the user to enter name and address (the input field and error messages are grouped in one cell with the help of `panelGroup`) as shown in Figure 4.11.

Figure 4.11　Submit button is pressed without the entries.

If we violate the validations, error message is also displayed in the same table cell where text box is kept as shown in Figure 4.12 (as we have grouped the text box and the error message in one cell with the help of panel group tag).

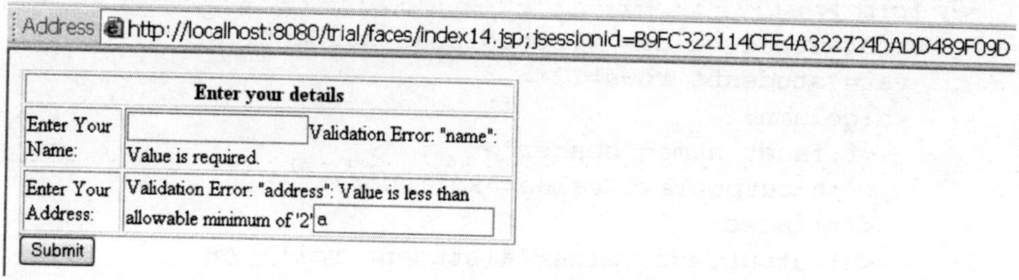

Figure 4.12　Display of error messages in the same table cell.

If we enter the data as per the validity rules, the output may be as shown in Figure 4.13.

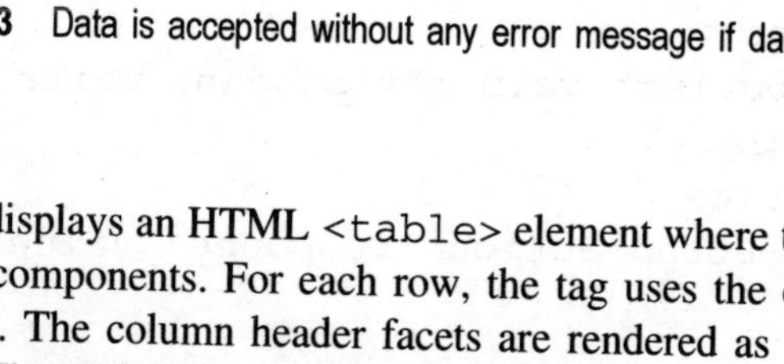

Figure 4.13　Data is accepted without any error message if data is valid.

h:dataTable

The `h:dataTable` tag displays an HTML `<table>` element where the columns are specified with the help of column components. For each row, the tag uses the column components as a template for each column. The column header facets are rendered as `<th>` elements within a separate `<tr>` element. The styles can be applied to header and footer cells with the help of CSS style classes specified by the `headerClass` and `footerClass` attributes. Similarly, the styles can be applied to rows and cells with the help of CSS style classes specified by the `rowClasses` and `columnClasses` attributes.

The following application demonstrates the use of h:dataTable tag. For this application, we are going to develop one page index15.jsp. This page displays two student records where each record consists of Roll No, Name and Marks. Let us first make a file index15.jsp with the below given contents in "webapps\trial" directory.

index15.jsp

```
<%@ taglib uri="http://java.sun.com/jsf/html" prefix="h" %>
<%@ taglib uri="http://java.sun.com/jsf/core" prefix="f" %>

<html>
  <head>
    <title> </title>
  </head>
  <body>
    <f:view>
      <h:form >
        <h:dataTable value="#{SchoolBean.studentlist}"
          var="student" rows="2">
          <h:column>
            <f:facet name="header">
              <h:outputText value="Roll No"/>
            </f:facet>
            <h:outputText value="#{student.roll}"/>
          </h:column>
          <h:column>
            <f:facet name="header">
              <h:outputText value="Name"/>
            </f:facet>
            <h:outputText value="#{student.name}"/>
          </h:column>
          <h:column>
            <f:facet name="header">
              <h:outputText value="Marks"/>
            </f:facet>
            <h:outputText value="#{student.marks}"/>
          </h:column>
        </h:dataTable>
        <h:commandButton action="response" value="Submit" />
      </h:form>
    </f:view>
  </body>
</html>
```

The statement `<h:dataTable value="#{SchoolBean.studentlist}" var="student" rows="2">` invokes `getStudentlist()` method of the JavaBean: **SchoolBean** and the contents of the array: `studentlist` returned by this method will be displayed in the form of a table. studentlist is an array of **User** objects. Also, the array returned will be referred to as `"student"` in the application.

Note:

(i) In this application, "User" class is made to store roll, name and marks of a student.

(ii) The array of "User" objects: **studentlist** returned by the **getStudentlist()** method of the JavaBean: **SchoolBean** is referred in this program as **student**.

Observe the following statements in the above program

```
<h:column>
    <f:facet name="header">
        <h:outputText value="Roll No"/>
    </f:facet>
    <h:outputText value="#{student.roll}"/>
</h:column>
```

The statement: `<h:outputText value= "RollNo" />` displays a column with heading as "Roll No". In the statement: `<h:outputext value= "#{student.roll}"/>`, **student** refers to **studentlist** that is the array of "User" objects returned by invocation of **getStudentlist()** method of the JavaBean:**SchoolBean**. So, student.roll will display all the roll numbers in the studentlist array. Similarly, "#{student.name}" and "#{student.marks}" will display all the names and marks in array: studentlist.

Since an array of User object is desired in JavaBean: `SchoolBean`, we first define a User class with three attributes : roll, name and marks and their respective setter and getter methods. Let's make a file `User.java` in "webapps\trial\WEB-INF\classes directory with the below given contents.

User.java

```
public class User {
    String name;
    Integer roll, marks;

    User(Integer r, String n, Integer m)
    {
        this.roll=r;
        this.name=n;
        this.marks=m;
    }
    public String getName() {
        return name;
    }
    public void setName(String n) {
```

```
            name = n;
        }
    public Integer getRoll() {
        return roll;
    }
    public void setRoll(Integer r) {
        roll = r;
    }
    public Integer getMarks() {
        return marks;
    }
    public void setMarks(Integer m) {
        marks = m;
    }
}
```

Compile the java program

Open the command prompt and go to the classes folder of our application (trial) and give following command:

```
C:\apache-tomcat-6.0.14\webapps\trial\WEB-INF\classes>    javac
User.java
```

Now we will create a bean that will hold the array of User objects and will return it through the respective getter method. We make a file `School.java` in "webapps\trial\WEB-INF\classes` directory with the below given contents.

School.java

```
public class School {
    private User[] studentlist={
    new User(101, "Johny",85),
    new User(102, "Peter",95)};

    public User[] getStudentlist()
    {
        return studentlist;
    }
}
```

In the JavaBean, we provide an array **studentlist** where each element of the studentlist array is an object of **User** class with three attributes: **roll**, **name** and **marks**.

Compile the JavaBean application

Open the command prompt and go to the classes folder of our application (trial) and give following command:

```
C:\apache-tomcat-6.0.14\webapps\trial\WEB-INF\classes>  javac
School.java
```

Let us create an application configuration file: `faces-config.xml` in WEB-INF folder of our application to specify the name our JavaBean. The contents of the `faces-config.xml` file are as follows:

faces-config.xml

```
<?xml version='1.0' encoding='UTF-8'?>
<!DOCTYPE faces-config PUBLIC
"-//Sun Microsystems, Inc.//DTD JavaServer Faces Config 1.1//EN"
"http://java.sun.com/dtd/web-facesconfig_1_1.dtd">
<faces-config>
    <managed-bean>
        <managed-bean-name>SchoolBean</managed-bean-name>
        <managed-bean-class>School</managed-bean-class>
        <managed-bean-scope>request</managed-bean-scope>
    </managed-bean>
</faces-config>
```

Above code specifies that the class name of the managed bean is `School.class` and is referred to in the application as `SchoolBean`.

Deployment Descriptor file will be the same as in earlier application: `web.xml` (in WEB-INF folder).

To run the application, run Tomcat and in the browser type: `http://localhost:8080/trial/faces/index15.jsp`. The application displays the student records returned in the form of array of User objects as shown in Figure 4.14.

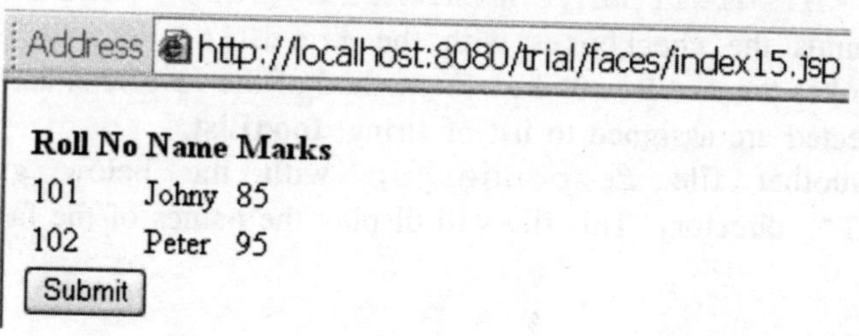

Figure 4.14   Display of student record using h:dataTable.

Demonstrating the use of `h:selectManyCheckbox` and `h:dataTable`

The following application demonstrates the use of `h:selectManyCheckbox` tag. For this application, we are going to develop two pages `index8.jsp` and `response.jsp`. The `index8.jsp` displays four items of fast food in the form of checkboxes and prompts the user to select all the food that he/she wants. User can select one or more items. The food selected in the page is binded with `FoodBean` (JavaBean) attribute: `foodList` (it is a List of String). The food selected by the user is then displayed through `response.jsp` page. Let us first make a file `index8.jsp` with the given contents in "`webapps\trial`" directory.

index8.jsp

```
<%@ taglib uri="http://java.sun.com/jsf/html" prefix="h" %>
<%@ taglib uri="http://java.sun.com/jsf/core" prefix="f" %>

<html>
    <head>
        <title> </title>
    </head>
    <body>
        <f:view>
            <h:form>
                <h:outputText value="Select your Fast Food:"/><br/>
                <h:selectManyCheckbox id="food"
                  value="#{FoodBean.foodList}">
                    <f:selectItem itemValue="pizza" itemLabel="Pizza"/>
                    <f:selectItem itemValue="burgar" itemLabel="Burgar"/>
                    <f:selectItem itemValue="chowmein"
                       itemLabel="Chowmein"/>
                    <f:selectItem itemValue="hotdog"itemLabel="HotDog"/>
                </h:selectManyCheckbox> <br/>
              <h:commandButton action="response" value="Submit" />
            </h:form>
        </f:view>
    </body>
</html>
```

The statement `<h:selectManyCheckbox id="food" value= "#{FoodBean. foodList}">` binds the checkboxes with the `foodList` attribute of the JavaBean: `FoodBean`. It invokes the `setFoodList()` method of the JavaBean and **itemValues** of all the checkboxes selected are assigned to list of string: **foodList**.

Also make another file `response.jsp` with the below given contents in "webapps\trial" directory. This file will display the names of the fast food selected by the user.

response.jsp

```
<%@ taglib uri="http://java.sun.com/jsf/html" prefix="h" %>
<%@ taglib uri="http://java.sun.com/jsf/core" prefix="f" %>
<html>
    <head>
        <title> </title>
    </head>
    <body>
        <f:view>
            <h:outputText value="You have selected" />
            <h:dataTable value="#{FoodBean.foodList}" var="food1">
```

```
        <h:column>
          <h:outputText value="#{foodl}"/>
        </h:column>
      </h:dataTable>
    </f:view>
  </body>
</html>
```

The statement `<h:dataTable value="#{FoodBean.foodlist}" var="foodl">` invokes `getFoodlist()` method of the JavaBean: **FoodBean** and the contents, of the List: `foodList` returned by this method will be displayed in the form of a table, **foodList** is a list of string. Also, the list returned will be referred to as `"foodl"` in the application.

Observe the following statements:

```
<h:column>
    <h:outputText value="#{foodl}"/>
</h:column>
```

These statements display a column in which the list of string represented by `foodl` (because `foodl` refers to the **foodList** which is nothing but the list of string designating the `itemValues` selected by the user) will be displayed.

Now we will create a JavaBean that will hold the list of string containing `itemValues` of the checkboxes selected and its respective setter and getter method. We make a file `Food.java` in `webapps\trial\WEB-INF\classes` directory with the below given contents.

Food.java

```java
import java.util.List;

public class Food {
   private List<String> foodList;

   public void setFoodList(List<String> items) {
       this.foodList = items;
   }
   public List<String> getFoodList() {
       return foodList;
   }
}
```

In the JavaBean, we provide a list of string **foodList** to store and retrieve the **itemValues** of the selected checkboxes.

Compile the JavaBean application

Open the command prompt and go to the classes folder of our application (trial) and give following command:

```
C:\apache-tomcat-6.0.14\webapps\trial\WEB-INF\classes>    javac
Food.java
```

Lets create an application configuration file: `faces-config.xml` in WEB-INF folder of our application to specify the name of JavaBean and also the condition of navigating to `response.jsp` page from `index8.jsp` page. The contents of the `faces-config.xml` file are as follows:

faces-config.xml

```
<?xml version='1.0' encoding='UTF-8'?>
<!DOCTYPE faces-config PUBLIC
"-//Sun Microsystems, Inc.//DTD JavaServer Faces Config 1.1//EN"
"http://java.sun.com/dtd/web-facesconfig_1_1.dtd">
<faces-config>
    <navigation-rule>
      <from-view-id>/index8.jsp</from-view-id>
      <navigation-case>
        <from-outcome>response</from-outcome>
        <to-view-id>/response.jsp</to-view-id>
      </navigation-case>
    </navigation-rule>
    <managed-bean>
      <managed-bean-name>FoodBean</managed-bean-name>
      <managed-bean-class>Food</managed-bean-class>
      <managed-bean-scope>request</managed-bean-scope>
    </managed-bean>
</faces-config>
```

Above code specifies that the class name of the managed bean is `Food.class` and is referred to in the application as `FoodBean`. It also specifies that if in `index8.jsp file`, the outcome of an event fired by the UI command component is `"response"`, then navigate to the `response.jsp page`.

The deployment descriptor file `web.xml` will be the same as that of earlier application.

To run the application, run Tomcat and in the browser type: `http://localhost: 8080/trial/faces/index8.jsp`. The application displays a list of Fast Food available in the form of checkboxes and the user can select any number of them. After selecting different types of fast foods, select `Submit` button (Figure 4.15).

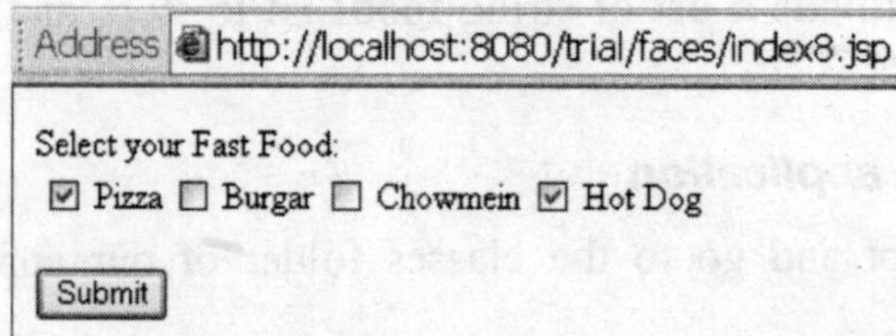

Figure 4.15   Selection of any no. of items from the checkbox.

We get the list of fast food selected by the user as shown in Figure 4.16.

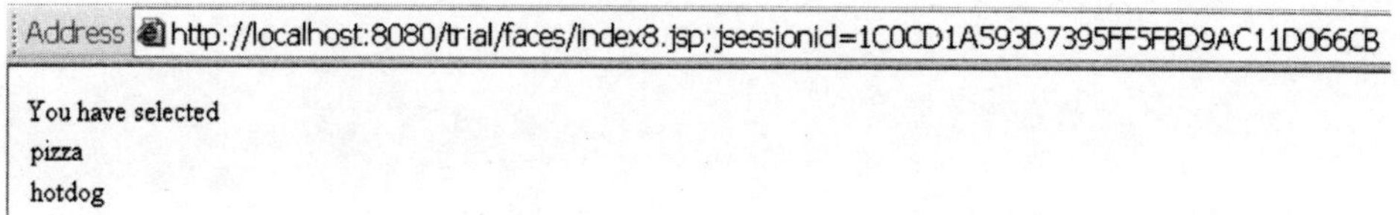

Figure 4.16 The selected items are displayed.

SUMMARY

This chapter briefly introduces different components that are essentially required in developing a web page. It also covers how these components can be practically used in web pages with the help of running examples. Not only this, the chapter also explains how the data is taken from the user using different controls, how it is binded with managed bean and finally how it is evaluated to display the desired information to the user. After learning the usage of these controls, we are ready to move ahead with deeper concepts like applying the concept of converters and validators.

REVIEW QUESTIONS

4.1 Write a JSF program that asks the customer to enter total amount of books purchased and choose customer type from a drop down list (selectOneMenu). The customer types stored in drop down list are: librarian, shop keeper and a private customer. According to the selected customer type, two things are computed and displayed: discount and net amount.

— If the customer type is librarian, the discount is 20% of the total amount.
— If the customer type is shop keeper, the discount is 10% of the total amount.
— If the customer type is a private customer, the discount is 5% of the total amount.

4.2 Write a JSF program that asks the user to fill up the sign up form. The form asks the user to enter:

Name (`inputText`),
Address (`inputTextarea`),
Sex (`selectOneRadio`) and
checkbox that says "`Accept Terms and Conditions`"
The information entered by the user is then displayed.

4.3 Write a JSF program to display Train Name, Train Number, and their Arrival and Departure times using panel grid. Display only 5 rows and apply certain styles also.

4.4 Consider you are running a hotel, write a JSF program to display customer names, the assigned room numbers and their check in date and time in the form of a data table.

5

Converters

In this chapter, we will learn:

- To apply DateTime converters to display dates in different patterns
- To convert date entered in one format into another format
- To display date in international locale
- To convert a number in different formats (decimal digits, currency format, etc.)
- To create our own custom converters

CONVERTERS

A converter is a process of converting, or transforming, one data type into another. For example, by using converters, we can format a number up till the desired number of decimals, date can be converted and displayed in short, long or medium format, etc.

Converters can also act as another form of validators if used along with input component. In that case, user's data will be accepted only if it is entered in the format specified by the converter. If the format of the input doesn't matches with the format specified, an exception is thrown and is displayed to the user.

JSF provides implicit conversion when we map a component's value to a managed bean property of a Java primitive type.

Example:

```
<h:inputText value="#{UserBean.amount}" id="amount"/>
```

Backing Bean:

```java
public class User {
    private int amount;

    public int getAmount() {
        return amount;
    }
    public void setAmount(int n) {
        amount = n;
    }
}
```

As, we can see that the amount entered in jsp page is implicitly converted into an **int** data type because of the reason that the attribute: **amount** is declared of type **int** in the backing bean.

The following JSF Tags supports converters:

- `<h:outputText>`
- `<h:outputFormat>`
- `<h:outputLink>`
- `<h:outputLabel>`
- `<h:inputText>`
- `<h:inputTextarea>`
- `<h:inputHidden>`
- `<h:inputSecret>`
- `<h:selectBooleanCheckbox>`
- `<h:selectManyListbox>`
- `<h:selectManyMenu>`
- `<h:selectOneRadio>`
- `<h:selectOneListbox>`
- `<h:selectOneMenu>`

Standard Converters available in JSF Implementation are given in Table 5.1.

We can register converters in one of the three ways:

1. Specify the converter identifier with a component tag's converter property.

   ```
   <h:outputText value="#{UserBean.dateField}"converter="dteConverter">
   ```

2. Nest the `<f:converter>` tag along with the converters's identifier inside the component tag.

   ```
   <h:outputText value="#{UserBean.dateField}">
   <f:converter converterId="dteConverter"/>
   </h:outputText>
   ```

3. Nest the converter's custom tag inside a component tag.

   ```
   <h:outputText value="#{UserBean.dateField}">
   <labelcomp:dteConverter/>
   </h:outputText>
   ```

Table 5.1   Standard Converters: Available in JSF Implementation

`BigDecimalConverter`	Used to convert the user input string values into values of type `java.math.BigDecimal`
`BigIntegerConverter`	Used to convert the user input string values into values of type `java.math.BigInteger`
`BooleanConverter`	Used to convert the user input string values into values of type `java.lang.Boolean`
`ByteConverter`	Used to convert the user input string values into values of type `java.lang.Byte`
`CharacterConverter`	Used to convert the user input string values into values of type `java.lang.Character`
`DateTimeConverter`	Used to convert the user input string values into values of type `java.util.Date` with a default format.
`DoubleConverter`	Used to convert the user input string values into values of type `java.lang.Double`
`EnumConverter`	Used to convert the user input string values into values of type `java.lang.Enum`
`FloatConverter`	Used to convert the user input string values into values of type `java.lang.Float`
`IntegerConverter`	Used to convert the user input string values into values of type `java.lang.Integer`
`LongConverter`	Used to convert the user input string values into values of type `java.lang.Long`
`NumberConverter`	Used to convert the user input string values into values of type `java.lang.Number`
`ShortConverter`	Used to convert the user input string values into values of type `java.lang.Short`

DateTime Converter

To format a Date object, JSF provides a converter tag `<f:convertDateTime>` which is nested inside a component tag that supports converters.

Example:

```
<h:outputText value="#{UserBean.dateField}">
<f:convertDateTime type="date" dateStyle="long"/>
</h:outputText>
```

The DateTime converter supports several attributes to configure the converter, like **type**, **dateStyle**, etc. The list of attributes that we can use with the DateTime converter is given in Table 5.2.

Table 5.2   Attributes used in DateTime converter

Attribute	Description
dateStyle	To specify the formatting style for the date part of the string. Valid options are short, medium (default), long and full
timeStyle	To specify the formatting style for the time part of the string. Valid options are short, medium (default), long and full
timeZone	To specify the time zone for the date. Default is Greenwich Mean Time (GMT)
locale	To specify the locale to be used for displaying the date.
pattern	To specify the date format pattern
type	To specify whether to display the date, time or both

The output that we get when we apply different dateStyle is shown in Table 5.3.

Table 5.3   Output of different dateStyle

default	Jan 1, 2008 2:30:15 PM
short	1/1/08 2:30:15 PM
medium	Jan 1, 2008 2:30:15 PM
long	January 1, 2008 2:30:15 PM
full	Tuesday, January 1, 2008 2:30:15 PM

Symbols that can be used in a date format pattern are shown in Table 5.4.

Table 5.4   Symbols used in date format pattern

Symbol	Meaning	Format	Example
G	Era designator	G	AD
y	Year	yyyy	2009
		yy	09
M	Month	MMMM	January
		MM	01
d	Day	dd	01
h	Hour in am/pm (1-12)	hh	4
H	Hour in day (0-23)	HH	16
m	Minute	mm	15
s	Second	ss	45
E	Day in week	EEEE	Monday
		EE	Mon
a	AM/PM	a	AM

ACCEPTING DATE IN A GIVEN FORMAT

The following application demonstrates the use of date and time converter. For this application, we are going to develop two pages index.jsp and response.jsp. The index.jsp prompts the user to enter a date in the specific format (converter acting as a validator). The date entered in the page is binded with **UserBean** (JavaBean) attribute: **dateBirth**. The date of birth entered by user is then displayed through response.jsp page.

Note: Through `index.jsp` page, we set the attribute: **dateBirth** of UserBean class (model) and through `response.jsp` page, we get the value stored in this attribute.

To try it practically, let's make a new application by name: trial8, i.e., we need to make a folder trial8 in Tomcat's webapps folder and make a file `index.jsp` with following contents:

index.jsp

```
<%@ taglib uri="http://java.sun.com/jsf/html" prefix="h" %>
<%@ taglib uri="http://java.sun.com/jsf/core" prefix="f" %>

<html>
    <head>
      <title> </title>
    </head>
    <body>
      <f:view>
         <h:form id="Converter">
           <h:outputText value="Enter your date of birth"/>
           <h:inputText value="#{UserBean.dateBirth}"
               id="dateBirth" required="true">
             <f:convertDateTime pattern="MMM-dd-yyyy" />
           </h:inputText> (MMM-dd-yyyy)
             <h:message for="dateBirth" />
             </p>
           <h:commandButton action="response" value="Submit" />
         </h:form>
      </f:view>
    </body>
</html>
```

As we can see in the above jsp program, that the date entered by the user is binded with **dateBirth** attribute of the JavaBean: **UserBean**. The statement: `<f:convertDateTime pattern="MMM-dd-yyyy" />` means that the user is supposed to enter date in the given pattern only else it won't be accepted and exception will be thrown. Recall, that converters can also act as validators if used along with input component.

Also make another file `response.jsp` with the below given contents in `"webapps\trial8"` directory. The `response.jsp` file is for displaying the date entered in `index.jsp` file.

response.jsp

```
<%@ taglib uri="http://java.sun.com/jsf/html" prefix="h" %>
<%@ taglib uri="http://java.sun.com/jsf/core" prefix="f" %>
<html>
    <head>
      <title></title>
    </head>
```

```
    <body>
      <f:view>
        <h:outputText value="Your date of birth is" /></br>
        <h:outputText value="#{UserBean.dateBirth}">
          <f:convertDateTime pattern="MMM-dd-yyyy"/>
        </h:outputText>
      </f:view>
    </body>
</html>
```

As we can see in the above jsp program, that the date binded with **dateBirth** attribute of the JavaBean: **UserBean** is displayed after converting it in the pattern specified. The statement: `<f:convertDateTime pattern="MMM-dd-yyyy" />` acts as a converter to convert the date in the given format and then displays it.

Now we will create a bean that will hold the date of birth entered by the user. We know that a JavaBean is nothing but a class file having attributes and their respective setter and getter methods. Let us make a file `User.java` in `webapps\trial8\WEB-INF\classes` directory with following contents:

User.java

```
import java.util.Date;
public class User {
    private Date dateBirth;
    public Date getDateBirth() {
        return dateBirth;
    }
    public void setDateBirth(Date dte) {
        dateBirth = dte;
    }
}
```

Compiling the JavaBean application

Open the command prompt and go to the classes folder of our application (trial8) and give following command:

```
C:\apache-tomcat-6.0.14\webapps\trial8\WEB-INF\classes> javac
User.java
```

Let us create an application configuration file: `faces-config.xml` in WEB-INF folder of our application to specify the name of our JavaBean and also the condition of navigating to `response.jsp` page from `index.jsp` page. The contents of the faces-config.xml file are as follows:

faces-config.xml

```xml
<?xml version='1.0' encoding='UTF-8'?>
<!DOCTYPE faces-config PUBLIC
"-//Sun Microsystems, Inc.//DTD JavaServer Faces Config 1.1//EN"
"http://java.sun.com/dtd/web-facesconfig_1_1.dtd">
<faces-config>
    <navigation-rule>
        <from-view-id>/index.jsp</from-view-id>
        <navigation-case>
            <from-outcome>response</from-outcome>
            <to-view-id>/response.jsp</to-view-id>
        </navigation-case>
    </navigation-rule>
    <managed-bean>
        <managed-bean-name>UserBean</managed-bean-name>
        <managed-bean-class>User</managed-bean-class>
        <managed-bean-scope>request</managed-bean-scope>
    </managed-bean>
</faces-config>
```

Above code specifies that the class name of the managed bean is User.class and is referred to in the application as **UserBean**. It also specifies that if in index.jsp file, the outcome of an event (i.e., the value of the action property of the UI command component–button) is "response", then navigate to the response.jsp page.

Note: The to-view-id element specifies the target page. The **from-outcome** value is the outcome of processing of the file specified in the from-view-id. This value comes from the action property of the UI command component that may be a button component in the file specified in **from-view-id**.

Also make a deployment descriptor file web.xml with the below given contents in WEB-INF folder of our application to register the FacesServlet (the engine of all JSF applications).

web.xml

```xml
<?xml version='1.0' encoding='UTF-8'?>
<!DOCTYPE web-app PUBLIC
"-//Sun Microsystems, Inc.//DTD Web Application 2.3//EN"
"http://java.sun.com/dtd/web-app_2_3.dtd">
<web-app>
<!"Faces Servlet">
    <servlet>
        <servlet-name>Faces Servlet</servlet-name>
        <servlet-class>javax.faces.webapp.FacesServlet
        </servlet-class>
        <load-on-startup> 1 </load-on-startup>
```

```
    </servlet>

<!"Faces Servlet Mapping">
    <servlet-mapping>
        <servlet-name>Faces Servlet</servlet-name>
        <url-pattern>/faces/*</url-pattern>
    </servlet-mapping>
</web-app>
```

Through `<servlet-mapping>` element we need to state that any request containing the pattern `/faces/` in the URL must be passed to the FacesServlet. Also, we set the "`load-on-startup`" element to true, so that the FacesServlet should be loaded when the application starts up.

Note: FacesServlet builds a *component tree* of the JSP page whose control fires an event. It also creates an Event object and passes it to any registered listener.

To test the application run Tomcat and in the browser type the following address: `http:/ /localhost:8080/trial8/faces/index.jsp`. We get following screen prompting us to enter date in the given format as shown in Figure 5.1.

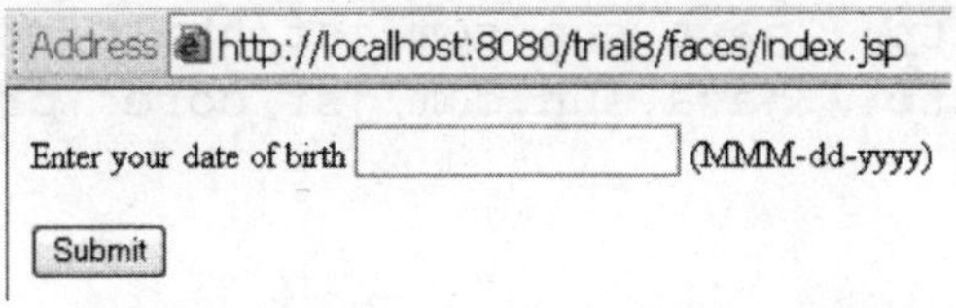

Figure 5.1   Enter date in the given format.

If we enter date in wrong format, we get a screen displaying conversion error as shown in Figure 5.2.

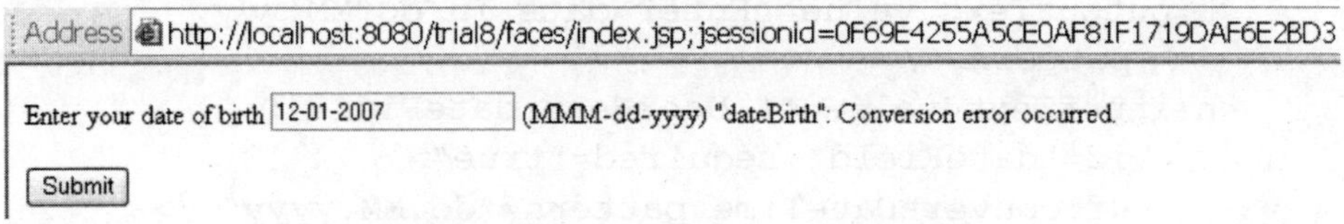

Figure 5.2   Conversion error displayed.

If we enter the date in the specified format, it is accepted and is displyaed in the desired format as shown in Figures 5.3 and 5.4.

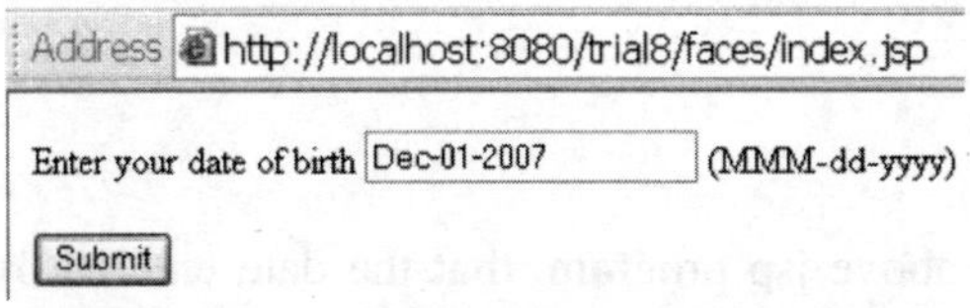

Figure 5.3   Re-entry of date in correct format.

Figure 5.4 Date is displayed.

DISPLAYING A DATE IN DIFFERENT FORMATS

The following application asks a user to enter a date which is then displayed in different styles and formats. For this application, we are going to develop two pages: `index.jsp` and `response.jsp`. The `index.jsp` prompts the user to enter a date in the specific format (converter acting as a validator). The date entered in the page is binded with UserBean (JavaBean) attribute: `dateField`. The date fed by the user is then displayed after converting in different formats through `response.jsp  page`.

Let us make a new application by name: trial10, i.e., we need to make a folder trial10 in Tomcat's webapps folder and make a file `index.jsp` with following contents:

index.jsp

```
<%@ taglib uri="http://java.sun.com/jsf/html" prefix="h" %>
<%@ taglib uri="http://java.sun.com/jsf/core" prefix="f" %>
<html>
    <head>
        <title> </title>
    </head>
    <body>
        <f:view>
        <h:form id="Converter">
            <h:outputText value="Enter date in dd.MM.yyyy
                pattern "/>
            <h:inputText value="#{UserBean.dateField}"
                id="dateField" required="true">
                <f:convertDateTime pattern="dd.MM.yyyy" />
            </h:inputText>
            </p>
            <h:commandButton action="response" value="Submit" />
        </h:form>
        </f:view>
    </body>
</html>
```

As we can see in the above jsp program, that the date entered by the user is binded with `dateField` attribute of the JavaBean: `UserBean`. The statement: `<f:convertDateTime pattern="dd.MM.yyyy"  />` means that the user is supposed to enter date in the given pattern only else it won't be accepted and exception will be thrown. That is, a converter acts as a form of validator when used with input component.

Also make another file `response.jsp` with the below given contents in "webapps\trial10" directory. The `response.jsp` file is for displaying the date entered in `index.jsp` file in different formats.

response.jsp

```
<%@ taglib uri="http://java.sun.com/jsf/html" prefix="h" %>
<%@ taglib uri="http://java.sun.com/jsf/core" prefix="f" %>
<html>
  <head>
    <title></title>
  </head>
  <body>
    <f:view>
      <h2>
      <h:outputText value="Dates in different format"/></h2></br>
      <h:outputText value="The date in long style is"/>
      <h:outputText value="#{UserBean.dateField}">
        <f:convertDateTime type="date" dateStyle="long"/>
      </h:outputText> </br>
      <h:outputText value="The date in medium style is"/>
      <h:outputText value="#{UserBean.dateField}">
        <f:convertDateTime type="date" dateStyle="medium"/>
      </h:outputText> </br>
      <h:outputText value="The date in short style is"/>
      <h:outputText value="#{UserBean.dateField}">
        <f:convertDateTime type="date" dateStyle="short"/>
      </h:outputText> </br>
      <h:outputText value="The time in full style is"/>
      <h:outputText value="#{UserBean.dateField}">
        <f:convertDateTime type="time" timeStyle="full"/>
      </h:outputText> </br>
      <h:outputText value="The date and time in full style in
        French locale is"/>
      <h:outputText value="#{UserBean.dateField}">
        <f:convertDateTime type="both" dateStyle="full"
          locale="fr"/>
      </h:outputText> </br>
      <h:outputText value="The date and time in full style in
        Russian locale is"/>
      <h:outputText value="#{UserBean.dateField}">
        <f:convertDateTime type="both" dateStyle="full"
          locale="ru"/>
      </h:outputText> </br>
```

```
    <h:outputText value="The date in dd.MM.yyyy HH:mm pattern
      is"/>
    <h:outputText value="#{UserBean.dateField}">
      <f:convertDateTime pattern="dd.MM.yyyy HH:mm"/>
    </h:outputText> </br>
  </f:view>
</body>
</html>
```

As we can see in the above jsp program, that the date binded with `dateField` attribute of the JavaBean: **UserBean** is displayed after converting in different styles like: **long**, **medium** and **short** formats. Also the time is displayed in **full style**. Beside this, the date and time are also displayed in **French** and **Russian** locale too. In the last, the date and time are displayed in the specific pattern also.

The language codes for different countries are:

Language codes	Countries
af	Afrikaans
da	Danish
de	German
el	Greek
en	English
es	Spanish
fr	French
ja	Japanese
pl	Polish
ru	Russian
sv	Swedish
zh	Chinese

Now we will create a bean that will hold the date entered by the user. JavaBean is a class file having attributes and their respective setter and getter methods. Let us make a file `User.java` in `webapps\trial10\WEB-INF\classes` directory with following contents:

User.java

```
import java.util.Date;
public class User {
   private Date dateField;
   public Date getDateField() {
        return dateField;
   }
   public void setDateField(Date d) {
        dateField = d;
   }
}
```

Compiling the JavaBean application

Open the command prompt and go to the classes folder of our application (trial10) and give following command:

```
C:\apache-tomcat-6.0.14\webapps\trial10\WEB-INF\classes>  javac
User.java
```

Let us create an application configuration file: `faces-config.xml` in WEB-INF folder of our application to specify the name of our JavaBean and also the condition of navigating to `response.jsp` page from `index.jsp` page. The contents of the `faces-config.xml` file are as follows:

faces-config.xml

```xml
<?xml version='1.0' encoding='UTF-8'?>
<!DOCTYPE faces-config PUBLIC
"-//Sun Microsystems, Inc.//DTD JavaServer Faces Config 1.1//EN"
"http://java.sun.com/dtd/web-facesconfig_1_1.dtd">
<faces-config>
    <navigation-rule>
        <from-view-id>/index.jsp</from-view-id>
        <navigation-case>
        <from-outcome>response</from-outcome>
        <to-view-id>/response.jsp</to-view-id>
        </navigation-case>
    </navigation-rule>
    <managed-bean>
        <managed-bean-name>UserBean</managed-bean-name>
        <managed-bean-class>User</managed-bean-class>
        <managed-bean-scope>request</managed-bean-scope>
    </managed-bean>
</faces-config>
```

Above code specifies that the class name of the managed bean is User.class and is referred to in the application as `UserBean`. It also specifies that if in `index.jsp` file, the outcome of an event fired by the UI command component is "response", then navigate to the `response.jsp  page`.

Also make a deployment descriptor file `web.xml` in WEB-INF folder of our application to register the FacesServlet which is the engine of all JSF applications. Through the `web.xml` `file`, we need to state that any request containing the pattern/faces/ in the URL must be passed to the FacesServlet. The contents of `web.xml` file is same as in earlier application.

To run the application, run Tomcat and in the browser type: `http://localhost:` `8080/trial10/faces/index.jsp`. The application asks the user to enter date in a particular format. After entering the date in the given format, press Submit button (Figure 5.5).

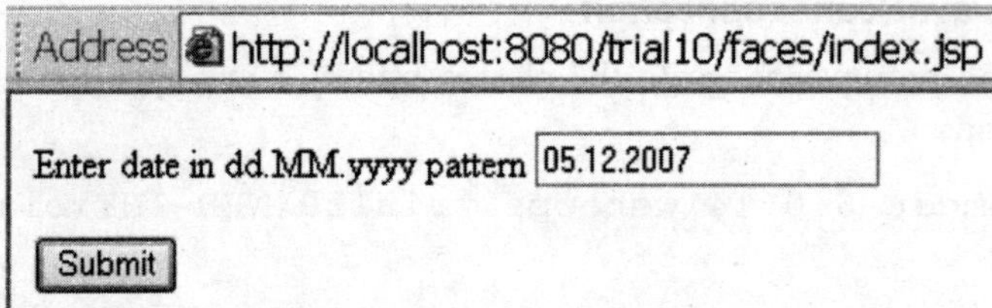

Figure 5.5   Enter the data in given format & press Submit button.

We get the date after being converted in different formats as shown in Figure 5.6.

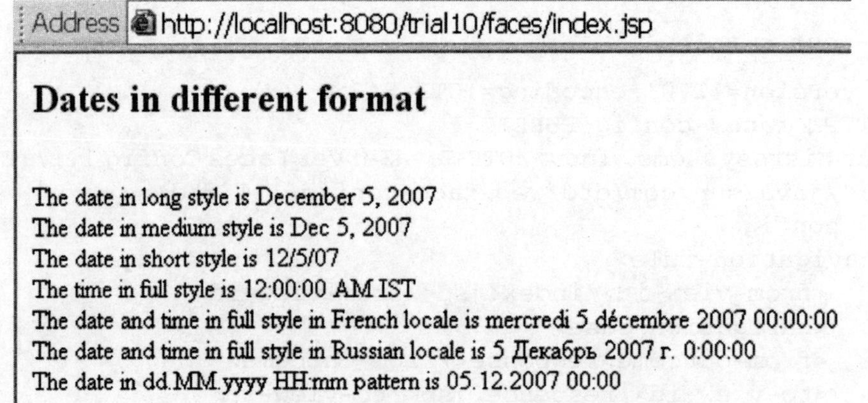

Figure 5.6   Data displayed in various formats.

Number Converter

Number converter is useful for displaying numbers in different formats. For example, to convert a number to a maximum of 3 integer digits, we write following code:

```
<h:outputText value="#{UserBean.amount}">
    <f:convertNumber type="number" maxIntegerDigits="3"/>
</h:outputText>
```

The attributes that can be used with Number converter are given in Table 5.5.

The following application converts a numerical number in different formats depending on the type of pattern applied onto it. For this application, we are going to develop two pages `index.jsp` and `response.jsp`. The `index.jsp` prompts the user to enter a numerical number. The number entered in the page is binded with **UserBean** (JavaBean) attribute: **amount**. The number fed by the user is then displayed after converting it in different formats through `response.jsp page`.

Let us make a new application by name: trial9, i.e., we need to make a folder trial9 in Tomcat's webapps folder and make a file `index.jsp` with following contents:

index.jsp

```
<%@ taglib uri="http://java.sun.com/jsf/html" prefix="h" %>
```

Table 5.5 Standard Number Converter Attributes

Attribute Name	*Description*
currencyCode	To specify a three-digit international currency code when the attribute type is currency. Example:"USD" for the United States Dollar, "EUR" for the Euro, etc.
currencySymbol	To specify a specific symbol, like $ to be used when the attribute type is currency. If the currencyCode is set then currencySymbol will be ignored
groupingUsed	It is a flag specifying whether formatted output will contain grouping separators like ",". Default value is true
integerOnly	It is set to true if we want that only the integer portion of the input value should be processed (all decimals will be ignored in that case). Default is false
locale	The locale to be used for displaying the number. It overrides the current locale set
minFractionDigits	Minimum number of fractional digits to display in the fractional portion of the output
maxFractionDigits	Maximal numbers of fractional digits to display
minIntegerDigits	Minimal numbers of integer digits to display
maxIntegerDigits	Maximal numbers of integer digits to display
pattern	To specify the custom formatting pattern which determines how the number string should be formatted and parsed ***Examples:*** ###,### 123,456 $###,###.## $123,456.99 #.### 1.789
type	To specify the number type. Valid values are "number", "currency", and "per cent". Default value is "number"

```
<%@ taglib uri="http://java.sun.com/jsf/core" prefix="f" %>
<html>
    <head>
      <title> </title>
    </head>
    <body>
      <f:view>
      <h:form id="Converter">
        <h:outputText value="Enter amount"/>
        <h:inputText value="#{UserBean.amount}" id="amount"
            required="true">
          </h:inputText>
        <h:commandButton action="response" value="Submit"/>
```

```
        </h:form>
      </f:view>
    </body>
</html>
```

As we can see in the above jsp program, that the amount entered by the user is binded with **amount** attribute of the JavaBean: **UserBean**.

Also make another file `response.jsp` with the below given contents in "webapps\trial9" directory. The `response.jsp` file is for displaying the amount entered in `index.jsp` file in different formats.

response.jsp

```
<%@ taglib uri="http://java.sun.com/jsf/html" prefix="h" %>
<%@ taglib uri="http://java.sun.com/jsf/core" prefix="f" %>

<html>
    <head>
      <title></title>
    </head>
    <body>
      <f:view>
        <h:outputText value="The amount in different format
            is"/></br>
        <h:outputText value="The amount with comma and 2 places of
            decimal"/>
        <h:outputText value="#{UserBean.amount}">
            <f:convertNumber pattern="#,###.00"/>
        </h:outputText> </br>
        <h:outputText value="The amount in integer format
            is"/>
        <h:outputText value="#{UserBean.amount}">
            <f:convertNumber integerOnly="true"/>
        </h:outputText> </br>
        <h:outputText value="The amount with maximum 3 integer
            digits is"/>
        <h:outputText value="#{UserBean.amount}">
            <f:convertNumber maxIntegerDigits="3"/>
        </h:outputText> </br>
        <h:outputText value="The amount in currency format
            is"/>
        <h:outputText value="#{UserBean.amount}">
            <f:convertNumber type="currency"
                currencySymbol="$"/>
        </h:outputText> </br>
```

```
                <h:outputText value="The amount with % symbol is"/>
                <h:outputText value="#{UserBean.amount}">
                  <f:convertNumber type="percent"/>
                </h:outputText> </br>
            </f:view>
        </body>
</html>
```

As we can see in the above jsp program, that the number binded with **amount** attribute of the JavaBean: **UserBean** is displayed after converting in different patterns like: two decimal places with comma separator, integer only format, currency format, with percentage symbol, etc.

Now we will create a bean that will hold the number entered by the user. JavaBean is a class file having attributes and their respective setter and getter methods. Let's make a file `User.java` in `webapps\trial9\WEB-INF\classes` directory with following contents:

User.java

```
    import java.util.Date;
    public class User {
       private Float amount;

       public Float getAmount() {
            return amount;
       }
       public void setAmount(Float n) {
            amount = n;
       }
    }
```

Compiling the JavaBean application

Open the command prompt and go to the classes folder of our application (trial9) and give following command:

```
C:\apache-tomcat-6.0.14\webapps\trial9\WEB-INF\classes>  javac
User.java
```

Let us create an application configuration file: `faces-config.xml` in WEB-INF folder of our application to specify the name of our JavaBean and also the condition of navigating to `response.jsp` page from `index.jsp page`. The contents of the `faces-config.xml` file are as follows:

faces.config.xml

```
<?xml version='1.0' encoding='UTF-8'?>
<!DOCTYPE faces-config PUBLIC
"-//Sun Microsystems, Inc.//DTD JavaServer Faces Config 1.1//EN"
"http://java.sun.com/dtd/web-facesconfig_1_1.dtd">
```

```
<faces-config>
    <navigation-rule>
        <from-view-id>/index.jsp</from-view-id>
        <navigation-case>
        <from-outcome>response</from-outcome>
        <to-view-id>/response.jsp</to-view-id>
        </navigation-case>
    </navigation-rule>
    <managed-bean>
        <managed-bean-name>UserBean</managed-bean-name>
        <managed-bean-class>User</managed-bean-class>
        <managed-bean-scope>request</managed-bean-scope>
    </managed-bean>
</faces-config>
```

Above code specifies that the class name of the managed bean is `User.class` and is referred to in the application as `UserBean`. It also specifies that if in `index.jsp file`, the outcome of an event fired by the UI command component (button) is "`response`", then navigate to the `response.jsp page`.

Also make a deployment descriptor file `web.xml` in WEB-INF folder of our application to register the FacesServlet which is the engine of all JSF applications. The contents of `web.xml  file` are same as earlier applications.

To run the application, run Tomcat and in the browser type the address: `http://localhost: 8080/trial9/faces/index.jsp`. The application asks the user to enter a numerical number. After entering a the number, select `Submit` button (Figure 5.7).

Figure 5.7   Enter a numerical number & press Submit button.

We get the number after being converted in different formats as shown in Figure 5.8.

Figure 5.8   The number is displayed in different formats.

Custom Converters

If the standard converters do not serve our purpose, then we may even create our own converters. There are several steps for creating a custom converter:

1. Create a class that implements `javax.faces.converter.Converter` interface.
2. Import necessary packages and classes.
3. Implement the `getAsObject()` and `getAsString()` methods within the converter class.

   - `getAsObject()` method converts the String (User Input) to Object (i.e., converts from the presentation view to the model view).
   - `getAsString()` method converts the Object to String to send back to the page (i.e., converts from the model view to the presentation view).

4. Configure the configuration file (`faces-config.xml`) by adding `<converter>` element. This element has child elements `<converter-id>` (name of the converter to be used while programming) and `<converter-class>` (name of the converter class).
5. Create view page where `<f:converter>` tag is used with attribute "converterId" which specifies the name of the converter specified in `<converter-id>` element of `<converter>` element in "faces-config. xml" file.
6. If the user doesn't enters data in correct format then display error message to show that the conversion was not successful. Use `<h:message>` tag to display the error message.

Custom Converter—`TimeConverter`

The following application creates a custom converter called `TimeConverter`, to convert the time entered into seconds. For example, if the time entered is 0:1:0 (hh:mm:ss) then the output displyaed is: 60. If the time entered is 1:0:0), then the output appears as :3600. For this application, we are going to develop a page `index.jsp` which prompts the user to enter time in `hh:mm:ss` format. The time entered in the page is binded with `TimeBean` (JavaBean) attribute: time. The time fed by user is then converted into seconds.

To try it practically, let's make a new application by name: trial17, i.e., we need to make a folder trial17 in Tomcat's webapps folder and make a file `index.jsp` with following contents:

index.jsp

```
<%@ taglib uri="http://java.sun.com/jsf/html" prefix="h" %>
<%@ taglib uri="http://java.sun.com/jsf/core" prefix="f" %>
<f:view>
    <html>
      <body>
        <h:form>
          <h2>Custom Converter to convert time into seconds </h2>
        <b>Enter time in below given format, it will be converted
            into seconds</b><br/>
            <h:inputText id="time" value="#{TimeBean.time}">
```

```
            <f:converter converterId="TimeConverter"/>
        </h:inputText><br/>
        Hours:Minutes:Seconds (Ex.01:05:40)<br/>
        <h:message for="time" style="color:RED"/><br/>
        <h:commandButton value="Submit"/>
     </h:form>
   </body>
</html>
</f:view>
```

`<f:converter>` tag is used to associate the converter to the component using **converter Id** attribute. **The** `TimeConverter` is attached to the **time** component. Now, the time entered in the **time** component will be automatically converted according to the rules specified in the Converter: **TimeConverter**.

Now, we will create a bean that will hold the time entered by the user. JavaBean is a class file having attributes and their respective setter and getter methods. Let's make a file `Timestore.java` in `webapps\trial17\WEB-INF\classes` directory with following contents:

Timestore.java

```
import javax.faces.component.UIComponent;
import javax.faces.context.FacesContext;
import javax.faces.convert.*;
import javax.faces.application.*;
public class Timestore {
    private String time;
    public String getTime(){
        return time;
    }
    public void setTime(String time)
    {
        this.time=time;
    }
}
```

To implement custom converter, we make a file `TimeConverter.java` in `webapps\trial17\WEB-INF\classes` directory with following contents:

TimeConverter.java

```
import javax.faces.component.UIComponent;
import javax.faces.context.FacesContext;
import javax.faces.convert.*;
import javax.faces.application.*;
public class TimeConverter implements Converter {

    public Object getAsObject(FacesContext context, UIComponent
```

```java
        component, String value){
        if(value==null){
            return null;
        }
        try {
            String t[] = value.split(":");
            int seconds =
            Integer.parseInt(t[0])*60*60 +
            Integer.parseInt(t[1])*60+
            Integer.parseInt(t[2]);
            Integer secs= new Integer(seconds);
            return secs;
        }
        catch (Exception exception) {
            throw new ConverterException(exception);
        }
    }

    public String getAsString(FacesContext context, UIComponent
    component, Object value) {
        if(value==null)
        {
            return null;
        }
        String sc=value.toString();
        return sc;
    }
}
}
```

All custom converters must implement the converter interface. This implementation must define how to convert data both ways between the two views of the data.

To define how the data is converted from the presentation view to the model view, the converter implementation must implement the getAsObject(FacesContext, UI component, string) method from the converter interface.

To define how the data is converted from the model view to the presentation view, the converter implementation must implement the getAsString(FacesContext, UI component, object) method from the converter interface.

During the Apply Request Values (refer Figure 1.3) phase, when the components' decode methods are processed, the JavaServer Faces implementation looks up the component's local value in the request and calls the getAsObject method. While calling this method, the JavaServer Faces implementation passes in the current **FacesContext**, the **component** whose data needs conversion and the bean **value** to be converted. In this class "value" represents the string provided by the user in the component. In getAsObject method, we can manipulate or convert the value as per our requirement and return the appropriate object. We can see in above coding that in getAsObject method, we are writing the local value to a character array separating hours, minutes and seconds. Splitting the data wherever : (colon) occurs in the input. Then the elements of array are multiplied by 60 after converting into Integer type to convert the time into seconds. The result is then returned. If there is any problem in this process we handle it by **try** and **catch** block. An exception is thrown if any error occurs in conversion process.

During the Render Response phase, the components encode methods are called *JSF* implementation calls, the `getAsString()` method in order to generate the appropriate output. The "`value`" parameter passed in `getAsString()` method represents the converted object in the previous method. This method is called while displaying the page. So we return the appropriate string by manipulating this **value** object.

Compiling the JavaBean and converter class

Open the command prompt and go to the classes folder of our application (trial17) and give following commands:

```
C:\apache-tomcat-6.0.14\webapps\trial17\WEB-INF\classes>  javac
Timestore.java

C:\apache-tomcat-6.0.14\webapps\trial17\WEB-INF\classes>  javac
TimeConverter.java
```

Let us create an application configuration file: `faces-config.xml` in WEB-INF folder of our application to specify the name of our JavaBean and also the details of the converter used. The contents of the `faces-config.xml` file are as follows:

faces-config.xml

```
<?xml version='1.0' encoding='UTF-8'?>
<!DOCTYPE faces-config PUBLIC
"-//Sun Microsystems, Inc.//DTD JavaServer Faces Config 1.1//EN"
"http://java.sun.com/dtd/web-facesconfig_1_1.dtd">
<faces-config>
    <converter>
        <converter-id>TimeConverter</converter-id>
        <converter-class>TimeConverter</converter-class>
    </converter>
    <managed-bean>
        <managed-bean-name>TimeBean</managed-bean-name>
        <managed-bean-class>Timestore</managed-bean-class>
        <managed-bean-scope>request</managed-bean-scope>
    </managed-bean>
</faces-config>
```

Above code specifies that the class name of the managed bean is `Timestore.class` and is referred to in the application as **TimeBean**. The converter element represents a converter implementation. The converter element contains required converter-id and converter-class elements.

The converter-id element is set to TimeConverter. It specifies the ID that is used by the converter attribute of a UI component tag to apply the converter to the component's data.

The converter-class element is also set to TimeConverter as it identifies the converter implementation.

Also make a deployment descriptor file `web.xml` in WEB-INF folder of our application to register the FacesServlet which is the engine of all JSF applications. Through the `web.xml` `file`, we need to state that any request containing the `pattern/faces/` in the URL must be passed to the FacesServlet. The contents of `web.xml` file are same as earlier applications:

To run the application, run Tomcat and in the browser type: `http://localhost:8080/trial17/faces/index.jsp`. We get the input screen as shown in Figure 5.9.

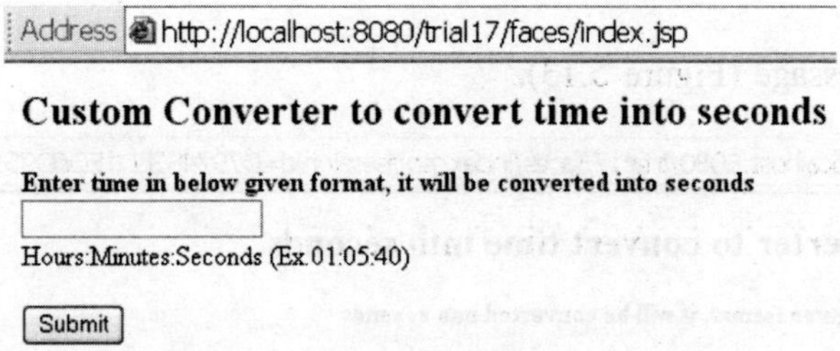

Figure 5.9 Display for entering the time.

The application asks the user to enter time in `hh:mm:ss` format. After entering the time, select `Submit` button (Figure 5.10).

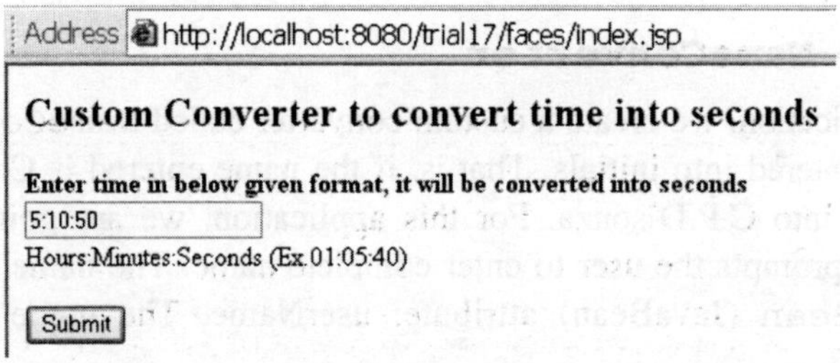

Figure 5.10 Time is feeded with the given format.

We get the time converted into seconds as shown in Figure 5.11.

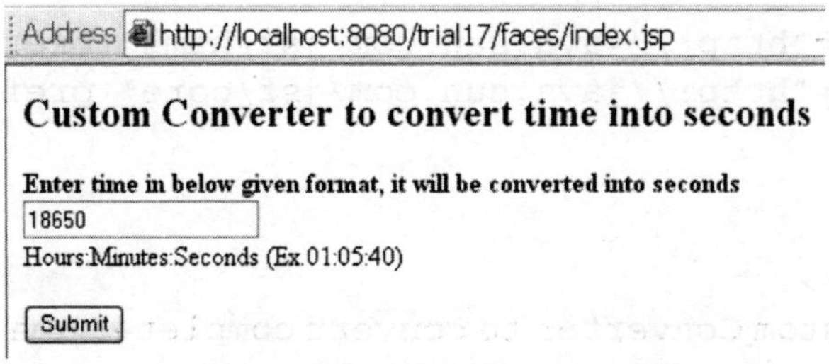

Figure 5.11 Time converted into seconds.

But if we don't enter the time as specified in the format, we get the conversion error as shown in Figure 5.12.

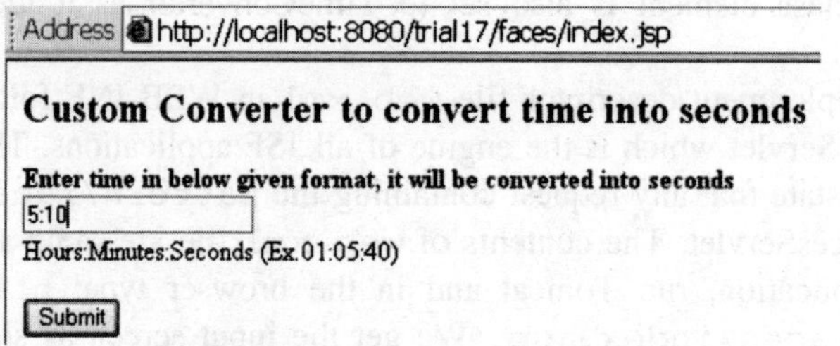

Address http://localhost:8080/trial17/faces/index.jsp

Custom Converter to convert time into seconds

Enter time in below given format, it will be converted into seconds

5:10

Hours:Minutes:Seconds (Ex. 01:05:40)

Submit

Figure 5.12   Time fed in wrong format.

We get error message (Figure 5.13).

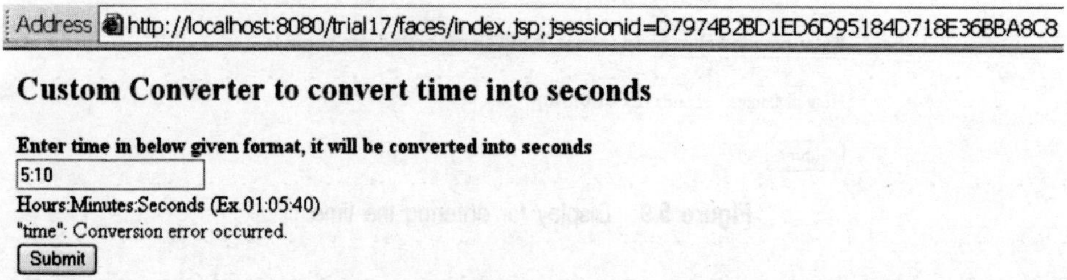

Address http://localhost:8080/trial17/faces/index.jsp;jsessionid=D7974B2BD1ED6D95184D718E36BBA8C8

Custom Converter to convert time into seconds

Enter time in below given format, it will be converted into seconds

5:10

Hours:Minutes:Seconds (Ex. 01:05:40)
"time": Conversion error occurred.
Submit

Figure 5.13   Error message is displayed.

Custom Converter—`NameConverter`

In the following application, we create a custom converter called `NameConverter`, to convert the complete name entered into initials. That is, if the name entered is Charles Peters D'souza, it will be converted into C.P.D'souza. For this application, we are going to develop a page `index.jsp` which prompts the user to enter complete name. The name entered in the page is binded with `UserBean` (JavaBean) attribute: userName. The name fed by user is then converted into initials.

Let us make a new application by name: trial18, i.e., we make a folder trial18 in Tomcat's **webapps** folder and make a `file index.jsp` with following contents:

index.jsp

```
<%@ taglib uri="http://java.sun.com/jsf/html" prefix="h" %>
<%@ taglib uri="http://java.sun.com/jsf/core" prefix="f" %>
<f:view>
    <html>
      <body>
        <h:form>
        <h2>Custom Converter to convert complete name into initials
        </h2>
        <b>Enter name in below given format, it will be converted
```

```
        into initials</b><br/>
    <h:inputText id="name" value="#{UserBean.userName}">
        <f:converter converterId="NameConverter"/>
    </h:inputText><br/>
    Ex: Charles Peters D'souza will be converted into
        C.P.D'souza<br/>
    <h:commandButton value="Submit"/>
    </h:form>
  </body>
 </html>
</f:view>
```

We can see in above code that `<f:converter>` tag is used to associate the converter to the component using **converter Id** attribute. The NameConverter is attached to the **name** component. With the help of this NameConverter, the name entered in the name component will be automatically converted into initials.

Now we will create a bean that will hold the name entered by the user. The bean is in the form of `User.java` file which we create in `webapps\trial18\WEB-INF\classes` directory with following contents:

User.java

```java
import javax.faces.component.UIComponent;
import javax.faces.context.FacesContext;
import javax.faces.convert.*;
import javax.faces.application.*;

public class User {
    private String userName;
    public String getUserName(){
        return userName;
    }
    public void setUserName(String name)
    {
        this.userName=name;
    }
}
```

As we know, a JavaBean is a class file having attributes and their respective setter and getter methods. So above `User.java` contains the setter and getter method of **userName** attribute.

To implement custom converter, we make a file `NameConverter.java` in "webapps\trial18\WEB-INF\classes directory with following contents:

NameConverter.java

```java
import java.util.StringTokenizer;
import javax.faces.component.UIComponent;
```

```java
import javax.faces.context.FacesContext;
import javax.faces.convert.*;
import javax.faces.application.*;
public class NameConverter implements Converter {
    public Object getAsObject(FacesContext context, UIComponent
        component,  String value){
        if(value==null){
           return null;
        }
        int x=0;
        StringBuffer shortname=new StringBuffer();
        StringTokenizer t = new StringTokenizer(value, " ");
        try {
           while (t.hasMoreTokens())
           {
               String token = t.nextToken();
               if (x == 0)
               {
                 String n=token.substring(0,1);
                 shortname.append(n);
                 shortname.append(".");
               }
               if (x == 1)
               {
                 String n=token.substring(0,1);
                 shortname.append(n);
                 shortname.append(".");
               }
               if (x == 2)
               {
                 shortname.append(token);
               }
               x++;
           }
        }
        catch (Exception exception) {
            throw new ConverterException(exception);
        }
        if(x<3)
        {
            throw new ConverterException();
        }
        return shortname;
    }
```

```
public String getAsString(FacesContext context, UIComponent
    component, Object value) {
    if(value==null)
    {
        return null;
    }
    String nm=value.toString();
    return nm;
}
}
```

As, we said earlier, all custom converters must implement the converter interface and the converter implementation must implement the `getAsObject(FacesContext, UI component, string)` to define how the data is converted from the presentation view to the model view and also the `getAsString(FacesContext, UI component, object)` method to define how the data is converted from the model view to the presentation view. During the Apply Request Values phase, the JavaServer Faces implementation looks up the component's value in the request and calls the `getAsObject` method. While calling this method, the JavaServer Faces implementation passes in the current FacesContext, the component whose data needs conversion and the bean value to be converted. In this class "`value`" represents the string provided by the user in the component. Now we can manipulate or convert the value as per our requirement. We can see in above coding that in `getAsObject` method, we break the value in separate parts using `StringTokenizer()` and then by using `substring()` method, we convert the name into initials. The result is then returned. If there is any problem in this process, we handle it by **try** and **catch** block. An exception is thrown if any error occurs in conversion process.

During the Render Response phase, JSF implementation calls the `getAsString()` method in order to generate the appropriate output. "`value`" parameter passed in `getAsString()` method represents the converted object in the previous method. The **value** object is converted into string format and is returned.

Compiling the JavaBean and Converter Class

Open the command prompt and go to the classes folder of our application (trial18) and give following commands:

```
C:\apache-tomcat-6.0.14\webapps\trial17\WEB-INF\classes> javac
User.java
C:\apache-tomcat-6.0.14\webapps\trial17\WEB-INF\classes> javac
NameConverter.java
```

Let us create an application configuration file: `faces-config.xml` in WEB-INF folder of our application to specify the name of our JavaBean and also the details of the converter used. The contents of the `faces-config.xml` file are as follows:

faces-config.xml

```
<?xml version='1.0' encoding='UTF-8'?>
```

```
<!DOCTYPE faces-config PUBLIC
"-//Sun Microsystems, Inc.//DTD JavaServer Faces Config 1.1//EN"
"http://java.sun.com/dtd/web-facesconfig_1_1.dtd">
<faces-config>
     <converter>
           <converter-id>NameConverter</converter-id>
           <converter-class>NameConverter</converter-class>
     </converter>
     <managed-bean>
           <managed-bean-name>UserBean</managed-bean-name>
           <managed-bean-class>User</managed-bean-class>
           <managed-bean-scope>request</managed-bean-scope>
     </managed-bean>
</faces-config>
```

Above code specifies that the class name of the managed bean is `User.class` and is referred to in the application as UserBean. The converter element represents a Converter implementation. The converter element contains required converter-id which is set to **NameConverter** and converter-class element which is also set to **NameConverter**. The converter-id specifies the ID that is used by the converter attribute of a UI component tag to apply the converter to the component's data and the converter-class element identifies the converter implementation.

Also make a deployment descriptor file `web.xml` in WEB-INF folder of our application to register the FacesServlet which is the engine of all JSF applications. Through the `web.xml` `file`, we need to state that any request containing the pattern/faces/ in the URL must be passed to the FacesServlet. The contents of `web.xml` file are same as above applications.

To run the application, run Tomcat and in the browser type: `http://localhost:8080/trial18/faces/index.jsp`. The application asks the user to enter complete name (consisting of three parts). If we don't enter complete name, no conversion will take place as shown in Figure 5.14.

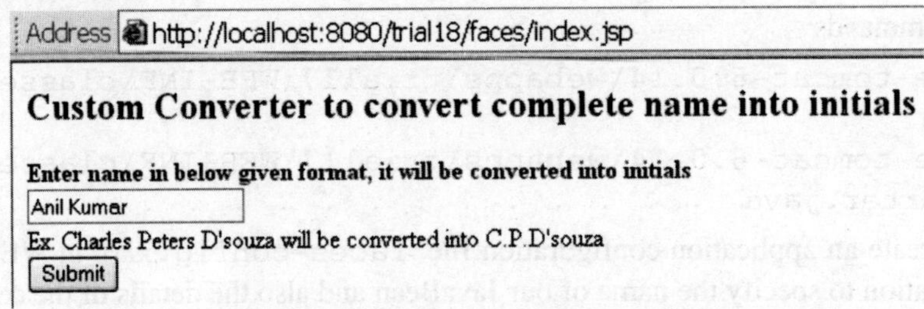

Figure 5.14   Complete name was not entered, no conversion took place.

If we enter complete name and press Submit button, conversion will take place (Figure 5.15).

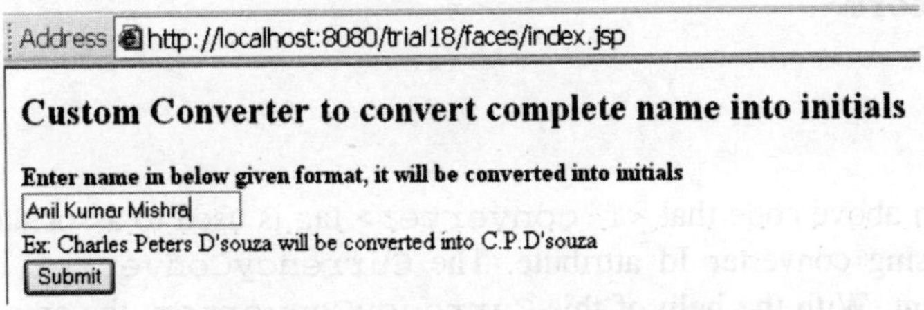

Figure 5.15 Complete name entered and Submit button was pressed.

The name will be converted into initials as shown in Figure 5.16.

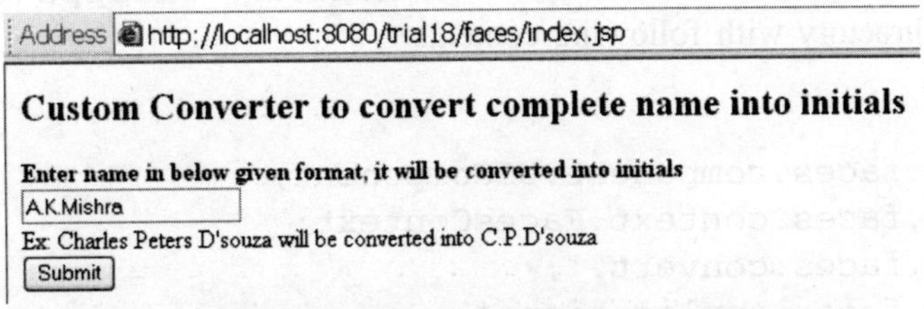

Figure 5.16 Name converted to Initials.

Custom Converter—`CurrencyConverter`

In the following application, we create a custom converter by name `CurrencyConverter` to convert the amount entered in rupees into dollars. That is, if the amount entered is 90, it will be converted into 2.0 (assuming 1 dollar = 45 Rs.). For this application, we are going to develop a page `index.jsp` which prompts the user to enter amount in rupees. The amount entered in the page is binded with test (JavaBean) attribute: **amount**. The amount fed by user is then converted into dollars.

Let us make a new application by name: trial19, i.e., we make a folder trial19 in Tomcat's webapps folder and make a file `index.jsp` with following contents:

index.jsp

```
<%@ taglib uri="http://java.sun.com/jsf/html" prefix="h" %>
<%@ taglib uri="http://java.sun.com/jsf/core" prefix="f" %>
<f:view>
    <html>
      <body>
        <h:form>
          <h2>Custom Converter to convert rupees into dollars </h2>
          <b>Assuming: 1 $ = 45 Rs. <br/>
          <b>Enter amount in rupees, it will be converted into
             dollars</b><br/>
          <h:inputText id="amount" value="#{test.amount}">
             <f:converter converterId="CurrencyConverter"/>
          </h:inputText><br/>
```

```
            <h:commandButton value="Submit"/>
        </h:form>
     </body>
   </html>
</f:view>
```

We can see in above code that `<f:converter>` tag is used to associate the converter to the component using converter Id attribute. The `CurrencyConverter` is attached to the **amount** component. With the help of this `CurrencyConverter`, the amount entered in the amount component will be automatically converted into dollars.

Now we will create a bean that will hold the amount entered by the user. The bean is in the form of `Test.java` file which we create in "webapps\trial19\WEB-INF\classes` directory with following contents:

Test.java

```
import javax.faces.component.UIComponent;
import javax.faces.context.FacesContext;
import javax.faces.convert.*;
import javax.faces.application.*;
public class Test {
    private Float amount;
    public Float getAmount(){
        return amount;
    }
    public void setAmount(Float amount)
    {
        this.amount=amount;
    }
}
```

A JavaBean is a class file having attributes and their respective setter and getter methods. So above `Test.java` contains the setter and getter method of **amount** attribute.

To implement custom converter, we make a file `CurrencyConverter.java` in "webapps\trial19\WEB-INF\classes` directory with following contents:

CurrencyConverter.java

```
import javax.faces.component.UIComponent;
import javax.faces.context.FacesContext;
import javax.faces.convert.*;
import javax.faces.application.*;
public class CurrencyConverter implements Converter {

    public Object getAsObject(FacesContext context, UIComponent
        component, String value){
        if(value==null){
```

```
            return null;
        }
        Float a;
        try {
            a=new Float(value);
            a=(float)a/45;
        }
        catch (Exception exception) {
            throw new ConverterException(exception);
        }
        return a;
    }

    public String getAsString(FacesContext context, UIComponent
        component, Object value) {
        if(value==null)
        {
            return null;
        }
        String am=value.toString();
        return am;
    }
}
```

The custom converter implements the Converter interface. And to define how the data is converted from the presentation view to the model view, the Converter implementation implements the getAsObject(FacesContext, UI component, string) and to define how the data is converted from the model view to the presentation view, the converter implementation implements the getAsString(FacesContext, UI component, object) method from the converter interface.

During the Apply Request Values phase, the JavaServer Faces implementation looks up the component's local value in the request and calls the getAsObject method. While calling this method, the JavaServer Faces implementation passes in the current **FacesContext**, the **component** whose data needs conversion and the bean **value** to be converted. In this class "value" represents the string provided by the user in the component. This string is passed to the getAsObject() method. Now we can manipulate or convert the value as per our requirement and return the appropriate object. We can see in above coding that in getAsObject method, we are dividing the local value by 45 after converting it into float data type (assuming 1 dollar = 45 Rs.). The result is then returned. If there is any problem in this process we handle it by **try** and **catch** block. An exception is thrown if any error occurs in conversion process.

During the Render Response phase, JSF implementation calls the getAsString() method in order to generate the appropriate output. "value" parameter passed in getAsString() method represents the converted object in the previous method. The **value** object is converted into string format and returned.

Compiling the JavaBean and Converter Class

Open the command prompt and go to the classes folder of our application (trial19) and give following commands:

```
C:\apache-tomcat-6.0.14\webapps\trial17\WEB-INF\classes> javac
Test.java
C:\apache-tomcat-6.0.14\webapps\trial17\WEB-INF\classes>javac
CurrencyConverter.java
```

Let us create an application configuration file: `faces-config.xml` in WEB-INF folder of our application to specify the name of our JavaBean and also the details of the converter used. The contents of the `faces-config.xml` file are as follows:

faces-config.xml

```
<?xml version='1.0' encoding='UTF-8'?>
<!DOCTYPE faces-config PUBLIC
"-//Sun Microsystems, Inc.//DTD JavaServer Faces Config 1.1//EN"
"http://java.sun.com/dtd/web-facesconfig_1_1.dtd">
<faces-config>
    <converter>
        <converter-id>CurrencyConverter</converter-id>
        <converter-class>CurrencyConverter</converter-class>
    </converter>
    <managed-bean>
        <managed-bean-name>test</managed-bean-name>
        <managed-bean-class>Test</managed-bean-class>
        <managed-bean-scope>request</managed-bean-scope>
    </managed-bean>
</faces-config>
```

Above code specifies that the class name of the managed bean is **Test.class** and is referred to in the application as **test**. The converter element represents a converter implementation. The converter element contains required converter-id which is set to **CurrencyConverter** and converter-class element which is also set to **CurrencyConverter**. The converter-id specifies the ID that is used by the converter attribute of a UI component tag to apply the converter to the component's data and the converter-class element identifies the converter implementation.

Also make a deployment descriptor file `web.xml` in WEB-INF folder of our application to register the FacesServlet which is the engine of all JSF applications. The contents of `web.xml  file` are same as above applications.

To run the application, run Tomcat and in the browser type: `http://localhost:8080/trial19/faces/index.jsp`. The application asks the user to enter amount in rupees and select Submit button (Figure 5.17).

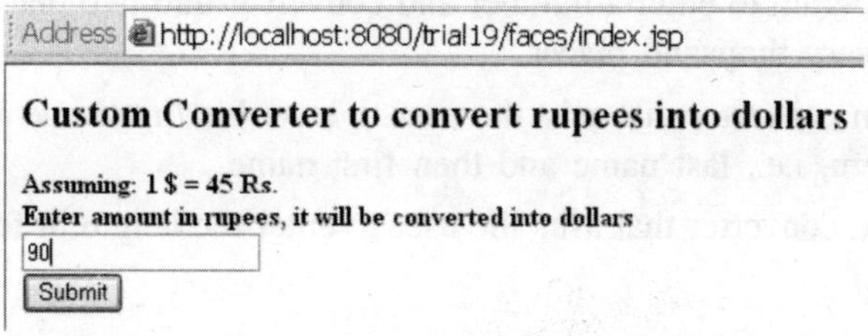

Custom Converter to convert rupees into dollars

Assuming: 1 $ = 45 Rs.
Enter amount in rupees, it will be converted into dollars

90

Submit

Figure 5.17   Enter the amount in Rs. & press Submit button.

The amount will be converted into dollars as shown below:

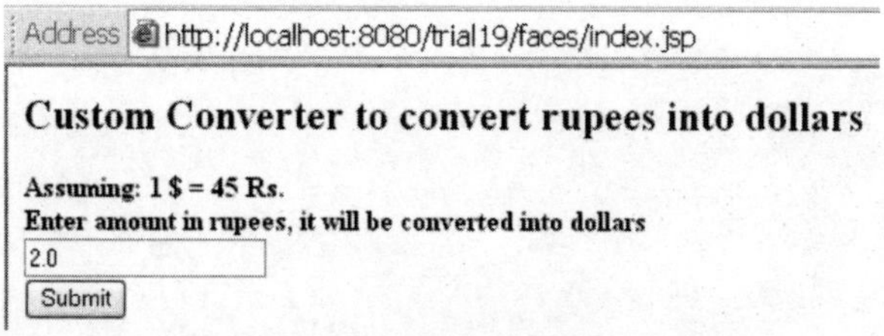

Custom Converter to convert rupees into dollars

Assuming: 1 $ = 45 Rs.
Enter amount in rupees, it will be converted into dollars

2.0

Submit

Figure 5.18   Amount converted in dollars.

SUMMARY

We have learnt different types of converters and how they are practically applied to convert data in the format required by an application. Date and time are extensively used in a web application to record order date, date of birth, date of reservation, etc. So, in this chapter, date time converters are explained deeply via different examples to convert them in the desired format. Also, how the date is converted in different country formats is covered. Similarly, how the numerical value can be converted into the desired number of decimal places is explained by applying Number converters.

The best part of JSF, i.e., how to create our own custom converters is also covered by creating three custom converters:

- Converting hours and minutes into seconds.
- Converting the complete name of the user into initials.
- Converting Rupees into Dollars.

REVIEW QUESTIONS

5.1   Write a JSF program to convert the date in MM-DD-YYYY format and print it in dd/mm/yy format.

5.2   Write a JSF program to enter a date in MM-DD-YYYY format and print it in Spanish locale.

5.3   Write a JSF program to enter a number (having decimal values) and convert it into integers.

5.4 Write a JSF program to enter a number and convert it into two places of decimals and "," (commas) at every thousand places.

5.5 Create a custom converter that asks the user to enter his first name and last name and then interchange them, i.e., last name and then first name.

5.6 Create a custom converter that asks the user to enter the length in feets and convert it into inches.

6

Validation

LEARNING OBJECTIVES

In this chapter, we will learn:

- How the validators are helpful in making the processing error free
- How to apply validators in compelling user to enter essential data
- How to constraint the user to enter data of the given length
- How to create our own customer validators: PhoneNumber validator, Email validator

Conversion is the process of ensuring that data is of right object or type. Validation ensures that data contains the expected content. The task of proper validation is done with the help of certain validators.

VALIDATORS

Validators are used for ensuring that data fed by the user is correct and has no error. JSF provides a set of validator classes for validating input values entered into input components. We can also write our own validator if none of the standard validator suits our needs.

We use a validator by nesting it inside an input component whose input needs to be validated. If the user's input is found invalid, the JSF servlet redisplays the JSP page from which the form was submitted, without updating the JavaBean attributes.

There are four forms of validations within JSF:

- Built-in validation components
- Application level validation
- Custom validation components (which implement the Validator interface)
- Validation methods in backing beans (inline)

Here's a list of the standard validation classes supplied by JSF (Table 6.1).

Table 6.1   Standard validation classes supplied by JSF

Validator Class	Description
DoubleRangeValidator	It validates that an input field provides a string that may be converted to a double and is within the supplied maximum and minimum values.
LengthValidator	It validates that an input field provides a string and its length is within the supplied maximum and minimum values.
LongRangeValidator	It validates that an input field provides a string that may be converted to a long and it is within the supplied maximum and minimum values.
RequiredValidator	It validates that an input field is not null. If the value is set to a string, the length of the string must be at least one character long.
StringRangeValidator	It validates that an input field provides a string and it is within the supplied maximum and minimum values.

Examples:

```
<h:inputText id="age" value="#{UserBean.age}">
    <f:validateLongRange maximum="150" minimum="0"/>
</h:inputText>
```

Above example accepts the age only if it is not less than 0 and not more than 150.

```
<h:inputText id="Name" value="#{UserBean.userName}">
    <f:validateLength minimum="2" maximum="25"/>
</h:inputText>
```

Above example accepts the name of the user only if its length is >=2 characters and is not more than 25 characters.

We can also write our own validator if none of the standard validator suits our needs.

Application level validation basically involves adding additional code to the backing bean methods in order to validate the data binded.

Suppose, the user clicks the Submit button, which is bound to the `save()` method of the application controller, we could add validation code to the `save()` method to determine whether the name field is left blank. If yes, we add a message to the FacesContext directing the associated component to return navigation to the current page.

The advantages of application-level validation are as follows:

- Easy to implement
- No need for a separate class
- No need to specify validator

The disadvantages of application level validation are as follows:

- Occurs after other forms of validation (standard, custom)
- Validation logic is limited to backing bean method, resulting in limited re-use
- It is difficult to manage in large applications

USING REQUIRED PROPERTY

Let us understand the concept of validation with the help of some practical examples. The following application demonstrates the use of **required property**. If this property is true, it forces the component to reject empty values. For this application, we are going to develop a page index4.jsp. The index4.jsp prompts the user to enter a name. If the user does not enter anything and presses Submit button, an error will be generated. Make a file index4.jsp with the below given contents in "webapps\trial" directory.

index4.jsp

```
<%@ taglib uri="http://java.sun.com/jsf/html" prefix="h" %>
<%@ taglib uri="http://java.sun.com/jsf/core" prefix="f" %>

<html>
    <head>
        <title> </title>
    </head>
    <body>
        <f:view>
            <h:form id="LoginForm">
            <p>
                <h:messages/>
            </p>
            <h1>
                <h:outputText value="Enter your details"/>
            </h1>
        <h:outputText value="Enter Your Name:"/>
        <h:inputText id="Name" value="#{UserBean.userName}"
                required="true"/>
        <h:commandButton action="welcome" value="Submit" />
            </h:form>
        </f:view>
    </body>
</html>
```

The statement `<h:messages/>` displays error messages if user violates any validation while feeding data. Since the required attribute is set to `"true"` in the statement `<h:inputText id="Name" value="#{UserBean.userName}" required="true"/>` it will generate error if **Name** textfield is left blank.

Now we will create a bean that will hold the data sent by index4.jsp page: userName. The JSF managed bean is a class file having attributes and their respective setter and getter methods. So, we make a file User.java in "webapps\trial\WEB-INF\classes directory with the below given contents. The bean simply captures the userName entered by a user after the user clicks the submit button. Here is the code of our managed bean (User.java):

```
User.java
```

```java
public class User {
    String userName;

    public String getUserName() {
        return userName;
    }
    public void setUserName(String name) {
        userName = name;
    }
}
```

Compile the JavaBean Application

Open the command prompt and go to the classes folder of our application (trial) and give following command:

```
C:\apache-tomcat-6.0.14\webapps\trial\WEB-INF\classes>  javac
User.java
```

Let us create an application configuration file: `faces-config.xml` in WEB-INF folder of our application. The contents of the `faces-config.xml` file are as follows:

faces-config.xml

```xml
<?xml version='1.0' encoding='UTF-8'?>
<!DOCTYPE faces-config PUBLIC
"-//Sun Microsystems, Inc.//DTD JavaServer Faces Config 1.1//EN"
"http://java.sun.com/dtd/web-facesconfig_1_1.dtd">
<faces-config>
<managed-bean>
        <managed-bean-name>UserBean</managed-bean-name>
        <managed-bean-class>User</managed-bean-class>
        <managed-bean-scope>request</managed-bean-scope>
</managed-bean>
</faces-config>
```

Above code specifies that the class name of the managed bean is `User.class` and is referred to in the application as UserBean.

Also make a deployment descriptor file `web.xml` in WEB-INF folder of our application to register the FacesServlet (the engine of all JSF applications). Through the `web.xml` file, we need to state that any request containing the pattern/faces/ in the URL must be passed to the FacesServlet. The contents of `web.xml` file are as follows:

web.xml

```xml
<?xml version="1.0"?>
<!DOCTYPE web-app PUBLIC
"-//Sun Microsystems, Inc.//DTD Web Application 2.3//EN"
"http://java.sun.com/dtd/web-app_2_3.dtd">
<web-app>
    <!"Faces Servlet">
    <servlet>
        <servlet-name>Faces Servlet</servlet-name>
        <servlet-class>javax.faces.webapp.FacesServlet</servlet-class>
        <load-on-startup> 1 </load-on-startup>
    </servlet>
    <!"Faces Servlet Mapping">
    <servlet-mapping>
        <servlet-name>Faces Servlet</servlet-name>
        <url-pattern>/faces/*</url-pattern>
    </servlet-mapping>
</web-app>
```

To run the application, run Tomcat and in the browser type: `http://localhost:8080/trial/faces/index4.jsp`. The browser asks the user to enter his name (Figure 6.1).

Figure 6.1 Browser asks to enter a name.

If we do not enter any data in Name textfield and select `Submit` button, we get an error message as shown in Figure 6.2.

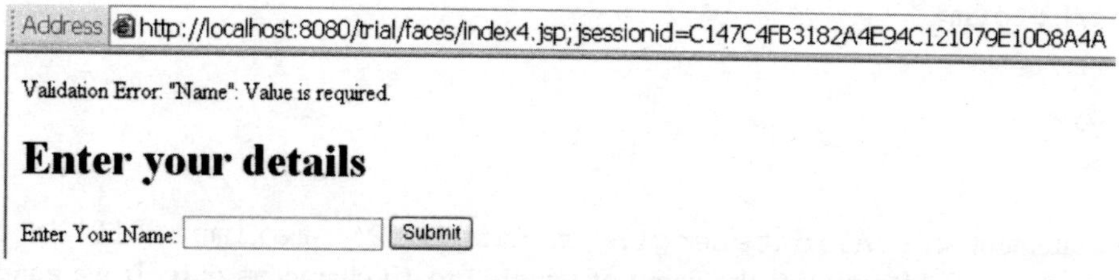

Figure 6.2 Error message is displayed if name is not entered.

f:validateLength

The following application demonstrates the use of `<f:validateLength>` tag. This validator verifies the length of the control's value. That is, we can compel a textfield to handle data within the specified size limits. For this application, we are going to develop a page `index4.jsp`. The `index4.jsp` prompts the user to enter a name. If the user name is within the size limits, i.e., if the length of user name is between 2 to 10 characters, then welcome message is displayed otherwise error message will be displayed. Let's make a file `index4.jsp` with the below given contents in "webapps\trial" directory.

index4.jsp

```
<%@ taglib uri="http://java.sun.com/jsf/html" prefix="h" %>
<%@ taglib uri="http://java.sun.com/jsf/core" prefix="f" %>

<html>
  <head>
    <title> </title>
  </head>
  <body>
    <f:view>
      <h:form id="LoginForm">
      <p>
        <h:messages/>
      </p>
      <h1>
      <h:outputText value="Enter your details"/>
      </h1>
      <h:outputText value="Enter Your Name:"/>
      <h:inputText id="Name" value="#{UserBean.userName}"
          required="true">
        <f:validateLength minimum="2" maximum="10"/></h:inputText>
        </br>
    <h:commandButton action="welcome" value="Submit"/>
      </h:form>
    </f:view>
  </body>
</html>
```

The statement `<f:validateLength minimum="2" maximum="10"/>` ensures that the **Name** textfield can store the name of length 2 to 10 characters only. If we enter name of more than 10 characters or less than 2 characters, a validation error occurs.

Next file is `welcome.jsp`, which displays the welcome message to the user. Let us make this file in "webapps\trial" directory with following contents:

welcome.jsp

```
<%@ taglib uri="http://java.sun.com/jsf/html" prefix="h" %>
<%@ taglib uri="http://java.sun.com/jsf/core" prefix="f" %>
<html>
    <head>
      <title> </title>
    </head>
    <body>
      <f:view>
        <h3>
          <h:outputText value="Welcome" />,
          <h:outputText value="#{UserBean.userName}" /> to our
            Shopping Mall
        </h3>
      </f:view>
    </body>
</html>
```

The code `<h:outputText value="#{UserBean.userName}"/>` is for retrieving the contents of the userName attribute stored in JavaBean: UserBean.

We will use the same JavaBean: User.java of the earlier example.

Let us create an application configuration file: `faces-config.xml` in WEB-INF folder of our application to specify the name of our JavaBean and also the condition of navigating to `welcome.jsp` page from `index4.jsp` page. The contents of the `faces-config.xml` file are as follows:

faces-config.xml

```
<?xml version='1.0' encoding='UTF-8'?>
<!DOCTYPE faces-config PUBLIC
"-//Sun Microsystems, Inc.//DTD JavaServer Faces Config 1.1//EN"
"http://java.sun.com/dtd/web-facesconfig_1_1.dtd">
<faces-config>
<navigation-rule>
    <from-view-id>/index4.jsp</from-view-id>
    <navigation-case>
        <from-outcome>welcome</from-outcome>
        <to-view-id>/welcome.jsp</to-view-id>
    </navigation-case>
</navigation-rule>
<managed-bean>
    <managed-bean-name>UserBean</managed-bean-name>
    <managed-bean-class>User</managed-bean-class>
```

```
        <managed-bean-scope>request</managed-bean-scope>
</managed-bean>
</faces-config>
```

Above code specifies that if in `index4.jsp` file, the outcome of an event (i.e., the value of the action property of the UI command component which triggers the ActionEvent) is "welcome", then navigate to the `welcome.jsp` page. It also specifies that the class name of the managed bean is User.class and is referred to in the application as UserBean.

To run the application, run Tomcat and in the browser type: `http://localhost: 8080/trial/faces/index4.jsp`. The browser asks the user to enter his name (Figure 6.3).

Figure 6.3   Name entered but not complete.

If we enter name of just 1 character, we get a validation error as shown in Figure 6.4.

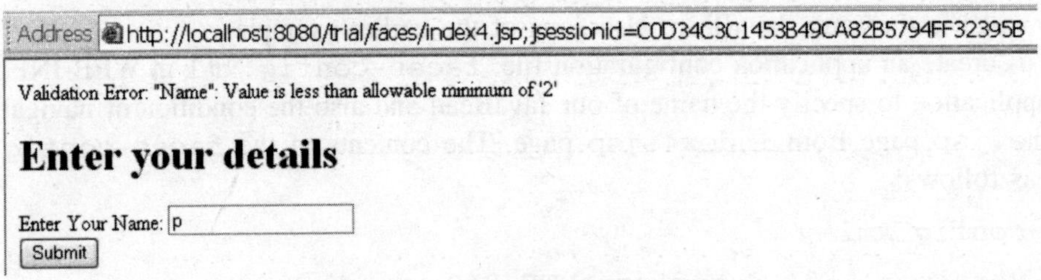

Figure 6.4   Display of validation error.

If we enter name of more than 10 characters, we get a validation error as shown in Figure 6.5.

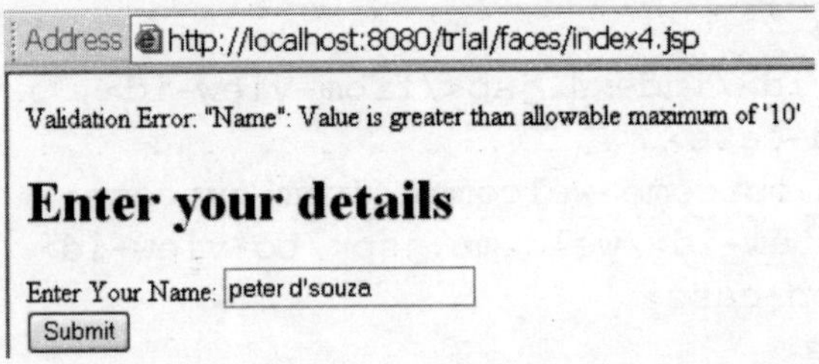

Figure 6.5   Validation error: Name is entered which is more than 10 characters.

If we enter the name within the range of 2 to 10 characters, we get a welcome message as shown in Figure 6.6.

Address | http://localhost:8080/trial/faces/index4.jsp

Enter your details

Enter Your Name: peter
Submit

Address | http://localhost:8080/trial/faces/index4.jsp;jsessionid=C0D34C3C1453B49CA82B5794FF32395B

Welcome, peter to our Shopping Mall

Figure 6.6   Correct name entered & display of welcome message.

Creating Custom Validation Components

The JSF standard validators provide common validation checks for numeric ranges and string lengths. If we need more complex validation rules and checks, we can implement our own validation code by either implementing a `javax.faces.validator. Validator` interface or creating a bean method that performs the custom validation.

We also need to build our own validators in cases where we want explicit control over the validation messages displayed to the end user.

The steps to create a custom validator are as follows:

1. Create a class that implements the validator interface
   (`javax.faces.validator.Validator`).
2. Implement the validate method.
3. Register our custom validator in the `faces-config.xml  file`.
4. Use the `<f:validator/>` tag in our JSPs.

Example to create a custom validator step by step:

Step 1: Implement the validator interface

The first step is to implement the validator interface.

```
import javax.faces.component.UIComponent;
import javax.faces.context.FacesContext;
import javax.faces.application.*;
import javax.faces.validator.Validator;
import javax.faces.validator.ValidatorException;

public class PhoneNumberValidator implements Validator{
    public PhoneNumberValidator() {
    }
```

Step 2: Implement the validate method

Next, we need to implement the validate method.

```java
public void validate(FacesContext context, UIComponent component,
Object value) throws ValidatorException {
   String strValue = (String)value;
   try{
     long phoneNumber = Long.parseLong(strValue);
   }catch (Exception exception){
     throwException("All Phone Digits must be of numbers only.");
   }
   if (strValue.length() != 10){
     throwException("Number of phone digits must be 10");
   }
}
private void throwException(String errMessage){
   FacesMessage message = new FacesMessage();
   message.setDetail(errMessage);
   message.setSummary(errMessage);
   message.setSeverity(FacesMessage.SEVERITY_ERROR);
   throw new ValidatorException(message);
}
}
```

Step 3: Register our custom validator with the FacesContext

The code to register the custom validator with the FacesContext is as follows:

```xml
<validator>
    <validator-id>PhoneNumberValidator</validator-id>
    <validator-class>PhoneNumberValidator
    </validator-class>
</validator>
```

Step 4: Use the `<f:validator/>` tag in the JSP pages

```xml
<h:inputText value="#{UserBean.phoneNo}" id="phoneNumber
TextField" required="true">
    <f:validator validatorId="PhoneNumberValidator"/>
</h:inputText>
<h:message for="phoneNumberTextField"/>
```

Overall, creating custom validators is fairly straightforward and makes validation reusable across many applications. The only drawback is that we do have to create another class and manage validator registration within the faces context.

Validation Methods in Backing Beans

Creating a bean method for performing validation is a good way to provide a custom validator as the method can access other instance fields of the class.

The bean method accepts a FacesContext, a UI component whose data is to be validated, and the data to be validated. We use the validator attribute of the component to reference the method via a method binding expression.

```
public void validate(FacesContext context, UIComponent component,
Object value){
    String strValue = (String)value;
    if  (strValue.length() != 10){
        ((UIInput)component).setValid(false);
        FacesMessage message = new FacesMessage("Number of phone
            digits must be 10");
        context.addMessage(component.getClientId(context),
            message);
    }
}
```

The validate method defined in JavaBean is used in the JSF tag via the validator attribute as:

```
<h:inputText value="#{UserBean.phoneNo}"
    id="phoneNumberTextField"
    validator ="#{UserBean.validate}" required="true">
</h:inputText>
```

The validate method is used by JSF to perform custom validation on an inputText component value bound to a **UserBean.phoneNo** attribute. If the phone number is invalid, then a message is added to the faces context for the associated component.

CUSTOM VALIDATOR: PHONE NUMBER VALIDATOR

The following application demonstrates the creation of a custom validator by name: "PhoneNumberValidator". This validator checks that while feeding the phone number, only numerals are entered and the number should be of exactly 10 digits. If either of the condition is violated, validation error is displayed. For this application, we are going to develop two pages index.jsp and response.jsp. The index.jsp prompts the user to enter a phone number. The phone number entered in the page is binded with **UserBean** (JavaBean) attribute: **phoneNo**. The JavaBean attribute: phoneNo is updated only if the phone number entered by the user satisfies the validation criteria. If the phone number is valid, it is then displayed through response.jsp page.

Let's make a new application by name: trial6, i.e., we need to make a folder trial6 in Tomcat's webapps folder and make a file index.jsp with following contents:

index.jsp

```
<%@ taglib uri="http://java.sun.com/jsf/html" prefix="h" %>
<%@ taglib uri="http://java.sun.com/jsf/core" prefix="f" %>
```

```
<html>
    <head>
        <title> </title>
    </head>
    <body>
        <f:view>
            <h:form id="CustomValidation">
            <h:outputText value="Enter your Phone number"/>
            <h:inputText value="#{UserBean.phoneNo}"
                id="phoneNumberTextField" required="true">
                <f:validator validatorId="PhoneNumberValidator" />
            </h:inputText>
            <h:message for="phoneNumberTextField"/>
            </p>
            <h:commandButton action="response" value="Submit"/>
            </h:form>
        </f:view>
    </body>
</html>
```

The statement `<f:validator validatorId="PhoneNumberValidator"/>` invokes the PhoneNumberValidator class to check whether the phone number entered is of exactly 10 digits and also it consists only of digits (no alphabet/symbol is entered).

The statement `<h:message for="phoneNumberTextField"/>` displays the error message if validation rules are violated.

Next file is response.jsp, that displays the valid phone number entered. Let us make this file in "webapps\trial6" directory with following contents:

response.jsp

```
<%@ taglib uri="http://java.sun.com/jsf/html" prefix="h" %>
<%@ taglib uri="http://java.sun.com/jsf/core" prefix="f" %>
<html>
    <head>
        <title></title>
    </head>
    <body>
        <f:view>
            <h:outputText value="The phone number entered is"/></br>
            <h:outputText value="#{UserBean.phoneNo}" />
        </f:view>
    </body>
</html>
```

The code `<h:outputText value="#{UserBean.phoneNo}"/>` retrieves the contents of the phoneNo attribute stored in JavaBean: **UserBean** and displays on the screen.

Now we will create a bean that will hold the data sent by index.jsp page: **phoneNo**. The JSF managed bean is a class file having attributes and their respective setter and getter methods. So, we make a file `User.java` in "webapps\trial6\WEB-INF\classes directory with the below given contents:

User.java

```java
public class User {
    String phoneNo;

    public String getPhoneNo() {
        return phoneNo;
    }
    public void setPhoneNo(String ph) {
        phoneNo = ph;
    }
}
```

In the same directory, i.e., "webapps\trial6\WEB-INF\classes directory let us make a validator class `PhoneNumberValidator.java` with following contents:

PhoneNumber,Validator.java

```java
import javax.faces.component.UIComponent;
import javax.faces.context.FacesContext;
import javax.faces.application.*;
import javax.faces.validator.Validator;
import javax.faces.validator.ValidatorException;

public class PhoneNumberValidator implements Validator{
    public PhoneNumberValidator() {
    }
    public void validate(FacesContext context, UIComponent component,
        Object value) throws ValidatorException {
        String strValue = (String)value;
        try{
            long phoneNumber = Long.parseLong(strValue);
        }catch (Exception exception){
            throwException("All Phone Digits must be of numbers only.");
        }
        if (strValue.length() != 10){
            throwException("Number of phone digits must be 10");
        }
    }
    private void throwException(String errMessage){
        FacesMessage message = new FacesMessage();
        message.setDetail(errMessage);
        message.setSummary(errMessage);
```

```
    message.setSeverity(FacesMessage.SEVERITY_ERROR);
    throw new ValidatorException(message);
    }
}
```

We can see in the above code that our custom validator class: PhoneNumberValidator implements the validator interface (`javax.faces.validator.Validator`) and also implements the validate method. While calling this validate method, the JavaServer Faces implementation passes in the current **FacesContext**, the **UI component** (whose data has to be validated) and the **data to** be validated. In this class `"value"` represents the data provided by the user in the component.

The `"value"` which is of Object type is first converted into string form. The first validation check is done to see if the data fed by the user contains only numerical or not. If the `"value"` contains any other matter besides numerical, an exception is thrown displaying the error message: "`All Phone Digits must be of numbers only`". Thereafter the length of the string is checked. If the length is exactly of 10 characters then the data entered by the user is valid else again an exception is thrown saying "`Number of phone digits must be 10`"

Compile the JavaBean and the validator class

Open the command prompt and go to the classes folder of our application (trial6) and give following commands:

```
C:\apache-tomcat-6.0.14\webapps\trial6\WEB-INF\classes>  javac
User.java
C:\apache-tomcat-6.0.14\webapps\trial6\WEB-INF\classes>  javac
PhoneNumberValidator.java
```

Let us create an application configuration file: `faces-config.xml` in WEB-INF folder of our application to specify the name our JavaBean and also the condition of navigating to `response.jsp` page from `index.jsp` page. The contents of the `faces-config.xml` file are as follows:

faces-config.xml

```
<?xml version='1.0' encoding='UTF-8'?>
<!DOCTYPE faces-config PUBLIC
"-//Sun Microsystems, Inc.//DTD JavaServer Faces Config 1.1//EN"
"http://java.sun.com/dtd/web-facesconfig_1_1.dtd">
<faces-config>
    <navigation-rule>
      <from-view-id>/index.jsp</from-view-id>
      <navigation-case>
        <from-outcome>response</from-outcome>
        <to-view-id>/response.jsp</to-view-id>
      </navigation-case>
```

```
    </navigation-rule>
    <managed-bean>
      <managed-bean-name>UserBean</managed-bean-name>
      <managed-bean-class>User</managed-bean-class>
      <managed-bean-scope>request</managed-bean-scope>
    </managed-bean>
    <validator>
      <validator-id>PhoneNumberValidator</validator-id>
      <validator-class>PhoneNumberValidator</validator-class>
    </validator>
</faces-config>
```

Above code specifies that if in `index.jsp` file, the outcome of an event (i.e., the value of the action property of the UI command component–button component) is `"response"`, then navigate to the `response.jsp` page. It also specifies that the class name of the managed bean is `User.class` and is referred to in the application as **UserBean**. We also register our custom validator with the help of validator element. The validator element represents a Validator implementation. The validator element contains required validator -id and validator-class elements.

The validator-id element is set to **PhoneNumberValidator**. It specifies the ID that is used by the validator attribute of a UI component tag to apply the validator to the component's data.

The validator-class element is set to **PhoneNumberValidator** as it identifies the validator implementation.

Also make a deployment descriptor file `web.xml` in WEB-INF folder of our application to register the FacesServlet (the engine of all JSF applications). Through the `web.xml file`, we need to state that any request containing the pattern/faces/ in the URL must be passed to the FacesServlet. The contents of `web.xml` file is same as earlier applications.

To run the application, run Tomcat and in the browser type: `http://localhost:8080/trial6/faces/index.jsp`. The browser asks the user to enter a phone number (Figure 6.7).

Figure 6.7 Enter a phone number.

If the phone number is of less than 10 digits, validation error is displayed as shown in Figure 6.8.

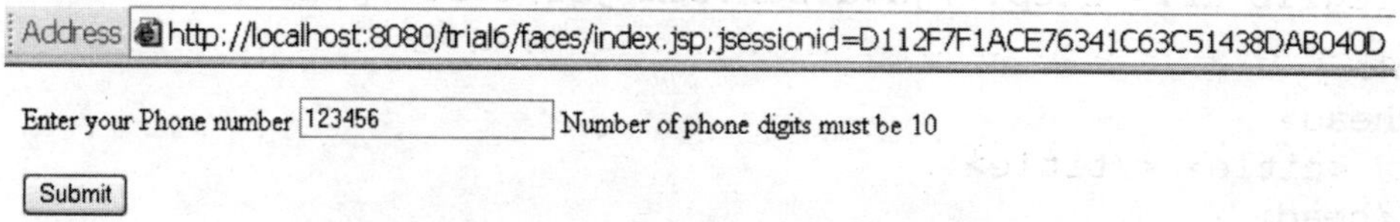

Figure 6.8 Validation error is displayed.

If the phone number contains any matter beside digits, validation error is displayed as shown in Figure 6.9.

Figure 6.9   Validation error is displayed.

If the phone number consists only of numericals and that also of exactly 10 digits, the phone number is accepted and is then displayed through `response.jsp` page as shown in Figure 6.10.

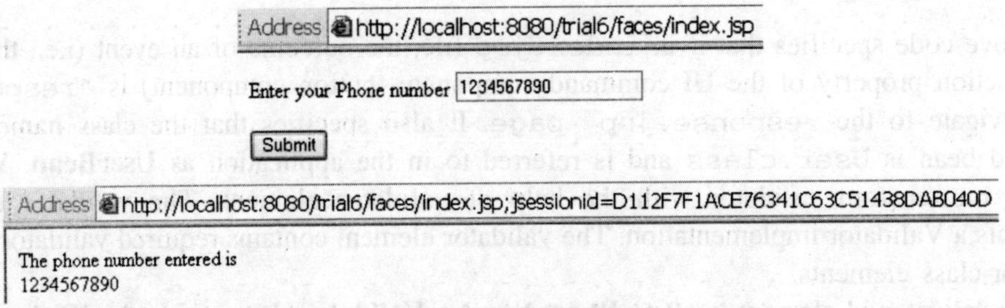

Figure 6.10   Display of the correct phone number.

CUSTOM VALIDATOR: EMAILVALIDATOR

The following application demonstrates the creation of a custom validator by name: "`EmailValidator`". This validator checks whether user has entered a valid email id or not. That is, it checks whether @ symbol exists or not in the email id entered by the user. If @ does not exist then validation error is displayed. For this application, we are going to develop two pages `index.jsp` and `response.jsp`. The `index.jsp` prompts the user to enter an email id. The email id entered in the page is binded with UserBean (JavaBean) `attribute: emailId`. The JavaBean `attribute: emailId` is updated only if the email id entered by the user satisfies the validation criteria. If the email id is valid, it is then displayed through `response.jsp` page.

Let us make a new application by name: trial7, i.e., we need to make a folder trial7 in Tomcat's webapps folder and make a file `index.jsp` with following contents:

index.jsp

```
<%@ taglib uri="http://java.sun.com/jsf/html" prefix="h" %>
<%@ taglib uri="http://java.sun.com/jsf/core" prefix="f" %>

<html>
  <head>
    <title> </title>
  </head>
  <body>
```

```
      <f:view>
        <h:form id="CustomValidation">
          <h:outputText value="Enter your email id"/>
          <h:inputText value="#{UserBean.emailId}" size="25"
            id="emailField" required="true">
            <f:validator validatorId="EmailValidator"/>
          </h:inputText>
          <h:message for="emailField"/>
          </p>
          <h:commandButton action="response" value="Submit"/>
        </h:form>
      </f:view>
    </body>
</html>
```

The statement `<f:validator validatorId="EmailValidator"/>` invokes EmailValidator class to check whether the email id entered by the user contains "@" symbol or not. If not, then exception is thrown.

The statement `<h:message for="emailField"/>` displays the error message if validation rules are violated.

Next file is `response.jsp`, which displays the valid email id entered. Let us make this file in "webapps\trial7" directory with following contents:

response.jsp

```
<%@ taglib uri="http://java.sun.com/jsf/html" prefix="h" %>
<%@ taglib uri="http://java.sun.com/jsf/core" prefix="f" %>

<html>
  <head>
    <title></title>
  </head>
  <body>
    <f:view>
      <h:outputText value="Your email id is"/></br>
      <h:outputText value="#{UserBean.emailId}"/>
    </f:view>
  </body>
</html>
```

The code `<h:outputText value="#{UserBean.emailId}"/>` retrieves the contents of the `emailld` attribute stored in JavaBean: UserBean and displays on the screen.

Now we will create a bean that will hold the data sent by `index.jsp` page: `emailId`. The JSF managed bean is a class file having attributes and their respective setter and getter methods. So, we make a file `User.java` in "webapps\trial7\WEB-INF\classes directory with the below given contents:

`User.java`

```java
public class User {
    String emailId;

    public String getEmailId() {
        return emailId;
    }
    public void setEmailId(String email) {
        emailId = email;
    }
}
```

In the same directory, i.e., "webapps\trial7\WEB-INF\classes directory, let us make validator class `EmailValidator.java` with following contents:

`EmailValidator.java`

```java
import javax.faces.component.UIComponent;
import javax.faces.context.FacesContext;
import javax.faces.application.*;
import javax.faces.validator.Validator;
import javax.faces.validator.ValidatorException;

public class EmailValidator implements Validator{
    public EmailValidator() {
    }

public void validate(FacesContext context, UIComponent component,
        Object value)   throws ValidatorException {
        String str = (String)value;
        if (str.indexOf('@')== -1){
            throwException("Invalid email id");
        }
    }
    private void throwException(String errMessage){
        FacesMessage message = new FacesMessage();
        message.setDetail(errMessage);
        message.setSummary(errMessage);
        message.setSeverity(FacesMessage.SEVERITY_ERROR);
        throw new ValidatorException(message);
    }
}
```

We can see in the above code that our custom validator class: **EmailValidator** implements the validator interface (`javax.faces.validator.Validator`) and also implements the **validate** method. While calling this validate method, the JavaServer Faces implementation passes in the current **FacesContext**, the UI **component** (whose data has to be validated) and the **data** to be validated. In this class "value" represents the data provided by the user in the component.

The "value" which is of object type is first converted into string form. Then it is checked that whether "@" symbol exists in it or not. If not, an exception is thrown displaying the error message: "Invalid email id".

Compile the JavaBean and the validator class

Open the command prompt and go to the classes folder of our application (trial7) and give following commands:

```
C:\apache-tomcat-6.0.14\webapps\trial7\WEB-INF\classes> javac
User.java

C:\apache-tomcat-6.0.14\webapps\trial7\WEB-INF\classes> javac
EmailValidator.java
```

Let us create an application configuration file: faces-config.xml in WEB-INF folder of our application to specify the name our JavaBean and also the condition of navigating to response.jsp page from index.jsp page. The contents of the faces-config.xml file are as follows:

faces-config.xml

```xml
<?xml version='1.0' encoding='UTF-8'?>
<!DOCTYPE faces-config PUBLIC
"-//Sun Microsystems, Inc.//DTD JavaServer Faces Config 1.1//EN"
"http://java.sun.com/dtd/web-facesconfig_1_1.dtd">
<faces-config>
    <navigation-rule>
        <from-view-id>/index.jsp</from-view-id>
        <navigation-case>
            <from-outcome>response</from-outcome>
            <to-view-id>/response.jsp</to-view-id>
        </navigation-case>
    </navigation-rule>
    <managed-bean>
        <managed-bean-name>UserBean</managed-bean-name>
        <managed-bean-class>User</managed-bean-class>
        <managed-bean-scope>request</managed-bean-scope>
    </managed-bean>
    <validator>
        <validator-id>EmailValidator</validator-id>
        <validator-class>EmailValidator
        </validator-class>
    </validator>
</faces-config>
```

Above code specifies that if in `index.jsp file`, the outcome of an event is "response", then navigate to the `response.jsp page`. It also specifies that the class name of the managed bean is **User.class** and is referred to in the application as **UserBean**. We also register our custom validator with the help of validator element. The validator element represents a validator implementation. The validator element contains required validator-id and validator-class elements.

The validator-id element is set to **EmailValidator**. It specifies the ID that is used by the validator attribute of a UI component tag to apply the validator to the component's data. The validator-class element is also set to **EmailValidator** as it identifies the validator implementation.

Also make a deployment descriptor file web.xml in WEB-INF folder of our application to register the FacesServlet (the engine of all JSF applications). The contents of web.xml file is same as earlier applications.

To run the application, run Tomcat and in the browser type: `http://localhost: 8080/trial7/faces/index.jsp`. The browser asks the user to enter an email id (Figure 6.11).

Figure 6.11 Browser asks to enter an email id.

If the email id entered does not contain "@" symbol, a validation error is displayed as shown in Figure 6.12.

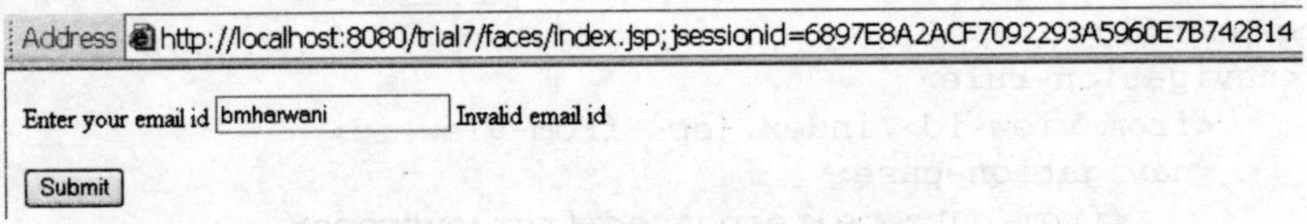

Figure 6.12 Validation error is displayed.

If the email id entered contains "@" symbol, it is accepted and is displayed through `response.jsp` page as shown in Figure 6.13.

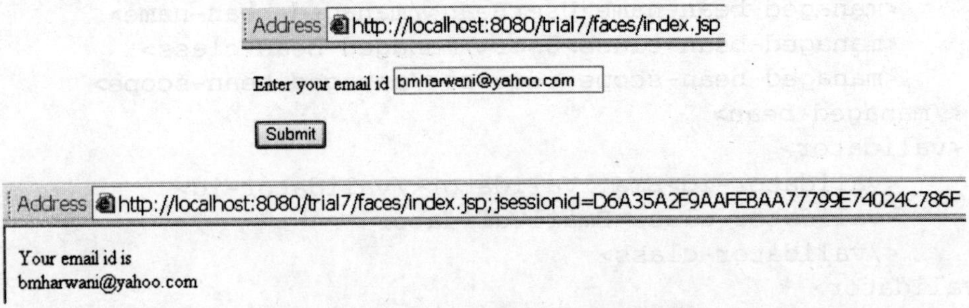

Figure 6.13 Display of correct email id feeded.

SUMMARY

This chapter explains different types of validators and how we can use them to check whether any essential field is left out, or whether the data entered by the user is within the given range length or not. With the practical examples, we have learnt how validators can be applied on different fields. Thereafter, we saw how to make custom validators: PhoneNumberValidator and EmailValidator step by step. Phone number validator checks that the phone number must not be less than 10 digits and should not contain any character or symbol. Similarly, the Email Id validators confirm the presence or "@" symbol in the email id entered.

REVIEW QUESTIONS

6.1 Write a JSF program that asks the user to enter password and displays an error if it is of less than 6 characters.

6.2 Write a JSF program that asks the user to enter his name and email id and displays an error if any of the field is left blank.

6.3 Create a custom validator that asks the user to enter a credit card number which should be of exactly 12 digits and should not contains any symbol or letter.

7

Event Handling

LEARNING OBJECTIVES

In this chapter, we will learn:

- How the events are handled in JSF
- How a control is binded with the action method
- How to store more than one option selected by the user in the Array List
- How to attach an actionListener to any component
- How to attach a valueChangeListener to any component

EVENT HANDLING

JavaServer Faces technology defines listeners and event classes that an application can use to handle events generated by UI components. An event object identifies the component that generates the event and stores information about the event. To be notified of an event, an application must provide an implementation of the listener class and register it on the component that generates the event. When the user activates a component, such as clicking a button, an event is fired. This causes the JavaServer Faces implementation to invoke the listener method that processes the event.

JSF uses JavaBeans to handle events with event listeners and handlers. Any component may fire one or more events. The most common events are:

- Value-change events (value change of a component)
- Action events (clicking on a button or link)

132

Event objects in JSF

All event objects in JSF must extend the `javax.faces.event.FacesEvent` class. The FacesEvent class is a subclass of the `java.util.EventObject class`.

The FacesEvent class has two subclasses:

- ActionEvent
- ValueChangeEvent

`ActionEvent class` : It represents the activation of the UI component, such as a UI command component.

`ValueChangeEvent class` : It represents a notification that the local value of a UI Input component has been changed. If the new value is not validated successfully, the `ValueChangeEvent` notification will not be fired. This class has two important methods: `getOldValue` and `getNewValue`. The `getOldValue` method returns the old value of the component that fired the event. The `getNewValue` method returns the new value.

Event listeners in JSF

To capture a JSF event, we use an event listener. All listeners in JSF applications must implement the `javax.faces.event.FacesListener` interface. This interface extends the `java.util.EventListener` interface, which is the interface that must be implemented by all Java event listeners.

The `FacesListener` interface has two subinterfaces:

- ActionListener
- ValueChangeListener

ActionListener: The ActionListener interface is the interface that must be implemented to capture an ActionEvent. This interface adds a new method: `processAction` that is invoked on occurrence of ActionEvent for which the ActionListener is registered. The Syntax of processAction method is:

```
public void processAction(ActionEvent event) throws
AbortProcessingException
```

ValueChangeListener: The `ValueChangeListener` interface is the interface implemented to capture a `ValueChangeEvent`. This interface adds one method: `processValueChange`. That is invoked on occurrence of `ValueChangeEvent` action observed by this listener. Syntax of the `processValueChange` method is:

```
public void processValueChange(ValueChangeEvent event)throws
AbortProcessingException
```

The UI command component supports method bindings for two types of methods:

- Action methods
- Action listener methods

Either type can be used to process an ActionEvent, but the action method type is the most commonly used. An action method has no parameters and returns a String value called the **action outcome**. The outcome value usually decides which view has to be displayed next. We can use the **action attribute** with a method binding expression to bind a UI command component to an action method.

An ActionEvent is handled by a listener that implements the ActionListener interface. To handle events, JSF implementation provides a listener called the default ActionListener. When a UI command component is asked to fire an ActionEvent, it first notifies all regular listeners attached to the component, if any. Then it checks if it is binded with some action method and creates an instance of the default ActionListener to handle that event. The default ActionListener evaluates the action method binding and invokes the method. The default ActionListener uses the action outcome value to decide which view to choose for the response.

DEMONSTRATIONS OF ACTION METHOD

Let us understand the concept of events with the help of some practical examples. The following application demonstrates the use action method of a UI component. For this application, we are going to develop a page `index.jsp`. The `index.jsp` prompts the user to enter two numbers. The numbers entered in the page are binded with **NumberBean** (JavaBean) attributes: `firstNumber` and `secondNumber`. On selecting submit button, the addition of two numbers will be then displayed. Let us make a new application by name: trial4, i.e., we need to make a folder trial4 in Tomcat's webapps folder and make a file `index.jsp` with following contents:

index.jsp

```
<%@ taglib uri="http://java.sun.com/jsf/html" prefix="h" %>
<%@ taglib uri="http://java.sun.com/jsf/core" prefix="f" %>
<html>
    <head>
        <title>Adding two numbers</title>
    </head>
    <body>
        <f:view>
            <h:form>
                <h3>Enter two numericals</h3>
                <table>
                    <tr>
                        <td>First Number:</td>
                        <td><h:inputText value=
                            "#{NumberBean.firstNumber}"/></td>
                    </tr>
                    <tr>
                        <td>Second Number:</td>
```

```
            <td><h:inputText value=
                "#{NumberBean.secondNumber}"/></td>
        </tr>
        <tr>
            <td>Addition:</td>
            <td><h:outputTextvalue=
                "#{NumberBean.totalValue}"/>
            </td>
        </tr>
    </table>
    <p>
    <h:commandButton value="Add" action=
    "#{NumberBean.sum}"/>
    </p>
        </h:form>
    </f:view>
  </body>
</html>
```

By the statement: `<h:commandButton value="Add" action="#{NumberBean.sum}"/>`, the command button is binded with the action method: **sum** which is defined in the JavaBean: **NumberBean**.

We now make a JavaBean by name `Number.java`. The overall structure of our web application is shown in Figure 7.1.

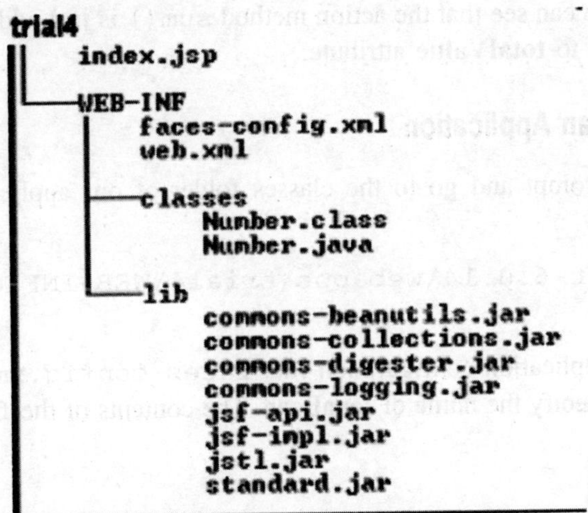

Figure 7.1 Structure of webapplication.

A bean is created to hold the values of two numbers entered by the user. Also, we know that a JavaBean is nothing but a class file having attributes and their respective setter and getter methods. The file `Number.java` is made in "webapps\trial4\WEB-INF\classes" directory with following contents:

Number.java

```
public class Number {
    private Integer firstNumber=null;
    private Integer secondNumber=null;
    private Integer totalValue=null;

    public Integer getFirstNumber() {return firstNumber;}
    public void setFirstNumber(Integer newValue)
        {firstNumber = newValue;}
    public Integer getSecondNumber() {return secondNumber;}
    public void setSecondNumber(Integer newValue)
        {secondNumber = newValue;}
    public Integer getTotalValue() {return totalValue;}
    public void setTotalValue(Integer newValue)
        {totalValue = newValue;}
    public void sum()
    {
        setTotalValue(firstNumber+secondNumber);
    }
}
```

totalValue is the attribute for storing addition of the attributes: `firstNumber` and `secondNumber`. We can see that the action method `sum()` is just adding the two numericals and assigning the sum to **totalValue** attribute.

Compile the JavaBean Application

Open the command prompt and go to the classes folder of our application (trial4) and give following command:

```
C:\apache-tomcat-6.0.14\webapps\trial4\WEB-INF\classes> javac
Number.java
```

Let us create an application configuration file: `faces-config.xml` in WEB-INF folder of our application to specify the name of JavaBean. The contents of the `faces-config.xml` file are as follows:

faces-config.xml

```
<?xml version='1.0' encoding='UTF-8'?>
<!DOCTYPE faces-config PUBLIC
"-//Sun Microsystems, Inc.//DTD JavaServer Faces Config 1.1//EN"
"http://java.sun.com/dtd/web-facesconfig_1_1.dtd">
<faces-config>
```

```
    <managed-bean>
        <managed-bean-name>NumberBean</managed-bean-name>
        <managed-bean-class>Number</managed-bean-class>
        <managed-bean-scope>request</managed-bean-scope>
    </managed-bean>
</faces-config>
```

Above code specifies that the class name of the managed bean is `Number.class` and is referred to in the application as NumberBean.

Also make a deployment descriptor file `web.xml.in` in WEB-INF folder of our application to register the FacesServlet. The contents of `web.xml` file are:

web.xml

```
<?xml version="1.0"?>
<!DOCTYPE web-app PUBLIC
"-//Sun Microsystems, Inc.//DTD Web Application 2.3//EN"
"http://java.sun.com/dtd/web-app_2_3.dtd">

<web-app>
    <!-- Faces Servlet -->
    <servlet>
        <servlet-name>Faces Servlet</servlet-name>
        <servlet-class>javax.faces.webapp.FacesServlet</servlet-class>
        <load-on-startup> 1 </load-on-startup>
    </servlet>
    <!-- Faces Servlet Mapping -->
    <servlet-mapping>
        <servlet-name>Faces Servlet</servlet-name>
        <url-pattern>/faces/*</url-pattern>
    </servlet-mapping>
</web-app>
```

There are two sections in the deployment descriptor. The `<servlet>` element registers the `FacesServlet`, and the `<servlet-mapping>` element states that any request containing the `pattern/faces/` in the URL must be passed to the FacesServlet.

The FacesServlet is the engine of all JSF applications. The servlet element identifies the FacesServlet, which processes the life cycle of the application. The load-on-startup element has a value of true, which indicates that the FacesServlet should be loaded when the application starts up.

To run the application, run Tomcat and in the browser type: `http://localhost:8080/trial4/faces/index.jsp`. The browser displays a JSP page which asks the user to enter two numbers. After feeding the two numbers, select `Submit` button (Figure 7.2).

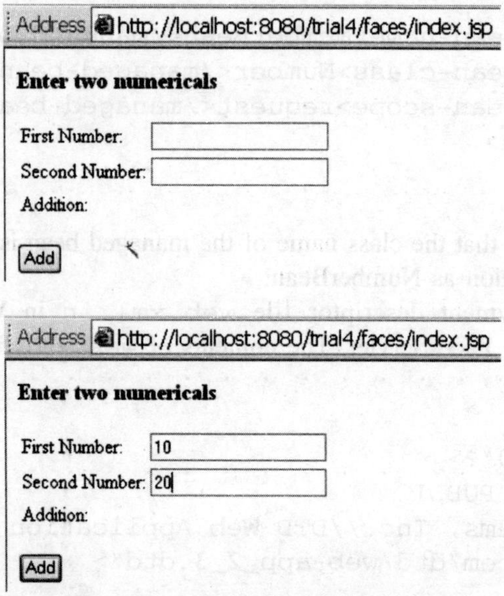

Figure 7.2 Two numbers are feeded.

We get the addition of two numbers entered as shown in Figure 7.3.

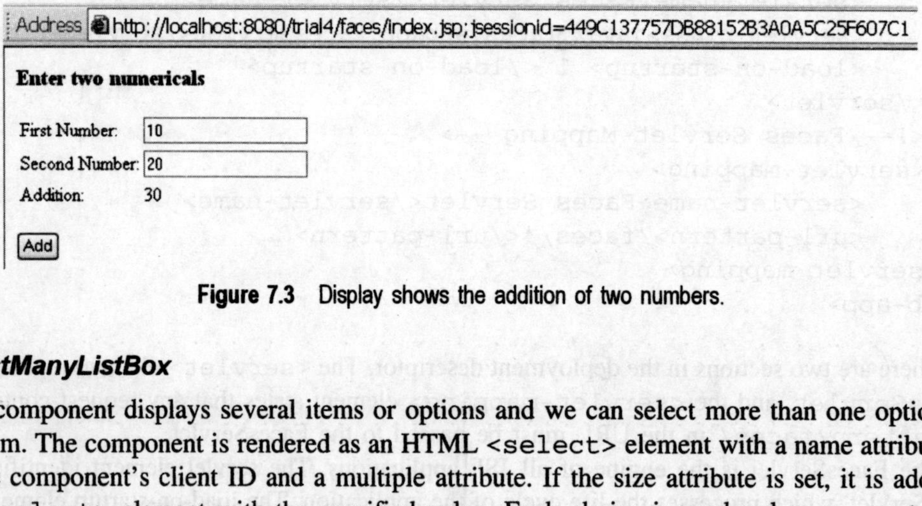

Figure 7.3 Display shows the addition of two numbers.

selectManyListBox

This component displays several items or options and we can select more than one option out of them. The component is rendered as an HTML <select> element with a name attribute set to the component's client ID and a multiple attribute. If the size attribute is set, it is added to the <select> element with the specified value. Each choice is rendered as an <option> element.

DEMONSTRATING ACTION METHOD WITH SELECT MANY LISTBOX COMPONENT

The following application demonstrates the use of <h:selectManyListbox> tag. For this application, we are going to develop two pages index7.jsp and response.jsp. The `index7.jsp` displays a list of fast foods and user can select any number of foods from it. The items selected in the page are binded with **FoodBean** (JavaBean) attribute: **foodList** (it is a list of strings). The list of fast food selected by the user are then displayed through `response.jsp` page. Make a file `index7.jsp` with the below given contents in "webapps\trial" directory.

index7.jsp

```
<%@ taglib uri="http://java.sun.com/jsf/html" prefix="h" %>
<%@ taglib uri="http://java.sun.com/jsf/core" prefix="f" %>

<html>
  <head>
    <title> </title>
  </head>
  <body>
    <f:view>
      <h:form>
        <h:outputText value="Select your Fast Food:"/><br/>
        <h:selectManyListbox id="food" value=
          "#{FoodBean.foodList}" size="3">
          <f:selectItem itemValue="pizza" itemLabel="Pizza" />
          <f:selectItem itemValue="burgar" itemLabel="Burgar" />
          <f:selectItem itemValue="chowmein"
            itemLabel="Chowmein" />
          <f:selectItem itemValue="hotdog" itemLabel="Hot Dog" />
        </h:selectManyListbox> <br/>
        <h:commandButton action="#{FoodBean.showSelectedFood}"
          value="Submit" />
      </h:form>
    </f:view>
  </body>
</html>
```

The statement `<h:selectManyListbox id="food" value="#{FoodBean.foodList}" size="3">` binds the Listbox with the **foodList** attribute of the JavaBean: **FoodBean**. It invokes the `setFoodList()` method of the JavaBean and **itemValues** of all the options selected are assigned to list of string: **foodList**.

The statement `<h:commandButton action="#{FoodBean.showSelected Food}" value="Submit"/>` binds the `commandbutton` with the action method `showSelectedFood`. When user clicks this buton, `showSelectedFood` method defined in the FoodBean will be invoked.

Also make another file `response.jsp` with the below given contents in "webapps\trial" directory. This file will display the names of the fast food selected by the user.

response.jsp

```
<%@ taglib uri="http://java.sun.com/jsf/html" prefix="h" %>
<%@ taglib uri="http://java.sun.com/jsf/core" prefix="f" %>
<html>
    <head>
      <title> </title>
    </head>
    <body>
      <f:view>
         <h:outputText value="You have selected" />
         <h:dataTable value="#{FoodBean.foodList}" var="foodl">
           <h:column>
              <h:outputText value="#{foodl}"/>
           </h:column>
         </h:dataTable>
      </f:view>
    </body>
</html>
```

The statement `<h:dataTable value="#{FoodBean.foodlist}" var="foodl">` invokes `getFoodlist()` method of the JavaBean: **FoodBean** and the contents of the List: `foodList` returned by this method will be displayed in the form of a table. **foodList** is a list of strings. Also, the list returned will be referred to as "`foodl`" in the application.

The following statements:

```
<h:column>
    <h:outputText value="#{foodl}"/>
</h:column>
```

displays a column in which the list of strings represented by **foodl** (because foodl refers to the **foodList** which is nothing but the list of strings designating the itemValues selected by the user) will be displayed.

Now we will create a bean that will hold the list of strings (to store itemValues of the options selected from the listbox) and its respective setter and getter method. We make a file `Food.java` in "`webapps\trial\WEB-INF\classes` directory with the below given contents.

Food.java

```
import java.util.List;
public class Food {
    private List<String> foodList;

    public void setFoodList(List<String> items) {
      this.foodList = items;
```

```
    }
    public List<String> getFoodList() {
      return foodList;
    }
    public String showSelectedFood() {
      return "response";
    }
  }
}
```

In the backing bean, we provide a list of strings **foodList** to store and retrieve the itemValues of the options selected from the listbox.

`showSelectedFood()` is an action method binded with the command button. Let us recall that to process an ActionEvent, action method type is a preferred approach. An action method has no parameters and returns a string value called the action outcome. This outcome value decides which view is to be displayed next. The action method returns `"response"` as action outcome which is then compared in the `faces-config.xml` file to decide which JSP page has to be opened next.

Compile the JavaBean Application

Open the command prompt and go to the classes folder of our application (trial) and give following command:

```
C:\apache-tomcat-6.0.14\webapps\trial\WEB-INF\classes>  javac
Food.java
```

Let us create an application configuration file: `faces-config.xml` in WEB-INF folder of our application to specify the name our JavaBean and also the condition of navigating to `response.jsp` page from `index7.jsp` page. The contents of the `faces-config.xml` file are as follows:

faces-config.xml

```xml
<?xml version='1.0' encoding='UTF-8'?>
<!DOCTYPE faces-config PUBLIC
"-//Sun Microsystems, Inc.//DTD JavaServer Faces Config 1.1//EN"
"http://java.sun.com/dtd/web-facesconfig_1_1.dtd">
<faces-config>
    <navigation-rule>
        <from-view-id>/index7.jsp</from-view-id>
        <navigation-case>
            <from-outcome>response</from-outcome>
            <to-view-id>/response.jsp</to-view-id>
        </navigation-case>
    </navigation-rule>
    <managed-bean>
        <managed-bean-name>FoodBean</managed-bean-name>
```

```
            <managed-bean-class>Food</managed-bean-class>
            <managed-bean-scope>request</managed-bean-scope>
      </managed-bean>
</faces-config>
```

Above code specifies that the class name of the managed bean is `Food.class` and is referred to in the application as **FoodBean**. It also specifies that if in `index7.jsp` file, the outcome of an event fired by the UI command component is `"response"`, then navigate to the `response.jsp` page.

Also make a deployment descriptor file `web.xml.in` in WEB-INF folder. The contents of `web.xml` file are same in earlier applications.

To run the application, run Tomcat and in the browser type: `http://localhost:8080/trial/faces/index7.jsp`. The browser displays a list of fast food available and asks user to select any number of fast foods out of them. Use Ctrl key for multiple selection. After selecting the foods, select `Submit` button (Figure 7.4).

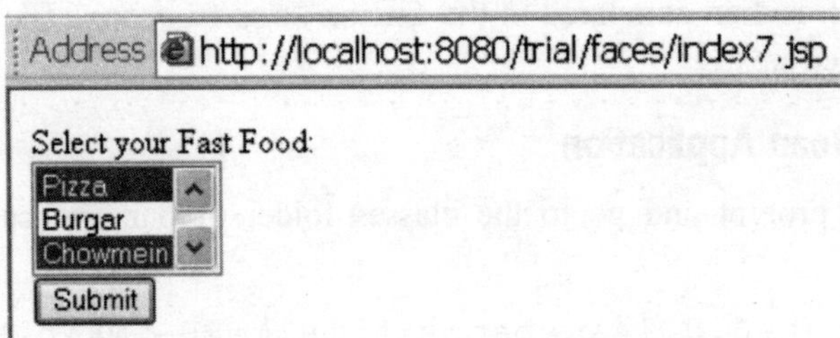

Figure 7.4   Selection of any number of items on list.

We get the list of fastfood selected as shown in Figure 7.5.

Figure 7.5   Output displayed.

Event Listeners

When the user clicks a button or link or changes a value in a field, or makes a selection in a list, an event is fired. There is a corresponding Listener Class for each type of events in JSF.

In case of **ActionEvent**, there exists an equivalent Listener class called **ActionListener**. Similarly, in case of **ValueChangeEvent**, the corresponding Listener class is **ValueChangeListener**.

Action Events

Action Events are emitted for UI command objects like command button or a hyperlink. Whenever a user presses a command button or clicks a hyperlink these events get generated.

We can attach any number of Listeners to these sources. For example:

```
<h:commandButton id="calculate" actionListener="#{UserBean.calc}"
value="Calculate"/>
```

In above example, we have defined an attribute called '**actionListener**' pointing to a method: **calc**. This method is defined in the managed bean with identifier '**UserBean**'. The syntax of the method for the actionListener attribute is:

public void anyMethod(ActionEvent actionEvent)

To conclude, there are two most commonly used event listeners:

- Action Listener
- Value-change Listener

Listeners can be declared in a managed bean or in a separate listener class. If we write listeners in a separate class, they can be used by several pages. A listener class must implement ActionListener or `ValueChangeListener` interfaces. A listener takes a FacesEvent object its only parameter. The FacesEvent provides information about the event such as the element which has fired the event.

DEMONSTRATION OF ACTION LISTENER

The following application demonstrates the use of action listener. For this application, we are going to develop two pages `index.jsp` and `response.jsp`. The `index.jsp` asks the user to enter employee's name, his basic salary and his designation. The details of the employee fed in the page are binded with UserBean (JavaBean) `attributes: userName, salary` and `desig`. On the basis of designation, HRA (House Rent Allowance) of the employee is computed and is displayed through `response.jsp` page. Let us make a new application by name: trial14, i.e., we need to make a folder trial14 in Tomcat's webapps folder and make a file `index.jsp` with following contents:

index.jsp

```
<%@ taglib uri="http://java.sun.com/jsf/html" prefix="h" %>
<%@ taglib uri="http://java.sun.com/jsf/core" prefix="f" %>
<html>
    <head>
      <title>Event Handling</title>
    </head>
    <body>
    <f:view>
      <h:form>
        <h2>Enter the following details</h2>
        <table>
          <tr>
            <td><h:outputText value="Name:"/></td>
            <td><h:inputText id="Name" value=
```

```
          "#{UserBean.userName}"/></td>
        </tr>
        <tr>
          <td><h:outputText value="Basic Salary:"/></td>
          <td><h:inputText id="salary" value=
          "#{UserBean.salary}"/></td>
        </tr>
        <tr>
          <td><h:outputText value="Designation:"/></td>
          <td><h:selectOneRadio id="Designation"
            value="#{UserBean.desig}">
            <f:selectItem itemValue="Officer"
              itemLabel="Officer"/>
            <f:selectItem itemValue="Worker"
              itemLabel="Worker"/>
            </h:selectOneRadio>
          </td>
        </tr>
      </table>
      <h:commandButton id="calculate" action="submit"
        actionListener="#{UserBean.calc}" value="Calculate" />
      </br>
    </h:form>
  </f:view>
  </body>
</html>
```

The statement `<h:commandButton id="calculate" action="submit" actionListener="#{UserBean.calc}" value="Calculate"/>` attaches an actionlistener with the command button. That means when the command button will be clicked, it will invoke the method **calc** defined in the JavaBean: **UserBean**. Besides this, the button also produces an action outcome: `"submit"` which will be used for navigation (by comparing this action outcome in the `faces-config.xml`, it will be decided that we have to navigate to which JSP page).

Also make another file `response.jsp` with the below given contents in "webapps\trial14" directory.

response.jsp

```
<%@ taglib uri="http://java.sun.com/jsf/html" prefix="h" %>
<%@ taglib uri="http://java.sun.com/jsf/core" prefix="f" %>

<html>
   <head>
     <title>Response Page</title>
   </head>
   <body>
```

```
    <f:view>
      <h:form>
        The details entered are </br>
        <h:outputText value="Name :" />
        <h:outputText value="#{UserBean.userName}"/> </br>
        <h:outputText value="Salary :" />
        <h:outputText value="#{UserBean.salary}"/> </br>
        <h:outputText value="Designation :" />
        <h:outputText value="#{UserBean.desig}"/> </br>
        <h:outputText value="HRA :" />
        <h:outputText value="#{UserBean.hra}"/> </br>
      </h:form>
    </f:view>
  </body>
</html>
```

As we can see in above coding that this file displays all the details of the employee like his name, salary, designation and HRA computed.

Now we will create a bean that will hold the data sent by `index.jsp` page: `userName`, `salary` and `desig`. The JSF managed bean is a JavaBean component whose property and methods are used by JSF components. It is a class file having attributes and their respective setter and getter methods. So, we make a file `User.java` in "webapps\trial14\WEB-INF\classes` directory with the below given contents. The bean simply captures the `userName`, `salary` and `desig` entered by a user after the user clicks the `Submit` button. The bean also contains `calc()` method which is invoked with the help of actionlistener attached to the command button. The `calc()` method computes HRA (House Rent Allowance) of the employee depending on the designation of the employee, i.e., whether the employee is a worker or an officer. HRA of officer is assumed to be Rs. 400 and that of worker as Rs. 200. Here is the code of our Managed Bean (`User.java`):

User.java

```java
import javax.faces.event.AbortProcessingException;
import javax.faces.event.ActionEvent;
import javax.faces.event.ActionListener;

public class User {
    private String userName;
    private Integer salary;
    private String desig;
    private Integer hra;

    public String getUserName() {return userName;}
    public void setUserName(String newValue) {userName = newValue;}
    public String getDesig() {return desig;}
    public void setDesig(String newValue) {desig = newValue;}
    public Integer getSalary() {return salary;}
```

```java
public void setSalary(Integer newValue) {salary = newValue;}
public void setHra(Integer newValue) {hra = newValue;}
public Integer getHra() {return hra;}
public void calc(ActionEvent ae)
{
  if(desig.equals("Officer"))
  {
    setHra(400);
  }
  else
  {
    setHra(200);
  }
}
}
```

Compile the JavaBean Application

Open the command prompt and go to the classes folder of our application (trial14) and give following command:

```
C:\apache-tomcat-6.0.14\webapps\trial14\WEB-INF\classes>  javac
User.java
```

Let us create an application configuration file: `faces-config.xml` in WEB-INF folder of our application to specify the name our JavaBean and also the condition of navigating to `response.jsp` page from `index.jsp` page. The contents of the `faces-config.xml` file are as follows:

faces-config.xml

```xml
<?xml version='1.0' encoding='UTF-8'?>
<!DOCTYPE faces-config PUBLIC
"-//Sun Microsystems, Inc.//DTD JavaServer Faces Config 1.1//EN"
"http://java.sun.com/dtd/web-facesconfig_1_1.dtd">
<faces-config>
    <navigation-rule>
      <from-view-id>/index.jsp</from-view-id>
      <navigation-case>
        <from-outcome>submit</from-outcome>
        <to-view-id>/response.jsp</to-view-id>
      </navigation-case>
    </navigation-rule>
    <managed-bean>
      <managed-bean-name>UserBean</managed-bean-name>
      <managed-bean-class>User</managed-bean-class>
```

```
    <managed-bean-scope>request</managed-bean-scope>
  </managed-bean>
</faces-config>
```

Above code specifies that the class name of the managed bean is `User.class` and is referred to in the application as UserBean. It also specifies that if in `index.jsp` file, the outcome of an event fired by the UI command component is `"submit"`, then navigate to the `response.jsp` page.

Note: The statement `<h:commandButton id="calculate" action="submit" actionListener="#{UserBean.calc}" value="Calculate"/>` defined in `index.jsp` attaches an actionlistener with the command button to invoke the method `calc()` defined in UserBean and also produces an action outcome: `"submit"`. This action outcome is used for navigating to `response.jsp` page.

Also make a deployment descriptor file `web.xml` in WEB-INF folder of our application to register the FacesServlet. The contents of `web.xml` file are same as earlier applications.

To run the application, run Tomcat and in the browser type: `http://localhost:8080/trial14/faces/index.jsp`. The browser displays a form to feed in the employees details. After feeding the employee's name, his basic salary and designation, select `Submit` button (Figure 7.6).

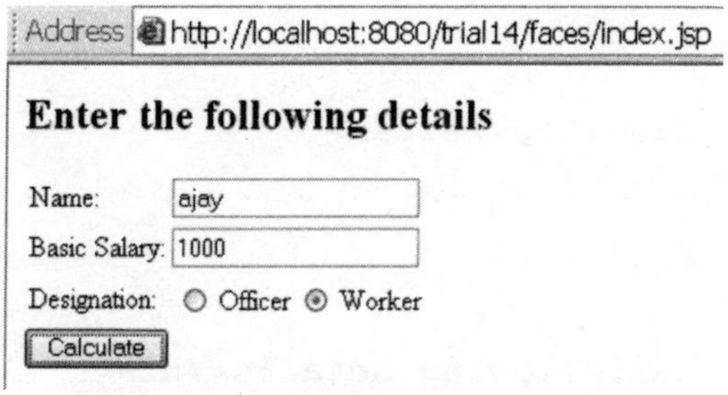

Figure 7.6 Browser asks to fill the form.

We get the details of the employee along with HRA computed on the basis of his designation as shown in Figure 7.7.

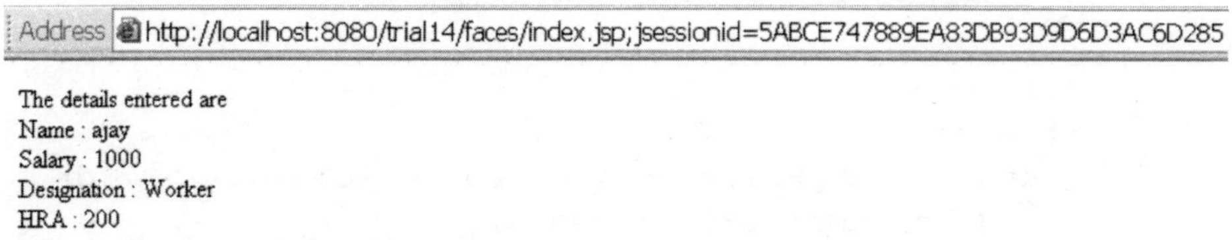

Figure 7.7 Calculation of HRA on the basis of salary.

ValueChangeEvent

`ValueChangeEvents` are applicable for UI components like Text Field, Check Box, List and Radio Buttons. A `ValueChangeEvent` is used to inform when there is a change in the value of a component, such as text modification in a text field or selection of a check box or a radio button.

When the user modifies the state of a component, the JSF implementation broadcasts the event to any registered listeners. The `ValueChangeEvent` provides the original value of the component and its new value (modified value) also.

DEMONSTRATION OF VALUE CHANGE LISTENER

The following application demonstrates the use of `valueChangeListener`. For this application, we are going to develop two pages `index.jsp` and `welcome.jsp`. The `index.jsp` asks the user to enter employee's name, his basic salary and his designation. The details of the employee fed in the page are binded with **UserBean** (JavaBean) attributes: `userName`, `salary` and `desig`. On the basis of designation, HRA (House Rent Allowance) of the employee is computed and is displayed through `welcome.jsp` page. Let us make a new application by name: trial12, i.e., we need to make a folder trial12 in Tomcat's webapps folder and make a file `index.jsp` with following contents:

index.jsp

```
<%@ taglib uri="http://java.sun.com/jsf/html" prefix="h" %>
<%@ taglib uri="http://java.sun.com/jsf/core" prefix="f" %>
<html>
    <head>
      <title>Event Handling</title>
    </head>
    <body>
    <f:view>
      <h:form>
        <h2>Enter the following details</h2>
          <table>
            <tr>
              <td><h:outputText value="Name:"/></td>
              <td><h:inputText id="Name"
                value="#{UserBean.userName}"/>
              </td>
            </tr>
            <tr>
              <td><h:outputText value="Basic Salary:"/></td>
              <td><h:inputText id="salary"
                value="#{UserBean.salary}"/>
              </td>
            </tr>
            <tr>
              <td><h:outputText value="Designation:"/></td>
              <td><h:selectOneRadio id="Designation"
```

```
              value="#{UserBean.desig}" valueChangeListener=
              "#{UserBean.desigSelected}">
              <f:selectItem itemValue="Officer"
                itemLabel="Officer"/>
              <f:selectItem itemValue="Worker"
                itemLabel="Worker"/>
              </h:selectOneRadio>
            </td>
          </tr>
        </table>
        <h:commandButton action="submit" value="Submit" />
      </h:form>
    </f:view>
  </body>
</html>
```

The statement `<h:selectOneRadio id="Designation"value="#{UserBean.desig}" valueChangeListener="#{UserBean.desigSelected}">` attaches a valueChangeListener with the radio button. That means, the moment user selects any of the option defined in radio button, it will invoke the method `designSelected()` defined in the JavaBean: **UserBean**.

Let us make another file `welcome.jsp` with the below given contents in "`webapps\trial12`" directory.

welcome.jsp

```
<%@ taglib uri="http://java.sun.com/jsf/html" prefix="h" %>
<%@ taglib uri="http://java.sun.com/jsf/core" prefix="f" %>

<html>
  <head>
    <title>Response Page</title>
  </head>
  <body>
    <f:view>
      <h:form>
        The details entered are </br>
        <h:outputText value="Name :" />
        <h:outputText value="#{UserBean.userName}"/> </br>
        <h:outputText value="Salary :" />
        <h:outputText value="#{UserBean.salary}"/> </br>
        <h:outputText value="Designation :" />
        <h:outputText value="#{UserBean.desig}"/> </br>
        <h:outputText value="HRA :" />
        <h:outputText value="#{UserBean.hra}"/> </br>
      </h:form>
```

```
   </f:view>
  </body>
</html>
```

As we can see in above coding that this file displays all the details of the employee like his name, salary, designation and HRA computed.

Now we will create a bean that will hold the data sent by `index.jsp` page: `userName`, `salary` and `desig`. Managed bean as we know is a class file having attributes and their respective setter and getter methods. So, we make a file `User.java` in "`webapps\trial12\WEB-INF\classes` directory with the below given contents. The bean simply captures the userName, salary and designation entered by a user. The bean also contains `desigSelected()` method which is invoked with the help of **valueChangeListener** attached to the radio button. The `desigSelected()` method computes HRA (House Rent Allowance) of the employee depending on the designation of the employee, i.e., whether the employee is a worker or an officer. For officer, the HRA is assumed to be Rs. 400 and for the worker, it is assumed to be Rs. 200. Here is the code of our managed bean (`User.java`):

User.java

```java
import javax.faces.event.AbortProcessingException;
import javax.faces.event.ValueChangeEvent;
import javax.faces.event.ValueChangeListener;

public class User {
  private String userName;
  private Integer salary;
  private String desig;
  private Integer hra;
  public String getUserName() {return userName;}
  public void setUserName(String newValue) {userName = newValue;}
  public String getDesig() {return desig;}
  public void setDesig(String newValue) {desig = newValue;}
  public Integer getSalary() {return salary;}
  public void setSalary(Integer newValue) {salary = newValue;}
  public void setHra(Integer newValue) {hra = newValue;}
  public Integer getHra() {return hra;}
  public void desigSelected(ValueChangeEvent event)
  {
    String str=(String) event.getNewValue();
    if(str.equals("Officer"))
    {
      setHra(400);
    }
    else
    {
      setHra(200);
```

```
        }
    }
}
```

Compile the JavaBean Application

Open the command prompt and go to the classes folder of our application (trial12) and give following command:

```
C:\apache-tomcat-6.0.14\webapps\trial12\WEB-INF\classes>  javac
User.java
```

Let us create an application configuration file: `faces-config.xml` in WEB-INF folder of our application to specify the name of JavaBean and also the condition of navigating to `welcome.jsp` page from `index.jsp` page. The contents of the `faces-config.xml` file are as follows:

faces-config.xml

```
<?xml version='1.0' encoding='UTF-8'?>
<!DOCTYPE faces-config PUBLIC
"-//Sun Microsystems, Inc.//DTD JavaServer Faces Config 1.1//EN"
"http://java.sun.com/dtd/web-facesconfig_1_1.dtd">
<faces-config>
    <navigation-rule>
      <from-view-id>/index.jsp</from-view-id>
      <navigation-case>
        <from-outcome>submit</from-outcome>
        <to-view-id>/welcome.jsp</to-view-id>
      </navigation-case>
    </navigation-rule>
    <managed-bean>
      <managed-bean-name>UserBean</managed-bean-name>
      <managed-bean-class>User</managed-bean-class>
      <managed-bean-scope>request</managed-bean-scope>
    </managed-bean>
</faces-config>
```

Above code specifies that the class name of the managed bean is `User.class` and is referred to in the application as **UserBean**. It also specifies that if in `index.jsp` file, the outcome of an event fired by the UI command component is `"submit"`, then navigate to the `welcome.jsp` page.

Note: The statement `<h:commandButton action="submit" value= "Submit" />` defined in `index.jsp` produces an action outcome: `"submit"` when command button is clicked. This action outcome is used for navigating to `welcome.jsp` page.

Also make a deployment descriptor file `web.xml.in` in WEB-INF folder of our application to register the FacesServlet. The contents of `web.xml` file are same as above applications.

To run the application, run Tomcat and in the browser type: `http://localhost:8080/trial12/faces/index.jsp`. The browser displays a form to feed in the employees details. After feeding the employee's name, his basic salary and designation, select `Submit` button (Figure 7.8).

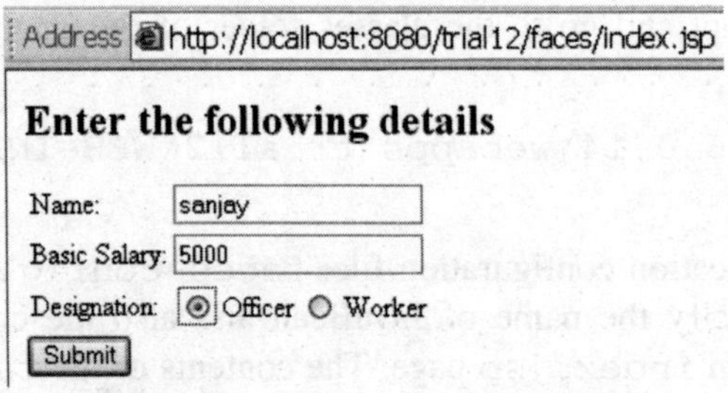

Figure 7.8 Browser asks to fill a form.

We get the details of the employee along with HRA computed on the basis of his designation as shown in Figure 7.9.

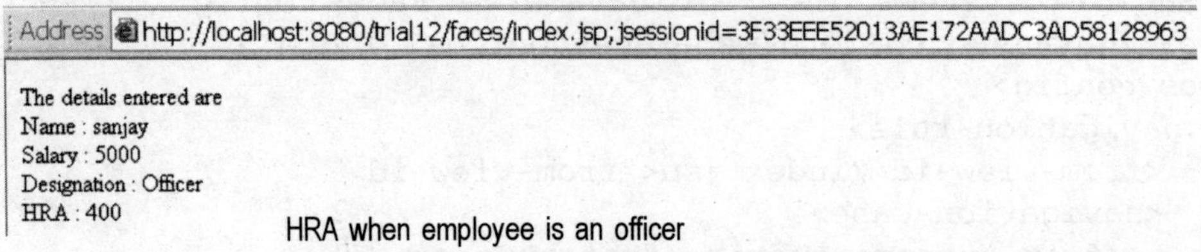

HRA when employee is an officer

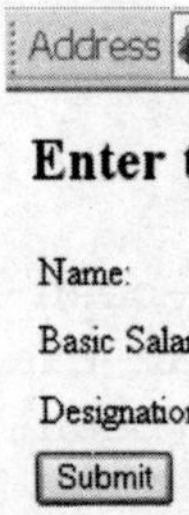

Browser asks to fill the form

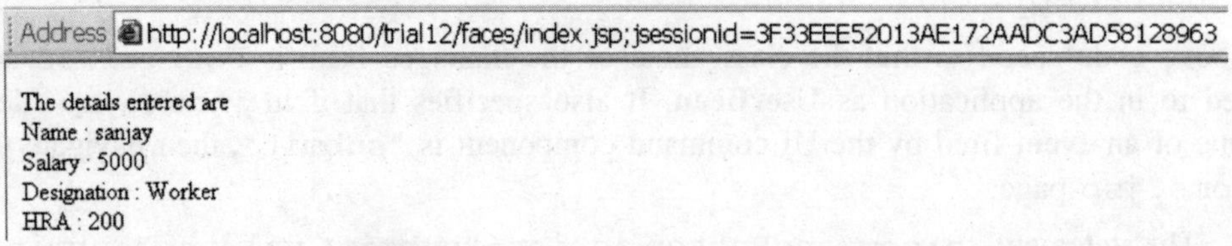

Figure 7.9 HRA when employee is a worker.

SUMMARY

In this chapter we saw how a command button is attached to an action button and helps in invoking the specified method when it is selected. Also, we saw the technique of storing more than one option selected by the user in `selectManyListbox` control in the array list. Beside this, the working of two event listeners: action listener and value change listener is explained via running examples. That is, how these listeners are used in invoking different methods to evaluate and display the desired information.

REVIEW QUESTIONS

7.1 Write a JSF program to make a mini calculator with four buttons having the symbols: "+", "–", "*" and "/". After feeding the two numerical values, when user selects a button, it displays the respective answer.

7.2 Write a JSF program to display three different types of rooms available in your hotel to the customer in the form of radio buttons (`selectOneradio`) and display the rent of that room. The three room types are:

Suite   Rent is Rs. 4500
AC Deluxe   Rent is Rs. 2500
Ordinary   Rent is Rs. 1000

Do this program using `valueChangeListener`.

7.3 Assuming that you are running a pizza parlour where a normal pizza is of Rs. 50 and extra charges for different toppings. The toppings will be displayed in the form of checkboxes and their cost will be added to Rs. 50 and the combined amount is displayed to the user. The different toppings and their prices are:

Extra Cheese   Rs. 10
Chicken   Rs. 25
Mushroom   Rs. 10

Write a JSF program to display the selected toppings and the computed bill.

8

Page Navigation

In this chapter, we will learn:

- How navigation rules are used for navigating from one page to another
- How to define global navigation rules
- How to define rule for a specific page
- How to use static and dynamic navigation
- How to use commandLink for navigating to the desired web page

User while visiting a web site can navigate from one page to another page. Navigation involves determining which page to go to when user selects a particular button or a hyperlink. Navigation through a JSF application is defined by navigation rules. These rules determine, based on outcomes specified by UI components, which page is displayed next when the UI component is clicked.

NAVIGATION RULES

Navigation rules determine the next page to display when a user clicks a navigation component, such as a button or a hyperlink. The navigation rule elements can contain any number of **navigation-case** elements, each of which defines the page to open next based on a logical outcome. The outcome can be defined by the **action** attribute of the UI command component that submits the form.

Each navigation rule can have one or more cases, which define where a user can go from the current page. For example, if a page has links to several other pages in the application, we can create a single navigation rule for that page and one navigation case for each link to the different pages.

Navigation Rule Elements

The general syntax of a JSF navigation rule element in the `faces-config.xml` file is as follows :

```
<navigation-rule>
   <from-view-id>page-or-pattern</from-view-id>
   <navigation-case>
      <from-action>action-method</from-action>
      <from-outcome>outcome</from-outcome>
      <to-view-id>destination-page</to-view-id>
      <redirect/>
   </navigation-case>
   <navigation-case>
      ...
   </navigation-case>
</navigation-rule>
```

A navigation rule can consist of the following elements:

navigation-rule: It is a wrapper element for navigation case elements.

from-view-id: Here, we specify the source web page from where navigation will take place. To make a global rule that applies to all pages, leave this element blank.

navigation-case: For every navigation, there is an individual navigation case. Each case defines the different navigation paths from the same page. A navigation rule must have at least one navigation case.

from-action: An optional element that defines navigation on the basis of outcomes from the specified action method.

from-outcome: A mandatory element that contains an outcome value that is expected from the action attribute of UI components.

to-view-id: A mandatory element where we specify the destination page where we want to navigate.

redirect: An optional element that indicates that the new view is to be requested through a redirect response instead of being rendering as the response to the current request. This element requires no value.

Example:

UI component defining the action in JSP page:

```
<h:commandButton action="login" value="Login" />
```

Example:

Specifying navigation rule in `faces-config.xml` file:

```
<navigation-rule>
    <from-view-id>/index.jsp</from-view-id>
```

```
<navigation-case>
  <from-outcome>login</from-outcome>
  <to-view-id>/login.jsp</to-view-id>
</navigation-case>
</navigation-rule>
```

`<navigation-case>` tag defines the circumstances of navigation. We can go to the different pages from one page. Tag `<navigation-case>` contains child tag `<to-view-id>` which describes the view to be next activated i.e. the target page we want to navigate at. This tag is not mandatory.

Tag `<from-outcome>` contains a string and if this string is equal to outcome of any component, the transfer to the mentioned page will be made. This tag is mandatory.

Defining page navigation for an application is a two-step process:

- First, we create navigation rules for all the pages in our application. Usually, we define one rule for each page in an application. However, we can also define pattern-based rules that affect groups of pages or global rules that affect all pages.
- Next, in each navigation component on the pages, such as a command button or link, we specify either a static or dynamic outcome value in the action attribute. Static outcome values are constants and don't change. Dynamic outcome values are derived from a binding on a backing bean method that returns an outcome value.

The Sun JSF Reference Implementation reads the navigation rules in the `faces-config.xml` file and calls the `NavigationHandler` class, which evaluates the navigation rules and determines which page to display. When evaluating which navigation rules to execute, the navigation handler looks for:

- The ID of the current page
- The action method used to handle the link
- The outcome string value of the action attribute, or the string returned by the action method

Defining pattern-based navigation rules for a group of pages

When we want to apply a navigation rule to a group of pages, we create a pattern-based rule. We identify the pages affected by the rule using a wildcard pattern, where the wildcard character (*) must be the last item in the pattern.

Example:

```
<navigation-rule>
    <from-view-id>/items/sales*</from-view-id>
    ...
</navigation-rule>
```

We can see that the `from-view-id` element contains a pattern instead of a specific page name. This pattern would cause the rule to apply to all pages in the **items** directory whose names start with **sales**.

Defining global navigation rules that apply to all pages

Sometimes, we may need to apply a navigation rule to all the pages, that rule is known as global rule. When we create a global rule, we exclude the `from-view-id` element, which causes the rule to apply to all pages. We can optionally include a `from-outcome` element, if we want to apply the rule whenever a UI component on any page returns a specific outcome.

Example:

```
<navigation-rule>
  <navigation-case>
     <to-view-id>/index.jsp</to-view-id>
     <from-outcome>submit</from-outcome>
  </navigation-case>
</navigation-rule>
```

It causes the index page to be displayed when any component on any page returns the value **submit**.

Defining default navigation cases in which no outcome is specified

Sometimes, we may expect outcome which may be one of multiple values and we want to create a navigation case for one or two specific outcomes and a default case for all other possible outcomes.

Note: Default navigation cases do not apply if a component specifies a null value in the action attribute. In this case, no navigation occurs and the same page is redisplayed.

Example:

```
<navigation-rule>
 <navigation-case>
   <to-view-id>/index.jsp</to-view-id>
 </navigation-case>
</navigation-rule>
```

We must supply a `to-view-id` value, to identify the destination of the navigation case, but can leave either or both the `from-action` and `from-outcome` elements empty. If we leave the from-action element empty, the case applies to the specified outcome regardless of how the outcome is returned. If we leave the `from-outcome` element empty, the case applies to all outcomes from the specified action method, thus creating a default navigation case for that method. If we leave both the `from-action` and the `from-outcome` elements empty, the case applies to all outcomes not identified in any other rules defined for the page, thus creating a default case for the entire page.

Navigation Rule for a Specific Page

Below is an example of a navigation rule with two cases defined in the `faces-config.xml` file. The first case navigates to the **login** page when the outcome specified in the action attribute of a component is **login**. The second case navigates to the new user page when the action attribute of a component is newuser.

```
<navigation-rule>
   <from-view-id>/index.jsp</from-view-id>
   <navigation-case>
      <from-outcome>login</from-outcome>
      <to-view-id>/login.jsp</to-view-id>
   </navigation-case>
   <navigation-case>
      <from-outcome>newuser</from-outcome>
      <to-view-id>/newuser.jsp</to-view-id>
   </navigation-case>
</navigation-rule>
```

The UI component defined in the JSP page may be as follows:

```
<h:commandButton action="login" value="Login" />
<h:commandButton action="newuser" value="New User" />
```

One button has string `login` in the action attribute and another one contains `newuser`. If we press the button `Login`, JSF will find all navigational rules in `faces-config.xml`. Further the comparison of the string `login` with values of all tags `<from-outcome>` will take place. If the value of any tag is equal to this string, JSF will move to the JSP page specified by its `<to-view-id>` tag. Similarly, if we press `New User` button, JSF will check for the `navigation-case` with `<from-outcome>` matching with string : `newuser` and if found, it navigates to the JSP page specified by its `<to-view-id>` tag.

Navigation Rule Defined with Redirect Rendering

Some of the cases use the redirect element, which causes JSF to send a redirect response that asks the browser to request the new page. When the browser requests the new page, the URL shown in the browser's address field is changed to show the actual URL for the new page. If a navigation case does not use the redirect element, the new page is rendered as a response to the current request, which means that the URL in the browser's address field does not change and it will show the address of the previous page. Any navigation case can be defined as a redirect. If we do not use redirect rendering, when a user bookmarks a page, the bookmark will not contain the URL of the current page; instead, it will contain the address of the previous page (i.e. source page).

Example:

```
<navigation-rule>
   <from-view-id>/index.jsp</from-view-id>
   <navigation-case>
      <from-outcome>login</from-outcome>
      <to-view-id>/login.jsp</to-view-id>
      <redirect/>
   </navigation-case>
   <navigation-case>
```

```
      <from-outcome>newuser</from-outcome>
      <to-view-id>/newuser.jsp</to-view-id>
      <redirect/>
   </navigation-case>
</navigation-rule>
```

Depending on the outcome of the UI component in `index.jsp` we will navigate either to `login.jsp` page or `newuser.jsp` page. The main thing to note is that when we navigate to either of the destination page, the URL in the browser changes to show the destinaion page as we have used the redirect element.

TYPES OF NAVIGATION

Broadly defined, there are two types of navigations:

- Static navigation
- Dynamic navigation

Static Navigation

When a component is defined using static navigation, the outcome value in the action attribute is a constant value that always triggers the same navigation case and hence, the same specific JSP page is displayed.

To use static navigation, we create the navigation case using a `from-outcome` value and not a `from-action` value. In the action attribute of the navigation button or link we specify a constant outcome value that matches the value we entered in the `from-outcome` element of the navigation case.

Example:

```
<navigation-rule>
    <from-view-id>/index.jsp</from-view-id>
    <navigation-case>
    <from-outcome>submit</from-outcome>
    <to-view-id>/response.jsp</to-view-id>
    </navigation-case>
</navigation-rule>
```

Once we have created the component, we can then specify the outcome value in the action attribute. When the user clicks the component, the application navigates to the page determined by the outcome value in navigation case.

For static navigation, the UI component in the JSP page may be defined as follows:

```
<h:commandButton action="submit" value="Submit" />
```

When the user clicks the button, the application navigates to the page determined by the outcome value: **submit**, i.e., to the `response.jsp` page.

Note: The outcome value we enter in the action attribute of an UI component must exactly match the outcome value in the navigation case, including uppercase and lowercase. If the outcome specified by an action does not match any outcome in a navigation case, the navigation will be handled by a default navigation rule (if one exists), or no navigation will occur.

Dynamic Navigation

In this navigation, we can dynamically determine the outcome by binding the action attribute of a navigation component to an action method defined in a backing bean. The action method may return any outcome depending on circumstances. Different outcomes could trigger different navigation cases, causing the application to navigate to one of several possible target pages. The method bound to a navigation component must be a public method with no parameters, and it must return a string representing the outcome of the action.

Example:

```
<h:commandButton value="Login" action="#{UserBean.chklogin}"/>
```

When user clicks the button, it will invoke `chklogin()` method in the backing bean. The value returned by this method determines the navigation rule that is implemented. The method may be as follows:

```
public String chklogin()
{
    if(userName.equals("peter")&& password.equals("peter"))
        return("success");
    else
        return("failure");
}
```

Above method checks the user name and password and then accordingly returns an outcome value to the page. The JSF navigation handler evaluates the outcome returned by the action method and matches it to a navigation case that has the same value defined in the `from-outcome` element. The matching rule is then implemented and the page defined in the rule's `to-view-id` element is displayed. If the method does not return an outcome or if the outcome does not match any of the navigation cases, the user remains on the current page.

DEMONSTRATION OF STATIC NAVIGATION

The following application demonstrates how static navigation is performed. For this application, we are going to develop three pages `index.jsp`, `login.jsp` and `newuser.jsp`. The `index.jsp` page displays a welcome message and two buttons where each button points to a unique JSP page. Clicking a button navigates to its designated JSP page. Let us make a new application by name: trial5, i.e., we need to make a folder trial5 in Tomcat's webapps folder and make a file `index.jsp` with following contents:

index.jsp

```
<%@ taglib uri="http://java.sun.com/jsf/html" prefix="h" %>
<%@ taglib uri="http://java.sun.com/jsf/core" prefix="f" %>
<html>
   <head>
      <title></title>
   </head>
   <body>
      <f:view>
         <h:form>
            <h2>Welcome to our Shopping Mall</br>
            But before purchasing you have to sign in </h2></br>
            <h:commandButton action="login" value="Login" />
            <h:commandButton action="newuser" value="New User" />
         </h:form>
      </f:view>
   </body>
</html>
```

We can see in code on the previous page that one button has string "login" in the action attribute and another one contains "newuser". If we press the button "Login", it will generate the outcome "login" and JSF will find all navigational rules in faces-config.xml and the navigation cases having the matching string "login" in <from-outcome> tag. If the value of any tag is equal to this string, JSF will move to the resource mentioned in <to-view-id> tag. Similarly, if we press "New User" button, JSF will check for the navigation-case with <from-outcome> matching with string: "newuser" and if found, it navigates to the JSP page specified by its <to-view-id> tag. We have to make two more JSP files: login.jsp and newuser.jsp. The overall structure of our webapplication is shown in Figure 8.1.

```
trial5
    index.jsp
    login.jsp
    newuser.jsp

    WEB-INF
        faces-config.xml
        web.xml

        classes
        lib
            commons-beanutils.jar
            commons-collections.jar
            commons-digester.jar
            commons-logging.jar
            jsf-api.jar
            jsf-impl.jar
            jstl.jar
            standard.jar
```

Figure 8.1 Structure of webapplication.

The main thing to note is that whatever the circumstance is, the "Login" button in `index.jsp` page will always navigate us to `login.jsp` page and not to any other page (static navigation). Similary, "New User" button will always navigate us to a fixed page : `newuser.jsp`.

Let us make another file `login.jsp` with the below given contents in "webapps\trial5" directory.

login.jsp

```
<%@ taglib uri="http://java.sun.com/jsf/html" prefix="h" %>
<%@ taglib uri="http://java.sun.com/jsf/core" prefix="f" %>
<html>
    <head>
        <title>Login Page</title>
    </head>
    <body>
        <f:view>
            <h:form>
                <h2>This is the login page </h2></br>
                <h:commandButton action="home" value="Home" />
            </h:form>
        </f:view>
    </body>
</html>
```

In code snippet on previous page, there is a string specifying that it is a login page and a button having a string "home" in its action attribute. If we press this button, it will generate the string "home" and JSF will check in `faces-config.xml` file for the `navigation-case` with `<from-outcome>` matching with string: "home" and if found, it navigates to the JSP page specified by its `<to-view-id>` tag. The home button is for navigating back to the source page i.e. `index.jsp` page.

Let us make another file `newuser.jsp` with the below given contents in "webapps\trial5" directory.

newuser.jsp

```
<%@ taglib uri="http://java.sun.com/jsf/html" prefix="h" %>
<%@ taglib uri="http://java.sun.com/jsf/core" prefix="f" %>
<html>
    <head>
        <title>New User Registration Page</title>
    </head>
    <body>
        <f:view>
            <h:form>
                <h2> This is the New User Registration page </h2></br>
                <h:commandButton action="home" value="Home" />
```

```
        </h:form>
      </f:view>
    </body>
</html>
```

In above code snippet, there is a string specifying that it is a New User Registration Page and a button having a string "home" in its action attribute. If we press this button, it will generate the outcome "home" and JSF will check in `faces-config.xml` file for the `navigation-case` with `<from-outcome>` matching with string: "home" and if found, it navigates to the JSP page specified by its `<to-view-id>` tag (i.e. source page : `index.jsp`).

Let us create an application configuration file: `faces-config.xml` in WEB-INF folder of our application to specify different conditions of navigating to `login.jsp` page or `newuser.jsp` page from `index.jsp` page. The contents of the `faces-config.xml` file are as follows:

faces-config.xml

```
<?xml version='1.0' encoding='UTF-8'?>
<!DOCTYPE faces-config PUBLIC
"-//Sun Microsystems, Inc.//DTD JavaServer Faces Config 1.1//EN"
"http://java.sun.com/dtd/web-facesconfig_1_1.dtd">
<faces-config>
   <navigation-rule>
      <from-view-id>/index.jsp</from-view-id>
      <navigation-case>
         <from-outcome>login</from-outcome>
         <to-view-id>/login.jsp</to-view-id>
      </navigation-case>
      <navigation-case>
         <from-outcome>newuser</from-outcome>
         <to-view-id>/newuser.jsp</to-view-id>
      </navigation-case>
   </navigation-rule>
   <navigation-rule>
      <from-view-id>/login.jsp</from-view-id>
      <navigation-case>
         <from-outcome>home</from-outcome>
         <to-view-id>/index.jsp</to-view-id>
      </navigation-case>
   </navigation-rule>
   <navigation-rule>
      <from-view-id>/newuser.jsp</from-view-id>
      <navigation-case>
         <from-outcome>home</from-outcome>
         <to-view-id>/index.jsp</to-view-id>
```

```
        </navigation-case>
    </navigation-rule>
</faces-config>
```

Above code specifies that there are three navigation rules. An individual rule for each JSP page: `index.jsp`, `login.jsp` and for `newuser.jsp` respectively. There are two `navigation-case` in case of `index.jsp` page. If in `index.jsp` file, the outcome of the UI command component is "login", then navigate to the `login.jsp` page. Similarly, if the outcome of the event is "newuser", then navigate to the `newuser.jsp` page.

Let us recall that the `to-view-id` element specifies the target page. The `from-outcome` value is the outcome of processing of the file specified in the `from-view-id`. This value comes from the action property of the UI command component that triggers the ActionEvent in the file specified in `from-view-id`.

There is one `navigation-case` in case of `login.jsp` page. If in `login.jsp` file, the outcome of an event is "home", then it will navigate to the `index.jsp` page. Also, there is one `navigation-case` in case of `newuser.jsp` page. If in `newuser.jsp` file, the outcome of an event is "home", then it will navigate to the `index.jsp` page.

These navigation cases makes it possible to navigate back to the source page : `index.jsp` from either of the pages : `login.jsp` or `newuser.jsp`.

Also make a deployment descriptor file `web.xml.in` in WEB-INF folder of our application to register the FacesServlet (the engine of all JSF applications). In this file, we set the `"load-on-startup"` element to true, so that the FacesServlet should be loaded when the application starts up.

Recall that FacesServlet builds a *component tree* of the JSP page whose control fires an event. It also creates an event object and passes it to any registered listener. The contents of `web.xml` file are:

web.xml

```
<?xml version='1.0' encoding='UTF-8'?>
<!DOCTYPE web-app PUBLIC
"-//Sun Microsystems, Inc.//DTD Web Application 2.3//EN"
"http://java.sun.com/dtd/web-app_2_3.dtd">
<web-app>
    <!-- Faces Servlet -->
    <servlet>
        <servlet-name>Faces Servlet</servlet-name>
        <servlet-class>javax.faces.webapp.FacesServlet</servlet-class>
        <load-on-startup> 1 </load-on-startup>
    </servlet>
    <!-- Faces Servlet Mapping -->
    <servlet-mapping>
        <servlet-name>Faces Servlet</servlet-name>
        <url-pattern>/faces/*</url-pattern>
```

```
    </servlet-mapping>
</web-app>
```

To test the application run Tomcat and in the browser type: `http://localhost:8080/trial5/faces/index.jsp`. The browser displays the welcome screen with two buttons (Figure 8.2).

Figure 8.2   Display of welcome screen.

If we select Login button, we get the login page as shown in Figure 8.3.

Figure 8.3   Display of Login page.

If we select New User button, we get the new user registration page as shown in Figure 8.4.

Figure 8.4   Display of new user registration page.

h:commandLink

The `h:commandLink` tag generates an HTML anchor element that acts like a form submit button. It generates JavaScript (onclick attribute) to make links act like buttons. When the link is clicked, the anchor element's value is set to the `h:commandLink`'s client ID and the enclosing form is submitted.

STATIC NAVIGATION USING `h:commandLink`

The following application demonstrates how `<h:commandLink>` tag can be used for navigating from one page to another. This application is exactly same as the earlier application we have just seen. The only difference is that instead of command buttons, we have used command links. Here also, we are going to develop three pages `index.jsp`, `login.jsp` and `newuser.jsp`. The `index.jsp` page displays a welcome message and two links where each link points to a unique JSP page. Clicking a link will navigate us to the designated JSP page. Let us make a new application by name: trial15, i.e., we need to make a folder trial15 in Tomcat's webapps folder and make a file `index.jsp` with following contents:

index.jsp

```
<%@ taglib uri="http://java.sun.com/jsf/html" prefix="h" %>
<%@ taglib uri="http://java.sun.com/jsf/core" prefix="f" %>
<html>
    <head>
        <title></title>
    </head>
    <body>
        <f:view>
            <h:form>
                <h2>Welcome to our Shopping Mall</br>
                But before purchasing you have to sign in  </h2></br>
                <h:commandLink action="login">
                    <h:outputText value="Login"/>
                </h:commandLink></br>
                <h:commandLink action="newuser">
                    <h:outputText value="New User" />
                </h:commandLink>
            </h:form>
        </f:view>
    </body>
</html>
```

Also make `login.jsp` file with following contents:

login.jsp

```
<%@ taglib uri="http://java.sun.com/jsf/html" prefix="h" %>
<%@ taglib uri="http://java.sun.com/jsf/core" prefix="f" %>
<html>
    <head>
        <title>Login Page</title>
    </head>
    <body>
        <f:view>
            <h:form>
                <h2>This is the login page </h2></br>
                <h:commandLink action="home"> <h:outputText
                    value="Home" />
                </h:commandLink>
```

```
            </h:form>
        </f:view>
    </body>
</html>
```

Also make a file `newuser.jsp` with following contents:

newuser.jsp

```
<%@ taglib uri="http://java.sun.com/jsf/html" prefix="h" %>
<%@ taglib uri="http://java.sun.com/jsf/core" prefix="f" %>
<html>
    <head>
        <title>New User Registration Page</title>
    </head>
    <body>
        <f:view>
            <h:form>
                <h2> This is the New User Registration page </h2></br>
                <h:commandLink action="home">
                    <h:outputText value="Home" />
                </h:commandLink>
            </h:form>
        </f:view>
    </body>
</html>
```

Let us create an application configuration file: `faces-config.xml` in WEB-INF folder of our application to specify different conditions of navigating to `login.jsp` page or `newuser.jsp` page from `index.jsp` page. The contents of the `faces-config.xml` file are as follows:

faces-config.xml

```
<?xml version='1.0' encoding='UTF-8'?>
<!DOCTYPE faces-config PUBLIC
"-//Sun Microsystems, Inc.//DTD JavaServer Faces Config 1.1//EN"
"http://java.sun.com/dtd/web-facesconfig_1_1.dtd">
<faces-config>
    <navigation-rule>
        <from-view-id>/index.jsp</from-view-id>
        <navigation-case>
            <from-outcome>login</from-outcome>
            <to-view-id>/login.jsp</to-view-id>
        </navigation-case>
        <navigation-case>
            <from-outcome>newuser</from-outcome>
```

```
            <to-view-id>/newuser.jsp</to-view-id>
        </navigation-case>
    </navigation-rule>
    <navigation-rule>
        <from-view-id>/login.jsp</from-view-id>
        <navigation-case>
            <from-outcome>home</from-outcome>
            <to-view-id>/index.jsp</to-view-id>
        </navigation-case>
    </navigation-rule>
    <navigation-rule>
        <from-view-id>/newuser.jsp</from-view-id>
        <navigation-case>
            <from-outcome>home</from-outcome>
            <to-view-id>/index.jsp</to-view-id>
        </navigation-case>
    </navigation-rule>
</faces-config>
```

Also make a deployment descriptor file `web.xml.in` in WEB-INF folder of our
application to register the FacesServlet which is the engine of all JSF applications. Through the
`web.xml` file, we need to state that any request containing the `pattern/faces/` in the
URL must be passed to the FacesServlet. The contents of `web.xml` file are same as earlier
applications.

To run the application, run Tomcat and in the browser type: `http://`
`localhost:8080/trial15/faces/index.jsp`. The browser displays the welcome
screen with two links (Figure 8.5).

Figure 8.5   Display of welcome screen.

If we select Login link, we get the login page as shown in Figure 8.6.

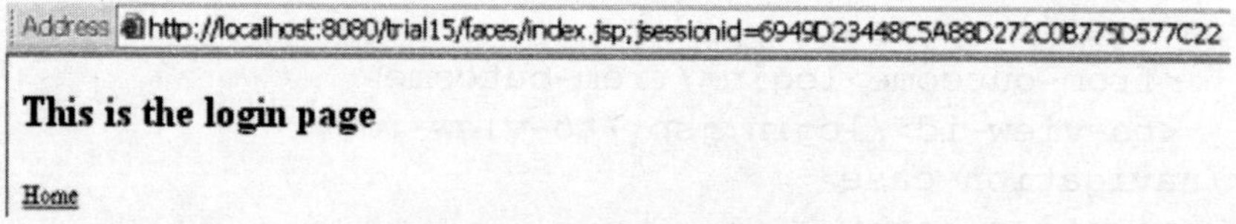

Figure 8.6   Display of login page.

If we select New User link, we get the new user registration page as shown in Figure 8.7.

Address   http://localhost:8080/trial15/faces/index.jsp

This is the New User Registration page

<u>Home</u>

Figure 8.7 Display of new user registration page.

DEMONSTRATING DYNAMIC NAVIGATION

The following application demonstrates dynamic navigation. We bind the action attribute of a navigation component (button) to an action method of a backing bean which returns an outcome value. The outcome value determines the next page that should be displayed. Different outcomes trigger different navigation cases, causing the application to navigate to one of several possible target pages.

For this application, we are going to develop three pages `index.jsp`, `welcome.jsp` and `unauthorised.jsp`. The `index.jsp` asks the user to enter User id and Password. If the User id and Password are correct, welcome page will be displayed otherwise page showing that user is an **unauthorised person** will be displayed. The User id and Password are binded with **UserBean** (JavaBean) attributes **userName** and **password**.

Let us make a new application by name: trial3, i.e., we need to make a folder trial3 in Tomcat's webapps folder and make a file `index.jsp` with following contents:

index.jsp

```
<%@ taglib uri="http://java.sun.com/jsf/html" prefix="h" %>
<%@ taglib uri="http://java.sun.com/jsf/core" prefix="f" %>
<html>
  <head>
    <title>Login Form</title>
  </head>
  <body>
    <f:view>
      <h:form>
        <h3>Please enter your userid and password.</h3>
        <table>
        <tr>
          <td>Userid:</td>
          <td><h:inputText value="#{UserBean.userName}"/></td>
        </tr>
        <tr>
          <td>Password:</td>
          <td><h:inputSecret value="#{UserBean.password}"/></td>
```

```
            </tr>
        </table>
        <p>
        <h:commandButton value="Login"
            action="#{UserBean.chklogin}"/>
        </p>
    </h:form>
  </f:view>
 </body>
</html>
```

As we can see in the above JSP program, that the user id and password entered by the user are binded with **userName** and **password** attribute of the JavaBean: **UserBean**. The statement: `<h:commandButton value="Login" action="#{UserBean.chklogin}"/>` means that when user clicks the command button, `chklogin()` method of the UserBean will be invoked.

Now we will create a bean that will hold the user id and password entered by the user. We know that a JavaBean is nothing but a class file having attributes and their respective setter and getter methods. Let us make a file `User.java` in "webapps\trial3\WEB-INF \classes directory. The overall structure of our webapplication is shown in Figure 8.8.

```
index.jsp
unauthorised.jsp
welcome.jsp

WEB-INF
        faces-config.xml
        web.xml

        classes
            User.class
            User.java

        lib
            commons-beanutils.jar
            commons-collections.jar
            commons-digester.jar
            commons-logging.jar
            jsf-api.jar
            jsf-impl.jar
            jstl.jar
            standard.jar
```

Figure 8.8   Structure of webapplication.

User.java

```java
public class User {
   private String userName;
   private String password;

   public String getUserName() {return userName;}
   public void setUserName(String newValue) {userName = newValue;}
   public String getPassword() {return password;}
```

```
    public void setPassword(String newValue) {password = newValue;}
    public String chklogin()
    {
        if(userName.equals("peter") && password.equals("peter"))
            return("success");
        else
            return("failure");
    }
}
```

`chklogin()` method checks the user name and password and then accordingly returns an outcome value as either "`success`" or "`failure`". The JSF navigation handler evaluates this outcome returned and matches it with a navigation case that has the same value defined in the **from-outcome** element. If any `<from-outcome>` tag has a matching string, it will navigate to the jsp page specified by its `<to-view-id>` tag.

Let us make a file `welcome.jsp` with following contents in trial3 folder:

welcome.jsp

```
<<%@ taglib uri="http://java.sun.com/jsf/html" prefix="h" %>
<%@ taglib uri="http://java.sun.com/jsf/core" prefix="f" %>

<html>
    <head>
      <title>Welcome Page</title>
    </head>
    <body>
      <f:view>
        <h:form>
          Welcome to our Web Site
          <h:outputText value="#{UserBean.userName}"/>
        </h:form>
      </f:view>
    </body>
</html>
```

Also make a file `unauthorised.jsp` with following contents in trial3 folder:

unauthorised.jsp

```
<%@ taglib uri="http://java.sun.com/jsf/html" prefix="h" %>
<%@ taglib uri="http://java.sun.com/jsf/core" prefix="f" %>
<html>
    <head>
      <title>Cancellation Page</title>
    </head>
    <body>
```

```
    <f:view>
     <h:form>
       Sorry Sir, you are not authorised :
       <h:outputText value="#{UserBean.userName}"/>!
     </h:form>
    </f:view>
   </body>
</html>
```

Let us create an application configuration file: `faces-config.xml` in WEB-INF folder of our application to specify the name of our JavaBean and also the condition of navigating to `welcome.jsp` page and `unauthorised.jsp` page from `index.jsp` page. The contents of the `faces-config.xml` file are as follows:

faces-config.xml

```
<?xml version='1.0' encoding='UTF-8'?>
<!DOCTYPE faces-config PUBLIC
"-//Sun Microsystems, Inc.//DTD JavaServer Faces Config 1.1//EN"
"http://java.sun.com/dtd/web-facesconfig_1_1.dtd">
<faces-config>
   <navigation-rule>
       <from-view-id>/index.jsp</from-view-id>
       <navigation-case>
           <from-outcome>success</from-outcome>
           <to-view-id>/welcome.jsp</to-view-id>
       </navigation-case>
       <navigation-case>
           <from-outcome>failure</from-outcome>
           <to-view-id>/unauthorised.jsp</to-view-id>
       </navigation-case>
   </navigation-rule>
   <managed-bean>
       <managed-bean-name>UserBean</managed-bean-name>
       <managed-bean-class>User</managed-bean-class>
       <managed-bean-scope>request</managed-bean-scope>
   </managed-bean>
</faces-config>
```

Above code specifies that the class name of the managed bean is User.class and is referred to in the application as **UserBean**. Also there is a navigation rule having two navigation-cases. If in `index.jsp` file, the outcome of an event (i.e., the value of the action property of the UI command component—command button) is "`success`", then navigate to the `welcome.jsp` page. Similarly, if the outcome of the event is "`failure`", then navigate to the `unauthorised.jsp` page.

Let us recall that the `to-view-id` element specifies the target page. The from-outcome value is the outcome of processing of the file specified in the `from-view-id`. This value comes from the action property of the UI command component that triggers the ActionEvent in the file specified in from-view-id.

Also make a deployment descriptor file `web.xml.in` in WEB-INF folder. The contents of `web.xml` file are same as earlier applications.

To run the application, run Tomcat and in the browser type: `http://localhost:8080/trial3/faces/index.jsp`. The browser prompts the user to enter userid and password. After feeding them, select `Submit` button (Figure 8.9).

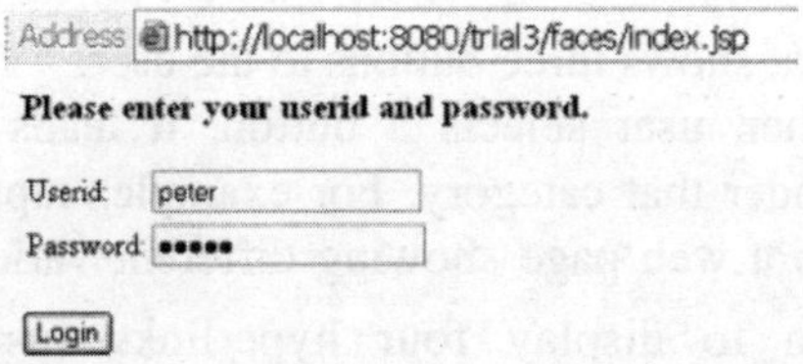

Figure 8.9 Press Login button on entering userid & password.

If the user id and password are correct, i.e., if user id and password both are entered as `"peter"`, we get a welcome message as shown in Figure 8.10.

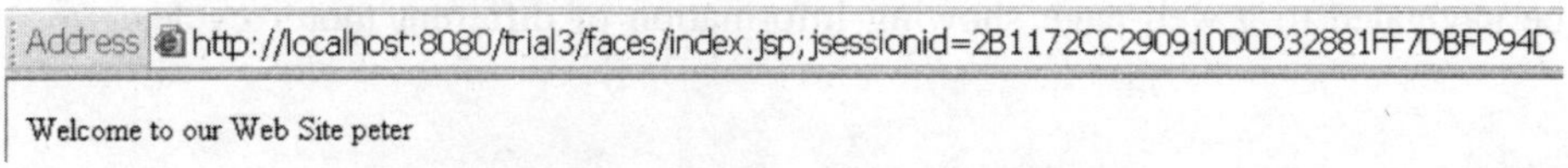

Figure 8.10 Display of welcome message.

If we enter userid and password other than `"peter"`, we get the message that the user is an unauthorised user (Figure 8.11).

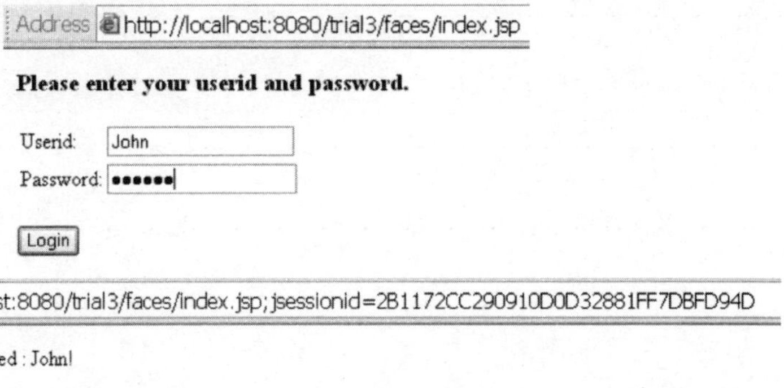

Figure 8.11 If wrong userid and password is entered, in authorised user message is displayed.

SUMMARY

In this chapter we saw that there are two types of navigations: static and dynamic. Static navigation always leads to the specific web pages and has nothing to do with the data entered by the user, whereas in dynamic navigation it may lead to any web page depending either on the evaluation of the expression or on the data provided by the user. We saw how to write navigation cases for different navigation rules. We have learnt through a practical examples that commandLink control can also be used for navigation to different web pages.

REVIEW QUESTIONS

8.1 Write a JSF program that shows three buttons to the user: `"Ice Creams"`, `"Juices"` and `"Candies"`. When user selects a button, it leads him to the respective page displaying the items under that category. For example, suppose user selects Ice Creams, he will be navigated to a web page showing different varieties of ice creams available.

8.2 Write a JSF program to display four hyperlinks (using commandLink control): `"Shimla"`, `"Goa"`, `"Kerala"` and `"Kashmir"`. When user clicks a link, he will be navigated to the web page showing the tourist places of the selected place.

8.3 Assuming that your site is selling scooter and motorcycle. User is provided a textfield to enter `"scooter"` or `"motor cycle"`. If he enters `"scooter"` he must be navigated to a page showing different models of scooters. And if he enters "Motor cycle" he must be navigated to a web page showing information of different motor cycles.

9

Using NetBeans IDE

── LEARNING OBJECTIVES ──

In this chapter, we will learn:

- How to use simple controls
- How to use managed bean
- How to navigate from one page to another
- How to perform dynamic navigation
- How to perform validation
- How to use drop down control
- How to use ListBox control
- How to use RadioButtonGroup control
- How to use CheckBoxGroup control
- How to use converters
- How to use DateTime converter
- How to make custom validator

NETBEANS IDE

NetBeans IDE is one of the popular emerging IDE for making Java based application. This chapter is devoted to understand how to use different controls of NetBeans in making java based application.

175

An IDE makes a software development quite easy. It provides a list of controls, properties, menus, database access, etc. at one place so the user finds everything very handy. The NetBeans IDE is open source and is written in the Java programming language. It is the first IDE which fully supports JDK 5.0 features.

NetBeans has following features:

- Syntax highlighting for Java, XML, HTML, CSS, JSP, IDL
- Customizable fonts, colours, and keyboard shortcuts
- Live parsing and error marking
- Pop-up Javadoc for quick access to documentation
- Advanced code completion
- Automatic indentation
- Matching brace highlighting
- Extensible component palette with preinstalled swing and AWT components
- Component Inspector showing a component's tree and properties
- JavaBeans support, including installing, using, and customizing properties, events, and customizers
- Database support—Database schema browsing to see the tables, views, and stored procedures defined in a database
- Data view to see data stored in tables
- SQL command execution to help us write and execute more complicated SQL commands

The NetBeans IDE also provides full-featured refactoring tools, which allow us to rename and move classes, fields, and methods, as well as change method parameters.

Within NetBeans, we work within the context of a project, which consists of an organized group of source files; project-specific properties files; and all the tools we'll need to write, compile, test, and debug our application.

NetBeans creates an environment when we create a project. That is, the moment we tell NetBeans the name of a new project, it then

- Creates a source tree with an optional skeleton class inside
- Sets classpaths for compiling, running, and testing
- Sets the Java platform the project is to run on

NetBeans IDE has several Palette of components. We can drag and drop any component from any palette on the web page and use it. Palettes have different categories of Components.

Component Categories

Components are grouped under categories (Palettes). Following are the categories:

Basic: The components that we are likely to use most often, like buttons, tables, drop down lists, and text fields, etc. are found in this category.

Layout:	Components whose main purpose is to organize or format a page, like the Grid Panel component that arranges components in a grid or the Group Panel component that groups components together, etc. are found in this category.
Composite:	Components with a more complex organization and a specialized purpose, like the Add Remove List component that displays a list of items or the Breadcrumbs component that displays a list of hyperlinks to previous pages in a site hierarchy, etc. are found in this category.
Validators:	Components to validate data entered by user are found in this category.
Converters:	A set of data converters that we can use with components to convert between the string data type and other data types as required are found in this category.
Standard:	The original set of standard JavaServer Faces components that are shipped with the IDE are placed in this category. They are not as sophisticated or easy to use as the basic, layout, and composite components. For example, the standard components cannot participate in a theme and their structure is also very complex.
Advanced:	The components in this category are for advanced users. These components have no visual appearance and are useful for advanced web developers.
Data Providers:	A set of components that provide an interface to data sources like database tables and JavaBeans objects are placed in this category.

Let us make few JSF applications in NetBeans IDE 6.0.

Using Simple Controls

In this application we will demonstrate how to use static text control and how to set its properties according to our needs. The steps are:

Select `File->New Project`. Select Web from Categories tab and Web Application from `Projects tab. Select Next button`. Give any name to Project Name say `Webex1`. Notice that the Context Path is `/Webex1`. Change the Project Location to any directory on the computer. The default Project Location that appears is: `C:\Documents and Settings\Administrator`. We will be referring to this directory now onwards as `:$PROJECTHOME`.

Select the server to which we want to deploy our application. Only servers that are registered with the IDE are listed. Let our server be: `GlassFish V2`. Leave the "`Set as Main Project`" checkbox selected. Click `Next` (Figure 9.1).

Select the Visual Web JavaServer Faces checkbox when prompted to select the framework and select `Finish` button (Figure 9.2).

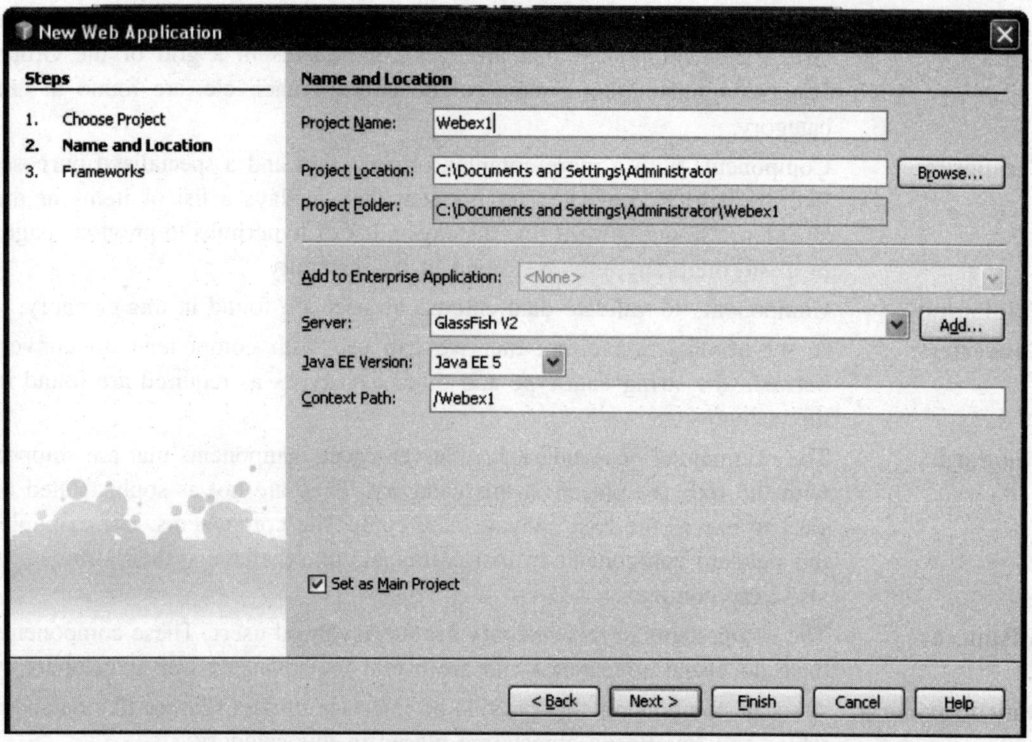

Figure 9.1   Screen of new web application.

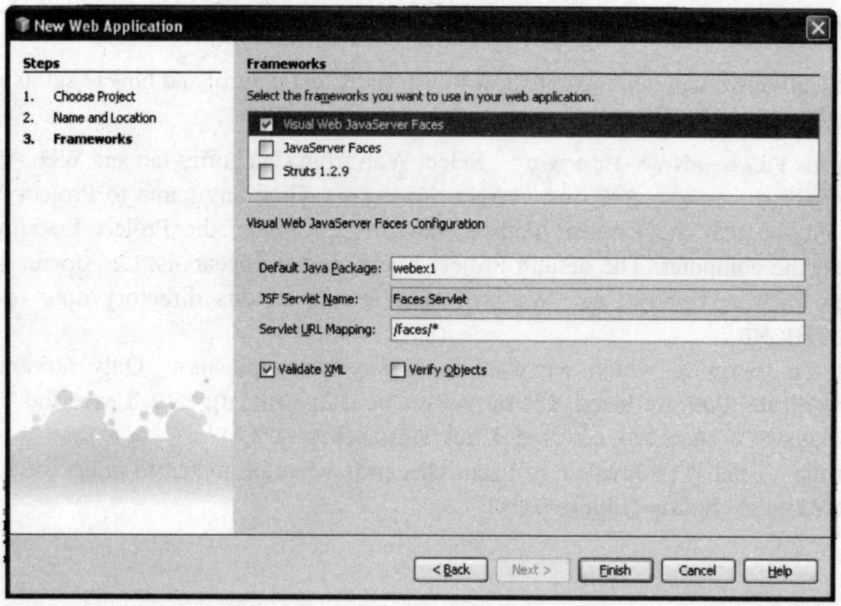

Figure 9.2   Selection of Visual Web JavaServer Faces checkbox.

By default `Page1.jsp file` is opened in design mode as shown in Figure 9.3.

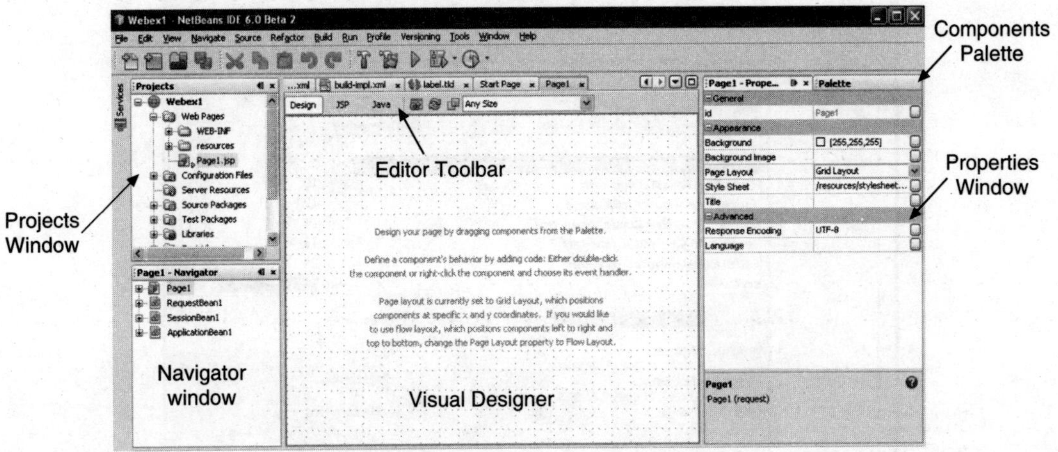

Figure 9.3   Display of design mode of Page1.jsp file.

The IDE creates the `$PROJECTHOME/Webex1` project folder for our application. The `Webex1` project opens in the IDE. We can view its logical structure in the `Projects` window and its file structure in the `Files` window.

Expand the `Webex1` project node and the Web Pages node. Note that the IDE has created a default JavaServer Pages file, `Page1.jsp`, for us.

In the Palette on the right side of the Visual Designer, expand Basic and drag the Static Text Component on the form and release the mouse button (Figure 9.4).

Figure 9.4   Screen after placing on the Static Text Component on the form.

Select the Properties tab to set the properties of the Static Text component and select style option and set the font and size as shown in Figure 9.5.

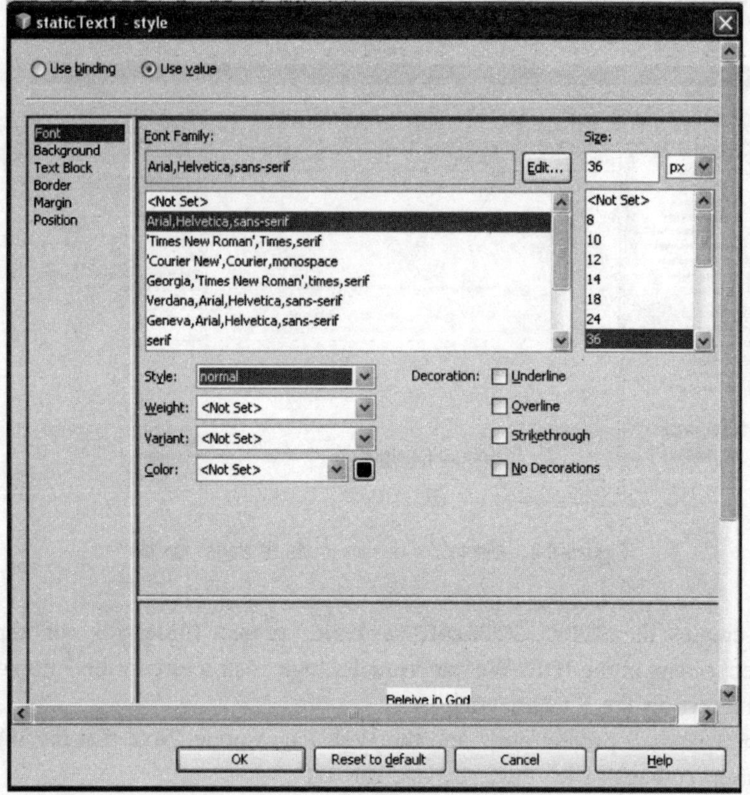

Figure 9.5   Setting the font and size by using style property.

Also set the text property to "Believe in God" (Figure 9.6).

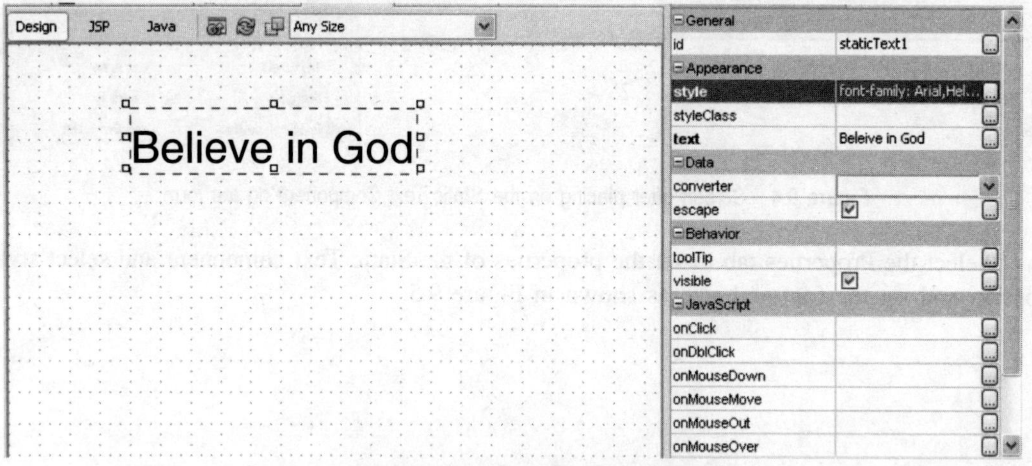

Figure 9.6   Setting the text property.

Run the project and we get the output as shown in Figure 9.7.

Figure 9.7   Output displayed.

This was a simple application to use a simple control.

Demonstrating How to Use Managed Bean and How to Navigate from One Page to Another

In this application we will ask a user to enter his name in a web page and when he selects submit button, a welcome page will be displayed to him. We will see how to bind a text field component to a managed bean attribute and also how we can navigate from one page to another page on clicking `Submit` button. The steps are as follows:

`Select File->New Project`. Select web from categories tab and web application from projects tab. Select `Next` button. Give any name to project name say `Webex2`. Notice that the context path is `/Webex2`. Select the server to be: `GlassFish V2`. Leave the "`Set as Main Project`" checkbox selected. Click `Next` (Figure 9.8).

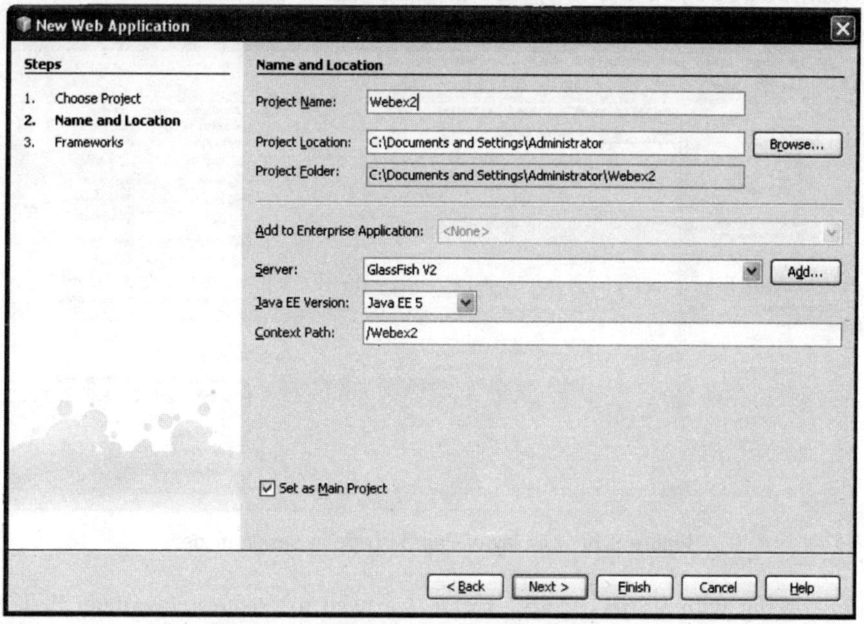

Figure 9.8   Screen of new web application.

Select the Visual Web JavaServer Faces checkbox when prompted to select the framework and select Finish button (Figure 9.9).

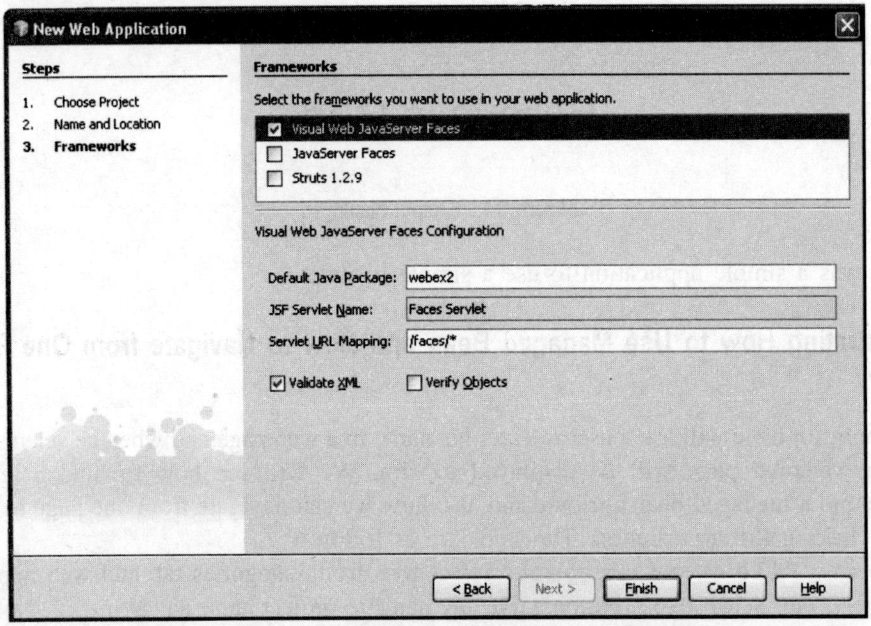

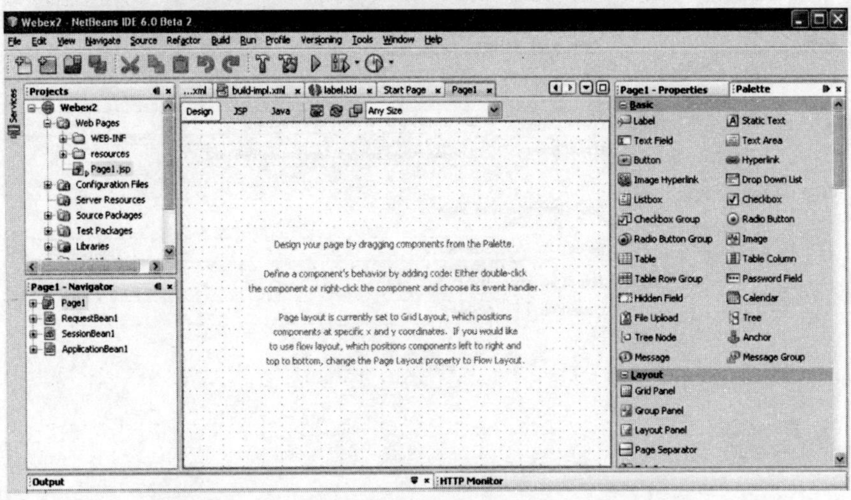

Figure 9.9   Selection of Visual Web JavaServer Faces checkbox.

By default `Page1.jsp` file is opened in design mode as shown in Figure 9.10.

Figure 9.10   Display of Page1.jsp file in design mode.

Before working with `Page1.jsp file`, we need to create a JavaBean first. So, right click on `Webex2` project node in Projects window, select New option and select JSF Managed Bean option. We get a screen to specify the class name as shown in Figure 9.11.

Assign the class name as `User` and select `Finish` button

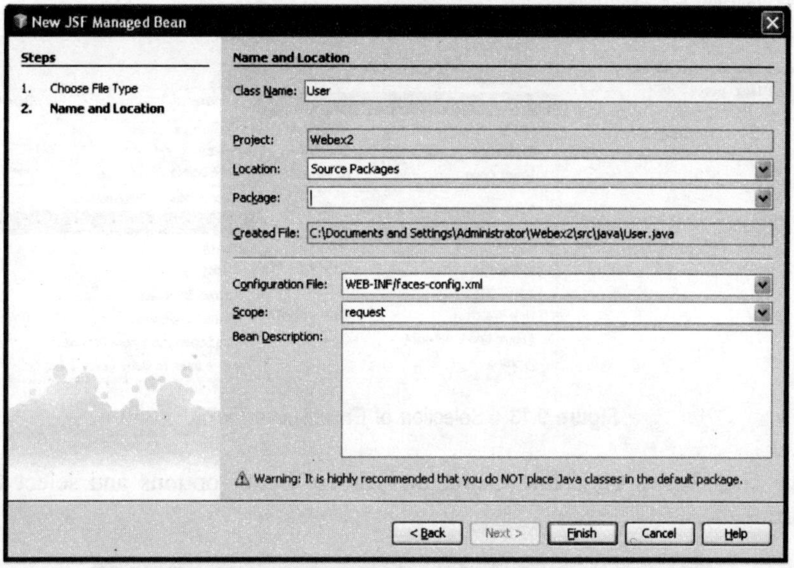

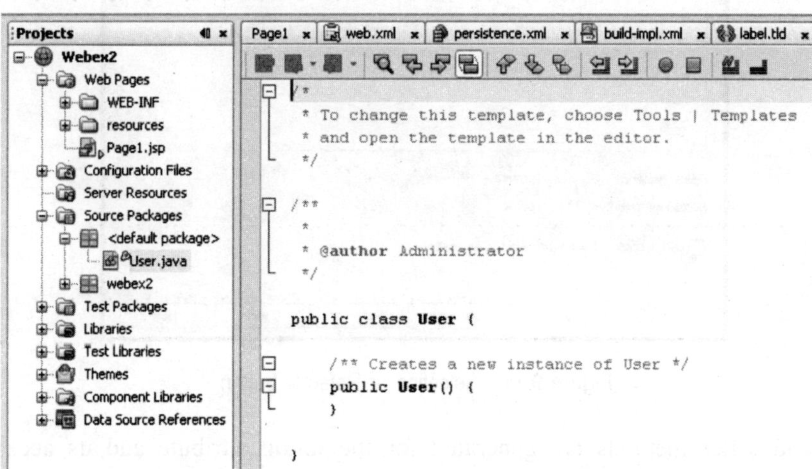

Figure 9.11   Creating a class: User.

`User.java` file gets opened in Source Editor with an empty constructor. We can create attributes for this Managed Bean now (Figure 9.12).

Figure 9.12   Creation of attributes for Managed Bean.

Declare a field by typing the following line directly below the class declaration:

```
String name;
```

To create setter and getter methods for our **name** attribute, right-click the string **name** in the Source Editor and choose Refactor -> Encapsulate Fields option (Figure 9.13).

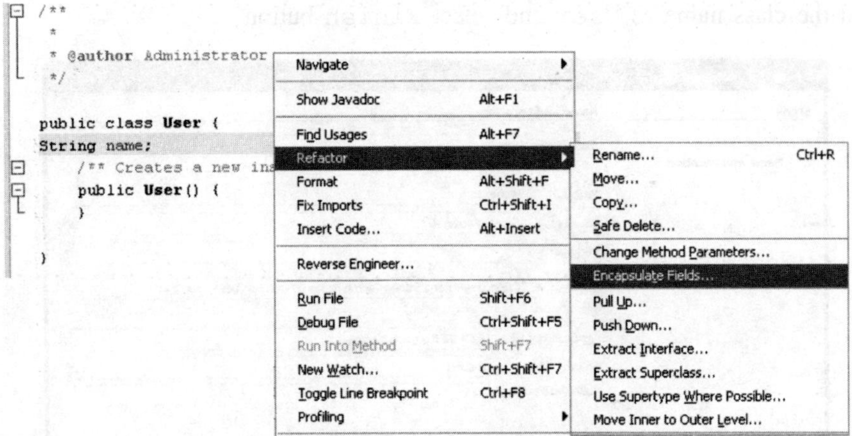

Figure 9.13   Selection of Encapsulate Fields.

Select the checkboxes of Create Getter and Create Setter options and select `Refactor` button (Figure 9.14).

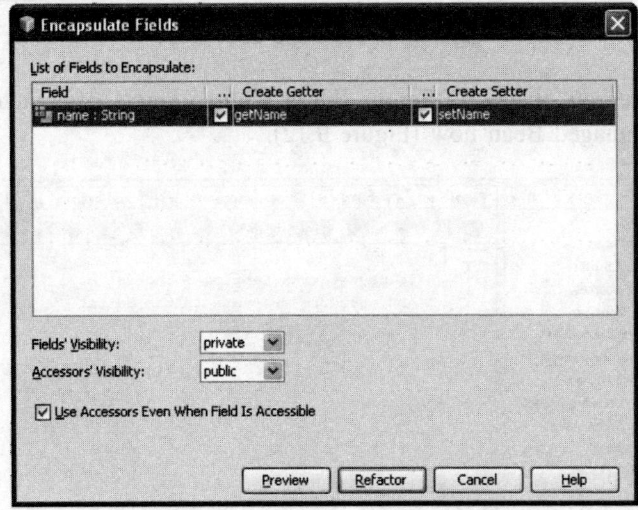

Figure 9.14   Selection of Refactor button.

Getter and setter methods are generated for the **name** attribute and its access level is changed to **private**. The Java class should now look similar to this:

User.java

```
public class User {
    private String name;
    public User() {
    }
```

```java
public String getName() {
    return name;
}
public void setName(String name) {
    this.name = name;
}
}
```

Now, we can set the managed bean property in `faces-config.xml` file. Expand the Configuration Files node, right click on `faces-config.xml` file and select Edit option. The contents of the `faces-config.xml` file that is displayed on the screen as:

```xml
<?xml version='1.0' encoding='UTF-8'?>

<!-- ====== FULL CONFIGURATION FILE =============================== -->

<faces-config version="1.2"

    xmlns="http://java.sun.com/xml/ns/javaee"
    xmlns:xsi="http://www.w3.org/2001/XMLSchema-instance"
    xsi:schemaLocation="http://java.sun.com/xml/ns/javaee
  http://java.sun.com/xml/ns/javaee/web-facesconfig_1_2.xsd">
    <application>
        <locale-config>
            <default-locale>en</default-locale>
            <supported-locale>en</supported-locale>
            <supported-locale>ja</supported-locale>
            <supported-locale>zh_CN</supported-locale>
            <supported-locale>pt_BR</supported-locale>
        </locale-config>
    </application>
    <managed-bean>
        <managed-bean-name>SessionBean1</managed-bean-name>
        <managed-bean-class>webex2.SessionBean1</managed-bean-class>
        <managed-bean-scope>session</managed-bean-scope>
    </managed-bean>
    <managed-bean>
        <managed-bean-name>Page1</managed-bean-name>
        <managed-bean-class>webex2.Page1</managed-bean-class>
        <managed-bean-scope>request</managed-bean-scope>
    </managed-bean>
    <managed-bean>
        <managed-bean-name>ApplicationBean1</managed-bean-name>
        <managed-bean-class>webex2.ApplicationBean1</managed-bean-class>
        <managed-bean-scope>application</managed-bean-scope>
```

```
</managed-bean>
<managed-bean>
     <managed-bean-name>RequestBean1</managed-bean-name>
     <managed-bean-class>webex2.RequestBean1</managed-bean-class>
     <managed-bean-scope>request</managed-bean-scope>
</managed-bean>
<managed-bean>
     <managed-bean-name>User</managed-bean-name>
     <managed-bean-class>User</managed-bean-class>
     <managed-bean-scope>request</managed-bean-scope>
</managed-bean>
</faces-config>
```

We delete the following lines from `faces-config.xml` file:

```
<managed-bean>
     <managed-bean-name>User</managed-bean-name>
     <managed-bean-class>User</managed-bean-class>
     <managed-bean-scope>request</managed-bean-scope>
</managed-bean>
```

It is so because we want to use `User.java` by the name UserBean in our application. Right click on the editor and select `JavaServerFaces->Add Managed Bean` option (Figure 9.15).

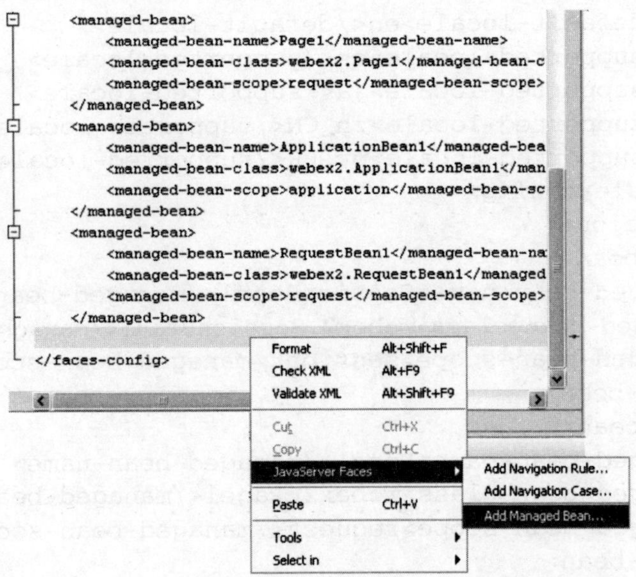

Figure 9.15   Selection of Add Managed Bean.

Specify the name of the Managed Bean as UserBean, class name as User, scope as request and select Add button (Figure 9.16).

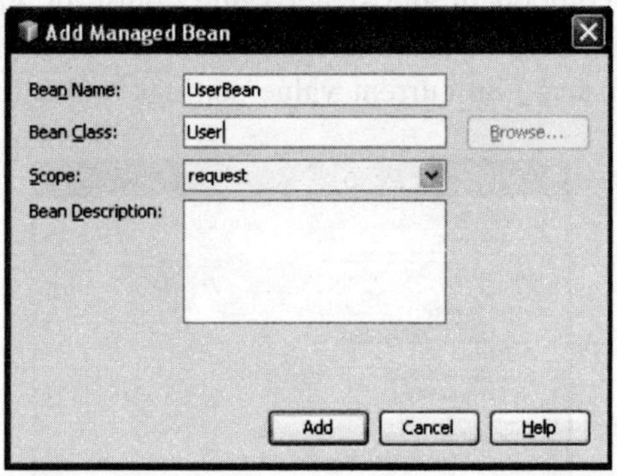

Figure 9.16   Fill the details & press Add button.

We get the following entries added to `Faces-config.xml` file:

```
<managed-bean>
    <managed-bean-name>UserBean</managed-bean-name>
    <managed-bean-class>User</managed-bean-class>
    <managed-bean-scope>request</managed-bean-scope>
</managed-bean>
```

Now open the `Page1.jsp` file in Design mode. In the Palette on the right side of the Visual Designer, expand Basic Palette and drag and drop the Static Text, Label and a Button component on the form. Also drag and drop Text Field Component from the Standard Palette on the form (Figure 9.17).

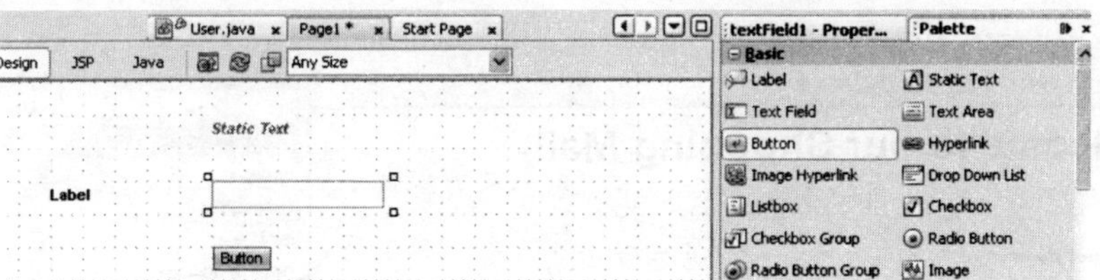

Figure 9.17   Selection from the Standard Palette.

Select the Static Text component change its text and style options from its `Properties` tab. Also select Label component and set its text property from its `Properties` tab to "Enter Your Name" as shown in Figure 9.18.

Figure 9.18   Selection of Properties tab.

Select `TextField1` component and select value option in `Properties` tab. We get a dialog box to specify the attribute of the Managed Bean to which this textfield is to be binded. We enter `#{UserBean.name}` in current value settings and select `OK` (Figure 9.19).

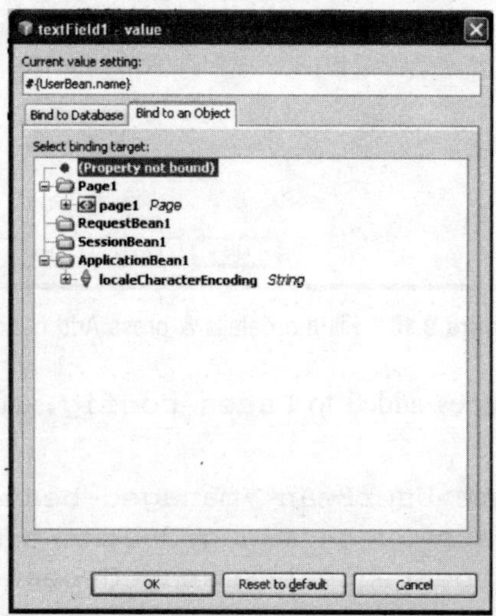

Figure 9.19   TextField1 is binded to Managed Bean attribute.

Select the button component and select its text property in the `Properties` window and set it to `"Submit"`. After making all these settings, our `Page1.jsp` should appear as shown in Figure 9.20.

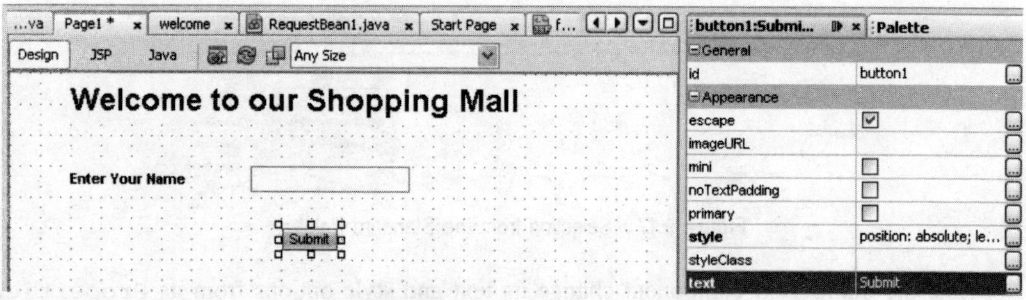

Figure 9.20   Display of Page1.jsp.

To make a welcome page, we right click on `Web Pages node` in Projects window, select `New` option and then select `Visual Web JSF Page` option. Assign the name as welcome and select `Finish` button (Figure 9.21).

`Welcome.jsp` page is opened in design mode. In the Palette on the right side of the Visual Designer, expand Basic Palette and drag and drop the Static Text and Label component on the form. Set the text property of the Static Text control to `"Welcome"` and select the Label component and set its text property to `#{UserBean.name}` in order to bind it to the **name** attribute of the Managed Bean component: UserBean (Figure 9.22).

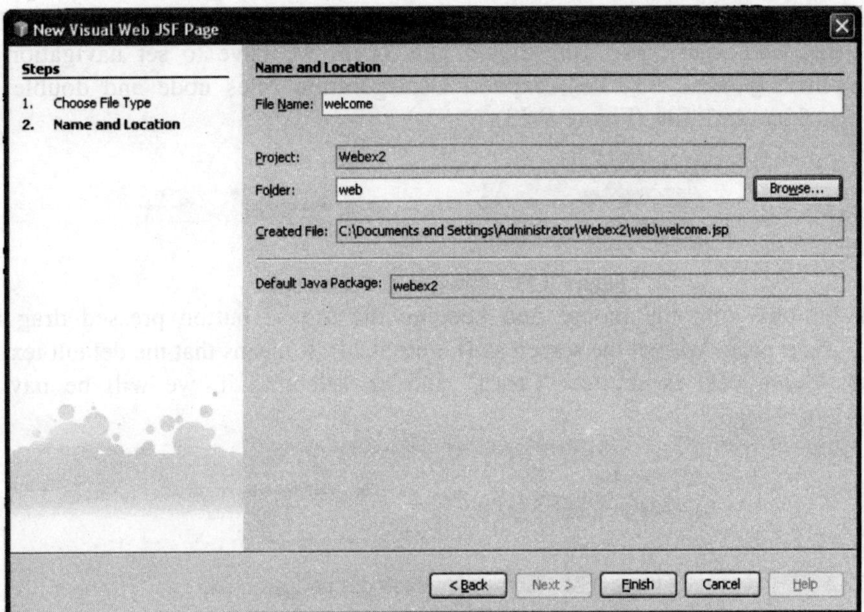

Figure 9.21   Screen for New Visual Web JSF Page: welcome.

Figure 9.22   Setting the text property of Label Control.

In order to set the navigation rule (i.e., if we want that on clicking `Submit` button in `Page1.jsp`, `welcome.jsp` file should gets open, we have to set navigation rules in (`faces-config.xml  file`), expand Configuration Files node and double click on `faces-config.xml` file (Figure 9.23).

Figure 9.23   Selection of Submit button.

Click button1 with the mouse and keeping the mouse button pressed drag it to the `welcome.jsp` page. We get the screen as (Figure 9.24). It means that the default text returned by button. Component is set to: "Case1" and on selecting it, we will be navigated to `welcome.jsp` page.

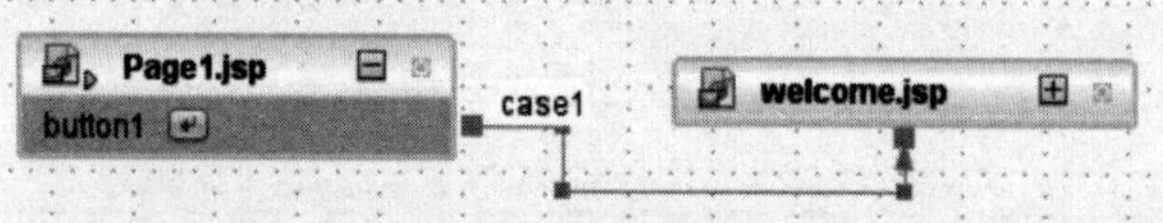

Figure 9.24   Screen for creating a navigation rule.

Above step will create following navigation rule in `faces-config.xml` file:

```
<navigation-rule>
   <from-view-id>/Page1.jsp</from-view-id>
   <navigation-case>
      <from-outcome>case1</from-outcome>
      <to-view-id>/welcome.jsp</to-view-id>
   </navigation-case>
</navigation-rule>
```

Our application is complete, let us run it. We get following output (Figure 9.25):

Figure 9.25   Enter a name and press Submit button.

Enter a name and press `Submit` button. We find that a welcome message is displayed (Figure 9.26).

Figure 9.26   Message displayed.

Using Managed Bean—IInd Method

This application is same as earlier application with a difference that instead of making a separate managed bean, we use the RequestBean provided by NetBeans (rest everything is same). The steps are:

```
Select File->New Project.
```
Select Web from Categories tab and Web Application from Projects tab. Select Next button. Give Project Name as `Webex2`. Let the server be: `GlassFish V2`. Click `Next`. Select the Visual Web JavaServer Faces checkbox when prompted to select the framework and select Finish button. By default `Page1.jsp` file is opened in design mode. The default name of the web page is `Page1.jsp`. We will rename it to `index.jsp` by right clicking on `Page1.jsp`, select `Refactor` option followed by `Rename`.

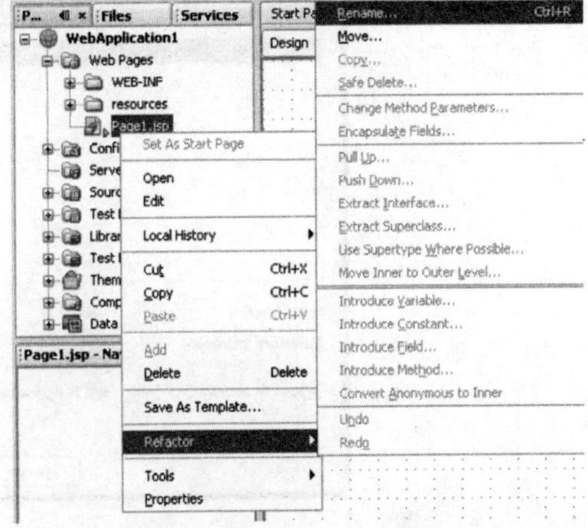

Figure 9.27   Selection of Refactor option.

We assign the new name as `Index.jsp`.

To create a Managed bean, expand the Source Package node in Projects window and double click on `RequestBean1.java` to open it. In RequestBean1.java file, add a field:

```
private String name;
```

To make its getter and setter methods, we right click on the editor and select Refactor option and select Encapsulate Fields as shown in Figure 9.28.

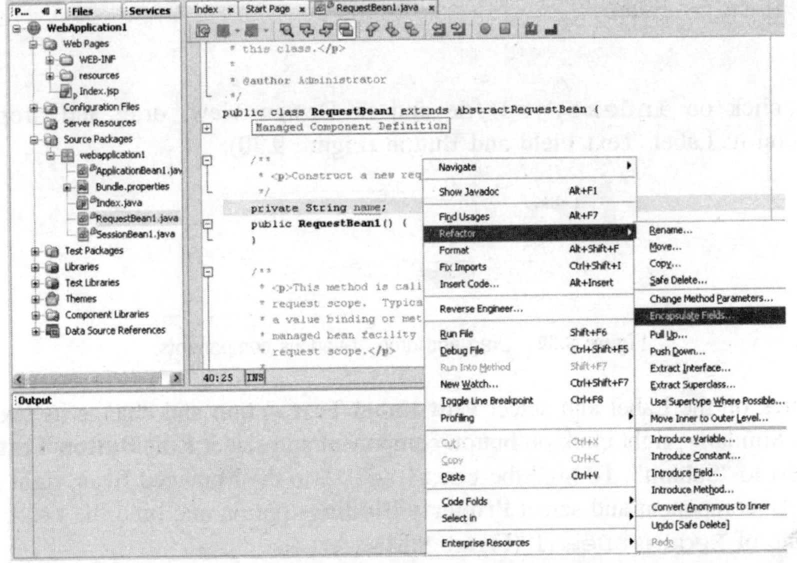

Figure 9.28   Selection of Encapsulate Fields.

Select the checkbox of `Create Getter` and `Create Setter` tabs and then press `Refactor` button as shown in Figure 9.29.

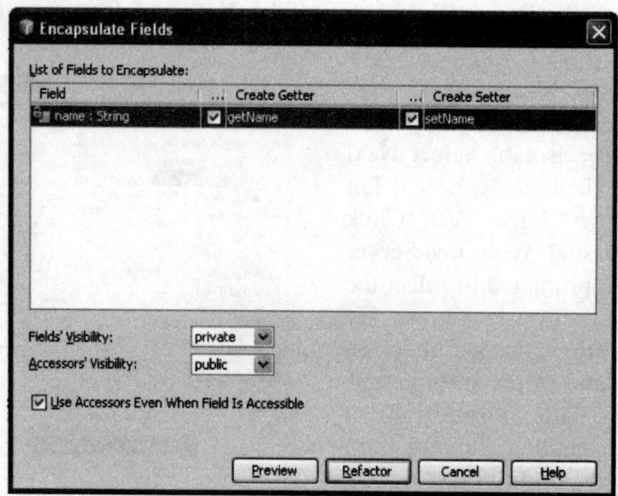

Figure 9.29   Press the Refactor button.

Refactoring will produce following setter and getter methods in `RequestBean1.java` file:

```
public String getName() {
    return name;
}
public void setName(String name) {
    this.name = name;
}
```

Double click on `Index1.jsp` file and in Design view, drag and drop following components on it: Label, Text Field and Button (Figure 9.30):

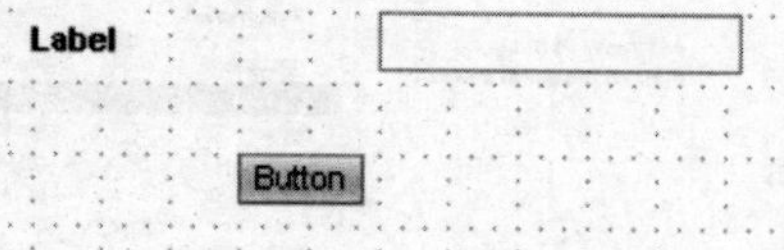

Figure 9.30   Drag and drop of various components.

Right click on the Label and select **Edit Label Text** option and change its text to: "Enter your name". Similarly, right click on button component and select **Edit Button Text** option and change its text to "Submit". To bind the `textField1` to the Managed Bean, right click on the `textField1` component and select **Property Bindings** option and bind the `textField1` to name attribute of `RequestBean1` (Figure 9.31).

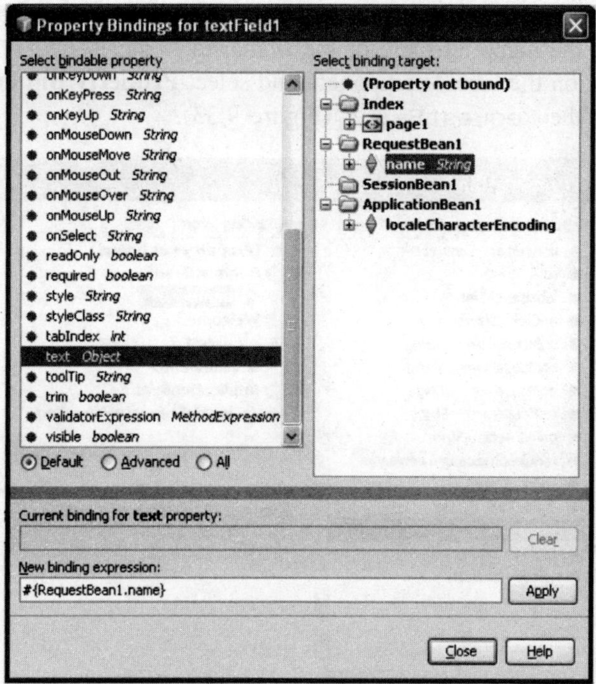

Figure 9.31   Selection of Property Bindings.

To add `Welcome.jsp` page, right click on the Web Application in Projects Window and select New option followed by Visual Web JSF Page as shown in Figure 9.32.

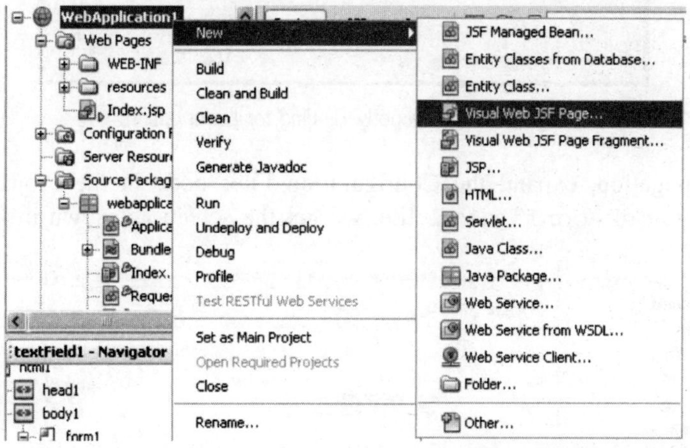

Figure 9.32   Steps for adding Welcome.jsp page.

Assign the name to the new page as `Welcome.jsp`. Drag and drop two Label components on Design form of `Welcome.jsp` page. Right click on the first Label component: label1 and select **Edit Label Text** option and change its text to **"Welcome"**. Also bind the second label component: label2 to the name attribute of the Managed Bean: `RequestBean1`. Binding is done by right clicking on the label2 component and select **Property Bindings** option and select the name attribute of the `RequestBean1` (Figure 9.33).

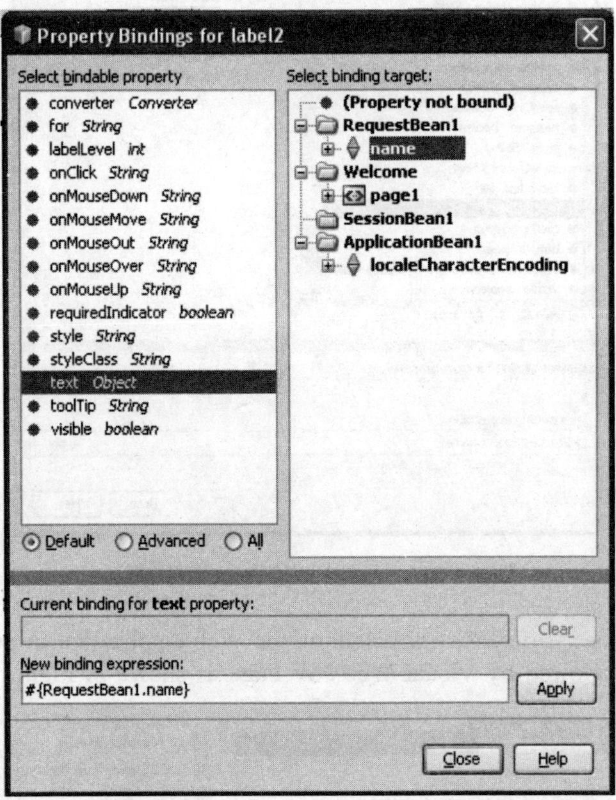

Figure 9.33   Property Binding for Label option.

To setup navigation, expand the Configuration Files node in the Projects Window and double click on `faces-config.xml` file, we get the screen as shown in Figure 9.34.

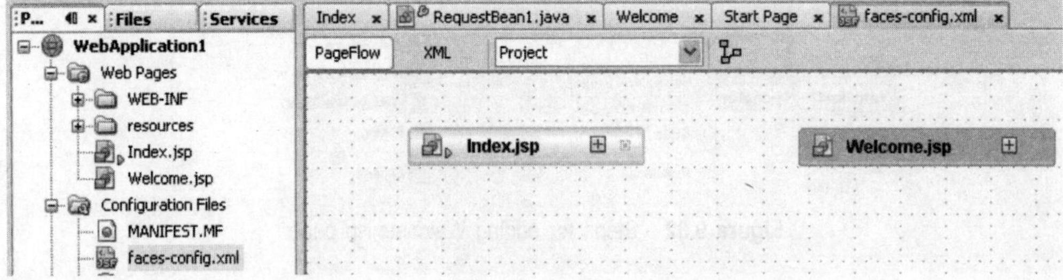

Figure 9.34   PageFlow view of faces-config.xml file.

Expand the `index.jsp` and click the mouse at button1 and drag it on `Welcome.jsp` as shown in Figure 9.35.

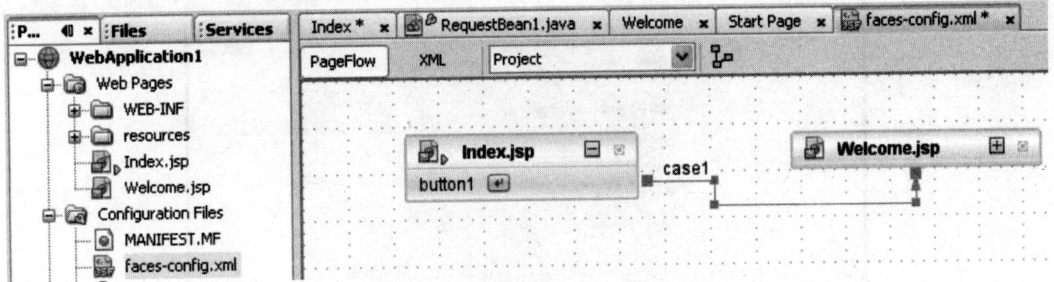

Figure 9.35   Dragging of Button1.

This means that when we click on submit button in `Index.jsp` file, we will be navigated to the `Welcome.jsp` file. When we run the application, we get the output as shown in Figure 9.36.

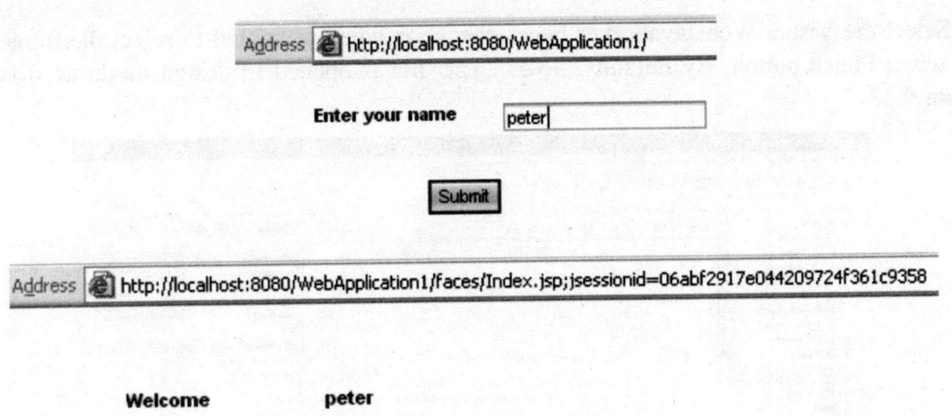

Figure 9.36   Name entered & output displayed.

Demonstrating Dynamic Navigation

In this application we demonstrate dynamic navigation. We ask user to enter userid and password. If userid and password entered are correct, welcome page will be opened else he will be navigated to another page displaying the message "`Sorry Sir, you are not authorized`". The steps are:

`Select File->New Project`. Select Web from Categories tab and Web Application from Projects tab. Select `Next` button. Give any name to Project Name say `Webex3`. Select the server as `GlassFish V2` to deploy our application. Click Next (Figure 9.37).

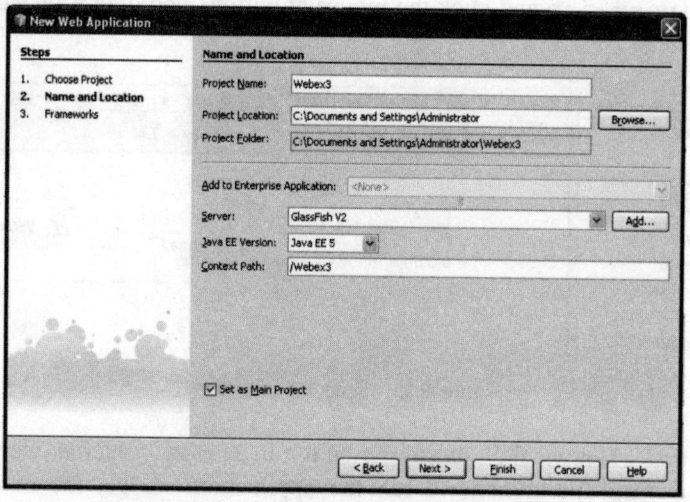

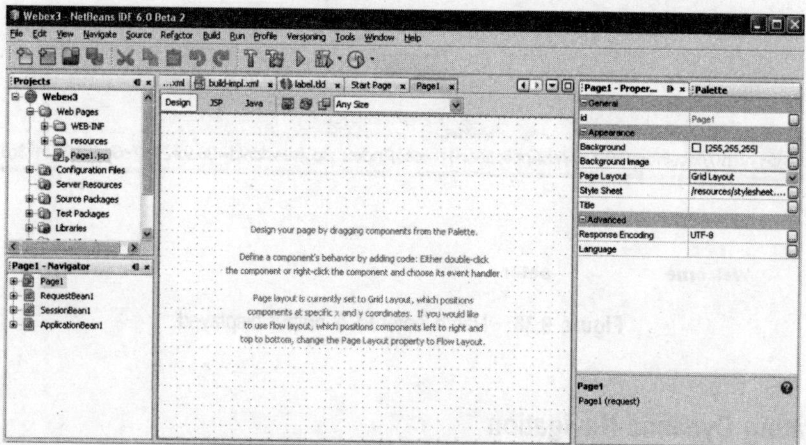

Figure 9.37   Screen for New Web Application.

Select the Visual Web JavaServer Faces checkbox when prompted to select the framework and select Finish button. By default `Page1.jsp` file is opened in design mode as shown in Figure 9.38.

Figure 9.38   Display of Page1.jsp file.

The IDE creates `Webex3` project folder. The IDE creates a default JavaServer Pages file: `Page1.jsp` for us. Before working with Page1.jsp file, we need to create a Managed Bean first. To create it, expand the Source Packages node in Projects Window and double click on `RequestBean1.java` and add two fields:

```
private String name;
private String password;
```

To make their getter and setter methods, right click on the editor and select Refactor option and select Encapsulate Fields as shown in Figure 9.39.

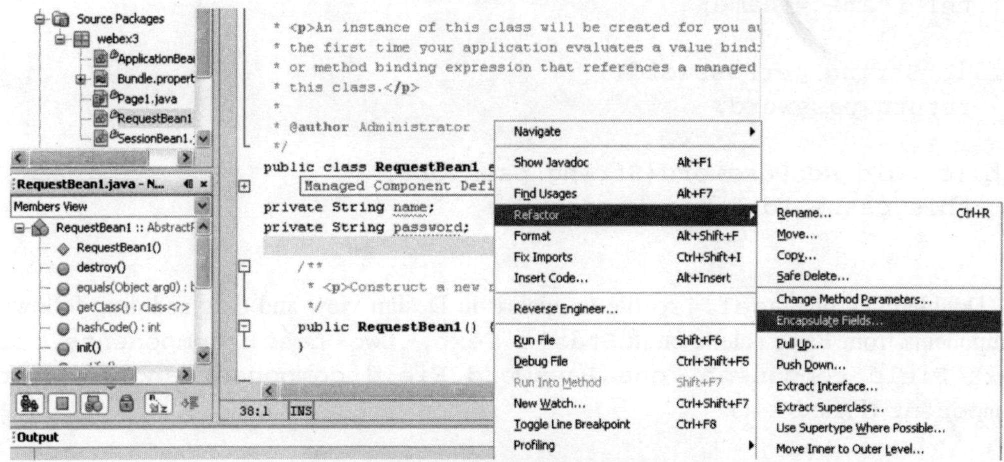

Figure 9.39   Selection of Encapsulate Fields.

Select the checkboxes of `Create Getter` and `Create Setter` tabs and then press `Refactor` button as shown in Figure 9.40.

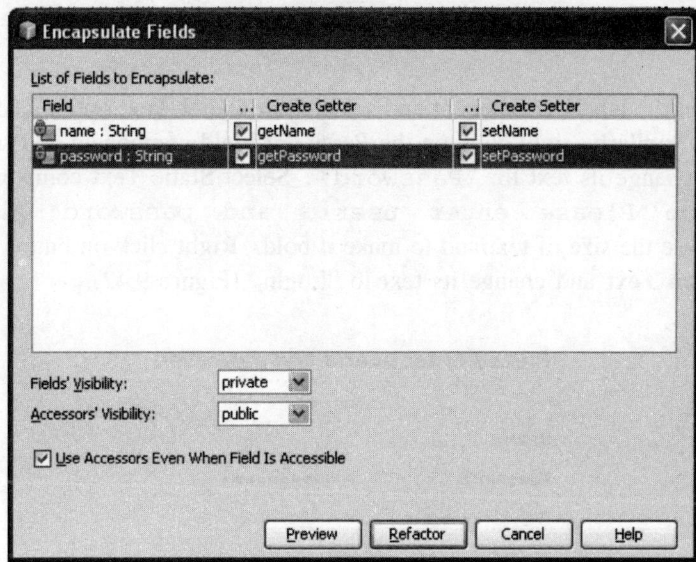

Figure 9.40   Press Refactor button.

Refactoring will produce following four methods in `RequestBean1.java` file:

```
public String getName() {
    return name;
}
public void setName(String name) {
```

```
    this.name = name;
}
public String getPassword() {
    return password;
}
public void setPassword(String password) {
    this.password = password;
}
```

Double click on `Page1.jsp` file to open it in Design view and drag and drop following components from Basic palette on it: `Static Text`, two `Label` components, one `Text Field` component, one `Password Field` component and a `Button` component (Figure 9.41).

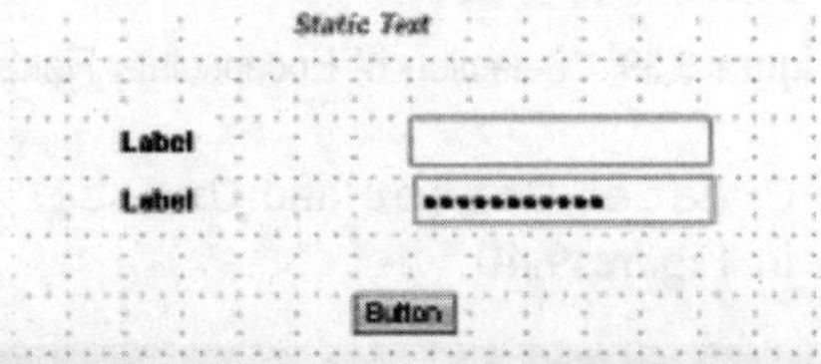

Figure 9.41   Placement of various components.

Right click on the label1 component and select **Edit Label Text** option and change its text to: "`Userid`". Similarly, right click on the Password Field component and select Edit Label Text option and change its text to: "`Password`". Select Static Text component and change its text property to "`Please enter userid and password`". Also use its **style** property to increase the size of text and to make it bold. Right click on button component and select **Edit Button Text** and change its text to "Login" (Figure 9.42).

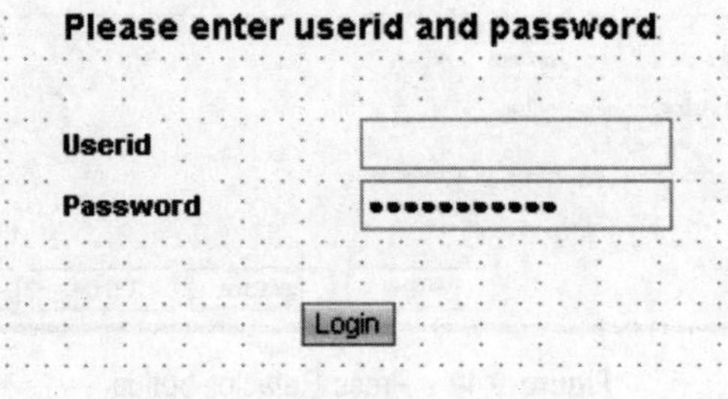

Figure 9.42   Components after setting their respective properties.

To bind the `textField1` to the Managed Bean, right click on the `textField1` component and select **Property Bindings** and bind the textField to **name** attribute of `RequestBean1` (Figure 9.43).

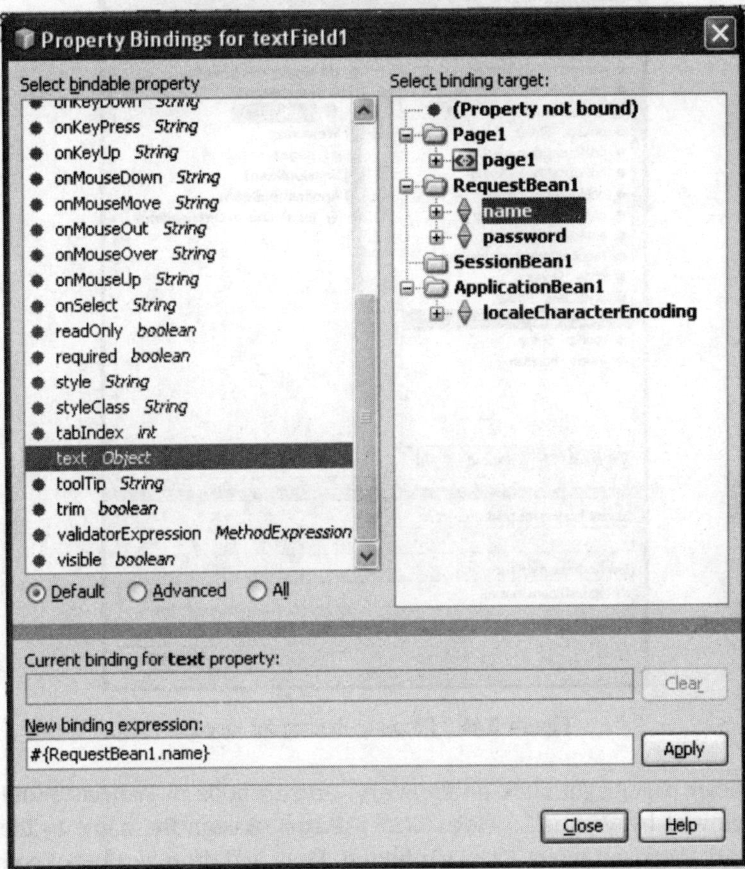

Figure 9.43   Property Binding for textField1.

Similarly, to bind the Password Field component to the Managed Bean, right click on the component and select **Property Bindings** and bind the component to **password** attribute of `RequestBean1`.

Now, we have to add two pages: `welcome.jsp` and `unauthorised.jsp`. To add `welcome.jsp` page, right click on the Web Pages node in Projects Window and select New option followed by Visual Web JSF Page. Assign the name to the new page as `welcome.jsp` and select `Finish` button. Drag and drop two Label components from the Basic palette on Design form of `welcome.jsp` page. Right click on the first Label component: label1 and select **Edit Label Text** option and change its text to "`Welcome to our Web Site`". Also bind the second label component: label2 to the **name** attribute of the Managed Bean: `RequestBean1`. Binding is done by right clicking on the label2 component and select **Property Bindings** option and select the **name** attribute of the `RequestBean1` (Figure 9.44).

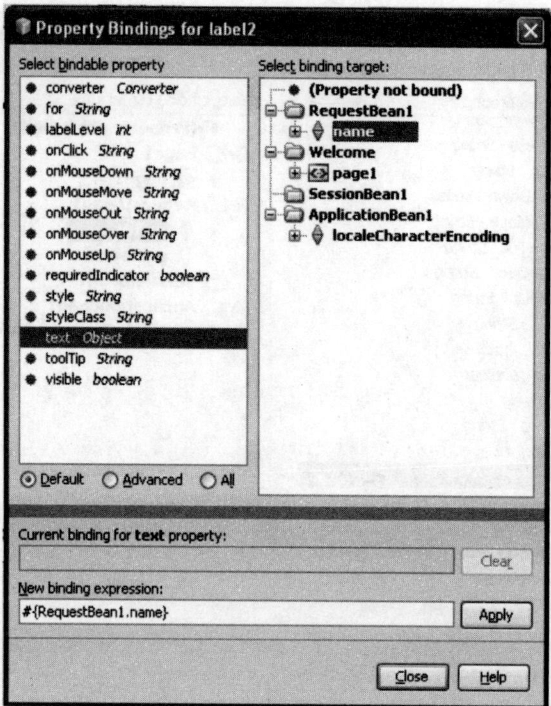

Figure 9.44   Property Binding for label2.

To add another page, right click on the Web Pages node in Projects Window and select New option followed by Visual Web JSF Page. Assign the name to the new page as unauthorized.jsp and select Finish button. Drag and drop two Label components from the Basic palette on Design form. Right click on the first Label component: **label1** and select **Edit Label Text** option and change its text to "Sorry Sir, you are not authorized:". Also bind the second label component: **label2** to the name attribute of the Managed Bean: RequestBean1. Binding is done by right clicking on the **label2** control and select **Property Bindings** option and select the **name** attribute of the RequestBean1.

To setup navigation, right click on Page1.jsp in design mode and select Page Navigation (or expand the Configuration files node in the Projects Window and double click on faces-config.xml file). We get the screen as shown in Figure 9.45.

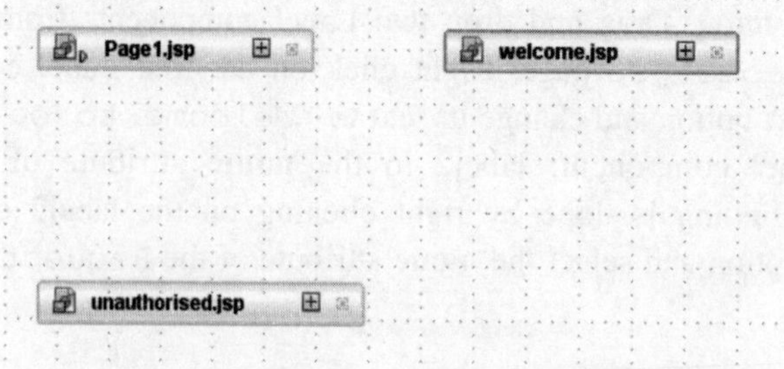

Figure 9.45   Screen on selecting page navigation.

Expand the `Page1.jsp` and click the mouse at button1 and drag it on `welcome.jsp` and also drag the mouse from button1 on `unauthorized.jsp` page. Double click on the connectors (navigation case) to edit them and make them appear as **success** and **failure** as shown in Figure 9.46.

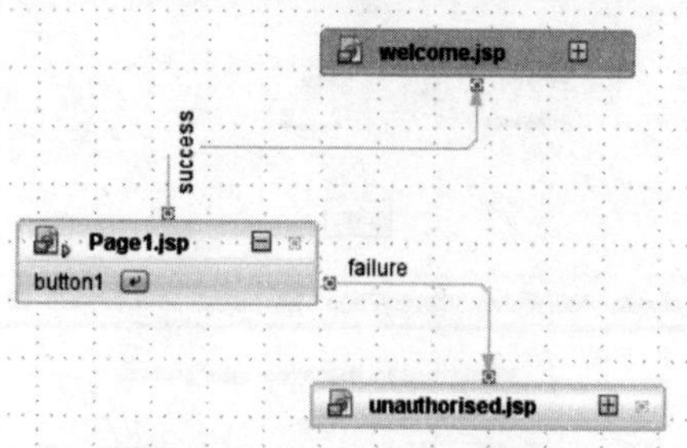

Figure 9.46   Dragging of Button1.

Now, double click on Login button in `Page1.jsp` file to write following code:

```
public String button1_action() {
    if(textField1.getValue().toString().trim().equals("peter") &&
        passwordField1.getValue().toString().trim().equals("peter"))
        return "success";
    else
        return "failure";
}
```

We can see in above coding that the button returns either string `"success"` or `"failure"` depending on whether the userid and password entered is correct or not and the returned string decides which JSP page to open up next. We assume that the correct userid and password is "peter".

Run the application. We get the screen asking us to enter userid and password (Figure 9.47).

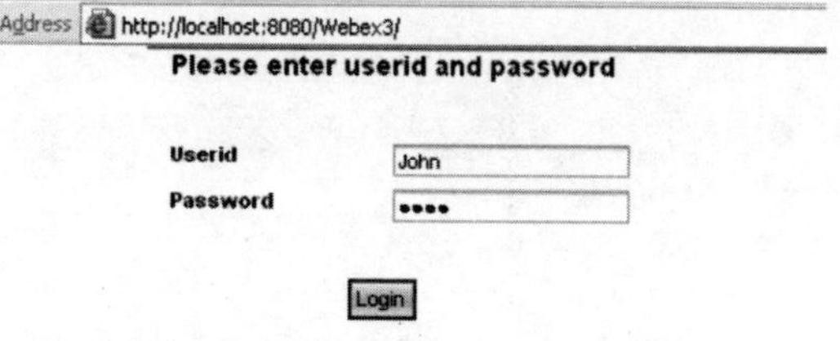

Figure 9.47   Enter the userid and password.

If we enter wrong user and password, we get the output declaring that the user is "not authorised" as shown in Figure 9.48.

Figure 9.48   Output displayed for wrong userid & password.

If we enter userid as peter and password also as "peter", we get the welcome message as shown in Figure 9.49.

Figure 9.49   Welcome screen displayed.

Demonstrating Validation

In this application we demonstrate how validation can be applied. We ask user to enter a name. The length of name must be between 2 to 20 characters. If the name entered is not of desired length, validation error will be displayed and if the length of name is between 2 to 20 characters, a welcome message will be displayed. The steps are: Select File->New Project. Select Web from Categories tab and Web Application from Projects tab. Select Next button. Give any name to Project Name say Webex4. Select the server as GlassFish V2 to deploy our application. Leave the "Set as Main Project" checkbox selected. Click Next (Figure 9.50).

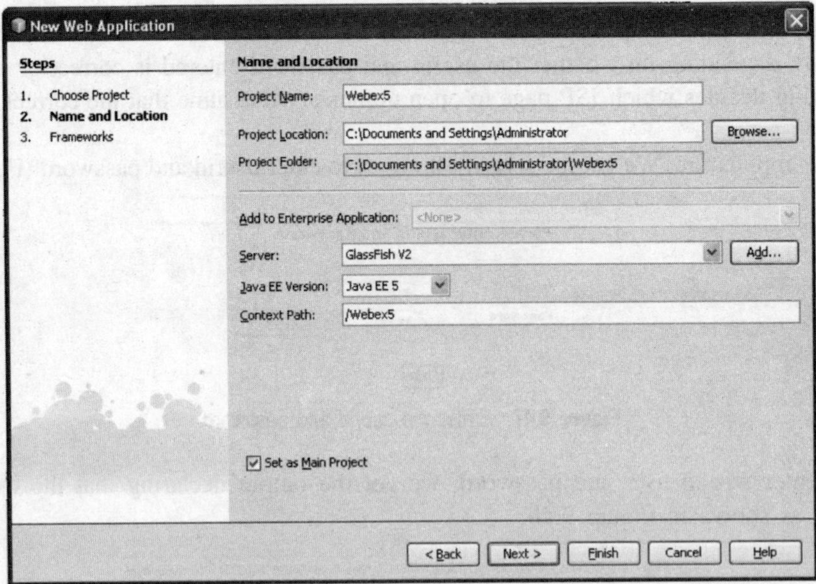

Figure 9.50   Screen of New Web Application.

Select the Visual Web JavaServer Faces checkbox when prompted to select the framework and select Finish button.

By default `page1.jsp` file is opened in design mode as shown in Figure 9.51.

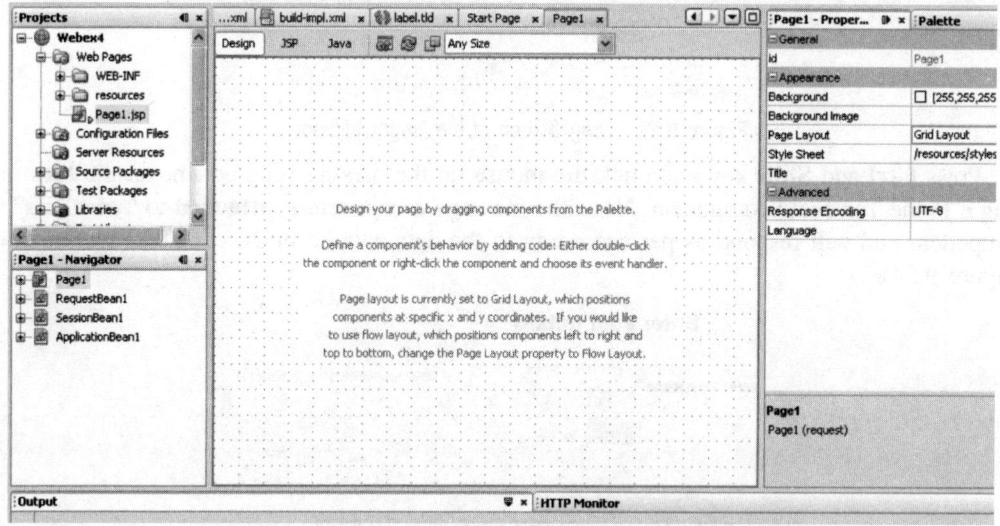

Figure 9.51 Display of Page1.jsp file.

From the Palette on the right side of the Visual Designer, expand Basic Palette and drag and drop the Static Text, Text Field and a Button component on the `Page1.jsp` file.

Change the text property of the Static Text component to "`Enter your details`". Also using its style property, increase its font size. Set the text property of Button component to "`Submit`". Set the lable property of `TextField1` component to "`Enter Your Name`" and also its **required** property to **true**. By selecting the **required check box**, we mean that the **TextField1** component cannot be left blank (Figure 9.52).

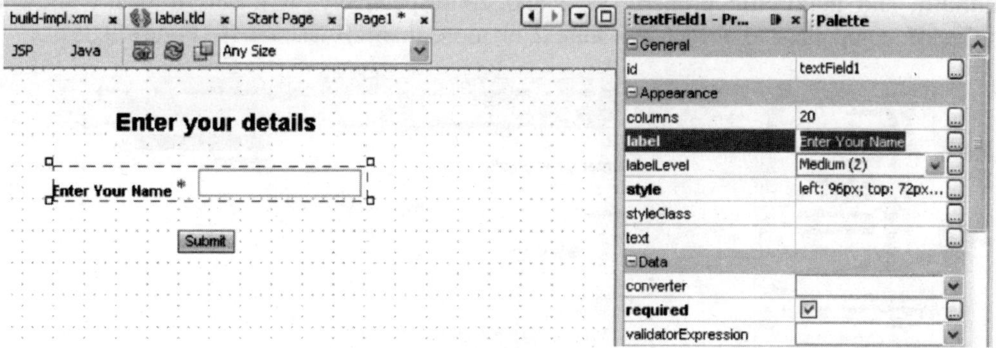

Figure 9.52 Setting the property.

Drag and drop the Length Validator component from the Validators palette on the `TextField1` component, Static Text component from the Basic palette at the bottom of the `Page1.jsp` and Message component beside the `TextField1` component (Figure 9.53).

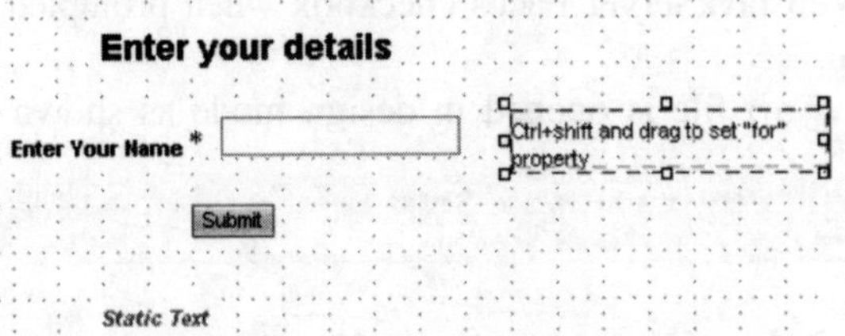

Figure 9.53   Drag & drop of the lengthValidator.

Press **Ctrl** and **Shift** key and click the mouse on the message component on the form and drag it to the TextField component. Now, the message component is **attached** to `TextField1` component and will respond as per according to the data entered in `TextField1` component (Figure 9.54).

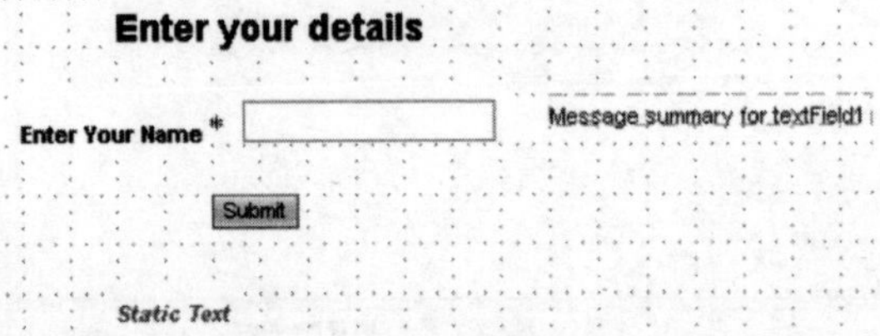

Figure 9.54   Message Control attached to TextField Component.

Double click on the Submit button to write following code into it:

```
public String button1_action() {
    staticText2.setText(" Welcome "+textField1.getText());
    return null;
}
```

Above coding assigns the String "Welcome"+username to staticText2 component on clicking the `Submit` button. The function returns null as we want to stay on the same page.

Select the `lengthValidator1` component in the Navigator window and set its **minimum** and **maximum** property to 2 and 20 respectively. It means it won't allow the TextField1 component to accept less than 2 or more than 20 characters (Figure 9.55).

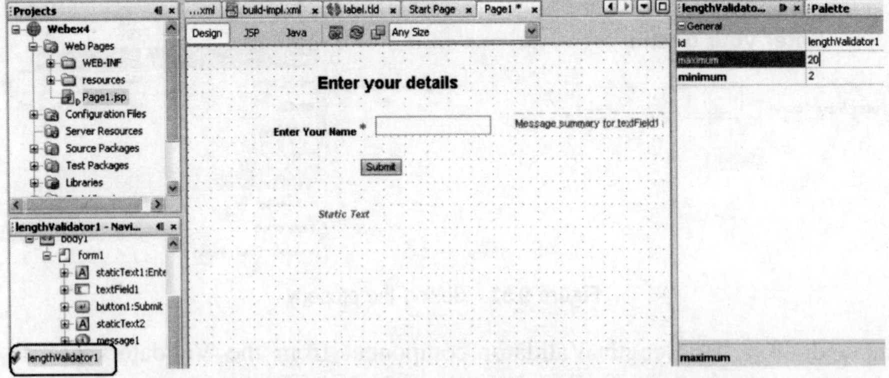

Figure 9.55   Setting property of lengthValidator1 Component.

Run the application. We get the initial screen as shown in Figure 9.56.

Figure 9.56   Initial screen displayed.

If we just select Submit button keeping the text field empty, we get the error message shown in Figure 9.57.

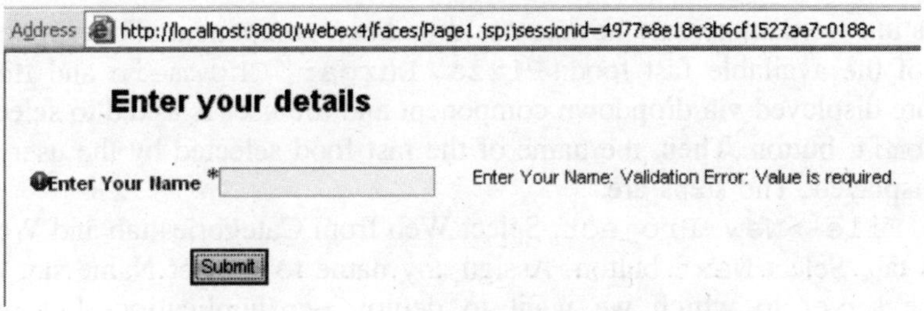

Figure 9.57   Error displayed if text field left empty.

If we enter a name of less than 2 characters, we get the error message shown in Figure 9.58.

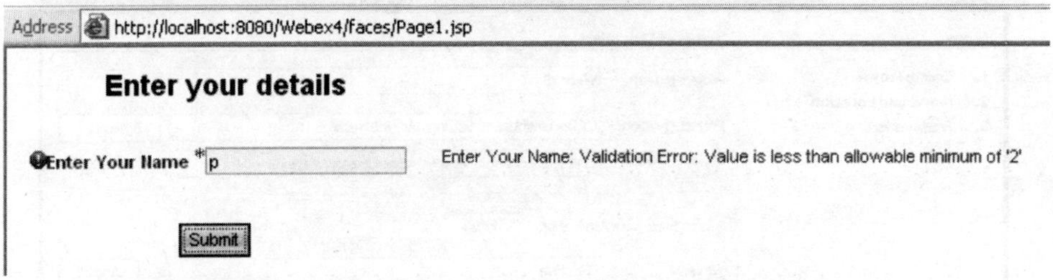

Figure 9.58   Error message displayed if text less than two characters.

If we enter a name of more than 20 characters, we get the error message shown in Figure 9.59.

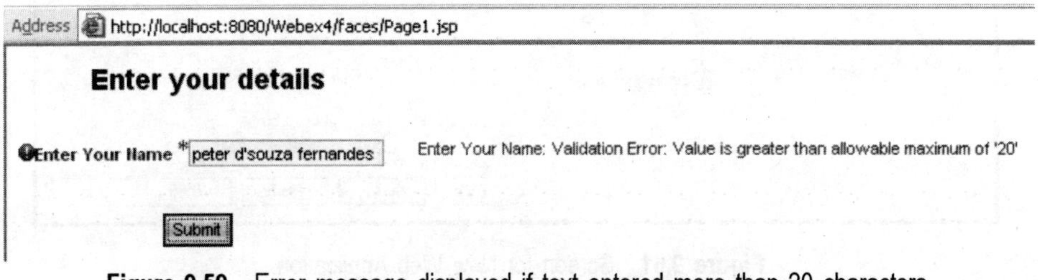

Figure 9.59   Error message displayed if text entered more than 20 characters.

If the name entered is within the given range, we get a welcome message shown in Figure 9.60.

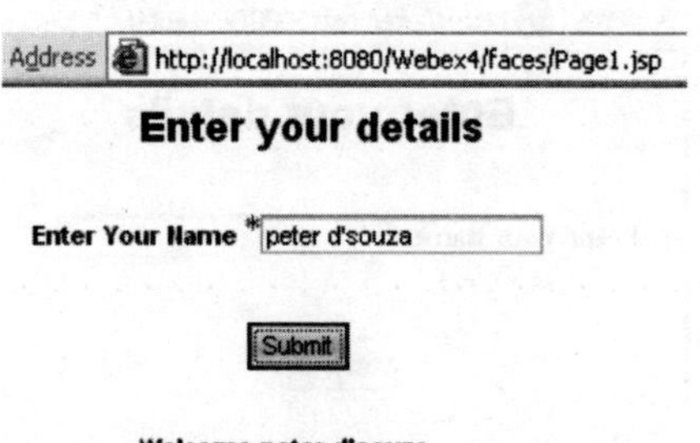

Figure 9.60   Welcome message displayed.

Demonstrating How to Use Dropdown Component

In this application we demonstrate how to use dropdown component. This application displays four options of the available fast food: `Pizza`, `Burgar`, `Chowmein` and `HotDog`. These four options are displayed via dropdown component and the user is asked to select one of them and press `Submit` button. Then, the name of the fast food selected by the user along with its bill will be displayed. The steps are:

`Select File->New Project`. Select Web from Categories tab and Web Application from Projects tab. Select `Next` button. Assign any name to Project Name say `Webex5`.

Select the server to which we want to deploy our application. Let our server be: `GlassFish V2`. Click `Next` (Figure 9.61).

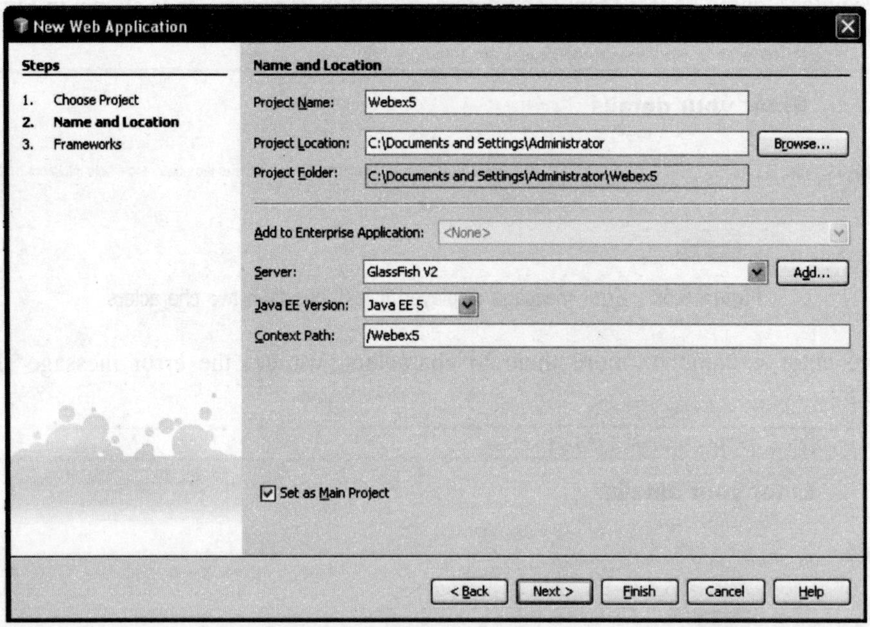

Figure 9.61   Screen for New Web Application.

Select the Visual Web JavaServer Faces check box when prompted to select the framework and select Finish button. By default Page1.jsp file is opened in design mode as shown in Figure 9.62.

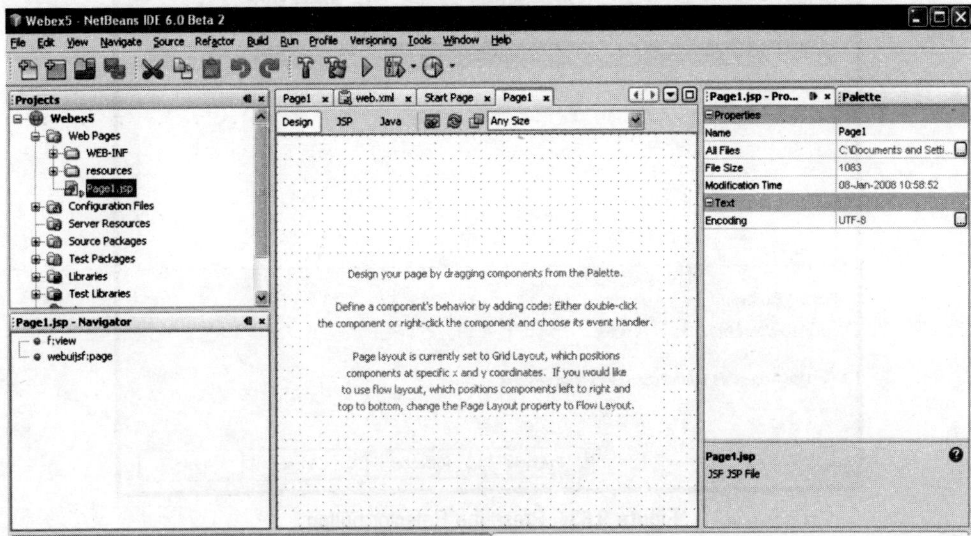

Figure 9.62   Display of Page1.jsp file.

To create a Managed bean, expand the Source Packages node in Projects window and double click on RequestBean1.java and add two fields:

```
private String foodName;
private Integer billAmt;
```

To make its getter and setter methods, right click on the editor and select Refactor option followed by Encapsulate Fields option. Select the checkboxes of Create Getter and Create Setter and then press Refactor button as shown in Figure 9.63.

Refactoring will produce following four methods in RequestBean1.java file:

```
public String getFoodName() {
    return foodName;
}
public void setFoodName(String foodName) {
    this.foodName = foodName;
}
public Integer getBillAmt() {
    return billAmt;
}
public void setBillAmt(Integer billAmt) {
    this.billAmt = billAmt;
}
```

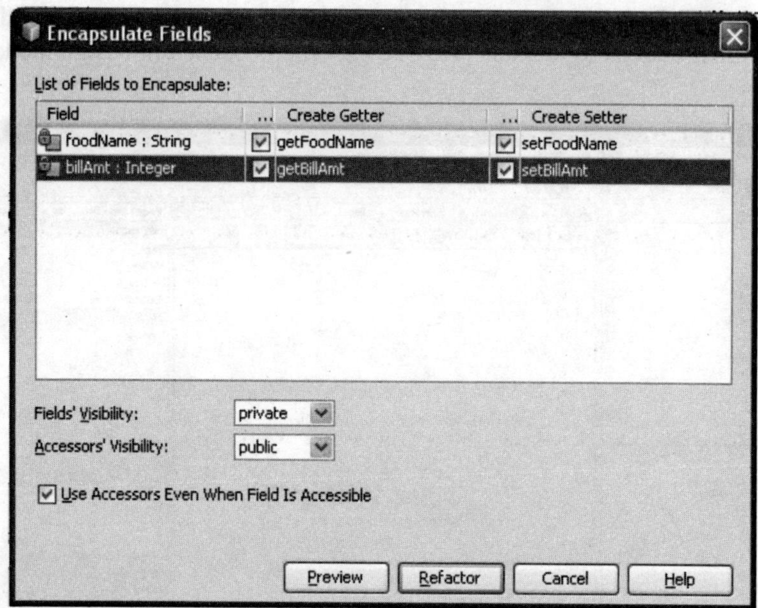

Figure 9.63   Press the Refactor button.

Double click on `Page1.jsp` file in Projects window to open it in Design view and from Basic palette, drag and drop `DropDown` List component and a Button component on it. Right click on button component and select `Edit ButtonText` and change its text to "`Submit`". Set the label property of the `DropDown List` component to "`Select your food`". Right click on the `DropDown List` component and select **Configure Default Options** in it. We get a screen to specify the items to be displayed in drop down list component (Figure 9.64).

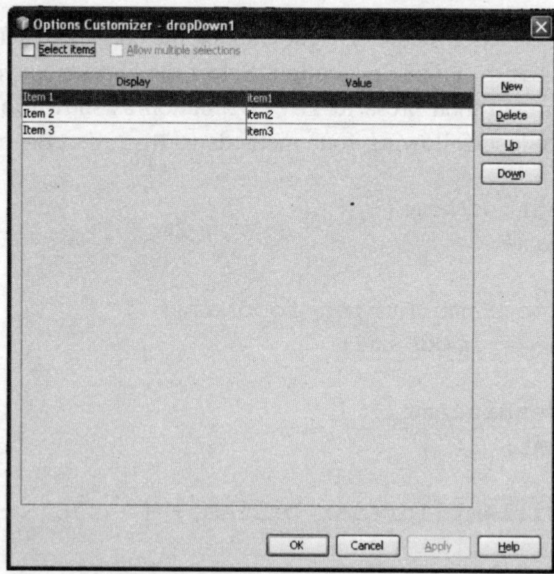

Figure 9.64   Screen for specifying the items in drop down list component.

Enter four items as shown in Figure 9.65.

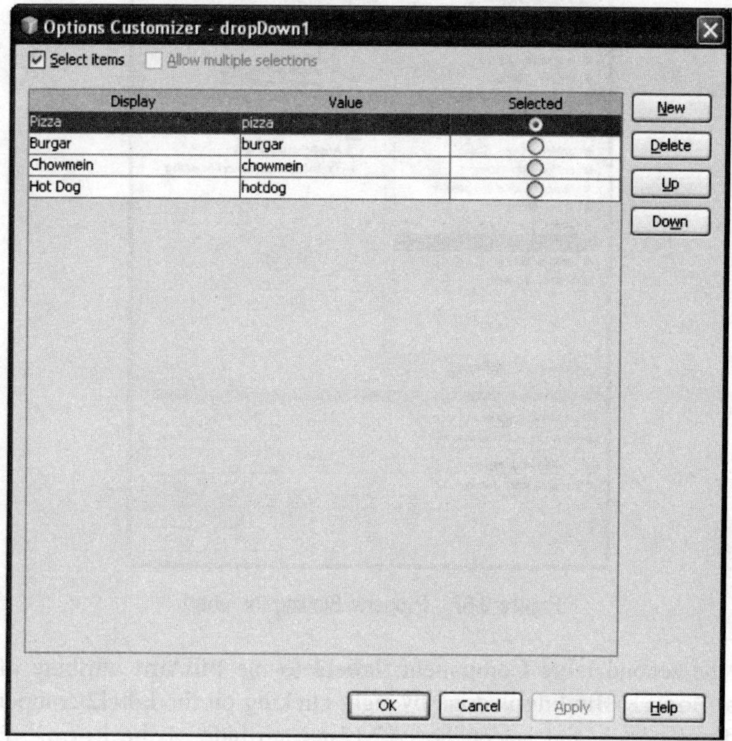

Figure 9.65 Four Items Entered.

Our `Page1.jsp` page may appear as shown in Figure 9.66.

Figure 9.66 Display of drop down list component on Page1.jsp in the Projects window.

Now, we will add a page: `bill.jsp`. To add this page, right click on the Web Pages node in Projects window and select New option followed by Visual Web JSF Page. Assign the name to the new page as **bill** and select Finish button. Drag and drop two Static Text components and two Label component from the Basic palette on Design form of `bill.jsp` page. Set the text property of first Static Text component to "`You have selected`" and the text property of second Static Text component to "`and your bill is`". Bind first label component: **label1** to the **foodName** attribute of the Managed Bean: `RequestBean1`. Binding is done by right clicking on the **label1** component and select **Property Bindings** option and select the **foodName** attribute of the `RequestBean1` (Figure 9.67).

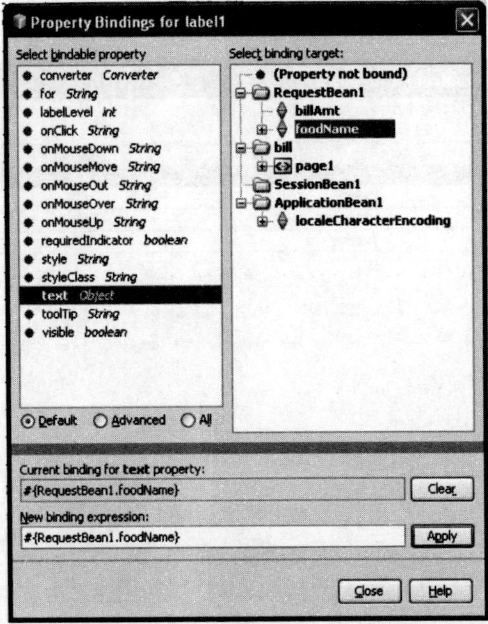

Figure 9.67   Property Binding for label1.

Also bind the second label Component: **label2** to the **billAmt** attribute of the Managed Bean: `RequestBean1`. Binding is done by right clicking on the **label2** component and select **Property Bindings** option and select the `billAmt` attribute of the `RequestBean1`. After doing all the above tasks, our `bill.jsp` file may appear as shown in Figure 9.68.

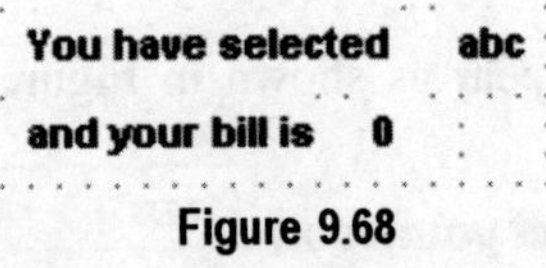

Figure 9.68

To setup navigation, right click on `Page1.jsp` in design mode and select **Page Navigation**. We get the screen as shown in Figure 9.69.

Figure 9.69   Navigation setup.

Expand the `Page1.jsp` and click the mouse at **button1** and drag it on `bill.jsp`. We can see that navigation case: **case1** has appeared as shown in Figure 9.70.

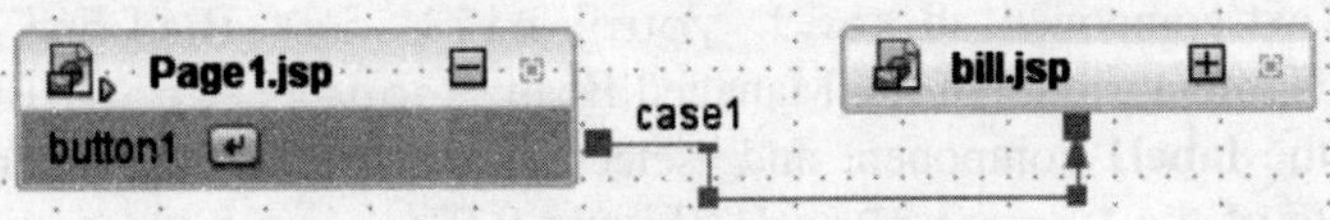

Figure 9.70   Setting up navigation case.

Now, double click on `Submit` button in `Page1.jsp` file to write following code:

```java
public String button1_action() {
    if(dropDown1.getSelected().equals("pizza"))
    {
        getRequestBean1().setFoodName("pizza");
        getRequestBean1().setBillAmt(80);
    }
    if(dropDown1.getSelected().equals("burgar"))
    {
        getRequestBean1().setFoodName("burgar");
        getRequestBean1().setBillAmt(30);
    }
    if(dropDown1.getSelected().equals("chowmein"))
    {
        getRequestBean1().setFoodName("chowmein");
        getRequestBean1().setBillAmt(40);
    }
    if(dropDown1.getSelected().equals("hotdog"))
    {
        getRequestBean1().setFoodName("hotdog");
        getRequestBean1().setBillAmt(25);
    }
    return "case1";
}
```

We can see in above coding that the values of attributes: `foodName` and `billAmt` of the Managed Bean: `RequestBean1` are set as per according to the option selected from the dropdown component. The function returns `"case1"` string to navigate to `bill.jsp` page. Let us run the application, we get the screen prompting to select the type of fast food we want (Figure 9.71).

Figure 9.71   Selection of type of fast food.

After selecting the food, select Submit button. We get the output as shown in Figure 9.72.

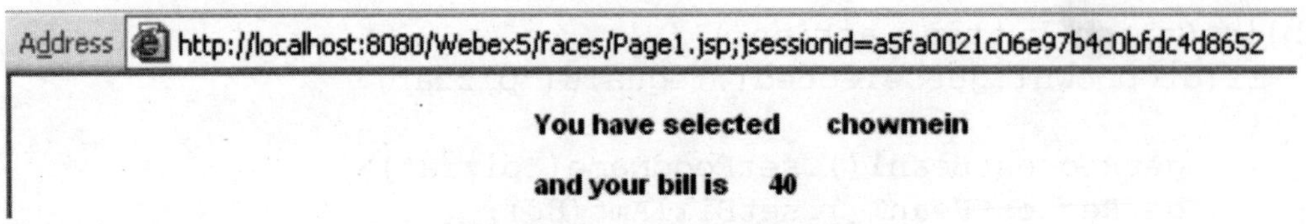

Figure 9.72   Output displayed.

Demonstrating How to Use ListBox and RadioButtonGroup Component

In this application we demonstrate how to use RadioButtonGroup and ListBox control. This application displays two radio buttons with text: "Male" and "Female" on it and user is asked to select his/her sex and also four options of the available fast food: Pizza, Burgar, Chowmein and HotDog are displayed with the help of listbox component and the user is asked to select any number of them (Multiselect) and press Submit button. The sex of the user and names of the fast food selected along with the bill will be then displayed. The steps are:

Select File->New Project. Select Web from Categories tab and Web Application from Projects tab. Select Next button. Give any name to Project Name say Webex6.

Select the server as: GlassFish V2. Click Next button (Figure 9.73).

Figure 9.73   Screen for New Web Application.

Select the Visual Web JavaServer Faces check box when prompted to select the framework and select Finish button. By default Page1.jsp file is opened in design mode.

From the Basic palette, drag and drop a Listbox component, a Radio button group component and a button component on the page1.jsp. Right click on button component and select **Edit button Text** and change its text to "`Submit`". Set the **label** property of the Listbox component to "`Select all the food that you want`". Right click on the Listbox component and select **Configure Default Options** in it. We get a screen to specify the **items** to be displayed in listbox component. Enter four items as shown in Figure 9.74.

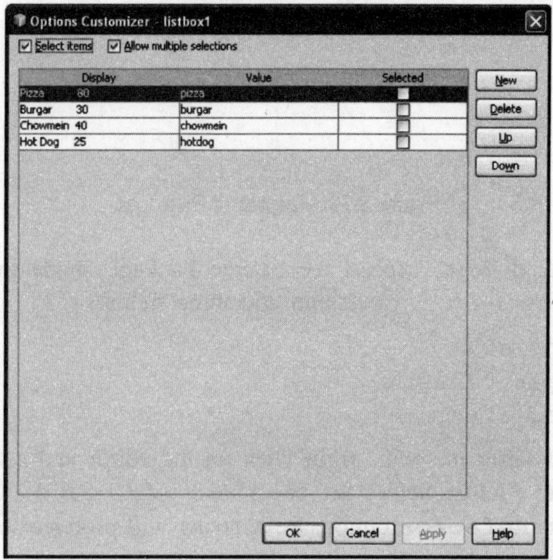

Figure 9.74   Specification of items in the Listbox.

Set the label property of the Radio Button Group component to "`Sex`". Right click on the component and select **Configure Default Options** in it. We get a screen to specify the **items** to be displayed in the control. Enter two items as shown in Figure 9.75.

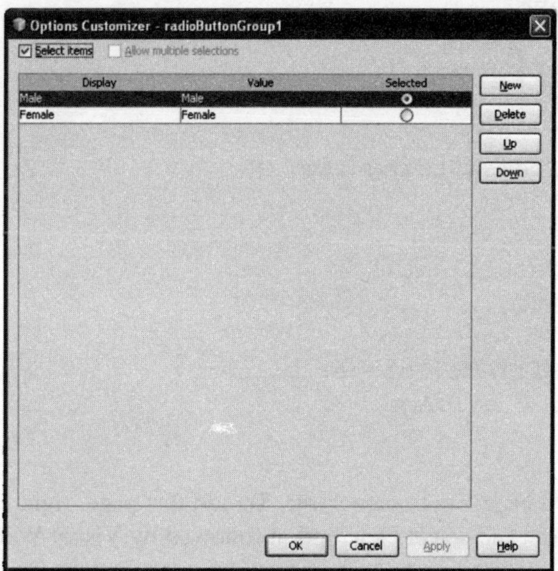

Figure 9.75   Specification of items in the Radio Button Group.

Our `Page1.jsp` page may appear as shown in Figure 9.76.

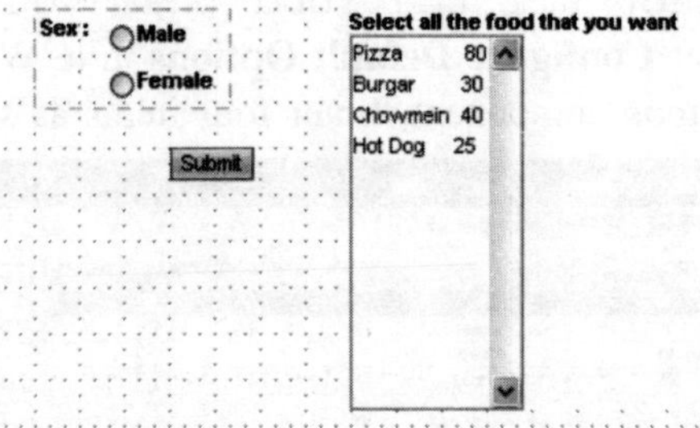

Figure 9.76   Display of Page1.jsp.

To create a Managed Bean, expand the Source Packages node in Projects window and double click on `RequestBean1.java` and add three fields:

```
private String sex;
private Integer billAmt;
private String items;
```

To make its getter and setter methods, right click on the editor and select `Refactor` option and select **Encapsulate Fields**. Select the checkboxes of `Create Getter` and `Create Setter` and then press **Refactor** button. Refactoring will produce setter and getter methods of all the three fields in `RequestBean1.java` file:

```
public String getSex() {
    return sex;
}
public void setSex(String sex) {
    this.sex = sex;
}
public String getItems() {
    return items;
}
public void setItems(String itm) {
    this.items = itm;
}
public Integer getBillAmt() {
    return billAmt;
}
public void setBillAmt(Integer billAmt) {
    this.billAmt = billAmt;
}
```

Now, we will add a page: `welcome.jsp`. To add this page, right click on the Web Pages node in Projects window and select New option followed by Visual Web JSF Page. Assign the name to the new page as "`welcome`" and select `Finish` button. Drag and drop three Static

Text components and two Label components from the Basic palette on Design form of `welcome.jsp` page. The two label components are placed adjacent to first and third Static Text component. Set the **text** property of first Static Text component to "`You are a`" and the text property of third Static Text component to "`and your bill is`". Bind second Static Text components to the **items** attribute of the Managed Bean: `RequestBean1`. Binding is done by right clicking on the `staticText2` Component and select **Property Bindings** option and select the **items** attribute of the `RequestBean1`. Bind first label component: label1 to the **sex** attribute of the Managed Bean: `RequestBean1`. Binding is done by right clicking on the **label1** component and select **Property Bindings** option and select the **sex** attribute of the `RequestBean1` (Figure 9.77).

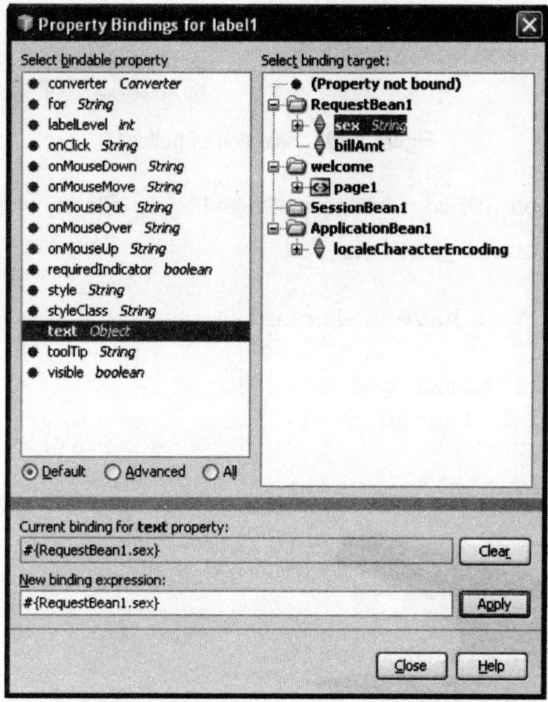

Figure 9.77   Property Binding for label1.

Also bind the second label component: label2 to the **billAmt** attribute of the Managed Bean: `RequestBean1`. Binding is done by right clicking on the **label2** component and select **Property Bindings** option and select the **billAmt** attribute of the `RequestBean1`. After doing all the above tasks, our welcome.jsp page may appear as shown in Figure 9.78.

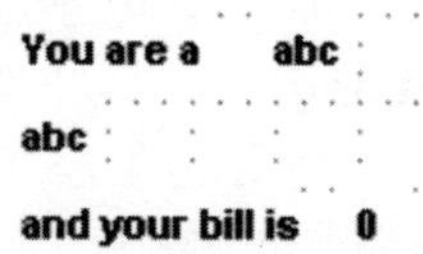

Figure 9.78   Display of welcome.jsp page.

To setup navigation, right click on Page1.jsp in design mode and select Page Navigation. We get the screen as shown in Figure 9.79.

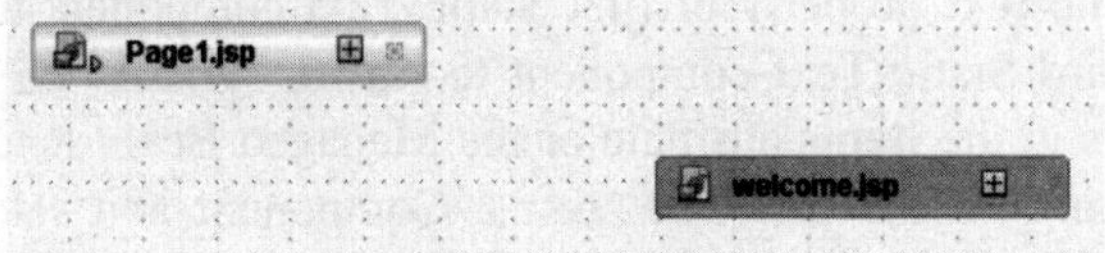

Figure 9.79   Navigation setup.

Expand the `Page1.jsp` and click the mouse at button1 and drag it on `bill.jsp`. We can see that default navigation case: **case1** has appeared as shown in Figure 9.80.

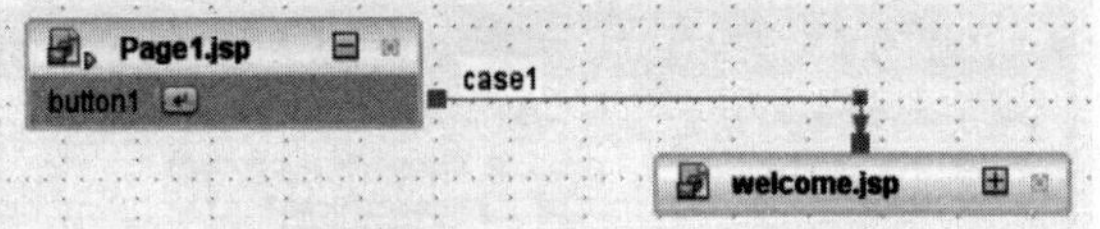

Figure 9.80   Selection of button1.

Now, double click on `Submit` button in `Page1.jsp` file to write following code:

```
public String button1_action() {
    String[] k;
    String itms="You have selected ";
    Integer b=0;
    k=(String[])listbox1.getValue();
    for(int i=0;i<k.length;i++)
    {
        if(k[i].equals("pizza"))
        {
            b=b+80;
            itms=itms+"pizza ";
        }
        if(k[i].equals("burgar"))
        {
            b=b+30;
            itms=itms+"burgar ";
        }
        if(k[i].equals("chowmein"))
        {
            b=b+40;
            itms=itms+"chowmein ";
        }
        if(k[i].equals("hotdog"))
        {
            b=b+25;
            itms=itms+"hotdog ";
```

```
        }
    }
    getRequestBean1().setBillAmt(b);
    getRequestBean1().setItems(itms);
    return "case1";
}
```

We can see in above coding that the String array **k** is declared and it is assigned the names of the fast food selected from the listbox. Using this String array k, we then compute the bill of the fast food selected. The bill computed and the String array containing the list of fast food selected are used to set the values of attributes: **billAmt** and **items** of the Managed Bean: `RequestBean1` to display the results. The function returns "case1" string to navigate to `welcome.jsp` page. Let us run the application. We get the screen to select sex and the fast food we want (Figure 9.81).

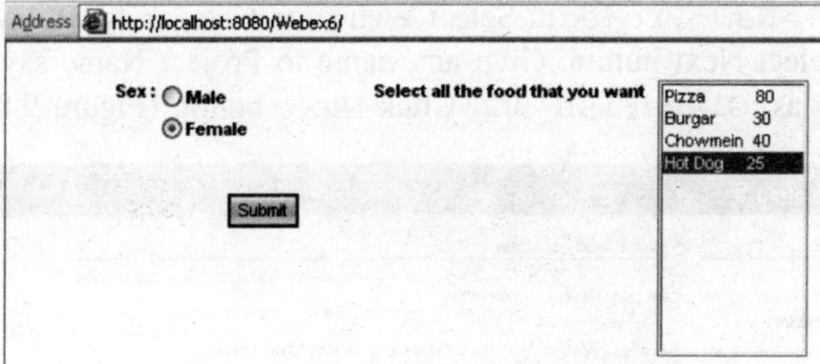

Figure 9.81   Selection of sex & food.

After selecting the sex and fast food, we select submit button. On selecting `Submit` button, we get the output as shown in Figure 9.82.

Figure 9.82   Output displayed.

We can select more than one fast food as shown in Figure 9.83.

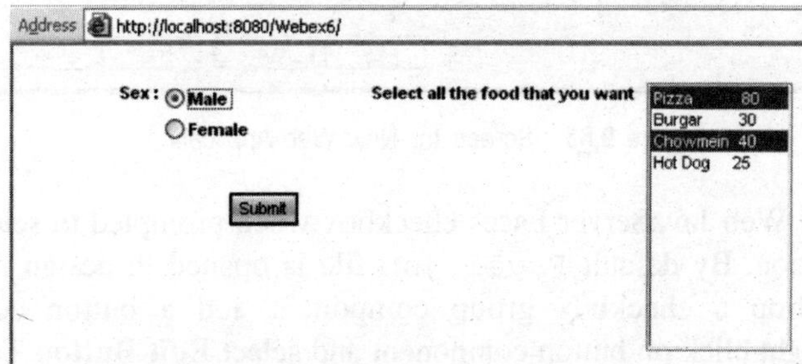

Figure 9.83   Selection of more than one food.

When we select `Submit` button, we get the output as shown in Figure 9.84.

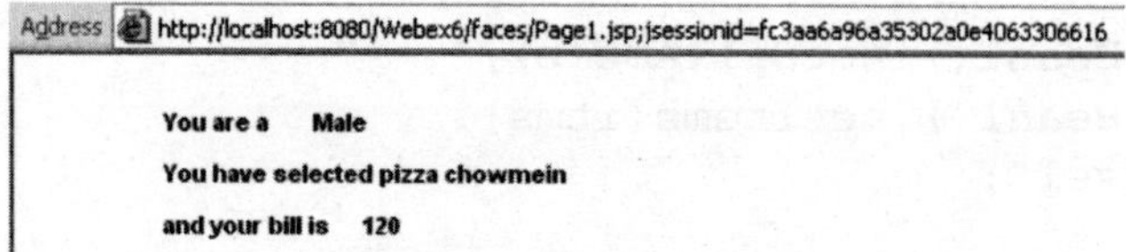

Figure 9.84   Output when more than one fast food is selected.

Demonstrating How to Use CheckBoxGroup Component

In this application we demonstrate how to use CheckBoxGroup Component. This application displays four options of the available fast foods: Pizza, Burgar, Chowmein and Hot Dog in the form of Checkbox and the user is asked to select any number of them and press Submit button. The names of all the fast food selected will be then displayed. The steps are:

`Select File->New Project`. Select Web from Categories tab and Web Application from Projects tab. Select Next button. Give any name to Project Name say `Webex7`.

Select the server as: `GlassFish V2`. Click `Next` button (Figure 9.85).

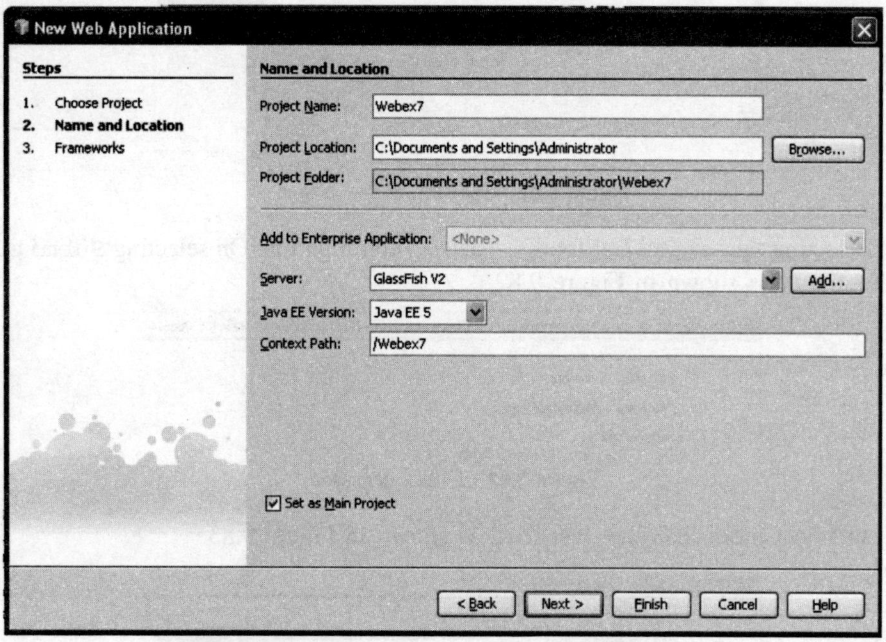

Figure 9.85   Screen for New Web Application.

Select the Visual Web JavaServer Faces checkbox when prompted to select the framework and select Finish button. By default `Page1.jsp` file is opened in design mode. From Basic palette, drag and drop a checkbox group component and a button component on the `Page1.jsp` file. Right click on button component and select **Edit Button Text** and change its **text** to `"Submit"`. Set the **label** property of the checkbox group Component to `"Select` all the food that you want". Right click on the checkbox component and select **Configure Default Options** in it. We get a screen to specify the **items** to be displayed in checkbox Group component. Enter four items as shown in Figure 9.86.

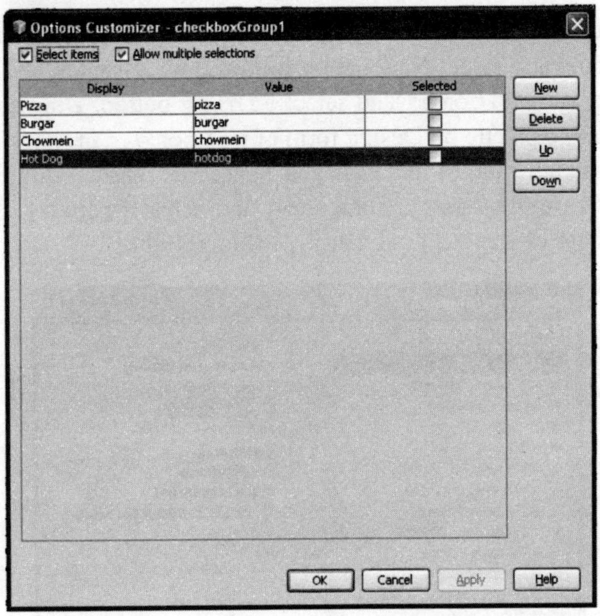

Figure 9.86 Specification of items in Checkbox Group.

Our Page1.jsp page may appear as shown in Figure 9.87.

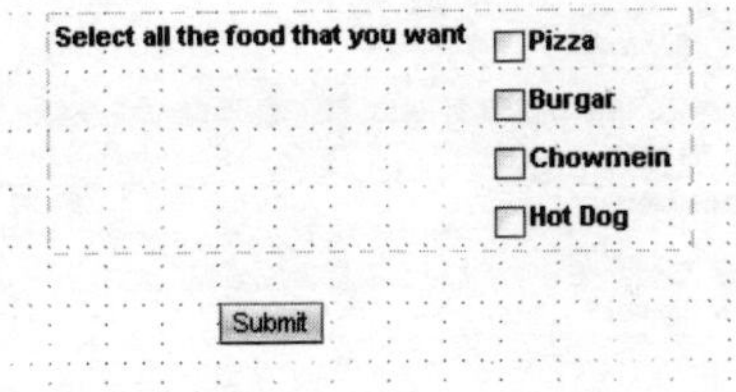

Figure 9.87 Display of Page1.jsp.

To create a Managed Bean, expand the Source Packages node in Projects window and double click on `RequestBean1.java` and add a field:

```
private String items;
```

To make its getter and setter methods, right click on the editor and select `Refactor` option and select **Encapsulate Fields** option. Select the checkboxes of `Create  Getter` and `Create  Setter` and then press `Refactor` button. Refactoring will produce following methods in `RequestBean1.java` file:

```
public String getItems() {
    return items;
}
```

```
public void setItems(String items) {
   this.items = items;
}
```

Now, we will add a page: `welcome.jsp`. To add this page, right click on the Web Pages node in Projects window and select New option followed by Visual Web JSF Page. Assign the name to the new page as `"welcome"` and select `Finish` button. Drag and drop a Static Text component from the Basic palette on Design form of `welcome.jsp` page. Bind the Static Text component to the **items** attribute of the Managed Bean: `RequestBean1`. Binding is done by right clicking on the `staticText1` Component and select **Property Bindings** option and select the **items** attribute of the `RequestBean1` (Figure 9.88).

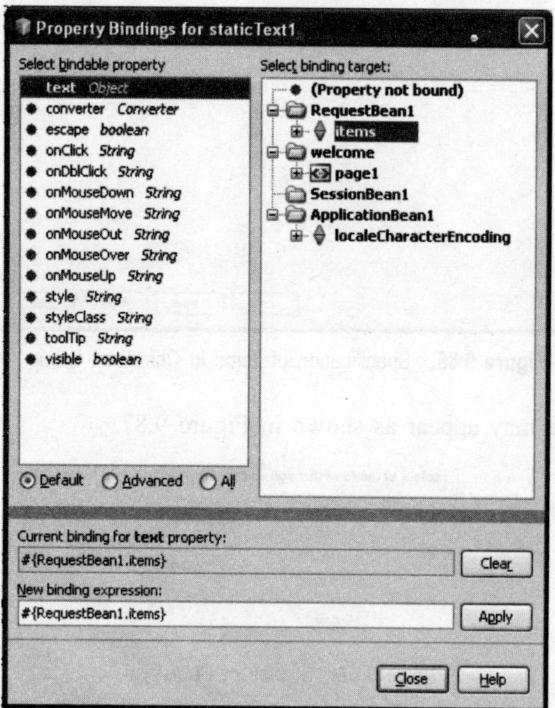

Figure 9.88 Property Binding for staticText1.

To setup navigation, right click on `Page1.jsp` in design mode and select `Page Navigation`. We get the screen as shown in Figure 9.89.

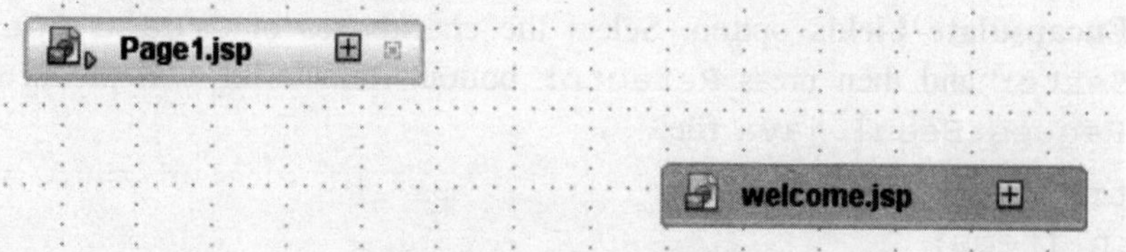

Figure 9.89 Navigation setup.

Expand the `Page1.jsp` and click the mouse at button1 and drag it on `bill.jsp`. We can see that navigation case: **case1** has appeared as shown in Figure 9.90.

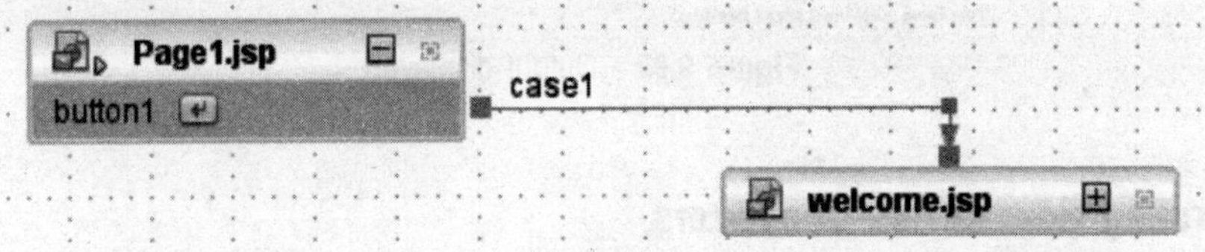

Figure 9.90   The default navigation case : case1 appears for navigation.

Now, double click on `Submit` button in `Page1.jsp` file to write following code:

```
public String button1_action() {
    String[] k;
    String itms="You have selected ";
    k=(String[])checkboxGroup1.getValue();
    for(int i=0;i<k.length;i++)
    {
        if(k[i].equals("pizza"))itms=itms+"pizza ";
        if(k[i].equals("burgar"))itms=itms+"burgar ";
        if(k[i].equals("chowmein"))itms=itms+"chowmein ";
        if(k[i].equals("hotdog"))itms=itms+"hotdog ";
    }
    getRequestBean1().setItems(itms);
    return "case1";
}
```

We can see in above coding that the string array **k** is declared and is assigned the **names** of the fast food selected from the checkboxgroup. Using this string array k, we assign the names of the selected fast food to a string variable **itms** which is then used to set the value of the attribute: **items** of the Managed Bean: `RequestBean1`. The attribute **items** of the Managed Bean is used to display the results. The function returns `"case1"` string to navigate to `welcome.jsp` page. Let us run the application. We get the screen to select all the fast food that we want (Figure 9.91).

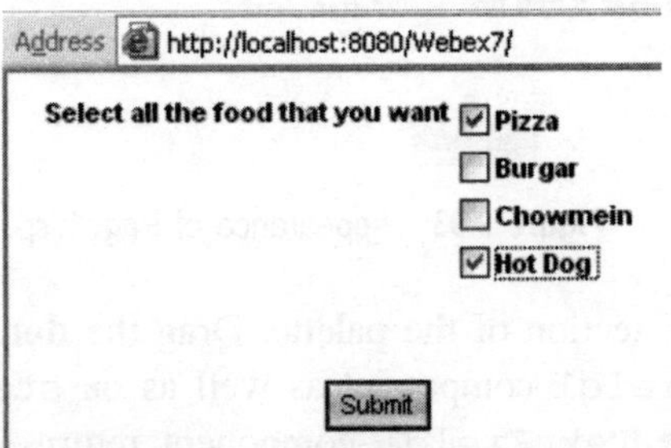

Figure 9.91   Selection of fast food.

We get the list of fast food selected as shown in Figure 9.92.

Figure 9.92   Output displayed.

Demonstrating How to Use Converters

In this application we demonstrate how to use converters. This application asks the user to enter a number and then that number is converted into different formats with the application of different converters. The formats in which the number will be converted are: currency format, integer format, double format and also according to a pattern `assigned`. The steps are:

`Select File->New Project`. Select Web from Categories tab and Web Application from Projects tab. Select `Next` button. Give any name to Project Name say `Webex8`.

Select the server as `GlassFish V2` to deploy our application. Click `Next`.

Select the Visual Web JavaServer Faces checkbox when prompted to select the framework and select `Finish` button.

By default `Page1.jsp` file is opened in design mode. From the Basic palette, drag and drop a TextField component, four Label component, four Static Text component, a Message component and a Button component on the `Page1.jsp` file. To attach the message component with the Text Field component, click the message component and after pressing **Ctrl+Shift key**, drag and drop the mouse on the Text Field1. Right click on button component and select **Edit Button Text** and change its **text** to "Submit". Set the **label** property of the **TextField1** component to "Enter a value". Set the **text** property of four labels as : "Double Format", "Integer Format" and "Currency Format", "In format #,##0.##" respectively. Our `Page1.jsp` may appear as shown in Figure 9.93.

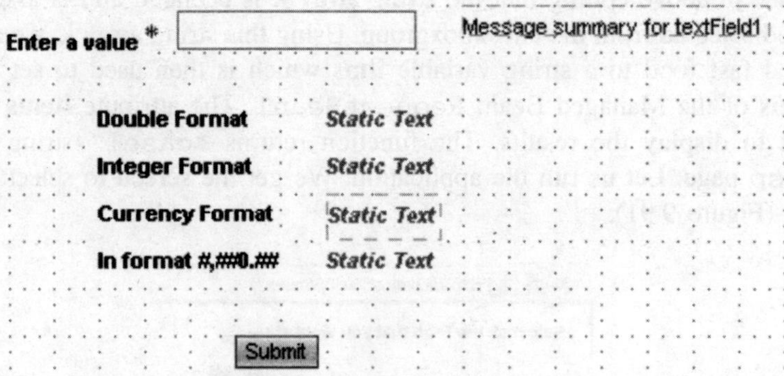

Figure 9.93   Appearance of Page1.jsp.

Expand the **converters** section of the palette. Drag the **double** converter from the palette and drop onto the `TextField1` component as well as on `staticText1` component. This converter specifies that the `TextField1` component returns a **double** value rather than a **string**. The default value `doubleConverter1` appears in the Properties window and in the

Navigator window. Again drag and drop the **number** converter from the palette and drop it onto the `staticText2` control. Set its `pattern`, `Integer    Only`, `maxIntegerDigits`, `minIntegerDigits` properties as shown in Figure 9.94.

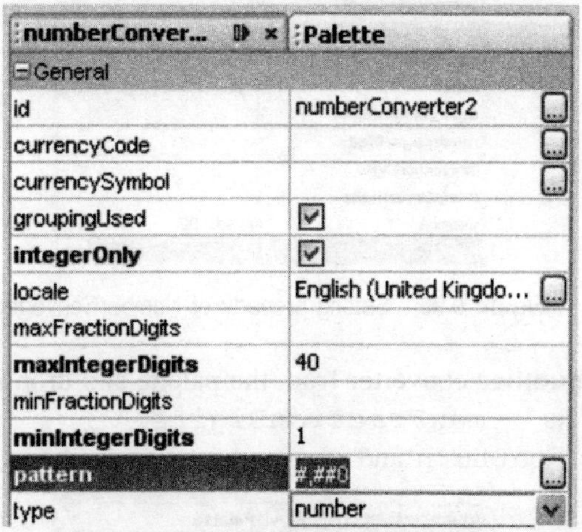

Figure 9.94   Number converter properties.

Drag and drop the `NumberConverter` from the palette and drop it onto the `staticText3` component. Set its `currencySymbol`,   `locale`, `maxFractionDigits`, `maxIntegerDigits`, `minIntegerDigits`, `pattern` and `type` properties as shown in Figures 9.95 and 9.96.

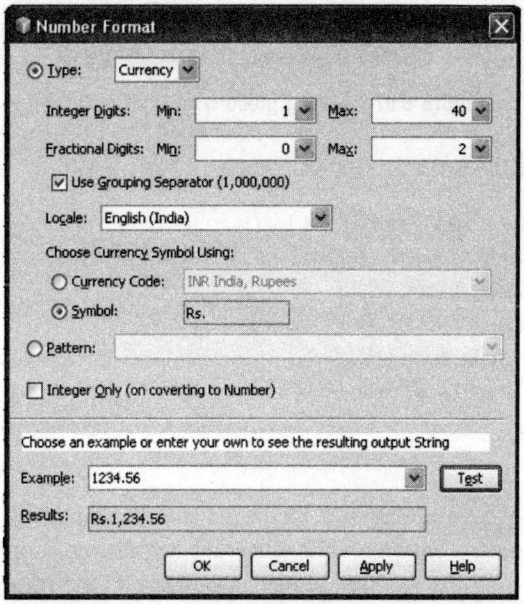

Figure 9.95   Setting properties of NumberConverter.

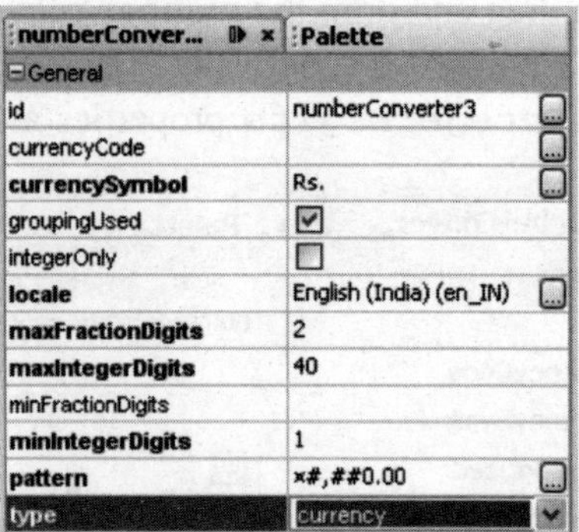

Figure 9.96 Setting property of NumberConverter.

Drag and drop the **number** converter from the palette and drop it onto the `staticText4` component. Set its `maxFractionDigits`, `maxIntegerDigits`, `minIntegerDigits`, `pattern` and `type` properties as shown in Figure 9.97.

Figure 9.97 Setting property of NumberConverter.

Now, double click on `Submit` button in `Page1.jsp` file to write following code:

```
public String button1_action() {
    double d = ((Double) textField1.getText()).doubleValue();
    staticText1.setText(d);
    staticText2.setText(d);
    staticText3.setText(d);
    staticText4.setText(d);
    return null;
}
```

We are assigning the value entered in the textfield component to all the four static text components. Since number converter with different formats are applied individually on each static component, they will display the number according to the format applied onto them. The function returns null as we want to stay on the same page. Let us run the application. If we do not enter a numerical expression, we get an error as shown in Figure 9.98.

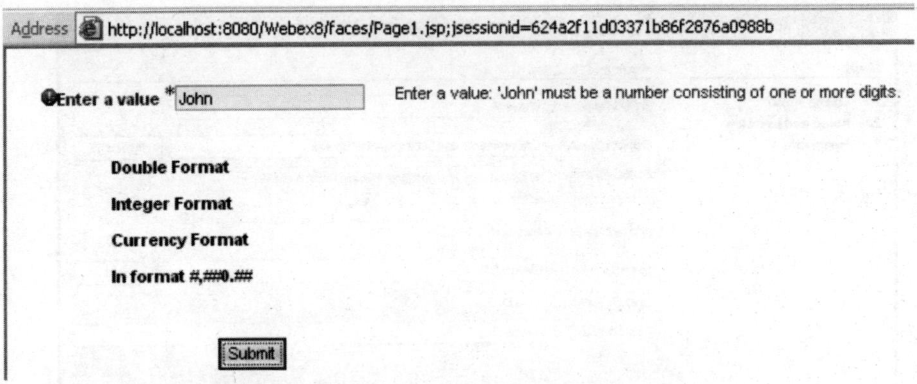

Address http://localhost:8080/Webex8/faces/Page1.jsp;jsessionid=624a2f11d03371b86f2876a0988b

Enter a value *John   Enter a value: 'John' must be a number consisting of one or more digits.

Double Format

Integer Format

Currency Format

In format #,##0.##

Submit

Figure 9.98   Error displayed as number not entered.

If we enter a numerical expression, we get the output converted in specified formats (Figure 9.99).

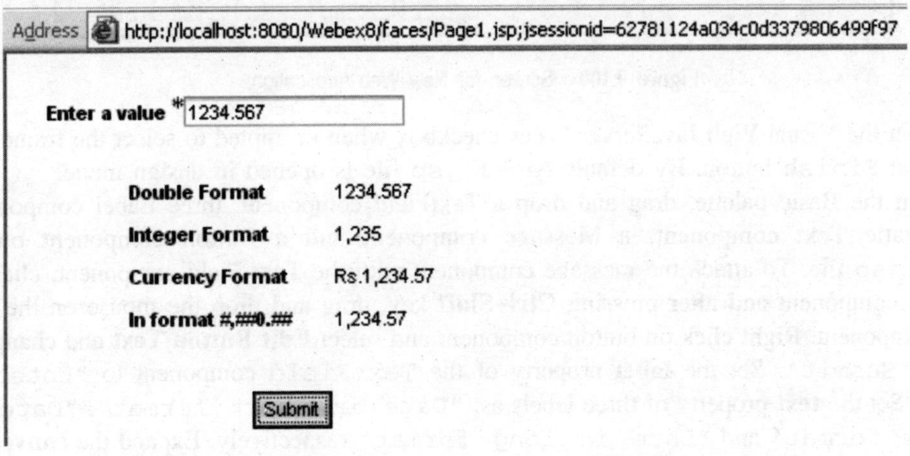

Address http://localhost:8080/Webex8/faces/Page1.jsp;jsessionid=62781124a034c0d3379806499f97

Enter a value *1234.567

Double Format	1234.567
Integer Format	1,235
Currency Format	Rs.1,234.57
In format #,##0.##	1,234.57

Submit

Figure 9.99   Output displayed in various format if number is entered.

Demonstrating How to Use DateTime Converter

In this application we demonstrate how to use `DateTimeConverters`. This application asks the user to enter a date in a specific format (displays error if date entered is not in the specified format) and then that date is converted into different formats: short, medium and long. The steps are:

`Select File->New Project`. Select Web from Categories tab and Web Application from Projects tab. Select `Next` button. Give any name to Project Name say Webex9.

Select the server as: `GlassFish V2`. Click `Next` button (Figure 9.100).

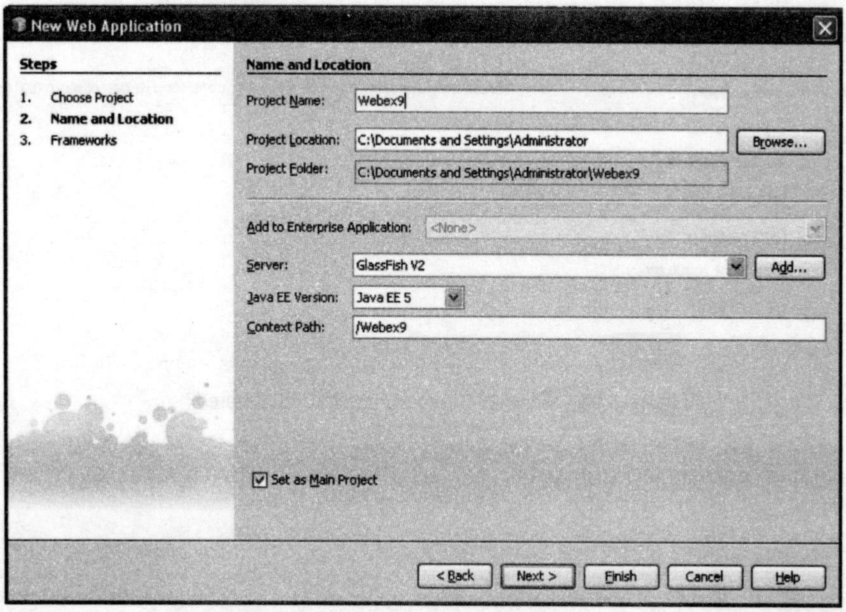

Figure 9.100   Screen for New Web Application.

Select the Visual Web JavaServer Faces checkbox when prompted to select the framework and select `Finish` button. By default `Page1.jsp` file is opened in design mode.

From the Basic palette, drag and drop a TextField component, three Label components, three Static Text component, a Message component and a Button component on the `Page1.jsp` file. To attach the message component with the Text Field component, click the message component and after pressing **Ctrl+Shift** key, drag and drop the mouse on the Text Field component. Right click on button component and select **Edit Button Text** and change its text to "`Submit`". Set the **label** property of the `TextField` component to "`Enter a Date`". Set the **text** property of three labels as: "`Date in short format`", "`Date in medium format`" and "`Date in long format`" respectively. Expand the **converters** section of the Palette. Drag the **Date Time Converter** from the Palette and drop onto the TextField1 component. This converter specifies that the TextField1 component returns a **Date** object rather than a **string**. Again drag and drop the **Date Time Converter** from the Palette and drop onto the three Static Text Fields. Our `Page1.jsp` may appear as (Figure 9.101):

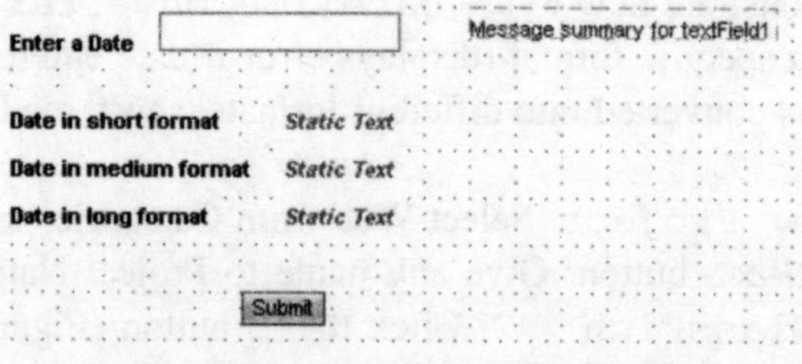

Figure 9.101   Appearance of Page1.jsp.

Select `dateTimeConverter1` control in `Navigator` window and set its `dateStyle` property to **short**. Also set its **pattern** property to: **dd-MM-yy** as shown in Figure 9.102.

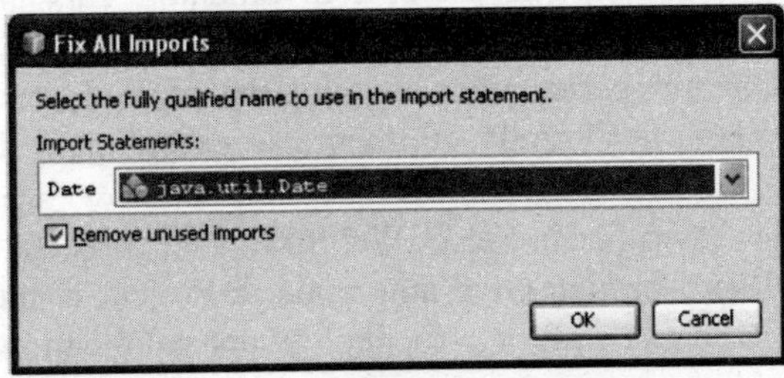

Figure 9.102   Setting pattern property of dateTime convertor.

Similarly, select `dateTimeConverter2` control in `Navigator` window and set its `dateStyle` property to **short**. Also set its **pattern** property to: **dd/MM/yy**. Select `dateTimeConverter3` control in `Navigator` window and set its `dateStyle` property to **medium**. Select `dateTimeConverter4` control in `Navigator` window and set its `dateStyle` property to **long**.

Now, double click on `Submit` button in `Page1.jsp` file to write following code:

```
public String button1_action() {
    Date date=(Date) textField1.getText();
    staticText1.setText(date);
    staticText2.setText(date);
    staticText3.setText(date);
    return null;
}
```

We are assigning the date entered in the textfield1 component to all the three static text components. Since datetime converters with different formats are applied individually on each static components, they will display the date according to the format applied onto them. The function returns **null** as we want to stay on the same page. We need to import the library for handling Date, so right click on the editor and select **Fix Imports** option. We get a dialog box displaying the library file to be imported as shown in Figure 9.103. Select OK.

Figure 9.103   Import of library for handling Date.

Run the application.

If we don't enter the date in the specified format, we get error as shown in Figure 9.104.

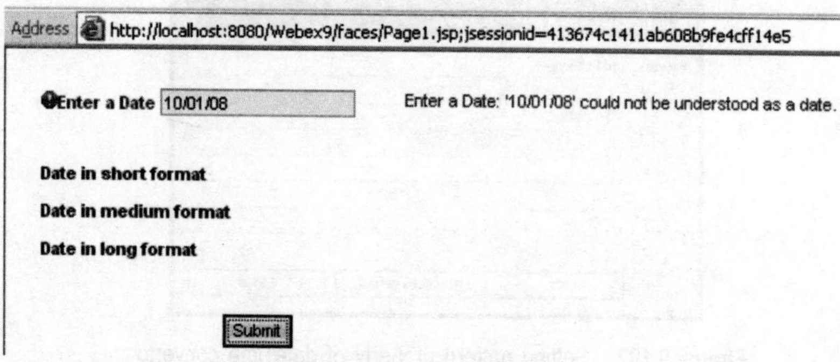

Figure 9.104   Error is displayed.

If we enter the date in correct format, we get the entered date in different formats as shown in Figure 9.105.

Figure 9.105   Output displayed if date in correct format is entered.

Demonstrating How to Make Custom Validator

In this application we demonstrate how to use custom validator. This application asks the user to enter a phone number which must contain any digit (no alphabet or symbol) and that also exactly 10 digits. If the phone number contains anything beside digits, exception will be thrown. Also, if the number of digits is not exactly 10, then also exception will be thrown. The steps are:

`Select File->New Project`. Select Web from Categories tab and Web Application from Projects tab. Select `Next` button. Give any name to Project Name say `Webex10`.

Select the server as `GlassFish V2` to deploy our application. Click `Next` button (Figure 9.106).

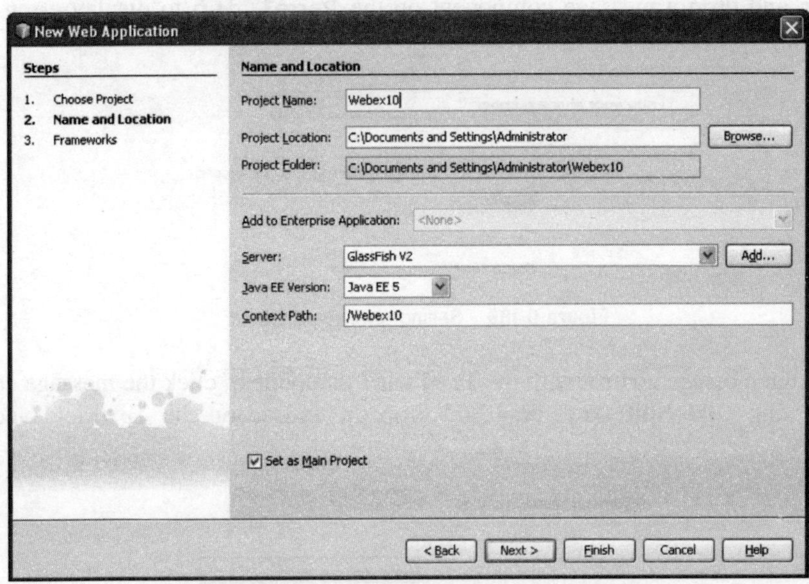

Figure 9.106   Screen for New Web Application.

Select the Visual Web JavaServer Faces checkbox when prompted to select the framework and select `Finish` button. By default `Page1.jsp` file is opened in design mode. Let the `Page1.jsp` file be open in Design view and from Basic palette, drag and drop a TextField Component, a Label Component, a Static Text component and a Button component on it (Figure 9.107).

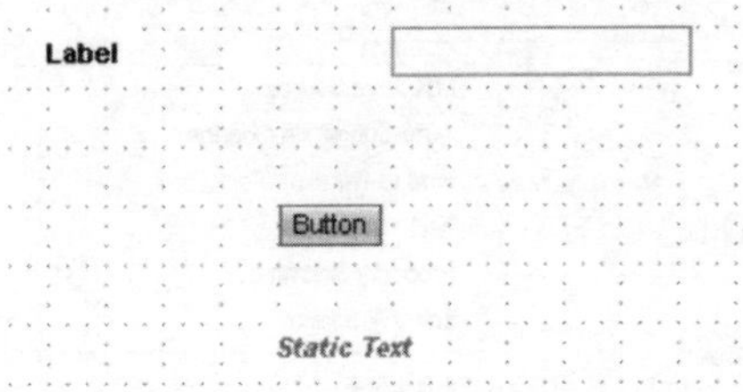

Figure 9.107   Display of Page1.jsp in Design view.

Set the **text** property of **label** component and button component to make them appear as shown in Figure 9.108.

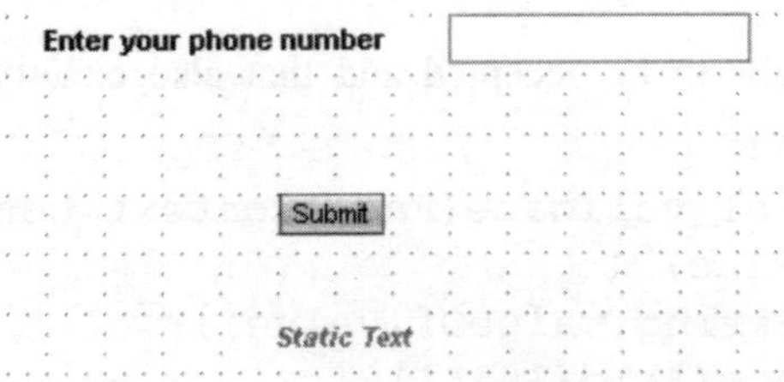

Figure 9.108   Components after setting their text property.

Also drag and drop a message component on the `Page1.jsp` to display error messages (Figure 9.109).

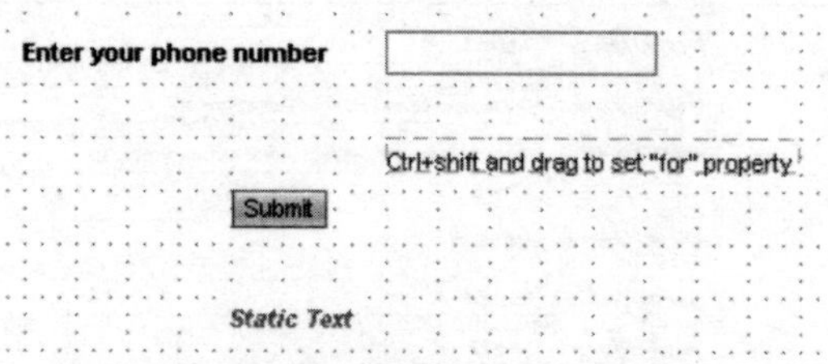

Figure 9.109   Setting error messages.

To attach the message control with the TextField1 component, click the message component and after pressing **Ctrl+Shift** key, drag and drop the mouse on the TextField1 component (Figure 9.110).

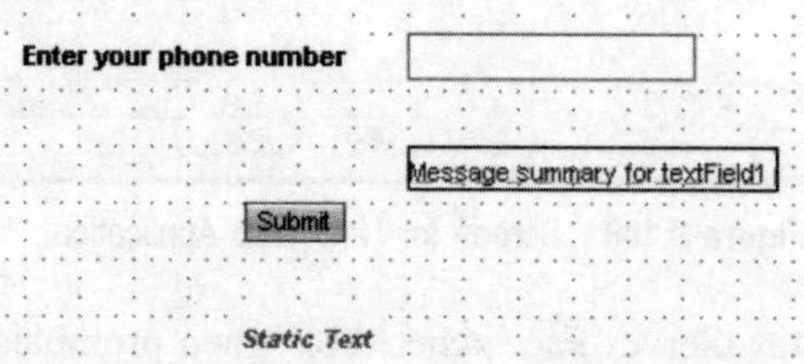

Figure 9.110   Attaching the message to TextField1 component.

To attach a validation rule to TextField1 component, right click on it, select `Edit Event Handler` option followed by **`validate`** option. We get a screen to specify the regular expression for the TextField1 component (Figure 9.111).

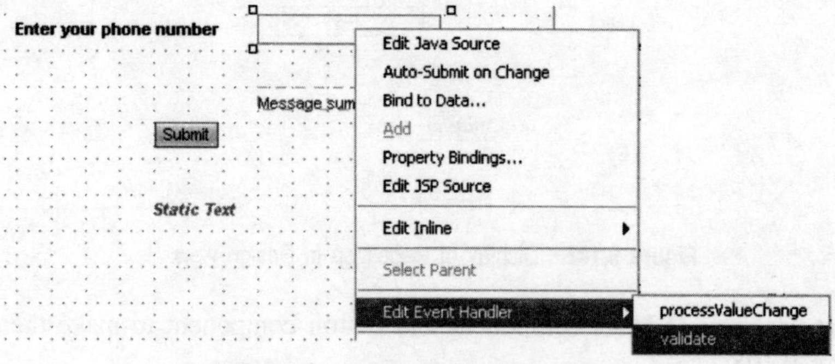

Figure 9.111   Attaching a validation rule.

Since we want only digits to be accepted and that also exactly 10 digits, we write the following regular expression:

```
public void textField1_validate(FacesContext context, UIComponent
component, Object value) {
    String phone = String.valueOf(value);
    if (!phone.matches("\\d{10}")) {
```

```
throw new ValidatorException(new FacesMessage(
    "Phone number can be of digits only -10 digits"));
    }
}
```

Note: \\ is the escape character and d stands for digits

1. w is for alphanumerical character
2. [A-Z] for capital letters
3. [A-Za-z] for all characters

While writing a regular expression validator, we may be requiring the constructs shown in Table 9.1.

Table 9.1 Constructs required to write a regular expression

Construct	Description
|	Or
^	Matches text beginning with the subsequent characters
$	Matches text ending with the preceding characters
\	Escape character. Necessary if we want to match to a period (.), bracket, brace or other special character
\n	New-line character
[r	Carriage-return character
[]	Used to delimit a set of characters
*	Zero or more occurrences of the previous character or set of characters
+	One or more occurrences of the previous character or set of characters

To import the libraries, right click on the editor and select Fix Imports option. We get a screen showing the name of the library file that will be imported as shown in Figure 9.112.

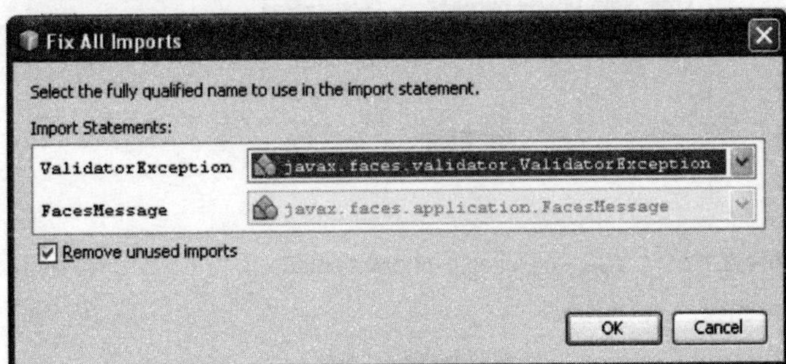

Figure 9.112 Importing Libraries.

Now double click on the Submit button and write following code in it:

```
public String button1_action() {
    staticText1.setText("Phone number entered is "
        +textField1.getText());
    return null;
}
```

Run the application, we get a screen to enter phone number. If we enter anything beside digits, we get an error as shown in Figure 9.113.

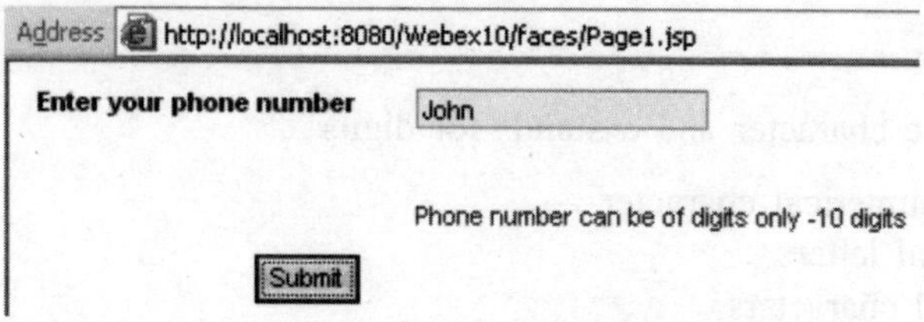

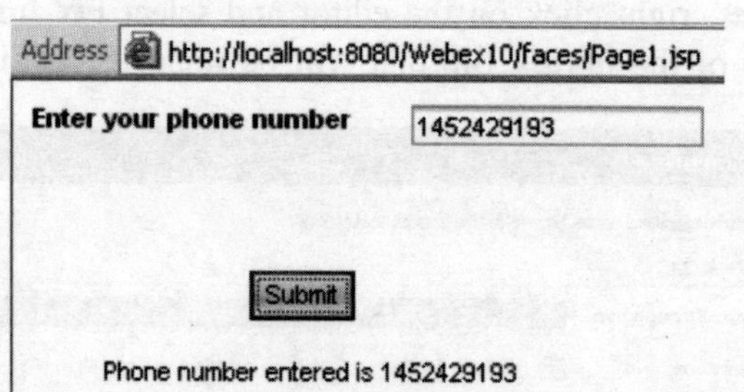

Figure 9.113   Error message is displayed if string is entered.

If we enter less than 10 or more than 10 digits, still we get an error as shown in Figure 9.114.

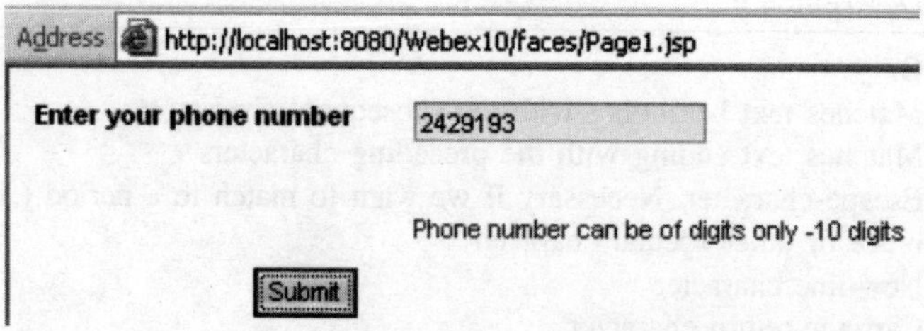

Figure 9.114   Error message is displayed if less digits are entered.

If we enter the phone number of 10 digits, it will be accepted and is displayed as shown in Figure 9.115.

Figure 9.115   Output displayed if phone number of 10 digits is entered.

SUMMARY

The main objective of this chapter is to give the complete idea of how to use different components in NetBeans IDE in order to make a web application quicker and with minimum errors. Not only we saw how to use managed bean and perform navigation to the desired pages but also how to apply validation and converters to get the data in the specified format. All the components like: Drop down component, ListBox component, RadioButtonGroup component, CheckBoxGroup component are practically explained. We have also learnt to make Customer validators using this IDE.

REVIEW QUESTIONS

Do all the programs through NetBeans IDE.

9.1 Write a JSF program that asks the customer to enter total amount of books purchased and choose customer type from a drop down list (`selectOneMenu`). The customer types stored in drop down list are: librarian, shop keeper and a private customer. According to the selected customer type, two things are computed and displayed: Discount and Net Amount.

- If the customer type is librarian, the discount is 20 per cent of the total amount.
- If the customer type is shop keeper, the discount is 10 per cent of the total amount.
- If the customer type is private customer, the discount is 5 per cent of the total amount.

9.2 Write a JSF program to convert the date in MMM-DD-YYYY format into dd/mm/yy format and print it.

9.3 Write a JSF program to enter a number (having decimal values) and convert it into integers.

9.4 Write a JSF program to display three different types of rooms available in your hotel to the customer in the form of radio button group and display the rent of that room. The three room types are:

Suite	Rent is Rs. 4500
AC Deluxe	Rent is Rs. 2500
Ordinary	Rent is Rs. 1000

10

Creating Custom Component

LEARNING OBJECTIVES

In this chapter, we will learn:

- To create a tag library descriptor file
- To create a tag handler class
- To create the component class
- To create the renderer class
- To register the custom component in faces-config.xml file

This chapter is devoted to creation of custom components. So, in this chapter we will learn all the steps that are necessary for creation of custom components.

Two custom components namely: Custom Label component and Email component are created and explained step by step in this chapter. The idea behind developing Custom UI components is to hide the complexity of UI functionality. A JSF component is a typical combination of three classes working closely together:

1. The **renderer** creates the client-side representation of the component. It takes any input (for input-type components) from the client and transforms it into the form the component can understand. The renderer implementation generates HTML.
2. The second class is a subclass of IO component (the **component class**). This class is responsible for the data and behaviour of the component on the server side.
3. The third class is the **tag handler**. This class is responsible for several tasks like creating the component, attaching the renderer to the component, and setting the fields on the component based on the values supplied in the JSP tag. The tag handler's tag are written in Tag Library Descriptor (TLD) file.

Steps to create a custom component are:

1. Create a new NetBeans Web Application Project
2. Create a Tag Library Descriptor File
3. Create a Tag Handler Class
4. Create the Component Class
5. Create the Renderer Class
6. Modify the `faces-config.xml` file
7. Modify the JSF Client Web Application Page

A Tag Library Descriptor (TLD) file is an XML document that contains information about a library as a whole and about tags and tag files contained in the library.

The term "`JSF UI Component`" is generally used to describe a set of sub-components, each perform their own specific task such as rendering the component, validating its input, and performing any data conversions. Each UI Components' sub-components can be individually customized and re-configured into new and varied combinations.

UI Component Class	A Java class derived from either the `UIComponentBase` or extended from an existing JSF UI component such as `outputText`. This is the actual Java class representing the core logic of the component. It can optionally contain the logic to "`render`" itself to a client, or rendering logic can be separated into a separate "`renderer`" class.
Renderer Class	This is a class that contains code to render a UI component. Rendering classes can provide different renderings for a UI component making it compatible with different types of clients.
UI Component Tag Class	This is a JSP tag handler class that allows the UI component to be used in a JSP. It can also associate a separate renderer class with a UI component class.
Tag Library Descriptor File	This is a standard J2EE JSP tag library descriptor (TLD) file which associates the tag handler class with a usable tag in a JSP page. Required only for JSP usage only.
Associated Helper Classes	These include a collection of standard (included in JSF RI) or custom helper classes such as Converters, Validators, ActionListeners, etc. that can be programmatically bound to UI components. For example a JSF UI Input Field component can be associated with different types of validators to ensure that the data entered is valid and is in format suitable for processing.

Creating a Custom Label Component

1. Create a new *NetBeans* web application project

The first step of creating a component is to create a new `NetBeans` web application project. So, we start `NetBeans` and select `File ->New Project` option. Select **web** from categories pane and **web application** from projects pane. Select `Next` button (Figure 10.1).

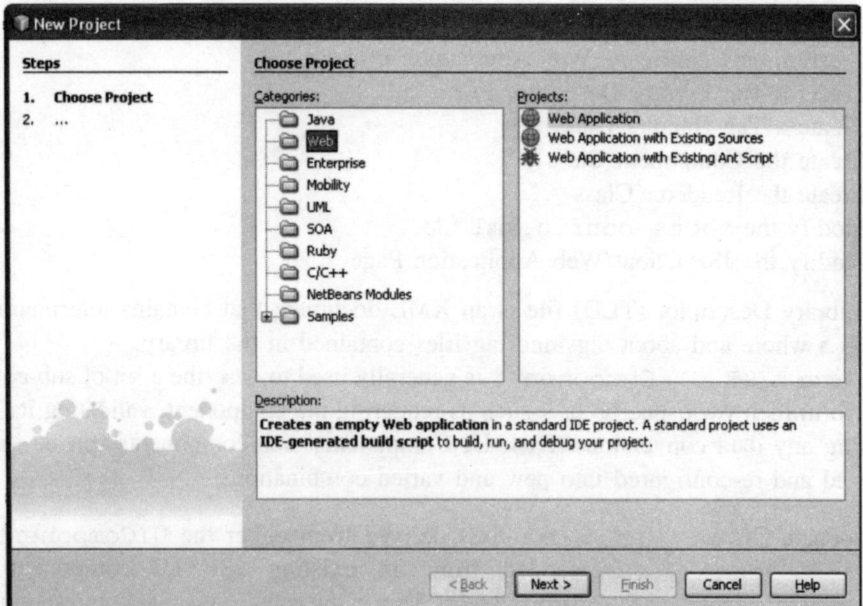

Figure 10.1   Screen of New Project.

Provide ContextPath as /LabelComp and select Next (Figure 10.2).

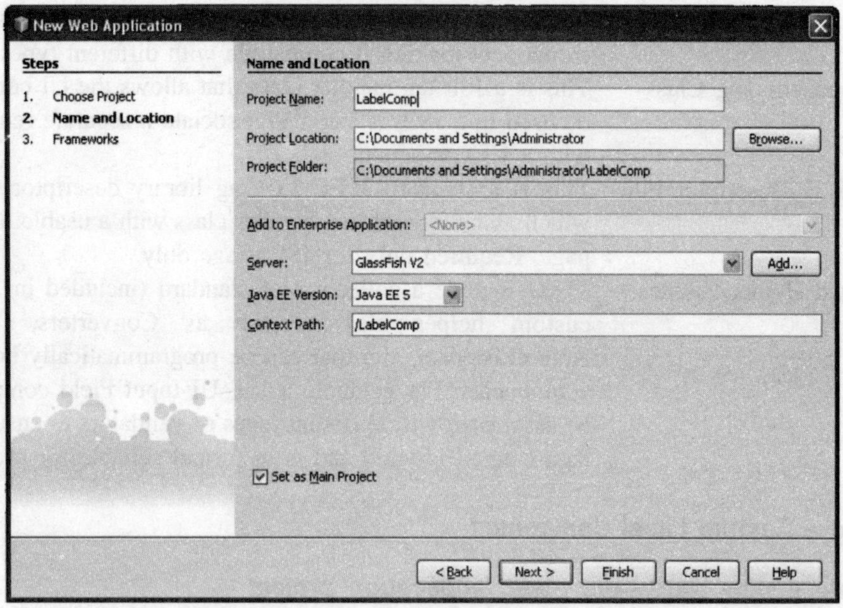

Figure 10.2   Screen of New Web Application.

Choose the framework as JavaServer Faces and select Finish (Figure 10.3).

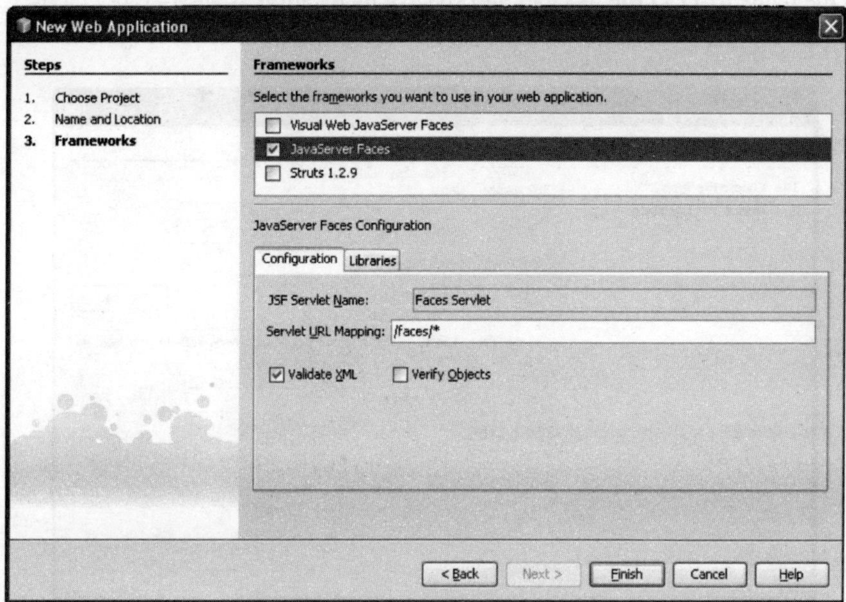

Figure 10.3 Selection of framework.

Create a `Tag Library Descriptor` file

To create a Tag Library Descriptor file, we right click on our `LabelComp Project` node and select `Tag Library Descriptor` option (Figure 10.4).

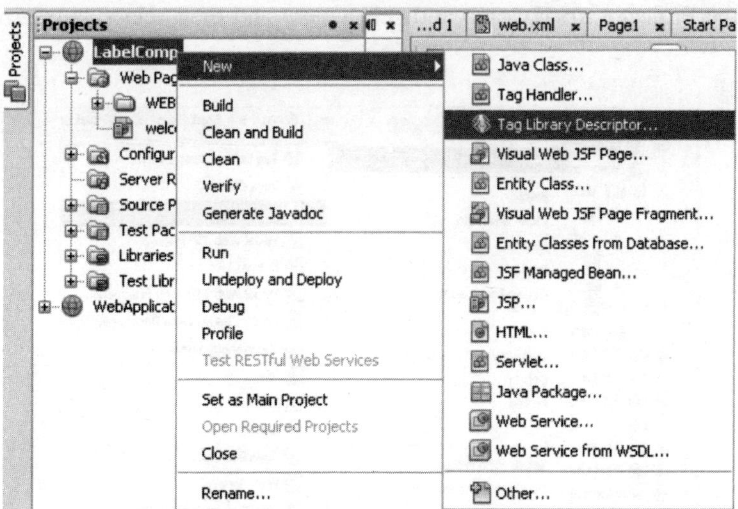

Figure 10.4 Selection of Tag Library Descriptor option.

Assign the name to TLD file as label and specify its location as `WEB-INF/tlds/` and URI will appear as `/WEB-INF/tlds/label` and select `Finish` button (Figure 10.5).

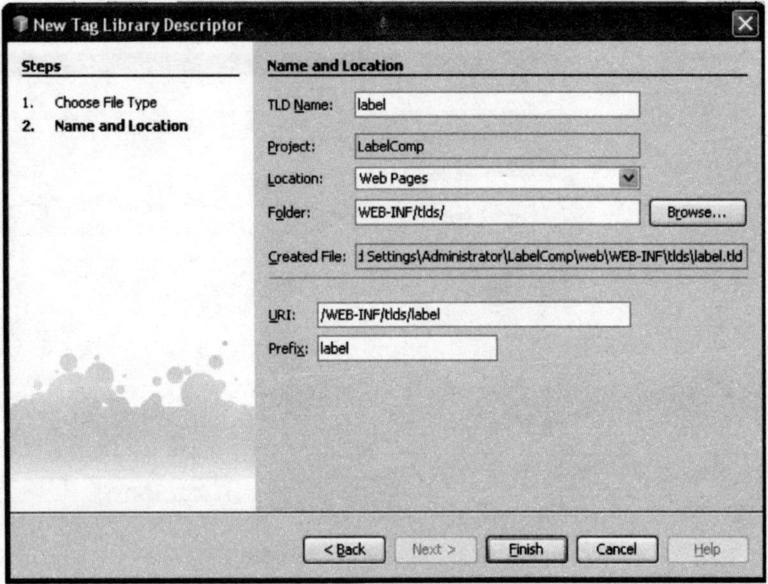

Figure 10.5 Assign name & specify location.

Create a `TagHandler` class

Right click on the Project `LabelComp` and select `New` and then select `TagHandler` option (Figure. 10.6).

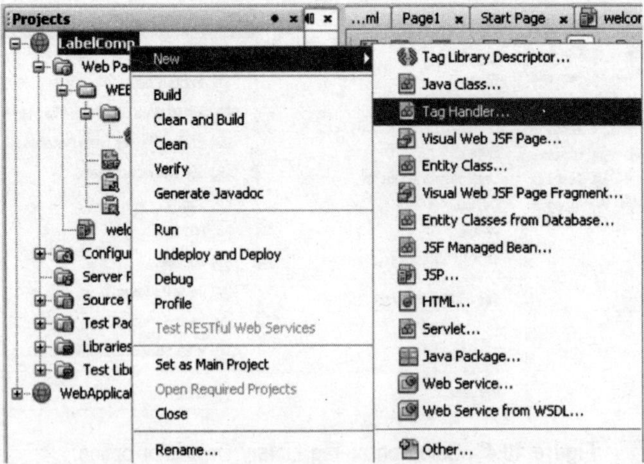

Figure 10.6 Selection of TagHandler option.

Assign the Class Name as `LabelTagHandler` and the Package name as `custom.comp.label` (Figure 10.7).

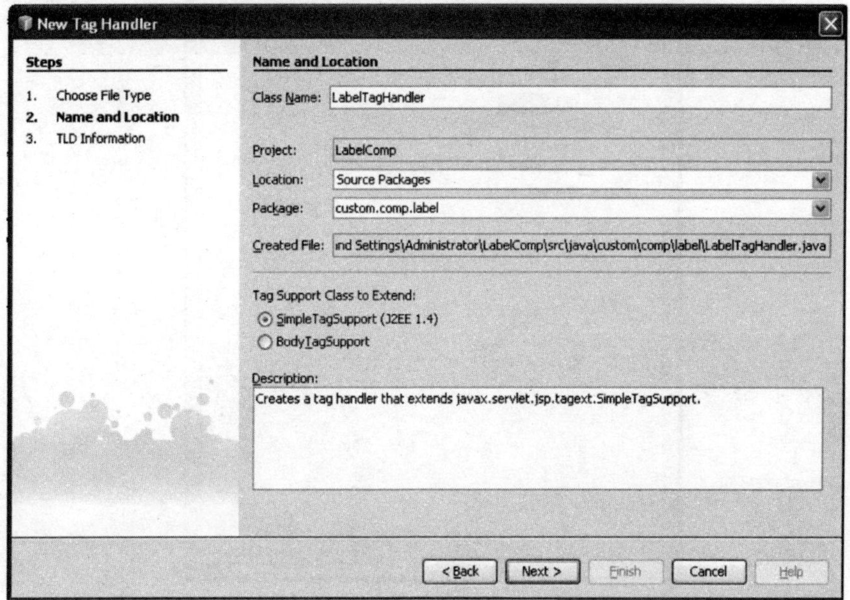

Figure 10.7   Assign the names.

We get a dialog to specify the name of TLD file (Figure 10.8).

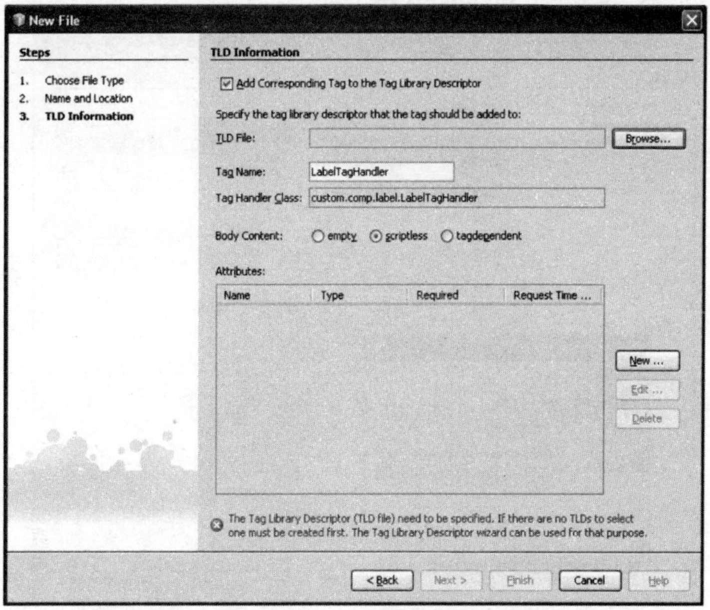

Figure 10.8   Dialog Box to specify the name of TLD file.

Select `Browse` button to specify the name of the TLD file: `label.tld` (Figure 10.9).

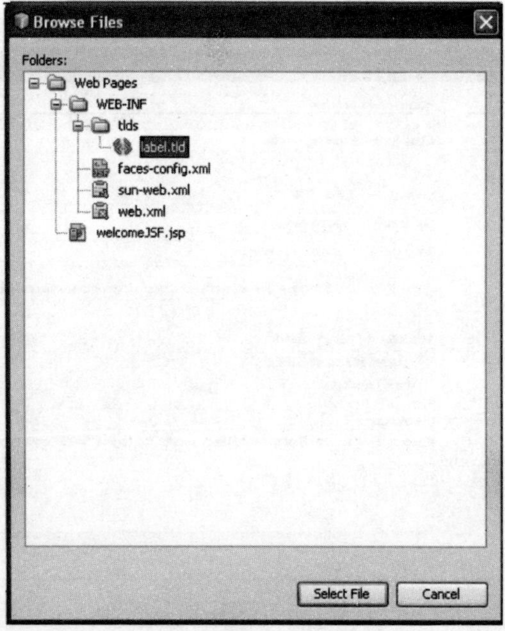

Figure 10.9   Selection of file name.

After choosing `label.tld  file`, select "`Select  File`" button.

Now select New button to specify the attribute of the component. We define an attribute: name of type string as shown in Figure 10.10:

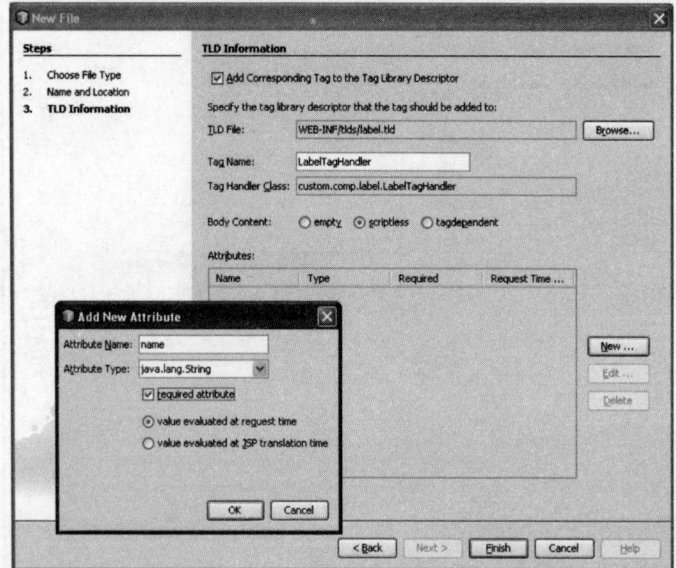

Figure 10.10   Definition of an attribute.

Select `Finish` to close this `TagHandler` class dialog box (Figure 10.11).

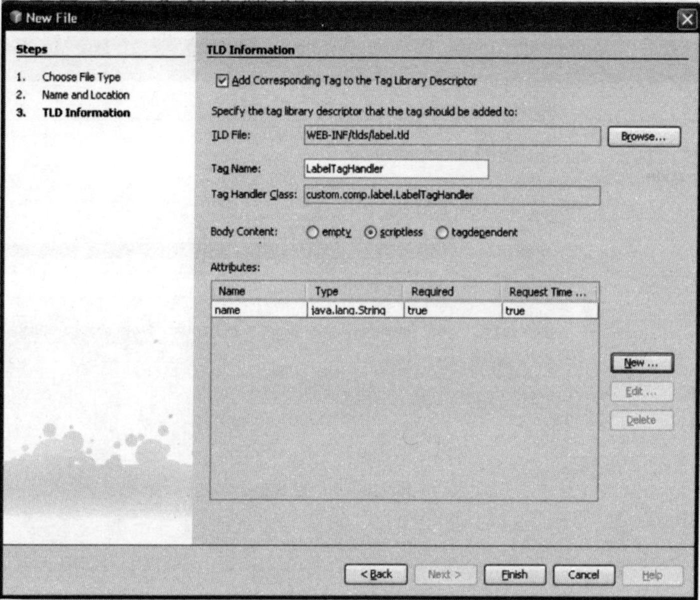

Figure 10.11   Selection of Finish to close this dialog box.

Create the component class

To create the component class, expand `Source Packages` node of our Project `LabelComp` and right click on `custom.comp.label` node and select New option and select `Java class` (Figure 10.12).

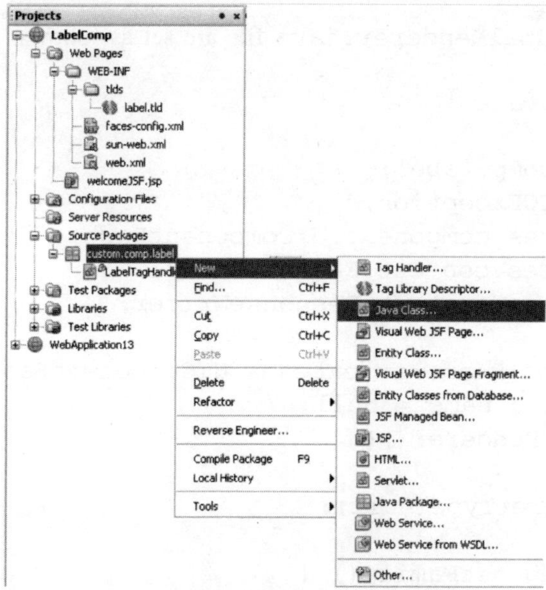

Figure 10.12   Selection of Java class.

Specify the class name as `LabelRenderer`, Package name as `custom.comp.label` and select `Finish` button (Figure 10.13).

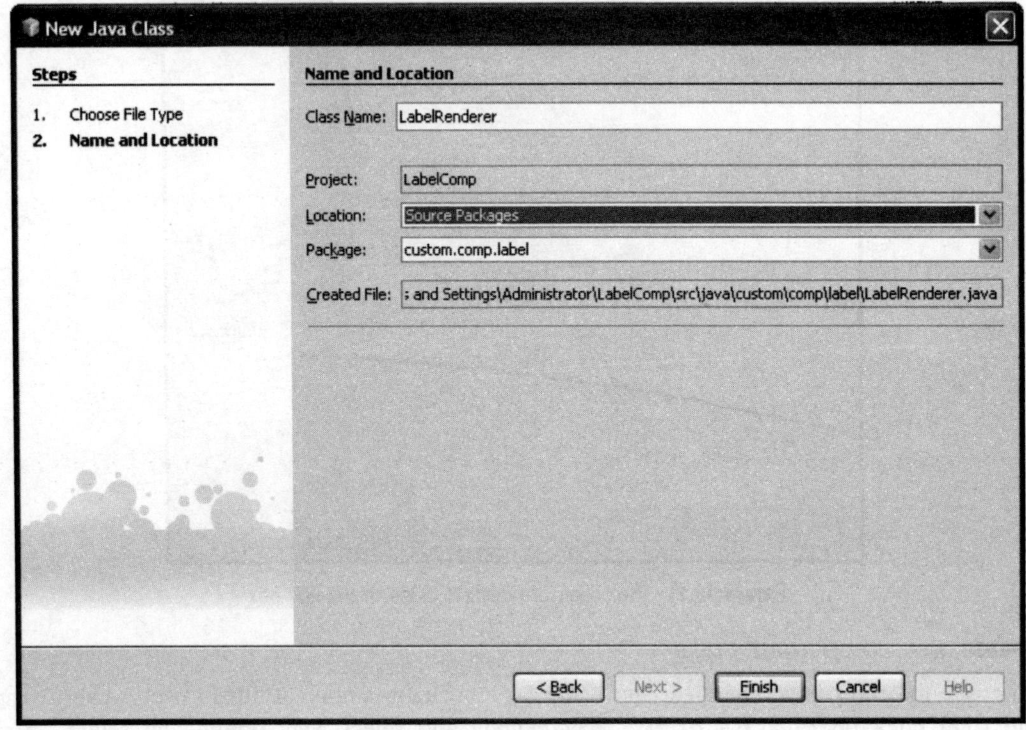

Figure 10.13 Specification of name.

The contents of `LabelRenderer.java` file are set as follows:

LabelRenderer.java

```java
package custom.comp.label;
import java.io.IOException;
import javax.faces.component.UIComponentBase;
import javax.faces.context.FacesContext;
import javax.faces.context.ResponseWriter;

public class LabelRenderer extends UIComponentBase {
    private String name = null;
    public LabelRenderer(){
        super();
        setRendererType(null);
    }
    public String getFamily() {
```

```java
        return null;
    }
    public void encodeBegin(FacesContext context) throws
IOException
    {
        ResponseWriter writer = context.getResponseWriter();
        String str = (String)getAttributes().get("name");
        writer.startElement("h2", this);
        if(str != null)
            writer.writeText(str, "name");
        else
            writer.writeText("Sorry no label", null);
        writer.endElement("h2");
    }
    public void setName(String txt) {
        this.name = txt;
    }
    public String getName() {
        return name;
    }
}
```

Let us recall again that to develop a component there are following steps:

1. The component must subclass one of the existing components such as `UIInput`, `UIOutput` or `UIData`. These classes subclass `UIComponentBase`.
2. Register it in a JSF configuration file (`faces-config.xml`).
3. Integrate it with a display technology (rendering it).

JSF components consist of two parts: the component and the renderer. The JSF Component class defines the state and behaviour of a UI component and a renderer defines how the component will be displayed. That is, renderer converts the values of the component to the appropriate markup.

Note: All UI components descend from the `javax.faces.component.UIComponent` abstract base class.

UI components are grouped into different families. Families help renderers decide how to handle a particular component. `getFamily()` method is actually required for UI components that extend `UIComponentBase` since it could come from any component family. Since in our example we won't be creating a new family of components, we can just return any String value or just null. Also, one of the following methods are overrided:

```java
public void encodeBegin(FacesContext context) throws IOException;
public void encodeChildren(FacesContext context) throws IOException;
public void encodeEnd(FacesContext context) throws IOException;
public void decode(FacesContext context);
```

Encode methods are for displaying the component and we begin encoding only if the rendered property is true. This method simply renders an HTML header (h2) with the custom message supplied. For this component a single `encodeBegin()` (or `encodeEnd()`) method is all that is needed to render the complete tag since it does not contain any children. The `encodeBegin` actually renders the beginning tag. UI components with children tags/components will override `encodeChildren()` along with `encodeEnd()`. The `encodeChildren()` method allows children components to be rendered and `encodeEnd()` renders the closing parent tag.

The `encodeBegin()` method has an argument: FacesContext. An extension to the servlet and JSP context, the FacesContext provides access to the many useful objects for JSF/JSP/Servlet development. Here, we simply extract a "`writer`" object in order to "`write`" our rendered response back to the client.

We first retrieve a `ResponseWriter` instance from a `FacesContext` in order to display data as it has several methods for generating markup.

Next we get the value of the attribute "`name`" which is passed from the tag from our JSP page using the method `getAttributes()`. The `getAttributes` method comes from the `UIComponentBase` class which is the base class for all UI components:

```
String str = (String)getAttributes().get("name");
```

When the attribute (name) or "`property`" is written to the client, an additional string value representing the name of the property "`name`" is also included as an argument to the `writeText()` method. The idea behind this is to provide development tools environments the ability to display the name of the property in a visual editor. We can also set the second argument as null.

```
writer.writeText(str, "name");
```

Decode method is used when our control accepts user input.

The custom component usually exposes its own set of new properties such as layout or pattern. These are JavaBean properties that affect the component's behaviour. We can enable value binding expressions by using the `getValueBinding` and method of UI component. That means components have a ValueBinding that must be bound to a JavaBean read-write property. For retrieving the property of a component, following principles are followed:

- If the value is set, return it
- If the value is not set, attempt to retrieve its value binding expression, evaluate it and return that value. The value binding expression is set with the `setValueBinding` method

Registering the custom UI component in `faces-config.xml`

Before moving on to building a `JSPtag` handler and a TLD file, we'll add a required entry for our custom component in the `faces-config.xml` file.

Expand the node of our project: `LabelComp` and right click on `faces-config.xml` node and select `Edit` option (Figure 10.14).

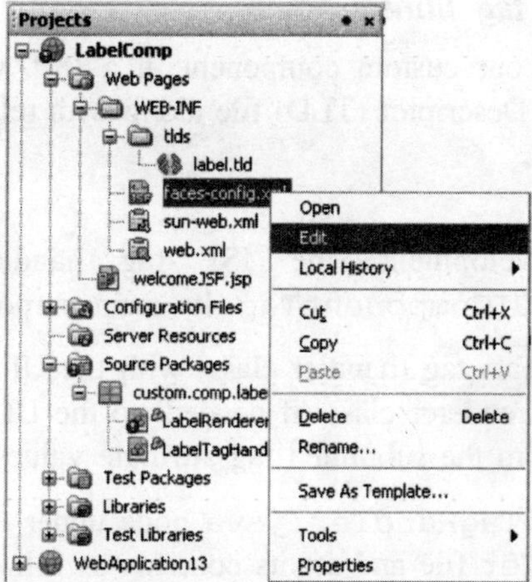

Figure. 10.14　Selection of Edit option.

Type the following contents in `faces-config.xml` file:

```xml
<?xml version='1.0' encoding='UTF-8'?>
<!- ====== FULL CONFIGURATION FILE ===================== ->
<faces-config version="1.2"
    xmlns="http://java.sun.com/xml/ns/javaee"
    xmlns:xsi="http://www.w3.org/2001/XMLSchema-instance"
    xsi:schemaLocation="http://java.sun.com/xml/ns/javaee
    http://java.sun.com/xml/ns/javaee/web-facesconfig_1_2.xsd">
    <component>
        <component-type>custom.comp.label</component-type>
        <component-class>custom.comp.label.LabelRenderer
        </component-class>
        <property>
            <property-name>name</property-name>
            <property-class>String</property-class>
        </property>
    </component>
</faces-config>
```

Every component has a type and it is the name by which the component will be referenced. We define component type with the help of `<component-type>` element. The `<component-class>` element specifies the name of the implementation class.

The `<property-name>` element is used for specifying the name of the attribute used with our custom component and `<property-class>` element is for defining the data type of the attribute.

Example:

```
public static final string COMPONENT_TYPE ="custom.comp.label";
```

That means the component will be referenced by "`custom.comp.label`".

Building a custom JSP tag library

In order to be able to use our custom component in a JSP, we need a custom tag library comprised of a Tag Library Descriptor (TLD) file along with references to taghandlers classes.

Building the Tag Handler

For JSF component development, the JSP tag handler class is derived from `javax.faces.webapp.UIComponentTag`. Its main purpose is to:

1. Associate a JSP callable tag (handler class) with the UI component.
2. Associate a separate renderer class (if needed) to the UI component.
3. Set the properties from the submitted tag attribute values to the UI component.

Double click on `LabelTagHandler.java` node under `Source Packages` node to open the `LabelTagHandler` file and set its contents as follows:

```
LabelTagHandler.java
package custom.comp.label;
import javax.faces.webapp.UIComponentTag;
import javax.faces.component.UIComponent;

public class LabelTagHandler extends UIComponentTag{
    private String name=null;
    public String getComponentType() {
        return "custom.comp.label";
    }
    public String getRendererType() {
        return null;
    }
    public void setName(String name) {
        this.name = name;
    }
    public String getName() {
        return name;
    }
    protected void setProperties(UIComponent component) {
        super.setProperties(component);
        LabelRenderer lbl = (LabelRenderer) component;
        if(name !=null){
            lbl.setName(name);
        }
    }
    public void release() {
        name = null;
        super.release();
    }
}
```

We can see in coding on the previous page that "`name`" property is defined of type string and its getter and setter methods are also specified in the class.

JSF provides two abstract base classes we can use for writing JSP component tags:

- `UIComponentTag`
- `UIComponentBodyTag`

We usually subclass `UIComponentTag` directly and if we need to process the body of the tag, we need to subclass `UIComponentBodyTag`. Beside subclassing either of the above base class, we need to declare the tag inside an XML file: TLD file which defines a set of tags.

So, to create a new component tag, we can subclass `javax.faces.webapp.UI componentTag` and associate it with a `component/renderer pair` by overriding two read only properties: componentType and rendererType.

These two methods associate the tag handler with our registered UI component: "`custom.comp.label`" as well as associate the renderer.

UI componentTag defines the component-Type property as:

```
public abstract String getComponentType();
```

Example:

```
public String getComponentType() {
    return "custom.comp.label";
}
```

We return a String representing the component's type. It basically associates the component class with component type.

Note: A component can be associated with many different tags. In addition to specifying the component type, we must specify the renderer type by overriding the rendererType property:

```
public abstract String getRendererType();
```

This property is a string that maps to a specific renderer type. Since we don't have a separate renderer class, this statement returns a null value.

Example:

```
public String getRendererType() {
    return null;
}
```

But, if rendering has to be done by some renderer, we have to specify its value. Example:

```
public String getRendererType() {
    return COMPONENT_RENDERER_TYPE;
}
```

The method `setProperties()`, sets the incoming values from the JSP tag by first calling the parent class' setProperties method along with custom code to set the value from the label tag attribute.

Tag handlers can also have properties which are exposed as element attributes. For example:

```
<lb:label name="Believe in God" />
```

The attribute `name` maps to a string property of the `LabelTaghandler` class. `LabelTagHandler` must map the name property to an attribute or property of Label component.

Note: UI `componentTag` supports a few basic component properties by default: id, renderType and renderer. If the customer component doesn't add any properties and the associated renderer doesn't require any special attributes, then there is no need to override any other methods.

If our custom component has its own properties, we also need to override the `setProperties` method:

```
protected void setProperties(UIComponent component);
```

In this method, we map properties of our tag class to properties or attributes of the component. But while implementing this method, we call the superclass's implementation otherwise the basic component properties like rendererType and renderer will not be updated properly. Besides this, for each property or attribute, we have to:

1. Add the property to the tag handler class
2. Associate the tag handler property with the appropriate component property or attribute in the setProperties method

For example our label component has name property, we expose it as properties of the `labelTagHandler` class:

```
public void setName(String name) {
    this.name = name;
}
public String getName() {
    return name;
}
```

Now, associate the tag handler property with the component property:

```
LabelRenderer lbl = (LabelRenderer) component;
if(name !=null){
    lbl.setName(name);
}
```

As, we can see that we first check that if the `labelTagHandler`'s name property is not null, we set the component's name property to be equal to the `labelTagHandler`'s name property. In short, `setProperties` method is used to set the component properties or attributes based on the properties of the tag handler class.

In order to add properties to the `labelTagHandler`, we have to override the release method:

```
public void release()
```

In this method, we release the resources that we have allocated as it is the standard method of the `javax.servlet.jsp.tagext.Tag` interface which `UIComponentTag` implements and is called before the tag is garbage collected.

```
public void release() {
    name = null;
    super.release();
}
```

As, we can see in above method, we are setting the instance variables (name) for the tag's properties to null.

In order for us to use our custom JSP tag handler class, we need to create an associated TLD file which contains the tag entry associated with the tag handler class. Here is an example of the TLD file needed for this tag. The TLD associates the tag name, "label" with the tag class "custom.comp.label.LabelTagHandler" along with its associated attributes.

Double click on `label.tld` file and we find its contents as follows:

label.tld

```
<?xml version="1.0" encoding="UTF-8"?>
<taglib version="2.0" xmlns="http://java.sun.com/xml/ns/j2ee"
    xmlns:xsi="http://www.w3.org/2001/XMLSchema-instance"
    xsi:schemaLocation="http://java.sun.com/xml/ns/j2ee
    web-jsptaglibrary_2_0.xsd">
    <tlib-version>1.0</tlib-version>
    <short-name>label</short-name>
    <uri>/WEB-INF/tlds/label</uri>
    <tag>
        <name>label</name>
        <tag-class>custom.comp.label.LabelTagHandler</tag-class>
        <body-content>scriptless</body-content>
        <attribute>
        <name>name</name>
        <required>true</required>
        <rtexprvalue>true</rtexprvalue>
        <type>java.lang.String</type>
        </attribute>
    </tag>
</taglib>
```

JSP custom tags are grouped into tag libraries through a TLD file which is an XML file located usually in `WEB-INF/lib` folder in a web application. It simply maps a custom tag handler class to a JSP tag and declares which properties should be exposed as JSP tag attributes.

All TLD files start with the library's description. The most important is `<uri>` node:

```
<uri>/WEB-INF/tlds/label</uri>
```

which has to be included in all JSP file which is supposed to use the custom component. Then comes is the tag descriptions which maps a tag name to a tag handler class and also describes each valid attribute. The attributes can belong to the custom component as well as those inherited from the parent component.

After the tag handler is registered with a tag library, we can use our custom component in a JSP file by following statement:

```
<lb:label name="Believe in God" />
```

To use the custom component, double click on welcomeJSF file and include the following taglib directives in the page:

```
<%@taglib uri="/WEB-INF/tlds/label" prefix="lb" %>
```

and then use the component with following statement:

```
<lb:label name="Believe in God" />
```

welcomeJSF.jsp

```
<%@page contentType="text/html"%>
<%@page pageEncoding="UTF-8"%>
<%@taglib prefix="f" uri="http://java.sun.com/jsf/core"%>
<%@taglib prefix="h" uri="http://java.sun.com/jsf/html"%>
<%@taglib uri="/WEB-INF/tlds/label" prefix="lb" %>

<!DOCTYPE HTML PUBLIC "-//W3C//DTD HTML 4.01 Transitional//EN"
    "http://www.w3.org/TR/html4/loose.dtd">
<html>
    <head>
        <meta http-equiv="Content-Type" content="text/html;
            charset=UTF-8">
        <title>Custom Component</title>
    </head>
    <body>
        <f:view>
            <lb:label name="Believe in God" />
        </f:view>
    </body>
</html>
```

Run the project and we get the output as shown in Figure 10.15.

Figure 10.15   Display of output.

Creating a Custom Email Component

Create a new NetBeans web application project

The first step of creating a component is to create a new NetBeans web application project. So, we start NetBeans, select `File ->New Project`. Select Web from categories pane and Web Application from Projects pane. Select `Next` button. Assign the Project name as `EmailComp`. Provide `ContextPath` as `/EmailComp` and select `Next` (Figure 10.16).

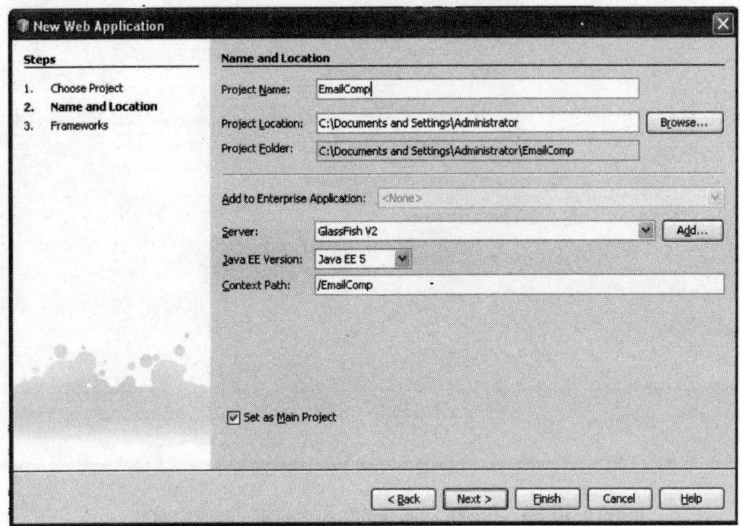

Figure 10.16   Screen for New Web Application.

Choose the framework as JavaServer Faces and select Finish.

Create a Tag Library Descriptor file

To create a Tag Library Descriptor file, we right click on our `EmailComp` Project node and select Tag Library Descriptor option (Figure 10.17)

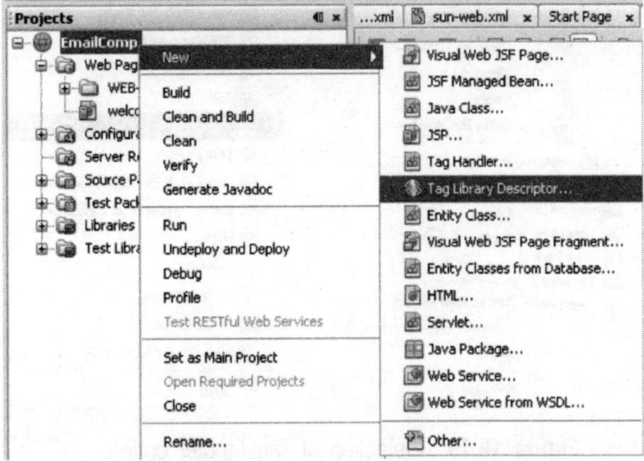

Figure. 10.17   Selection of Tag Library Descriptor option.

Assign the name to tld file as linkemail and specify its location as WEB-INF/tlds/ and URI will appear as /WEB-INF/tlds/linkemail and select Finish button (Figure 10.18).

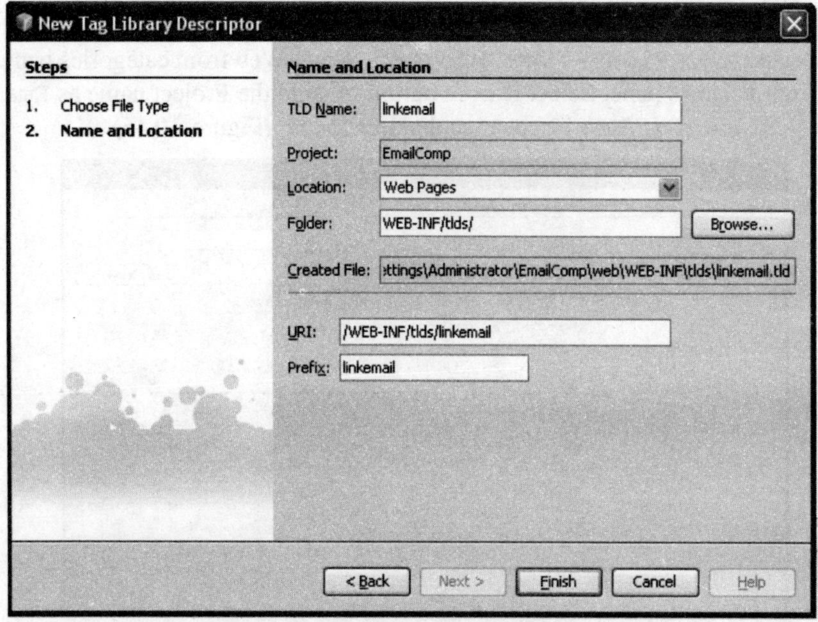

Figure 10.18   Assign the name & specify the location.

Create a TagHandler class

Right click on the Project EmailComp and select New and then select TagHandler option (Figure 10.19).

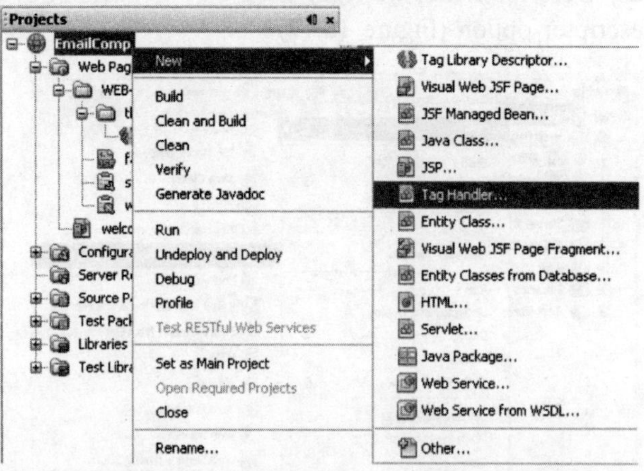

Figure 10.19   Selection of TagHandler option.

Assign the Class Name as `EmailTagHandler` and the Package name as `custom.comp.email` and select `Next` button.

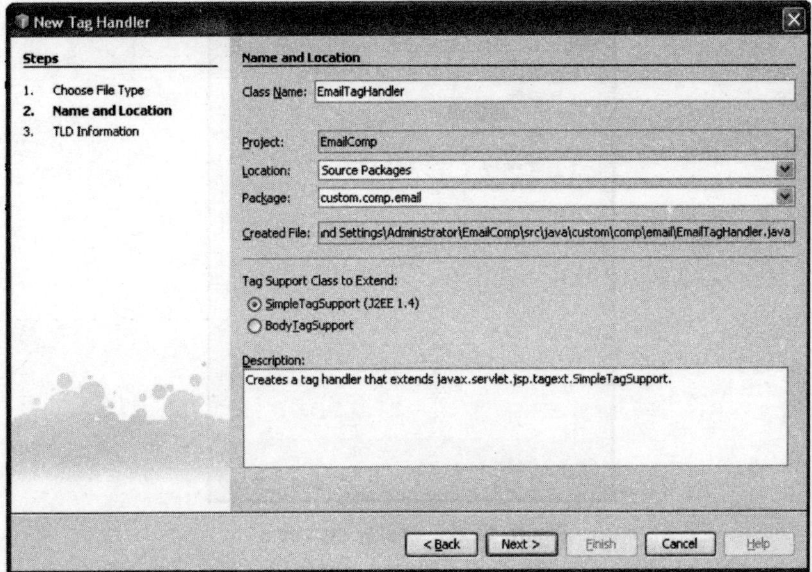

Figure 10.20   Assign the names.

We get a screen to specify the name of the TLD file (Figure 10.21).

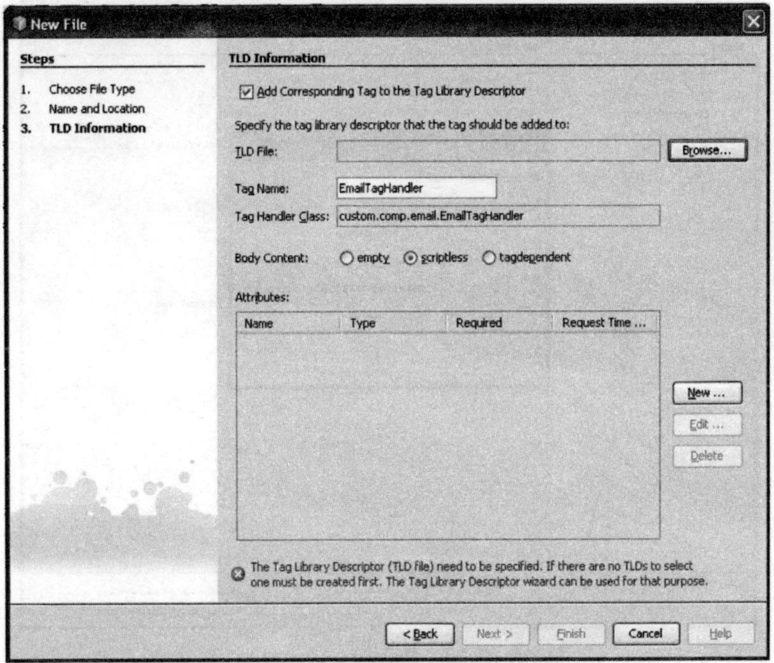

Figure 10.21   Dialog Box for specification of TLD file name.

Select Browse button to specify the name of the TLD file: `linkemail.tld` (Figure 10.22).

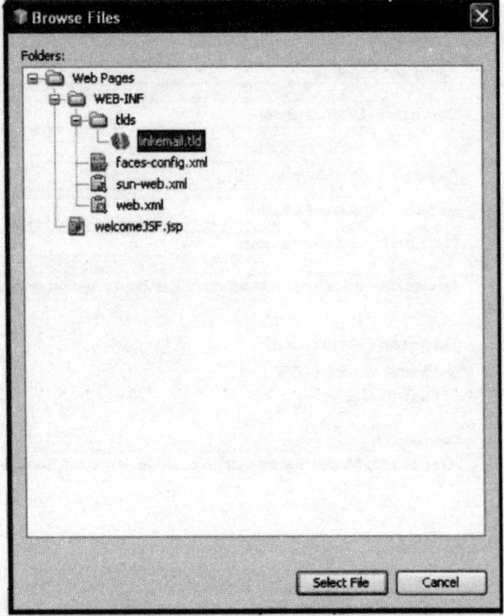

Figure 10.22   Specify the name.

After choosing `linkemail.tld` file, select "`Select File`" button.

Now select New button to specify the attribute of the component. We define two attributes: email and label of type string as shown in Figure 10.23.

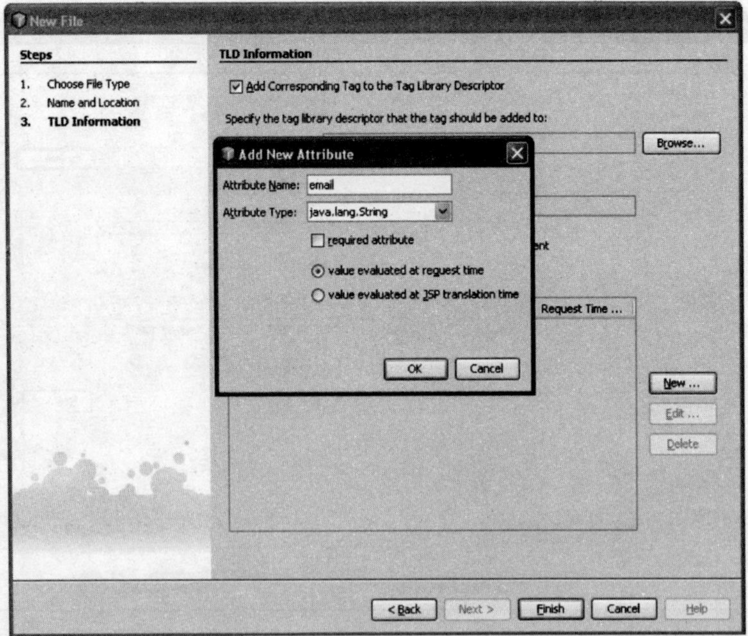

Figure 10.23   Definition of attributes.

Select Finish to close this `TagHandler class` dialog box.

Create the component class

To create the component class, expand Source Packages node of our Project `EmailComp` and right click on `custom.comp.email` node and select New option and select Java class (Figure 10.24).

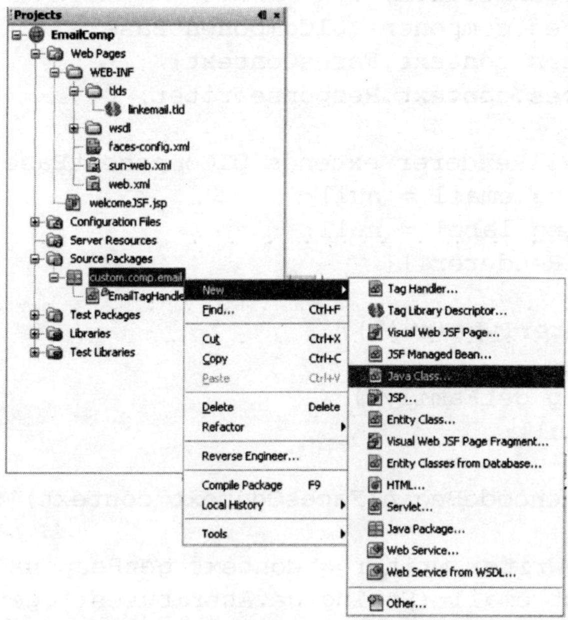

Figure 10.24 Selection of Java class option.

Specify the class name as `EmailRenderer`, Package name as `custom.comp.email` and select `Finish` button (Figure 10.25).

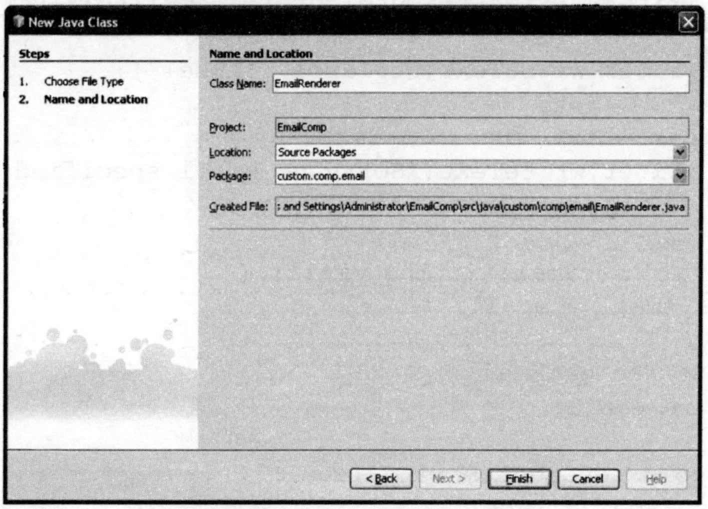

Figure 10.25 Specification of names.

The contents of `EmailRenderer.java` file are set as follows:

EmailRenderer.java

```java
package custom.comp.email;
import java.io.IOException;
import javax.faces.component.UIComponentBase;
import javax.faces.context.FacesContext;
import javax.faces.context.ResponseWriter;

public class EmailRenderer extends UIComponentBase{
    private String email = null;
    private String label = null;
    public EmailRenderer(){
        super();
        setRendererType(null);
    }
    public String getFamily() {
        return null;
    }
    public void encodeBegin(FacesContext context) throws
IOException {
        ResponseWriter writer = context.getResponseWriter();
        String stremail=(String)getAttributes().get("email");
        String strlabel=(String)getAttributes().get("label");
        writer.startElement("a", this);
        if(stremail !=null)
        {
            writer.writeAttribute("href", "mailto:"+stremail,
"email");
            writer.writeText(strlabel, "label");
        }
        else
            writer.writeText("Sorry no email specified",null);
            writer.endElement("a");
    }
    public void setEmail(String email) {
        this.email = email;
    }
    public String getEmail() {
        return email;
    }
    public void setLabel(String label) {
        this.label = label;
    }
}
```

```
    public String getLabel() {
        return label;
    }
}
```

JSF components consist of two parts: the component and the renderer. The JSF component class defines the state and behaviour of a UI component and a renderer defines how the component will be displayed. That is, renderer converts the values of the component to the appropriate markup.

Note: All UI components descend from the `javax.faces.component.UIComponent` abstract base class.

UI components are grouped into different families. Families help renderers decide how to handle a particular component. `getFamily()` method is actually required for UI components that extend `UIComponentBase` since it could come from any component family. Since in our example we won't be creating a new family of components, we can just return any string value or just null. Also, one of the following methods are overrided.

```
public void encodeBegin(FacesContext context) throws IOException;
```

Encode methods are for displaying the component and we begin encoding only if the rendered property is true. This method simply renders an HTML (a) with the custom message supplied. The `encodeBegin` actually renders the beginning tag. This method has an argument: `FacesContext`. An extension to the servlet and JSP context, the FacesContext provides access to the many useful objects for `JSF/JSP/Servlet` development. Here, we simply extract a "writer" object in order to "write" our rendered response back to the client.

We first retrieve a `ResponseWriter` instance from a FacesContext in order to display data as it has several methods for generating markup.

Next we get the values of the two attributes "email" and "label" which are passed from the tag from our JSP page using the method `getAttributes()`. The `getAttributes` method comes from the `UIComponentBase` class which is the base class for all UI components:

```
String stremail=(String)getAttributes().get("email");
String strlabel=(String)getAttributes().get("label");
```

When the attribute (label) or "property" is written to the client, an additional string value representing the name of the property "label" is also included as an argument to the `writeText()` method. The idea behind this is to provide development tools environments the ability to display the name of the property in a visual editor. We can also set the second argument as null.

```
writer.writeText(strlabel, "label");
```

Registering the custom UI component in *faces-config.xml*

Before moving on to building a JSP tag handler and a TLD file, we'll add a required entry for our custom component in the `faces-config.xml` file.

Expand the node of our project: `EmailComp` and right click on `faces-config.xml` node and select Edit option (Figure 10.26).

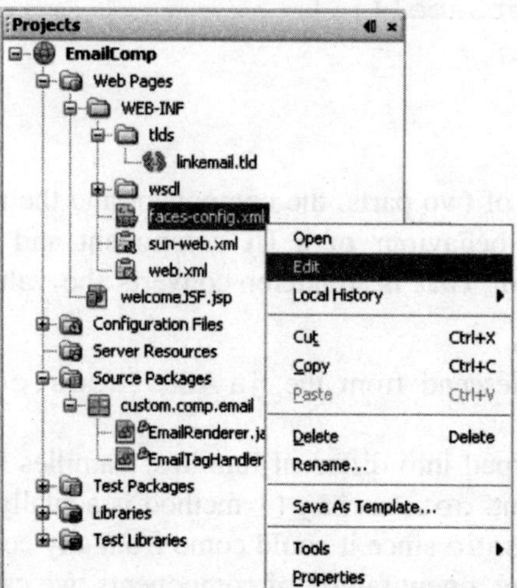

Figure 10.26   Selection of Edit option.

Type the following contents in `faces-config.xml` file:

```xml
<?xml version='1.0' encoding='UTF-8'?>
<!-- ====== FULL CONFIGURATION FILE =============================== -->
<faces-config version="1.2"
    xmlns="http://java.sun.com/xml/ns/javaee"
    xmlns:xsi="http://www.w3.org/2001/XMLSchema-instance"
    xsi:schemaLocation="http://java.sun.com/xml/ns/javaee
    http://java.sun.com/xml/ns/javaee/web-facesconfig_1_2.xsd">

    <component>
        <component-type>custom.comp.email </component-type>
        <component-class>custom.comp.email.EmailRenderer
        </component-class>
        <property>
            <property-name>email</property-name>
            <property-class>String</property-class>
        </property>
        <property>
            <property-name>label</property-name>
            <property-class>String</property-class>
        </property>
    </component>
</faces-config>
```

Every component has a type and it is the name by which the component will be referenced. We define component type with the help of `<component-type>` element. The `<component-class>` element specifies the name of the implementation class.

The `<property-name>` element is used for specifying the name of the attribute used with our custom component and `<property-class>` element is for defining the data type of the attribute.

Building a custom JSP tag library

In order to be able to use our custom component in a JSP, we need a custom tag library comprised of a Tag Library Descriptor (TLD) file along with references to taghandlers classes.

Building the Tag Handler

For JSF component development, the JSP taghandler class is derived from `javax.faces.webapp.UIComponentTag`. Its main purpose is to:

1. Associate a JSP callable tag (handler class) with the UI component.
2. Associate a separate renderer class (if needed) to the UI component.
3. Set the properties from the submitted tag attribute values to the UI component.

Double click on `EmailTagHandler.java` node under Source Packages node to open the `EmailTagHandler` file and set its contents as follows:

EmailTagHandler.java

```java
package custom.comp.email;
import javax.faces.component.UIComponent;
import javax.faces.webapp.UIComponentTag;

public class EmailTagHandler extends UIComponentTag {
    private String email = null;
    private String label = null;
    public String getComponentType() {
        return "custom.comp.email";
    }
    public String getRendererType() {
        return null;
    }
    public void setEmail(String email) {
        this.email = email;
    }
    public String getEmail() {
        return email;
    }
    public void setLabel(String label) {
        this.label = label;
    }
    public String getLabel() {
        return label;
    }
```

```
    protected void setProperties(UIComponent component) {
        super.setProperties(component);
        EmailRenderer eml = (EmailRenderer) component;
        if(null != email){
            eml.setEmail(email);
        }
        if(null != label){
            eml.setLabel(label);
        }
    }
    public void release() {
        email = null;
        label = null;
        super.release();
    }
}
```

We can see in above coding that "`email`" and "`label`" property is defined of type string and their getter and setter methods are also specified in the class.

JSF provides two abstract base classes we can use for writing JSP component tags:

- `UIComponentTag`
- `UIComponentBodyTag`

We usually subclass `UIComponentTag` directly and if we need to process the body of the tag, we need to subclass `UIComponentBodyTag`. Beside subclassing either of the above base class, we need to declare the tag inside an `XML file: tld file` which defines a set of tags.

So, to create a new component tag, we can subclass `javax.faces.webapp.` `UIComponentTag` and associate it with a `component/renderer` pair by overriding two read only properties: `componentType` and `rendererType`.

These two methods associate the tag handler with our registered UI component: "`custom.comp.label`" as well as associate the renderer.

`UIComponentTag` defines the component-Type property as:

```
    public abstract String getComponentType();
```

Example:

```
    public String getComponentType() {
        return "custom.comp.email";
    }
```

We return a string representing the component's type. It basically associates the component class with component type.

Note: A component can be associated with many different tags. In addition to specifying the component type, we must specify the renderer type by overriding the `rendererType` property:

```
public abstract String getRendererType();
```

This property is a string that maps to a specific renderer type. Since we don't have a separate renderer class, this statement returns a null value.

Example:

```
public String getRendererType() {
    return null;
}
```

But, if rendering has to be done by some renderer, we have to specify its value.

Example:

```
public String getRendererType() {
    return COMPONENT_RENDERER_TYPE;
}
```

The method `setProperties()`, sets the incoming values from the JSP tag by first calling the parent class' `setProperties` method along with custom code to set the value from the email tag attribute. Tag handlers can also have properties which are exposed as element attributes.

The attribute `email` maps to a String property of the `EmailTaghandler` class. `EmailTagHandler` must map the email property to an attribute or property of email component. Similarly, the label property is also mapped to an attribute of email component

Note: `UIComponentTag` supports a few basic component properties by default: id, `renderType` and renderer. If the customer component does not add any properties and the associated renderer doesn't require any special attributes, then there is no need to override any other method.

If our custom component has its own properties, we also need to override the `setProperties` method:

```
protected void setProperties(UIComponent component);
```

In this method, we map properties of our tag class to properties or attributes of the component. But while implementing this method, we call the superclass's implementation otherwise the basic component properties like `rendererType` and renderer will not be updated properly. Beside this, for each property or attribute, we have to:

1. Add the property to the tag handler class
2. Associate the tag handler property with the appropriate component property or attribute in the `setProperties` method

For example our email component has email property, we expose it as properties of the `EmailTagHandler` class:

```
public void setEmail(String email) {
    this.email = email;
}
public String getEmail() {
    return email;
}
```

Same thing we do for the label property also.

Now, associate the taghandler property with the component property:

```
EmailRenderer eml = (EmailRenderer) component;
if(null != email){
    eml.setEmail(email);
}
```

Repeat the same for label property also

As, we can see that we first check that if the `EmailTagHandler`'s email property is not null, we set the component's email property to be equal to the `EmailTagHandler`'s email property. In short, `setProperties` method is used to set the component properties or attributes based on the properties of the tag handler class.

In order to add properties to the `labelTagHandler`, we have to override the release method:

```
public void release()
```

In this method, we release the resources that we have allocated as it is the standard method of the `javax.servlet.jsp.tagext.Tag` interface which `UIComponentTag` implements and is called before the tag is garbage collected.

```
public void release() {
    email = null;
    label = null;
    super.release();
}
```

As, we can see in above method, we are setting the instance variables (email and label) for the tag's properties to null.

In order for us to use our custom JSP tag handler class, we need to create an associated TLD file which contains the tag entry associated with the tag handler class. Here is an example of the TLD file needed for this tag. The TLD associates the tag name, "`linkemail`" with the tag class "`custom.comp.emaill.EmailTagHandler`" along with its associated attributes.

Double click on `linkemail.tld` file and we find its contents as follows:

linkemail.tld

```
<?xml version="1.0" encoding="UTF-8"?>
<taglib version="2.0" xmlns="http://java.sun.com/xml/ns/j2ee"
xmlns:xsi="http://www.w3.org/2001/XMLSchema-instance"
xsi:schemaLocation="http://java.sun.com/xml/ns/j2ee web-
jsptaglibrary_2_0.xsd">
  <tlib-version>1.0</tlib-version>
  <short-name>linkemail</short-name>
  <uri>/WEB-INF/tlds/linkemail</uri>
<tag>
```

```
        <name>linkemail</name>
        <tag-class>custom.comp.email.EmailTagHandler</tag-class>
        <body-content>scriptless</body-content>
        <attribute>
            <name>email</name>
            <rtexprvalue>true</rtexprvalue>
            <type>java.lang.String</type>
        </attribute>
        <attribute>
            <name>label</name>
            <rtexprvalue>true</rtexprvalue>
            <type>java.lang.String</type>
        </attribute>
    </tag>
</taglib>
```

JSP custom tags are grouped into tag libraries through a TLD file which is an XML file located usually in `WEB-INF/lib` folder in a web application. It simply maps a custom tag handler class to a JSP tag and declares which properties should be exposed as JSP tag attributes.

All TLD files start with the library's description. The most important is `<uri>` node:

```
<uri>/WEB-INF/tlds/linkemail</uri>
```

which has to be included in JSP file which is supposed to use the custom component. Then comes is the tag descriptions which maps a tag name to a tag handler class and also describes each valid attribute.

After the tag handler is registered with a tag library, we can use our custom component in a JSP file by following statement:

```
<em:linkemail email="bmharwani@yahoo.com" label="bmharwani" />
```

To use the custom component, double click on `welcomeJSF` file and include the following taglib directives in the page:

```
<%@taglib uri="/WEB-INF/tlds/linkemail" prefix="em" %>
```

and then use the component with following statement:

```
<em:linkemail email="bmharwani@yahoo.com" label="bmharwani" />
```

welcomeJSF.jsp

```
<%@page contentType="text/html"%>
<%@page pageEncoding="UTF-8"%>
<%@taglib prefix="f" uri="http://java.sun.com/jsf/core"%>
<%@taglib prefix="h" uri="http://java.sun.com/jsf/html"%>
<%@taglib uri="/WEB-INF/tlds/linkemail" prefix="em" %>

<!DOCTYPE HTML PUBLIC "-//W3C//DTD HTML 4.01 Transitional//EN"
  "http://www.w3.org/TR/html4/loose.dtd">
```

```
<html>
    <head>
        <meta http-equiv="Content-Type" content="text/html;
            charset=UTF-8">
        <title>Custom Component</title>
    </head>
    <body>
        <f:view>
            <em:linkemail email="bmharwani@yahoo.com"
label="bmharwani" />
        </f:view>
    </body>
</html>
```

Run the application, we get a link for the email as shown in Figure 10.27.

Figure 10.27   Link for the email.

If we select the link, Outlook express will get open to do email (Figure 10.28).

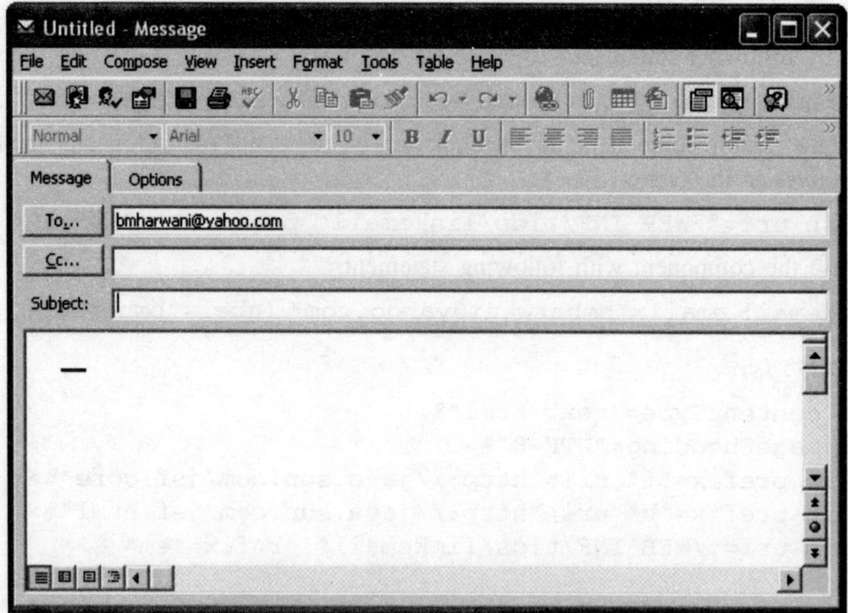

Figure 10.28   Outlook express will open.

SUMMARY

We have learnt how to create two custom components: custom label component and email component. Label component is for displaying different messages, whereas the email component displays a link which when selected invokes the outlook express so the user can send email.

REVIEW QUESTION

10.1 Write down all the steps to create a custom component that appears in the form of a link which when selected navigates us to the desired web page.

11

AJAX with RichFaces Using JBoss

LEARNING OBJECTIVES

In this chapter, we will learn:

- What is AJAX
- Installation of softwares required to apply AJAX in JSF like: JBoss, Eclipse, RichFaces, Ajax4Jsf, etc.
- Making RichFaces application
- Making Ajax4Jsf based application

AJAX BASICS

AJAX stands for Asynchronous JavaScript and XML. Usually in a traditional web application, when we want to access certain data from the database on server, an HTTP request from client is made to the server either in GET or POST method. After receiving the data from server, the web page needs to be *reloaded* to show the fetched data. Whereas in AJAX technology we can request and receive the data from server in background and can display it on the page without a reload.

With AJAX, JavaScript communicates directly with the server, through the JavaScript XMLHttpRequest object (XML over HTTP) and it is with the help of this object that a web page can make a request to, and get a response from a web server without reloading the page.

A traditional web page takes a longer time to get the desired results because of the *round trip*. Round trip means, all the information entered by the user on the form is sent from the client to the web server. The web server processes the data and the desired information is sent back to the client. Even if small changes are made in the form, still the whole data on the form is sent to the web server and the entire page is refreshed. In a traditional web application, we do not have any facility to refresh only a small portion of the web page instead the complete page is refreshed which is very time consuming.

In Figure 11.1 we can clearly see the three steps of communication performed in the traditional web application model:

1. Client makes an HTTP Request to the Web Server.
2. The Web Server searches for the desired data from the database, and
3. The fetched data (from the database) is sent back (postback) to the client (whole page is reloaded with the new information).

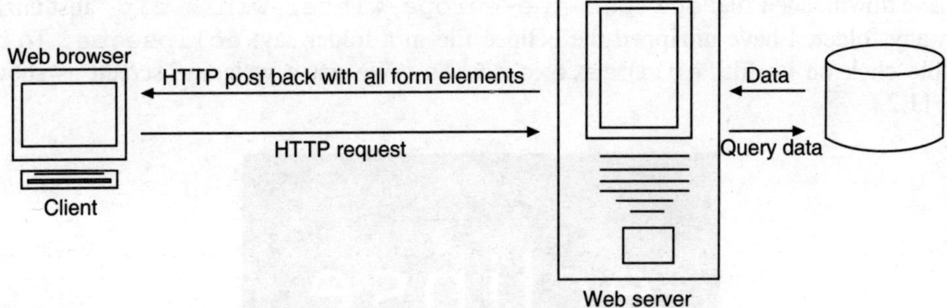

Figure 11.1 Traditional web application model.

To sum up, we face following limitations in a conventional web application:

Limitations of Traditional Web Applications

Whole data of the form is sent to web server, even if small changes are made. Results in network congestion because of large amount of data transferred during a postback. Until and unless user clicks a button or another control that posts data back to the server, no result will be displayed.

In AJAX, A stands for *Asynchronous* and it means getting server response without refreshing the whole page. We can even update a portion of a web page with this technology. So, lets go more deeper understanding what AJAX consists of. With AJAX all the above limitations of traditional web applications are removed as it consists of following items:

- XMLHttpRequest
- JavaScript
- DOM (Document Object Model)
- CSS (Cascading Style Sheets)

To develop JSF applications using RichFaces, we need following files to be downloaded from the net:

- JBoss tools — `JBossTools-2.1.1.GA-ALL-win32.zip`
- RichFaces jar files — `richfaces-ui-3.2.1.GA-bin.zip`
- Ajax4jsf jar files — `ajax4jsf-1.1.1.jar`
- JBoss Server — `JBoss-5.0.0.Beta4.zip`
- Eclipse — I have downloaded file: `eclipse-jee-europa-winter-win32.zip`

Just unzip the files in four different folders.

Installing Eclipse

Eclipse is an open source stack of developer tools that includes a widely used Java IDE and a developer tools plug-in framework heavily used in the software industry. Eclipse Europa is the new version of Eclipse's open source framework and components involving 17 million lines of code.

I have downloaded file: `eclipse-jee-europa-winter-win32.zip`. Just unzip the files in any folder. I have unzipped the eclipse file in a folder say: `eclipsejee`. To install it, double click on its file: `eclipse.exe  file`. We get a welcome screen as shown in Figure 11.2.

Figure 11.2   Welcome screen.

Eclipse asks for a workspace before beginning with any web project. It is a folder where all the configuration settings for the web project are placed. The workspace folder is used as the default content area for our project. We can provide any directory name (directory will be automatically created if it does not exist) (Figure 11.3).

Figure 11.3   Enter the directory name.

Select OK and the workspace will be created.

Since we want to work with AJAX and RichFaces, we need to install its features. We take the help of JBoss tools. But let us first understand what is JBoss tools and its features.

WHAT IS JBOSS TOOLS

JBoss Tools is a set of Eclipse based plugins for JBoss related technology such as Seam, JSF EJB, etc. It has nice functions to build RichFaces JSF pages. So, let us unzip its file: `JBossTools-2.1.1.GA-ALL-win32.zip` to any folder.

To install JBoss Tools in Eclipse, Select `Help->Software  Updates->Find` and Install option (Figure 11.4).

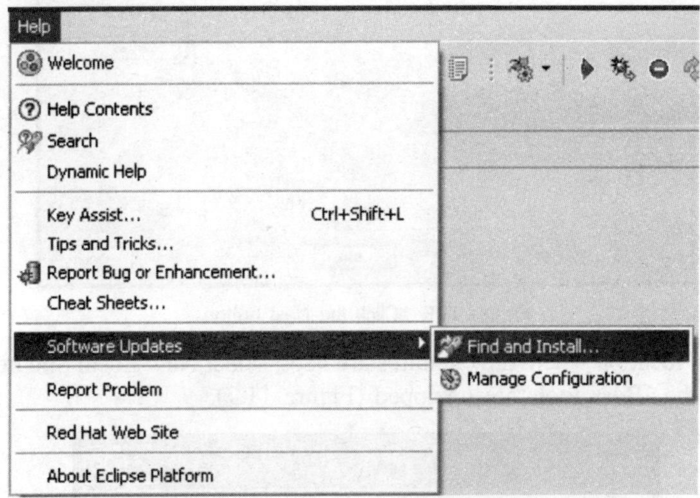

Figure 11.4   Selection of find and Install option.

Select the option: Search for new features to install (Figure 11.5).

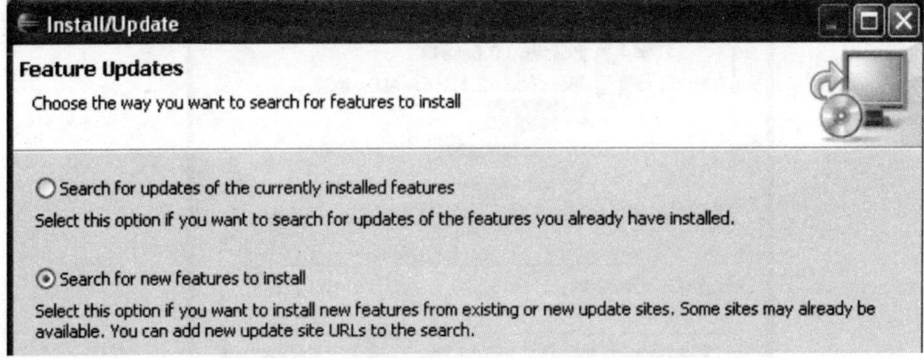

Figure 11.5   Selection of new features to install.

After selecting the above given option, click Next button (Figure 11.6).

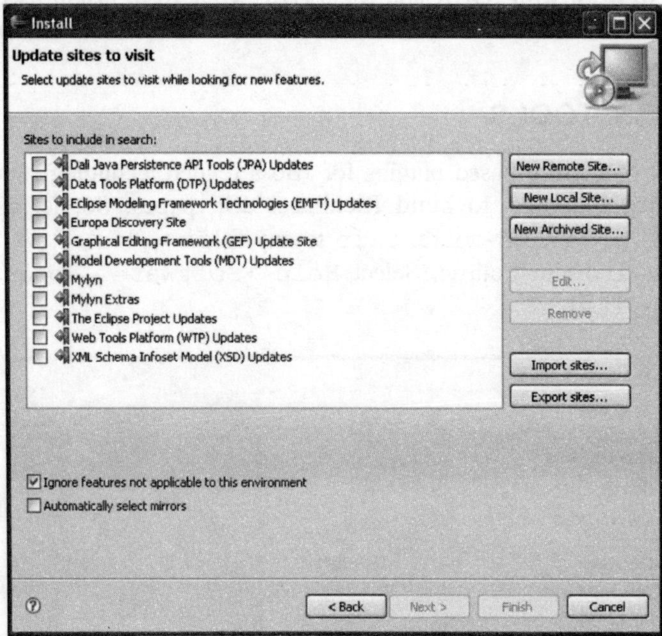

Figure 11.6 Click the Next button.

To specify the location where new features are kept, select New Local Site button and select the folder where the JBoss tools are unzipped (Figure 11.7).

Figure 11.7 Selection of folder where JBoss tools are unzipped.

After specifying the folder, select OK button (Figure 11.8).

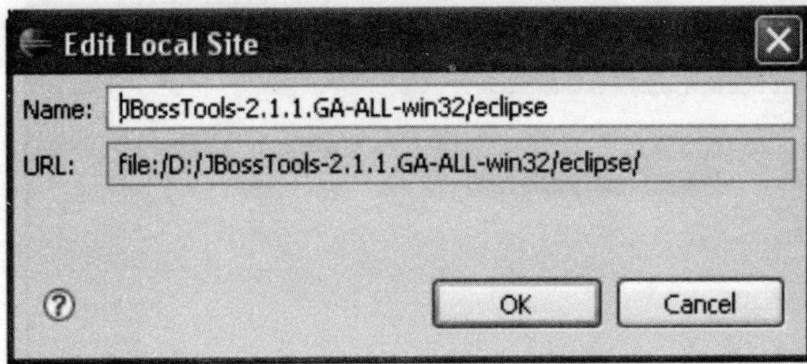

Figure 11.8　Selection of OK button.

We find that JBoss Tools checkbox is selected (Figure 11.9).

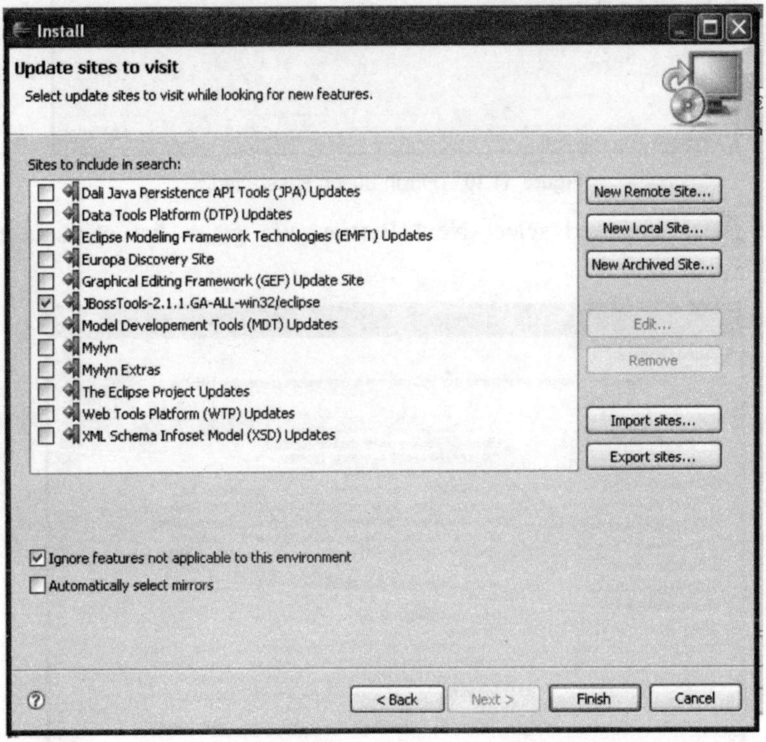

Figure 11.9　JBoss Tools are selected.

Select Finish button (Figure 11.10).

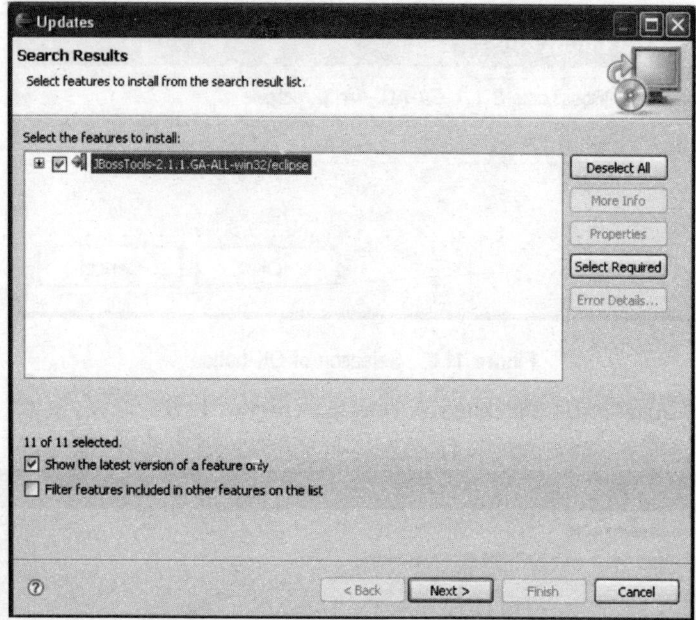

Figure 11.10   Finish button is selected.

Select the check box and select Next Button. We get a list of features to install (Figure 11.11).

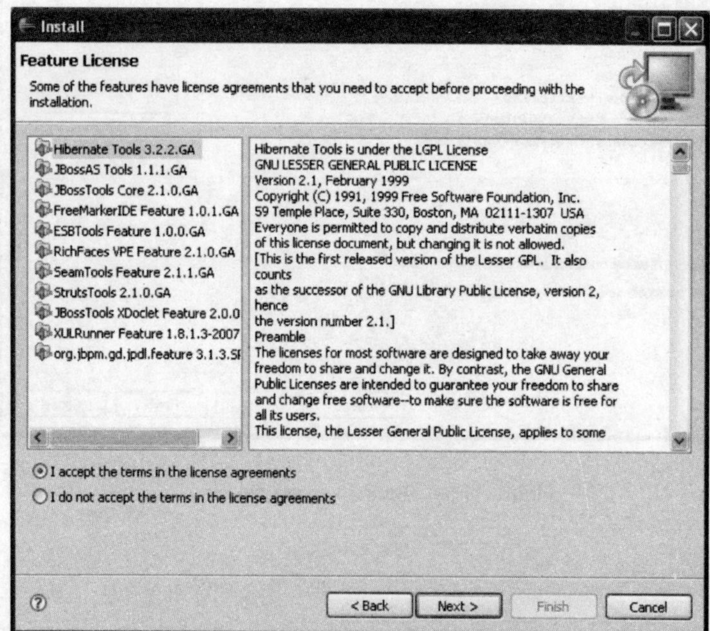

Figure 11.11   List of features for installation.

Accept the license terms and agreements and select Next button (Figure 11.12).

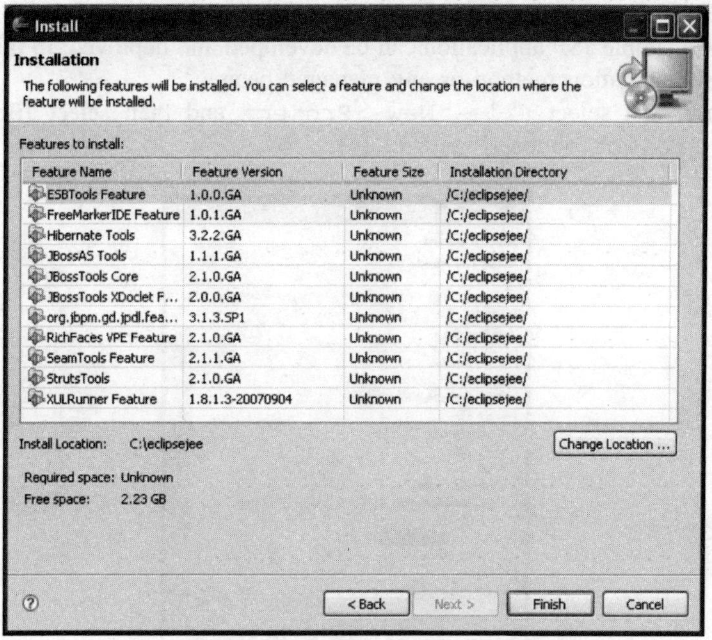

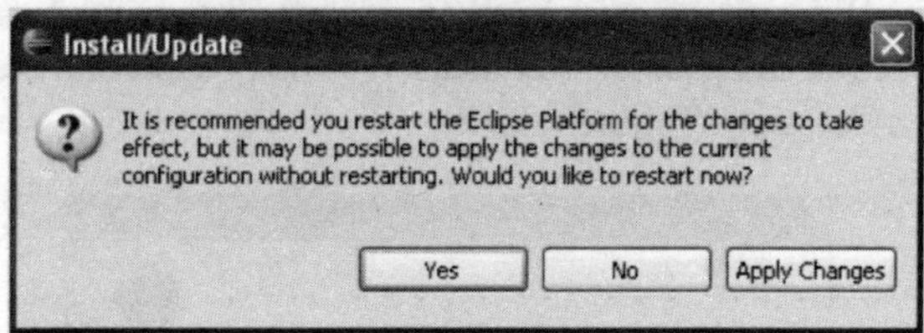

Figure 11.12　Accepting the terms & agreements.

Select Finish button and all the plugins will be installed. Eclipse requires a restart to utilize the plugins. Select Yes button to restart the computer (Figure 11.13).

Figure 11.13　Selection of Yes button to restart the computer.

JBoss Tools is installed.
Now, we need to unzip JBoss Server files.

WHAT IS JBOSS SERVER

JBoss Server is a next generation of the JBoss Application Server build on top of JBoss Microcontainer. JBoss Microcontainer is a lightweight container for managing and deploying POJOs. It provides the full range of J2EE 1.4 features as well as extended enterprise services including clustering, caching and persistence. Let us unzip its file: `JBoss-5.0.0.Beta4.zip` to any folder.

Now, we are ready to develop JSF projects in Eclipse.

First Application

This is a simple application that just displays a welcome message to the user. The idea is to understand how a simple JSF application can be developed and deployed. In this application we will not use any navigation method or any managed bean.

Start Eclipse, and select `File->New->Project` and then select JBoss Tools `Web->JSF->JSF Project` option (Figure 11.14).

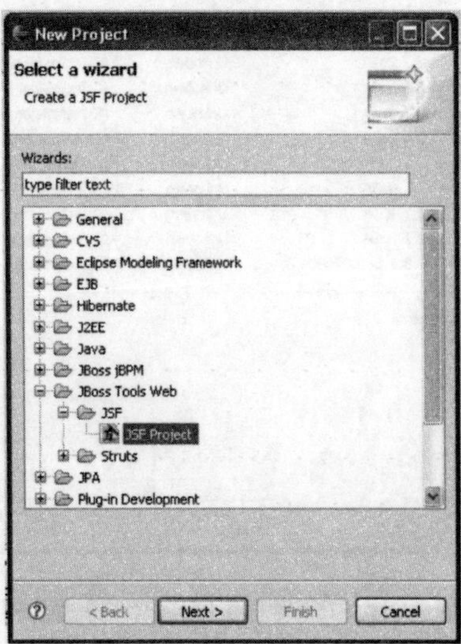

Figure 11.14   Selection of JSF Project option.

Select Next button. We will be prompted to specify the project name as well as the JSF implementation to be used in the project. Let us assign the project name as: `demorichfaces1` and use JSF 1.2 implementation (Figure 11.15).

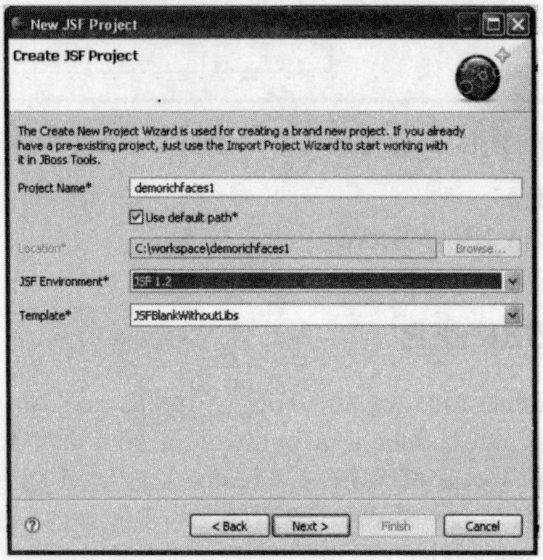

Figure 11.15   Specification of project name.

Leave the template as it is and select Next button. We get a dialog box to specify the Server details. Since we have downloaded the JBoss Server. We specify it by selecting New button of Target Server section (Figure 11.16).

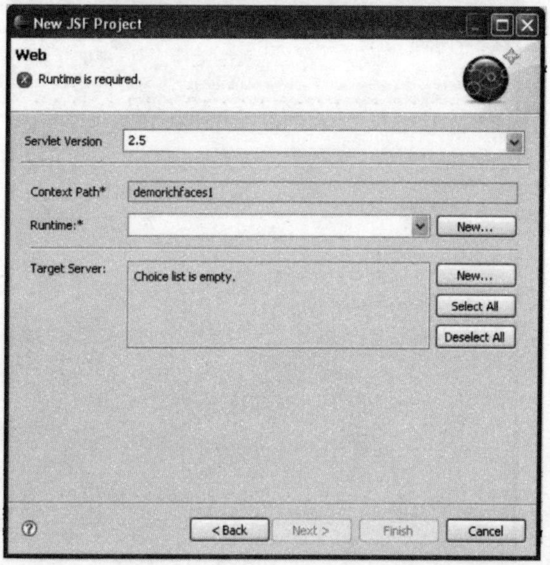

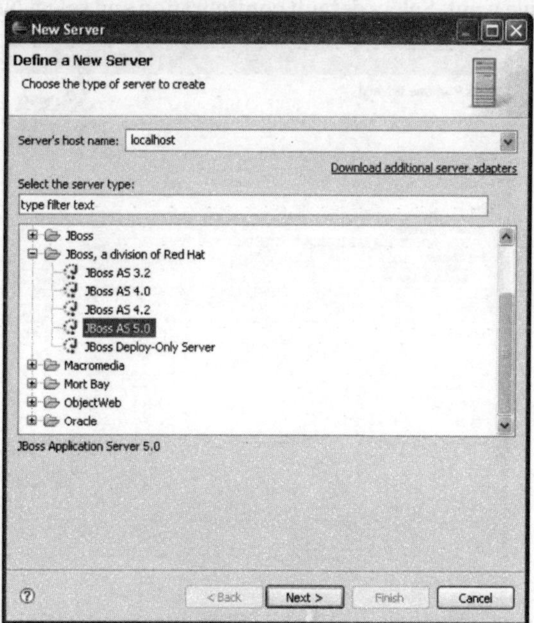

Figure 11.16   Selection of New button of Target Server section.

We get a dialog box to select the server type. Select JBoss AS 5.0 (a server provided by Red Hat—this is what we have downloaded from the net) and select Next button (Figure 11.17).

Figure 11.17   Selection of JBoss AS 5.0 as server.

We will be asked to provide the folder where JBoss Server files are unzipped. Select Browse button to specify that folder (Figure 11.18).

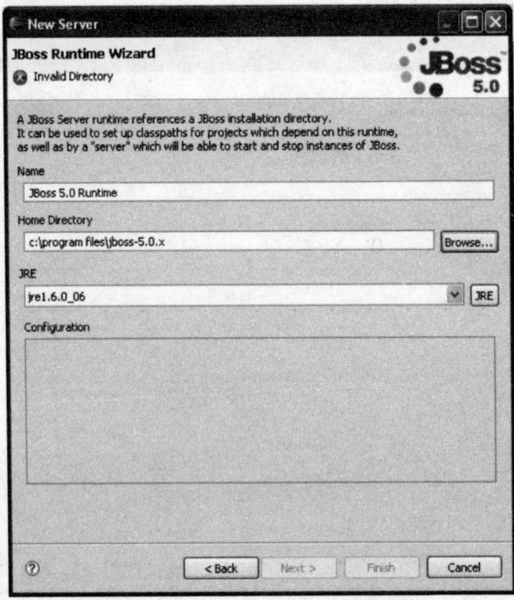

Figure 11.18   Specify the folder name.

Since, we have downloaded the JBoss Server files in `jboss-5.0.0.Beta4` folder of drive C, we select that directory and select Next button. We will be asked to specify the type of configuration of server we want. Select default configuration and select Next button (Figure 11.19).

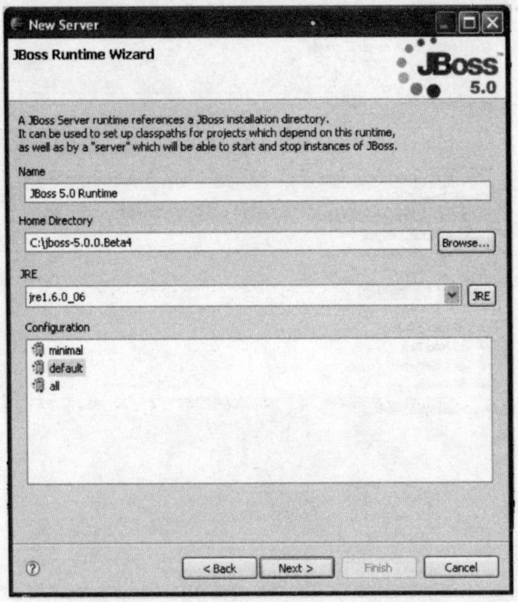

Figure 11.19   Selection of default configuration & select Next button.

We will get a dialog box to specify the login credentials. We do not want to specify any credentials, so will select Next button (Figure 11.20).

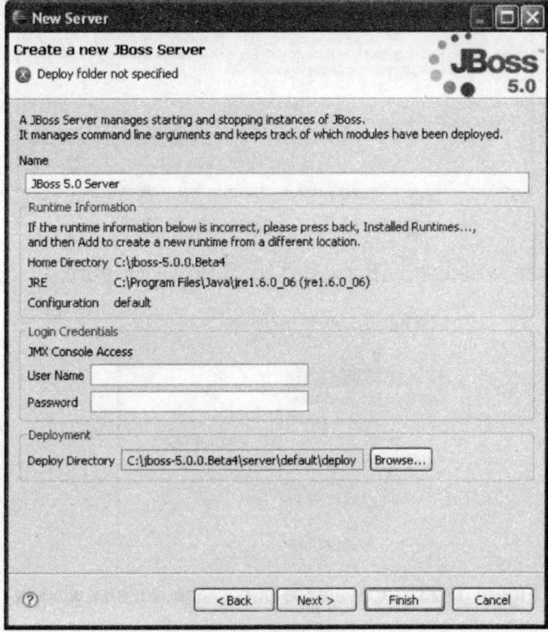

Figure 11.20 Selection of Next button.

We get a screen to confirm the target server selected. If everything is fine, select Finish button (Figure 11.21).

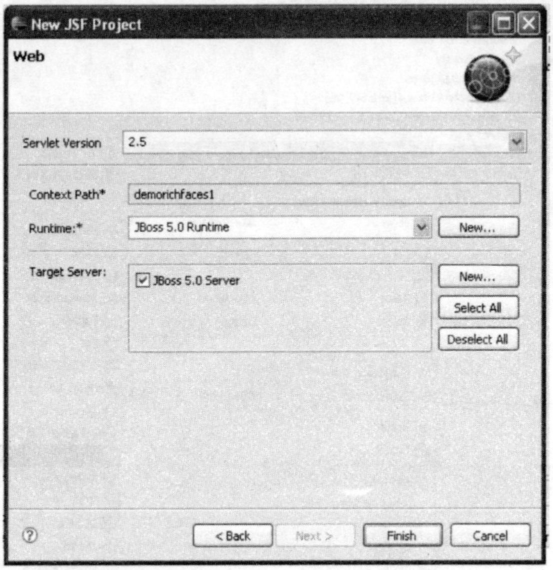

Figure 11.21 Selection of Finish button.

We will be asked to open the web development perspective. Select Yes button (Figure 11.22).

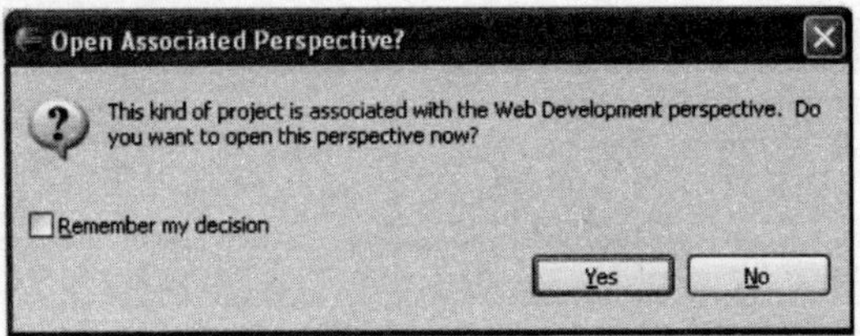

Figure 11.22 Select Yes button.

Our package explorer window will appear as follows (Figure 11.23).

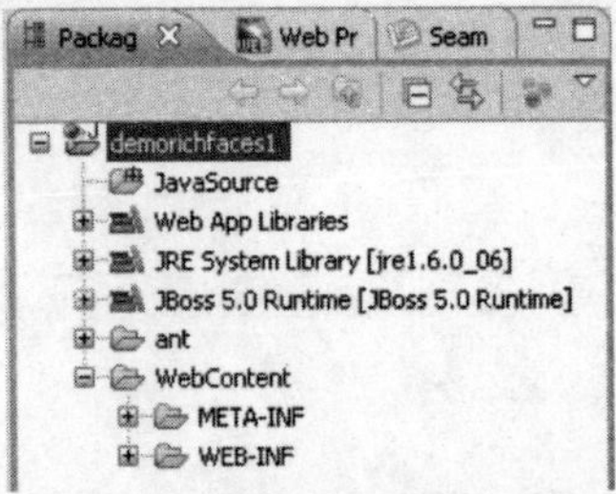

Figure 11.23 Appearance of package explorer window.

Let us add a `index.jsp` file to our web project: `demorichfaces1`. So in the packages explorer window, right click on WebContents node and select `New->JSP File` option (Figure 11.24).

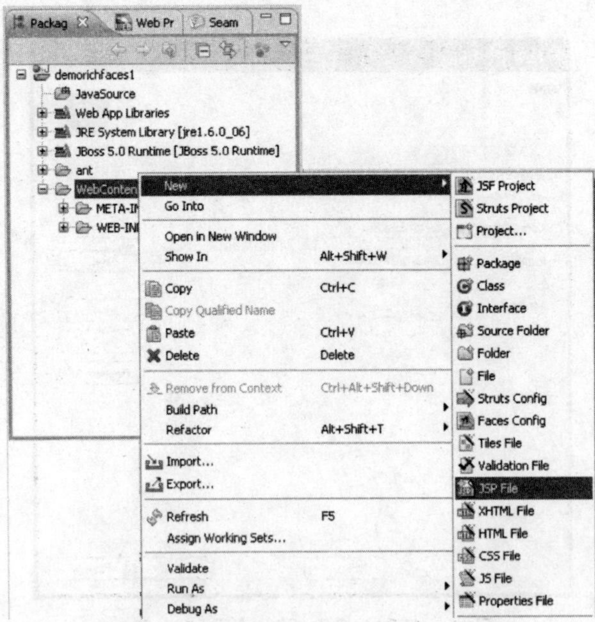

Figure 11.24 Selection of JSP File option.

Specify the file name and the template for the file. The file name we assign is: `index.jsp` and the template we use for our JSF file is: `JSFBasePage`. Then select Next button (Figure 11.25).

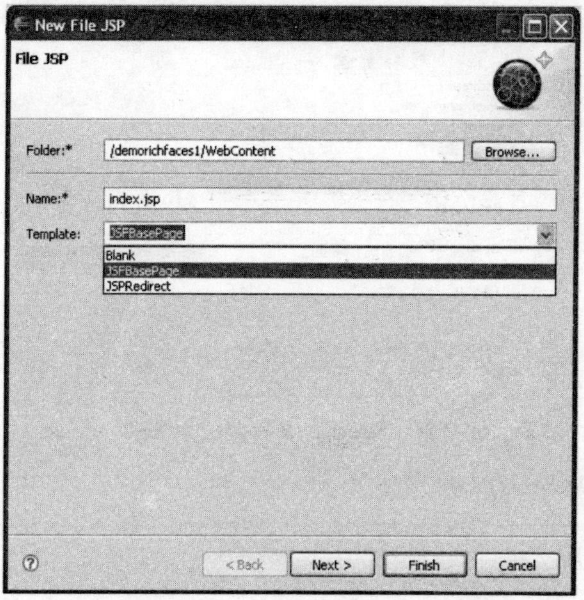

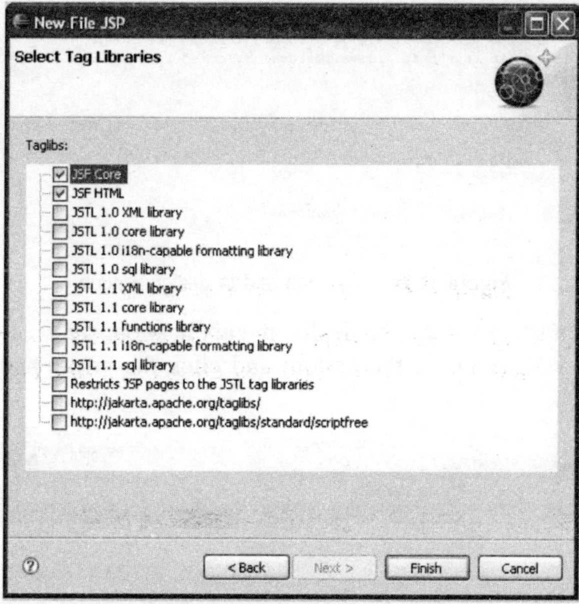

Figure 11.25   Specification of file name & template.

We get a dialog box to include the required tag libraries. Since this is a simple JSF application, we select JSF Core and JSF HTML tag libraries (Figure 11.26).

Figure 11.26   Selection of tag libraries.

On selecting Finish button, we find that `index.jsp` file is made and is opened in JSP Editor (default). We will open the `index.jsp` file in Web Page Editor as it is more comfortable for developing a web page. So, right click on `index.jsp` file in WebContent node and select Open `With->Web Page Editor` option (Figure 11.27).

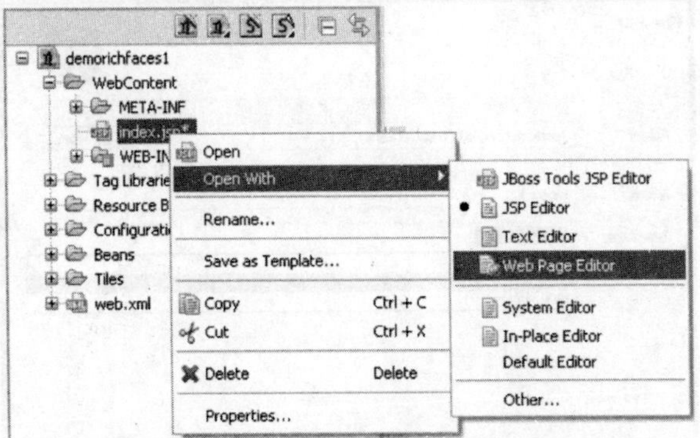

Figure 11.27   Selection of Web Page Editor option.

In the design window, type the text: `Welcome to JBoss RichFaces` (Figure 11.28).

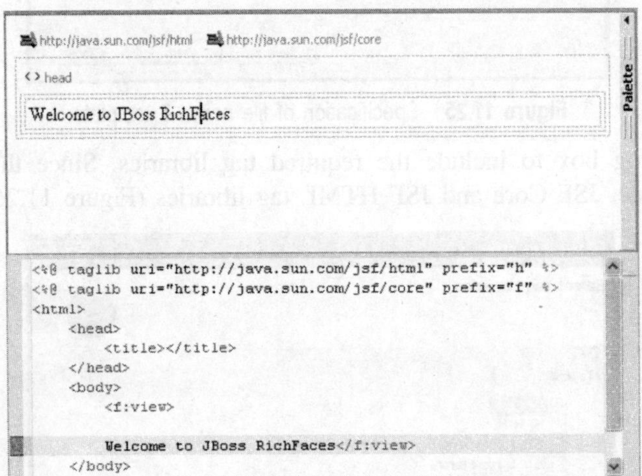

Figure 11.28   Type the text in design window.

The coding is automatically done. To deploy the application, we need to start the server. So, select the JBoss Server View tag at the bottom and click the arrow button to start the JBoss Server (Figure 11.29).

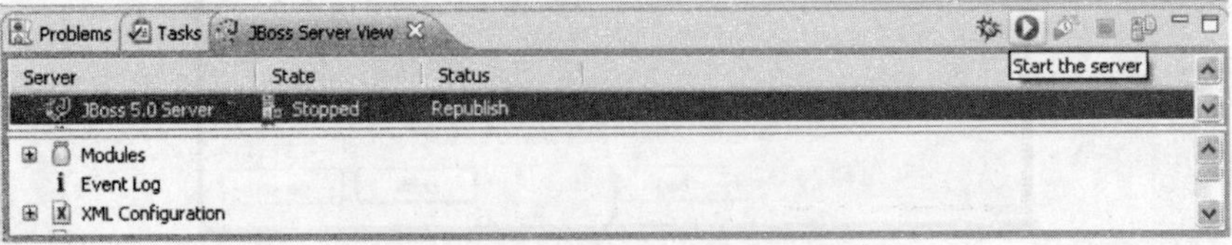

Figure 11.29   Click the arrow button.

We can see the JBoss Server booting in the console window (Figure 11.30).

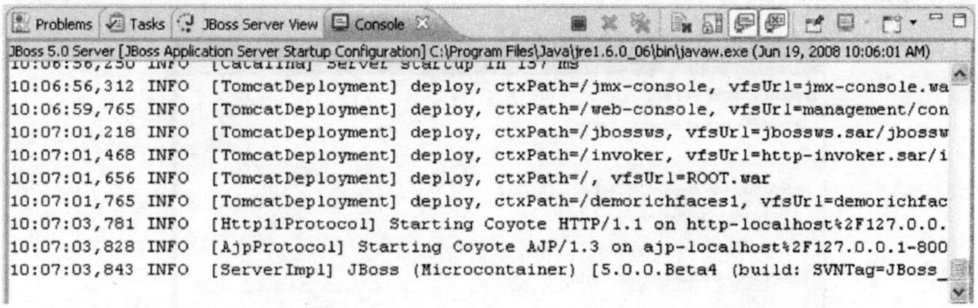

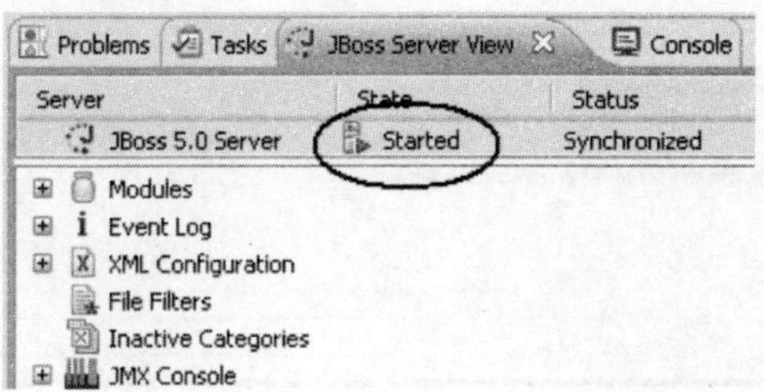

Figure 11.30　Booting of JBoss Server.

The icon designating *Started* in JBoss Server View tag specifies that JBoss is ready to deploy our web application (Figure 11.31).

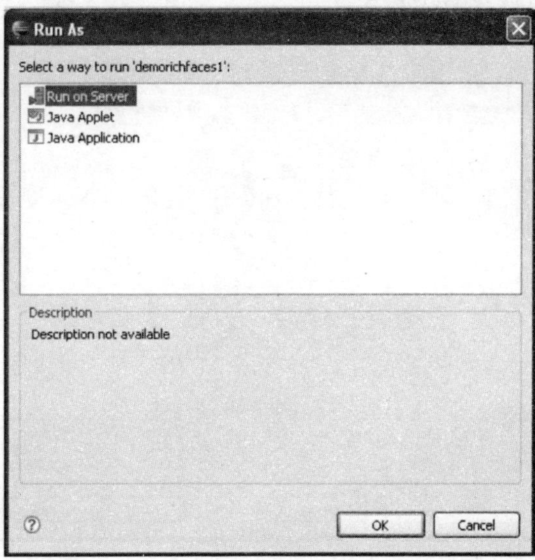

Figure 11.31　JBoss is ready to deploy.

We select the `index.jsp` file in the Web Content node and select the run icon in the toolbar. We get the dialog box asking how to run the application. We select "Run on Server" option (Figure 11.32).

Figure 11.32　Selection of Run on Server option.

Choose OK. We get a dialog box to select the server. We select JBoss Server to deploy our application (Figure 11.33).

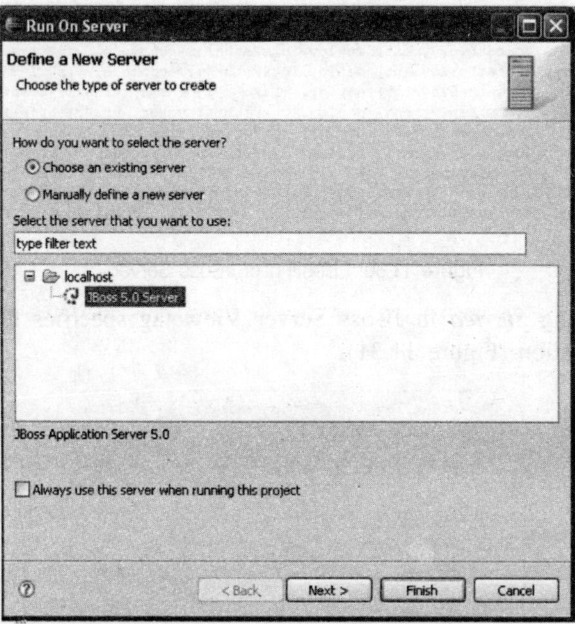

Figure 11.33   Selection of JBoss Server.

Select the web project: `demorichfaces1` and select Finish button (Figure 11.34).

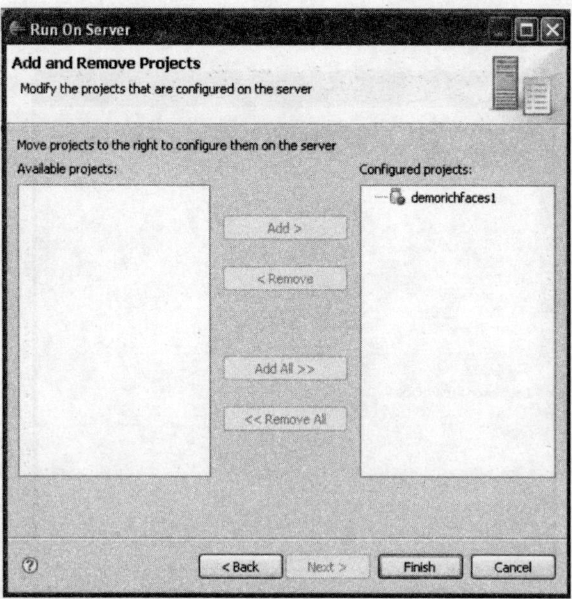

Figure 11.34   Select the web project & select Finish button.

We get the output as shown in Figure 11.35.

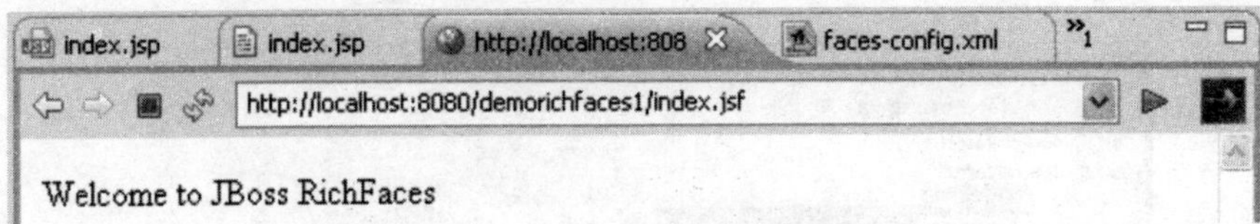

Figure 11.35   Output displayed.

Second Application

In this application, we will make two jsp pages and understand how navigation is performed between them and also how the data is maintained via managed bean.

`Select File->New->Project` and then select JBoss Tools Web->JSF->JSF Project option and select Next button. Specify the project name as: demorichfaces2 and select JSF 1.2 implementation as JSF environment:

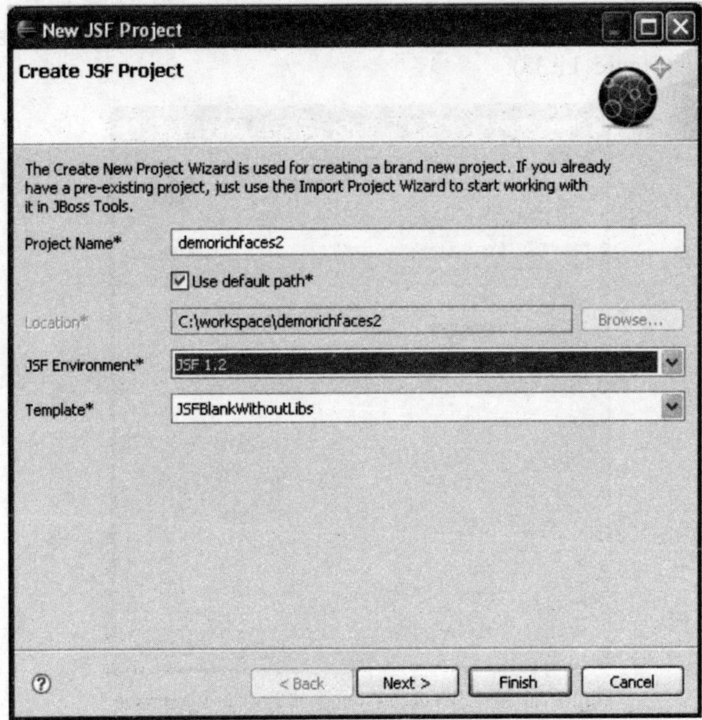

Figure 11.36   Screen for New JSF Project.

Leave the Template as it is and select Next button. We get a dialog box to specify the Server details. Select JBoss AS 5.0 server with default configuration and select Finish button.

Then, add a `index.jsp` file to our web project: `demorichfaces2` by right clicking on WebContents node and select `New->File->JSP` option (Figure 11.37).

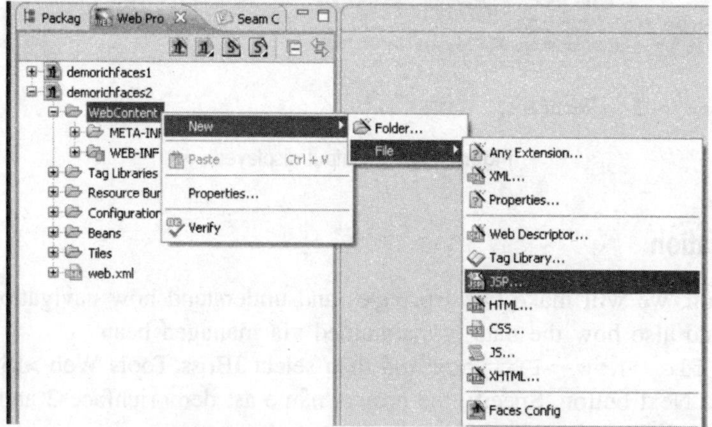

Figure 11.37   Selection of JSP option.

Specify the file name as `index.jsp` and the template for the file as: `JSFBasePage` and select Next button (Figure 11.38).

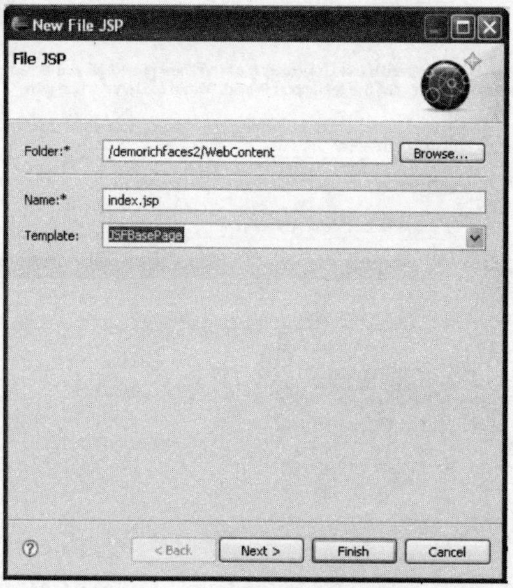

Figure 11.38   Select the name of the file & template.

We get a dialog box to include the required tag libraries. Select JSF Core and JSF HTML tag libraries and select Finish button. Since in this web application, we want to demonstrate how navigation takes place between two jsp pages. We need another jsp file: welcome.jsp. So let us repeat the same procedure to create another jsp file: `welcome.jsp` (Figure 11.39).

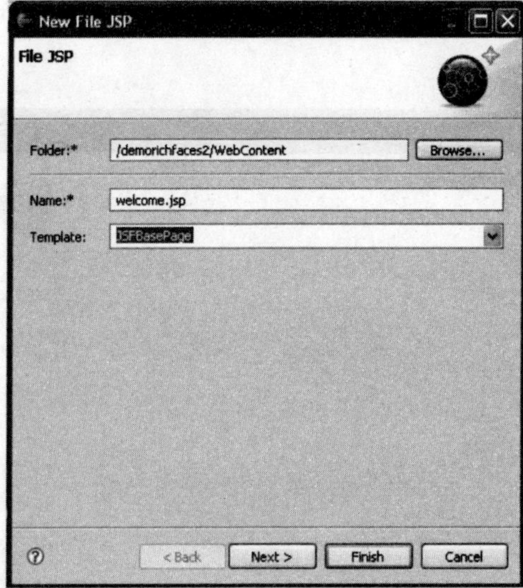

Figure 11.39   Creation of a new file.

To specify navigation from index.jsp page to welcome.jsp page, we make use of the configuration file: faces-config.xml. So double click on its node in web projects window (Figure 11.40).

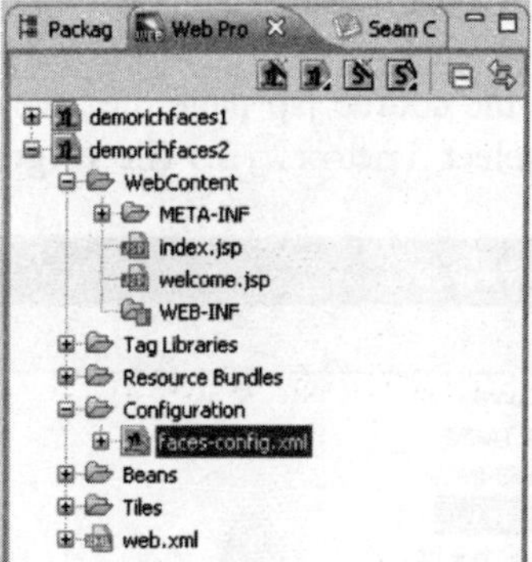

Figure 11.40   Use of configuration file.

The faces-config.xml file can be viewed in three modes: Diagram, Tree and Source. Select Diagram mode (Figure 11.41).

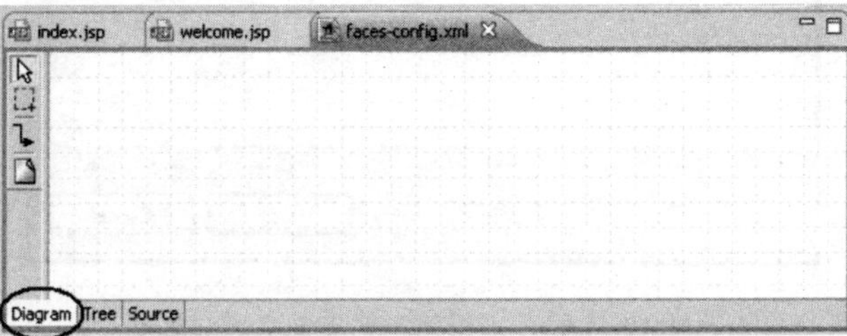

Figure 11.41   Diagram mode of the file.

Right click on the blank space and select New View option from the popup menu that appears (Figure 11.42).

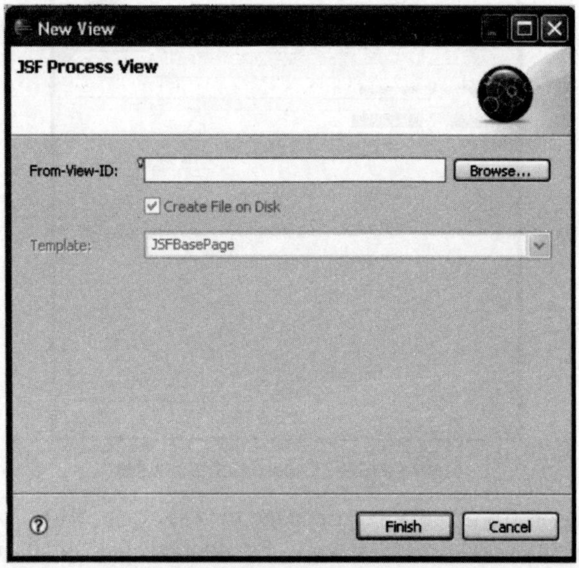

Figure 11.42   Selection of New View option.

We are prompted to specify the source jsp page, i.e., we have to specify: "navigate from" file. Select Browse button and select `index.jsp` file (Figure 11.43).

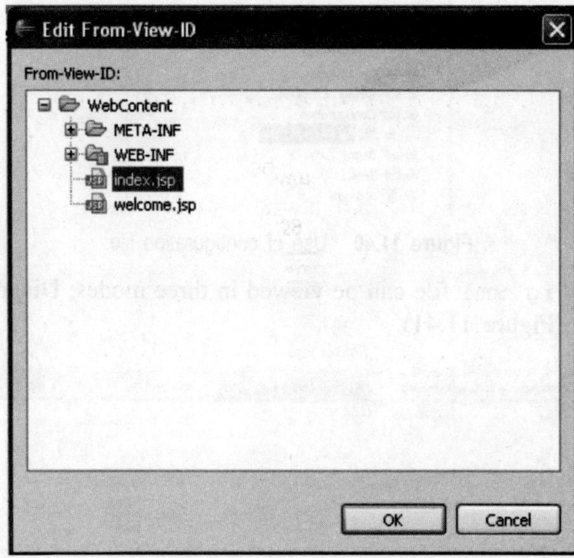

Figure 11.43   Selection of source jsp page.

After selecting the `index.jsp  page`, select OK button (Figure 11.44).

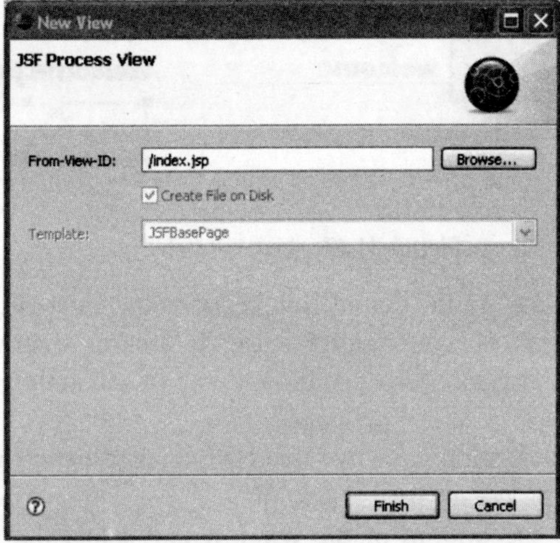

Figure 11.44 Select OK button & then Finish.

Select Finish.

Repeat the same procedure for the `welcome.jsp  page` (Figure 11.45).

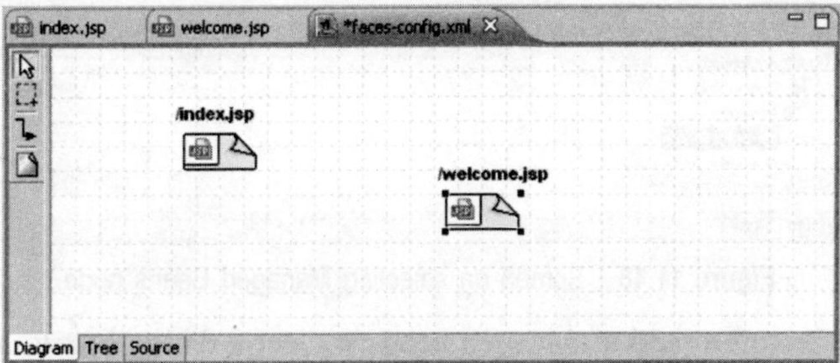

Figure 11.45 Same procedure applied to other file.

To create the connection between the two jsp pages, we make use of the "Create New Connection" tool (Connection is for applying navigation among jsp pages) (Figure 11.46).

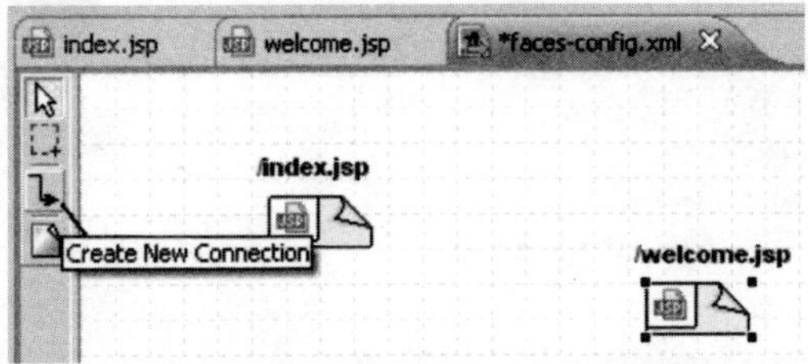

Figure 11.46 Selection of Create New Connection tool.

Click on the Create New Connection tool on the left side, we get an arrow cursor. Click with it on the `index.jsp` page icon and drag it and drop it on the `welcome.jsp` page icon. We get a link created between them (Figure 11.47).

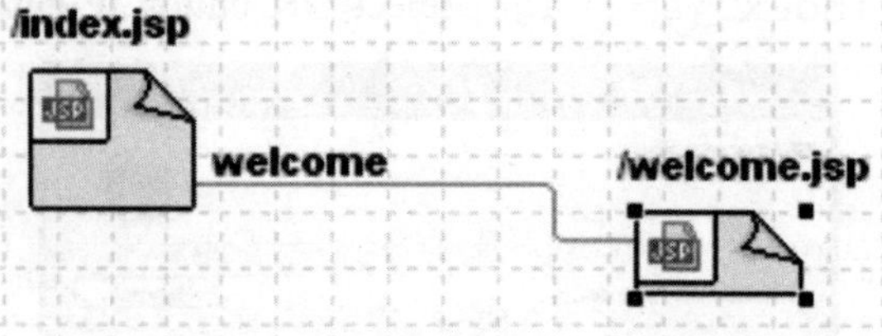

Figure 11.47   Link is established.

Note the word: "welcome" in the connection between the `index.jsp` and `welcome.jsp` page. This word "welcome" is a navigation case. It assures that when the navigation case "welcome" appears in the `index.jsp` (as an outcome of the action on any command button), we will be navigated to `welcome.jsp` page.

After providing the navigation case, we need a managed bean to maintain the information among jsp pages. So, let us create it:

Select the Tree tab at the bottom of the window and select the Managed Beans node, we get a screen as shown in Figure 11.48.

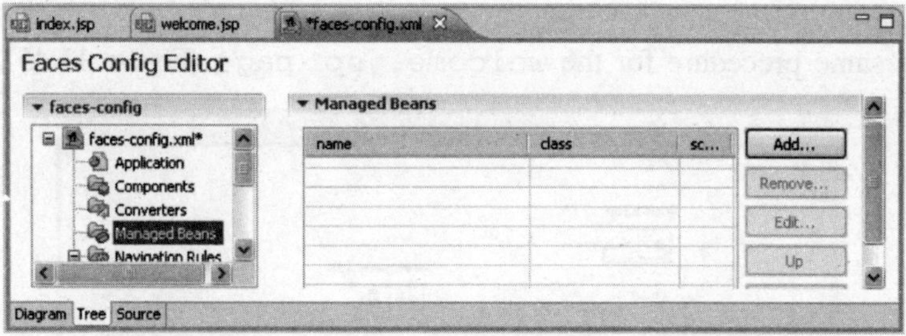

Figure 11.48   Screen on selecting Managed Beans node.

Select the Add button to add a managed bean. We get a dialog box to specify the scope of the managed bean and the name of its Class file and also the name by which it will be referred in the application (Figure 11.49).

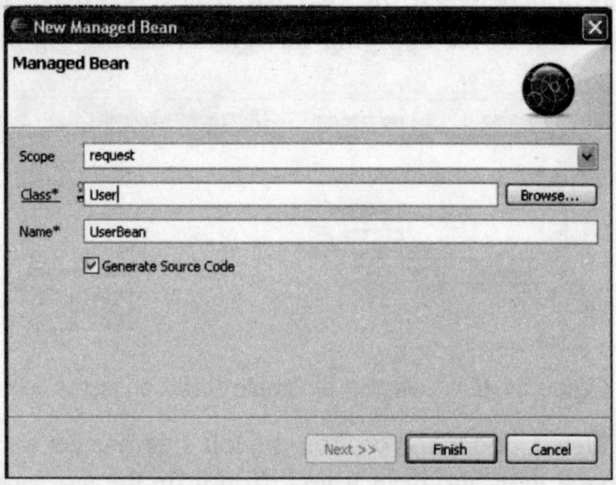

Figure 11.49   Dialog Box to specify the scope, class and name.

After specifying the details of the managed bean as shown above, select Finish button. We find that a managed bean by name: UserBean appears (Figure 11.50).

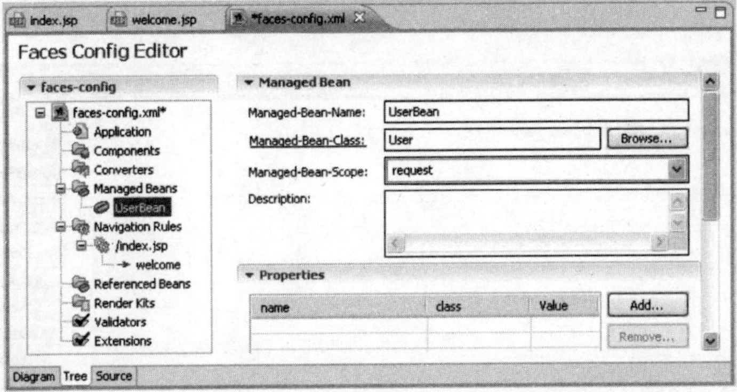

Figure 11.50 Appearance of UserBean.

Select `File->Save All` option to save whatever is done up till now. In order to define attribute for the managed bean, we need to open its class file: User.java (Figure 11.51).

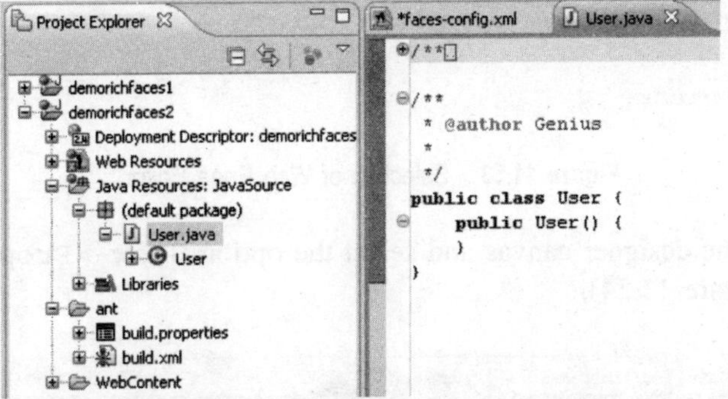

Figure 11.51 Selection of User.java file.

Double click on the `User.java` file under Java Resources node.

In the Java editor that opens up, define an attribute: name of type String below the class declaration and type its contents as shown in Figure 11.52.

```java
public class User {
    String name;

    public User() {
    }

    public String getName(){
        return name;
    }
    public void setName(String name)
    {
        this.name=name;
    }
}
```

Figure 11.52 Typing of contents in the file.

Managed bean is made. Its time to write something in the `index.jsp` page. Right click on the `index.jsp` file and select the option: `Open With->Web Page Editor` (Figure 11.53).

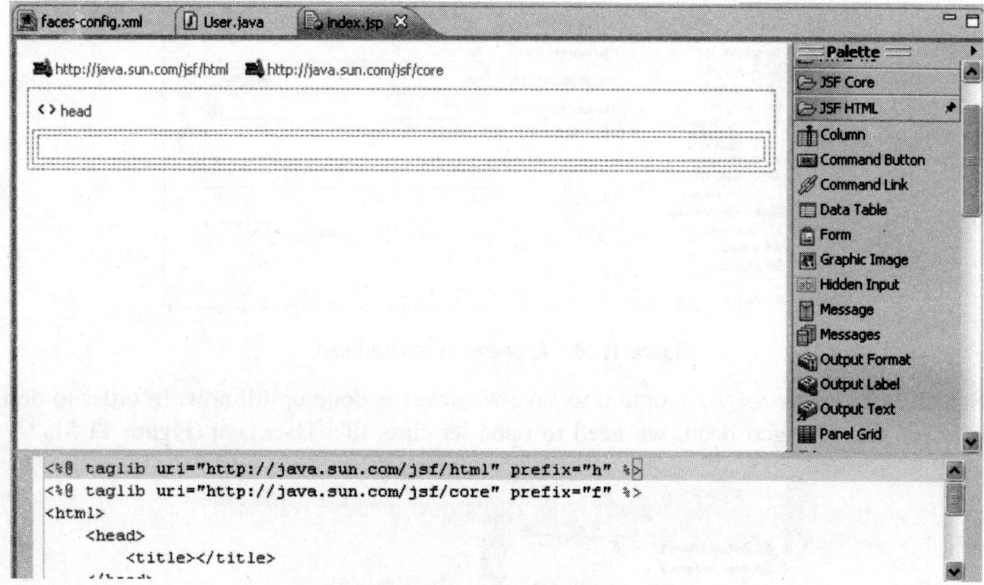

Figure 11.53   Selection of Web Page Editor.

Right click on the designer canvas and select the option `Show->Properties` to get the properties view (Figure 11.54).

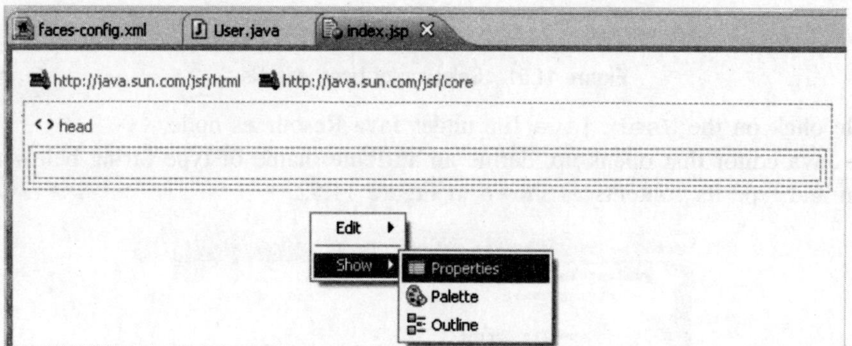

Figure 11.54   Selection of properties view.

From the Palette window, click on the JSF HTML section and drag and drop the Form component on the canvas. Note, the code is automatically generated (Figure 11.55).

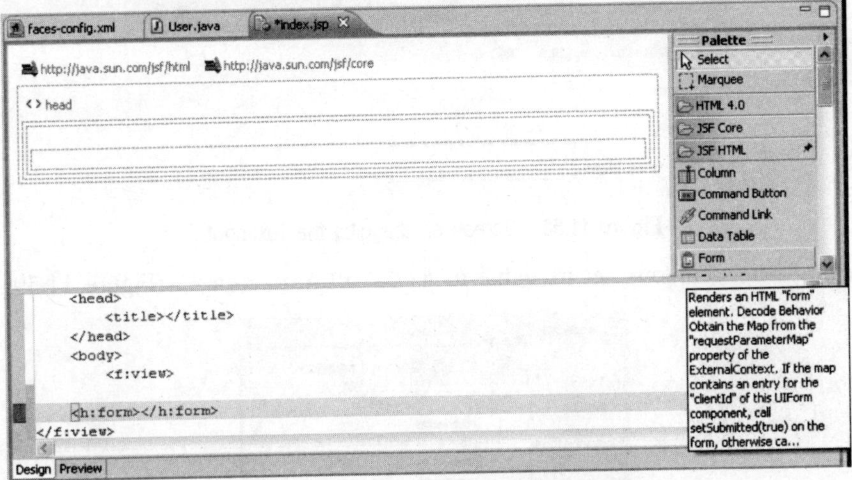

Figure 11.55   Generation of code automatically.

Drag and drop Output Text control in the `<h:form>` tag. Then in the Properties window, set its value to "Enter your Name" as shown in Figure 11.56.

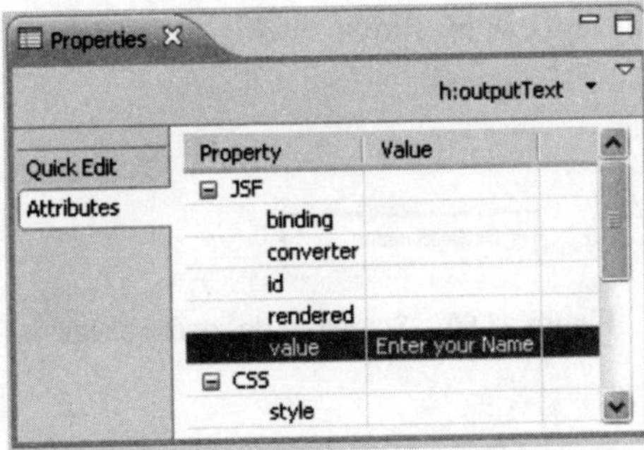

Figure 11.56   Set the Properties window.

We get the following line of code added (Figure 11.57).

```
<h:outputText value="Enter your Name"></h:outputText>
```

Figure 11.57   Addition of line of code.

Drag the component: TextInput and drop it in `<h:form>` after the `h:outputText` tag. We get a screen as shown in Figure 11.58.

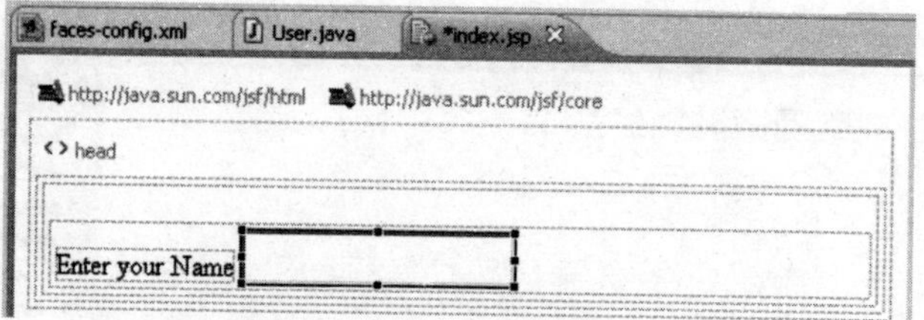

Figure 11.58   Screen on dragging the TextInput.

In the properties window, set its value to `#{UserBean.name}` (Figure 11.59).

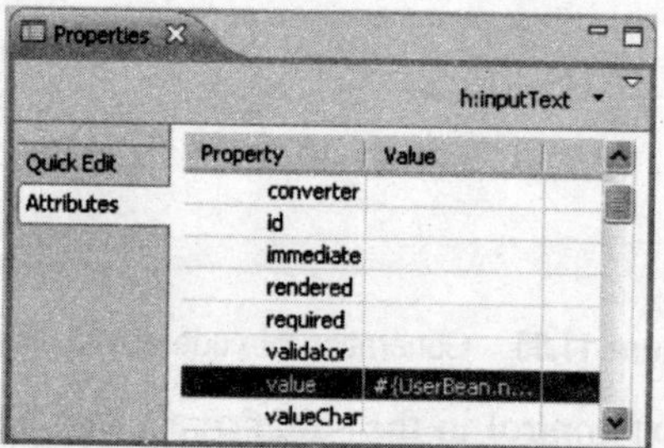

Figure 11.59   Set its value.

The designer canvas may appear as shown in Figure 11.60.

Figure 11.60   Screen of designer canvas.

The code that is added is:

```
<h:inputText value="#{UserBean.name}"></h:inputText>
```

Drag and drop the Command Button component after the inputText and press Enter key between them if we want the command button on the next line (Figure 11.61).

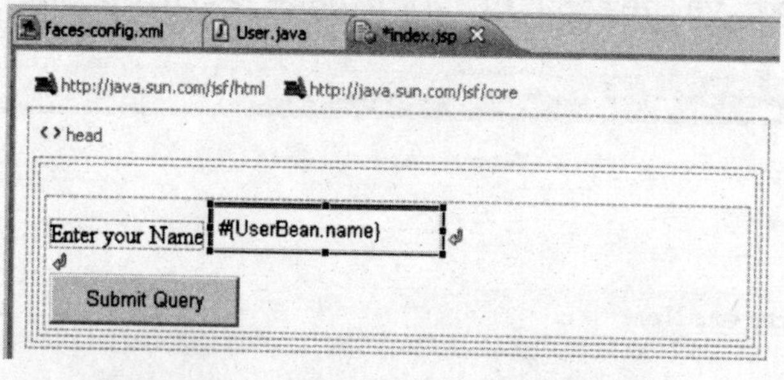

Figure 11.61   Drag & drop of command button.

Set the action and value property of the command button to: "welcome" and "Submit" respectively: The action property is set to "welcome" as it is the navigation case for navigating from the `index.jsp` page to the `welcome.jsp` page (we have specified above). So, when the command button will be pressed in the `index.jsp` page, it will generate action as "welcome" and this outcome will be used for navigation (Figure 11.62).

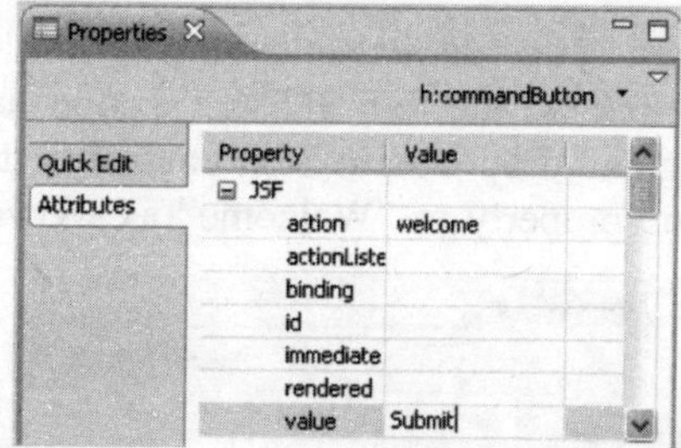

Figure 11.62   Setting the action and value property.

We get the following code added:

```
<h:commandButton action="welcome" value="Submit"></
h:commandButton>
```

and the canvas appears as shown in Figure 11.63.

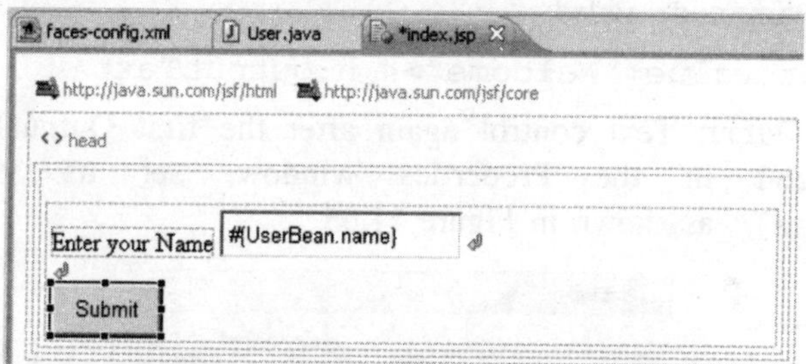

Figure 11.63   Canvas appears after the code added.

The overall code may appear as:

```
<%@ taglib uri="http://java.sun.com/jsf/html" prefix="h" %>
<%@ taglib uri="http://java.sun.com/jsf/core" prefix="f" %>
<html>
    <head>
        <title></title>
    </head>
    <body>
        <f:view>
    <h:form>
        <h:outputText value="Enter your Name"></h:outputText>
        <h:inputText value="#{UserBean.name}"></
                                        h:inputText><br><br>
        <h:commandButton action="welcome"
```

```
value="Submit"></h:commandButton>
   </h:form>
</f:view>
   </body>
</html>
```

Right click on the `welcome.jsp` file and select the option: `Open With->Web Page Editor`. In the Palette View, click on the JSF HTML section and drag and drop the Form component on the canvas. Drag and drop Output Text control in the `<h:form>` tag and in the Properties window, set its value property to "Welcome" as shown in Figure 11.64.

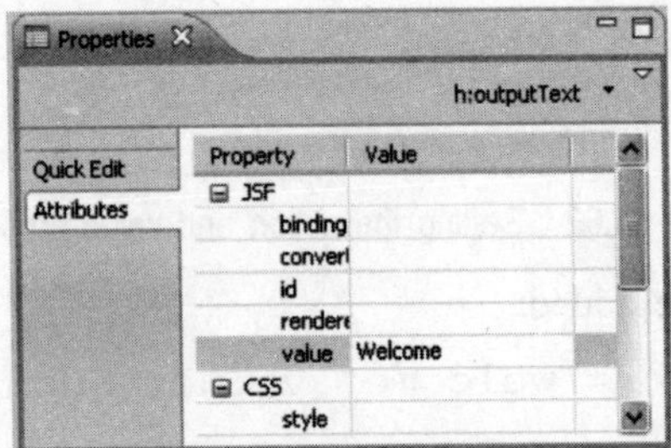

Figure 11.64   Set the value property of Output Text control.

We get the following code added:

```
<h:outputText value="Welcome"></h:outputText>
```

Drag and drop Output Text control again after the first OutputText control in the `<h:form>` tag and in the Properties window, set its value property to "`#{UserBean.name}`" as shown in Figure 11.65.

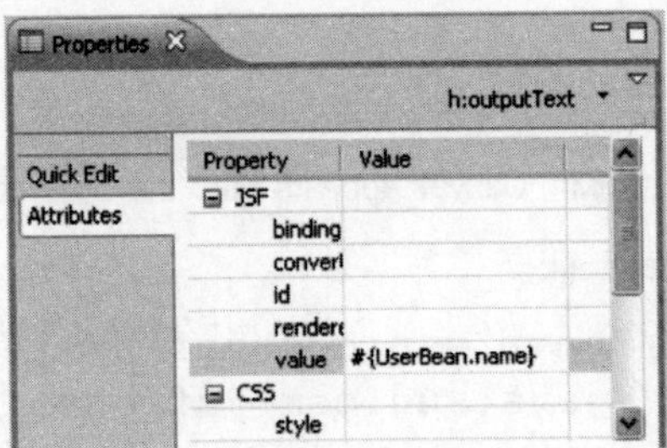

Figure 11.65   Value Property setted to # {UserBean . name}.

Canvas appears as shown in Figure 11.66.

Figure 11.66   Appearance of canvas.

The overall code of `welcome.jsp` page may appear as:

```
<%@ taglib uri="http://java.sun.com/jsf/html" prefix="h" %>
<%@ taglib uri="http://java.sun.com/jsf/core" prefix="f" %>
<html>
    <head>
        <title></title>
    </head>
    <body>
        <f:view>
            <h:form>
                <h:outputText value="Welcome"></h:outputText>
                <h:outputText
value="#{UserBean.name}"></h:outputText>
            </h:form>
        </f:view>
    </body>
</html>
```

Let us run the application now. To run the application, select the `index.jsp` file in Project Explorer window and select Run button. We get screen to specify (Figure 11.67).

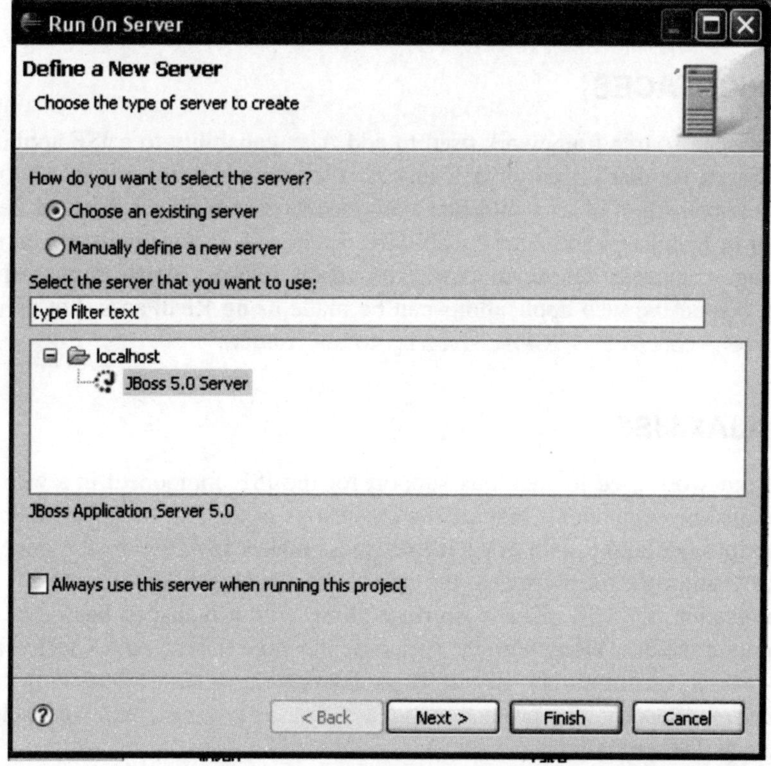

Figure 11.67   Screen for Run on server.

Enter any user name and press Submit button (Figure 11.68).

Figure 11.68   Press Submit button.

We get a welcome message on the screen (Figure 11.69).

Figure 11.69   Result displayed.

Third Application

In this application we will be using RichFaces also.

WHAT IS RICHFACES

RichFaces is an open source framework used to add Ajax capability to a JSF application. If we are using RichFaces, we don't need to write any JavaScript code to include AJAX functionality. It provides a new collection of user interface components suitable for JSF (Java Server Faces). It provides built in JavaScript and Ajax capabilities. RichFaces suite is built on and merged with Ajax4jsf making it suitable for developing RIA (Rich Internet Applications) and rich web clients. Highly responsive web applications can be made using RichFaces. Let us unzip its zip file—`richfaces-ui-3.2.1.GA-bin.zip` to any folder.

WHAT IS AJAX4JSF

Ajax4jsf is a framework used to add Ajax support for the JSF component in a web application. Its library contains the components that are the extensions of the JSF components that internally use the JavaScript code along with XMLHttpRequest that is invisible to the developer and is handled by the framework itself making the job of the developer quite easy.

In this application, we will make a jsp page along with a managed bean that will quickly display the name of the user along with the welcome message (Using AJAX technology). Select `File->New->Project` and then select JBoss Tools `Web->JSF->JSF` Project option and select Next button. Specify the project name as: `demorichfaces3` and select JSF 1.2 implementation as JSF environment:

Leave the template as it is and select Next button. We get a dialog box to specify the Server details. Select JBoss AS 5.0 server with default configuration and select Finish button. In this application, instead of making `index.jsp` or `welcome.jsp` pages, we begin with creation of managed bean first.

Select the Tree tab at the bottom of the window and select the Managed Beans node, we get a screen as shown in Figure 11.70.

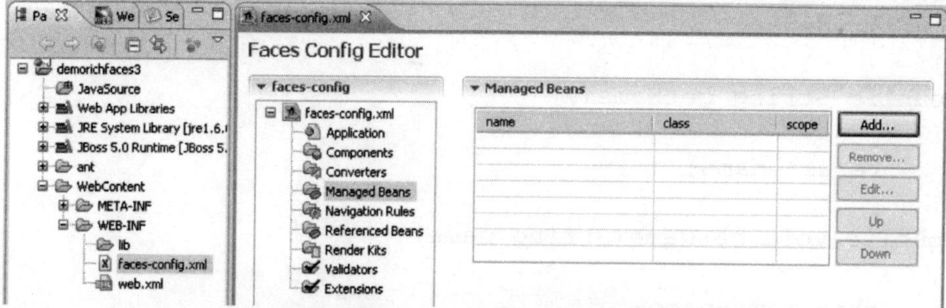

Figure 11.70 Screen for Managed Bean.

Select the Add button to add a managed bean. We get a dialog box to specify the scope of the managed bean, the class file name of the bean and also the name by which it will be referred in the web application (Figure 11.71).

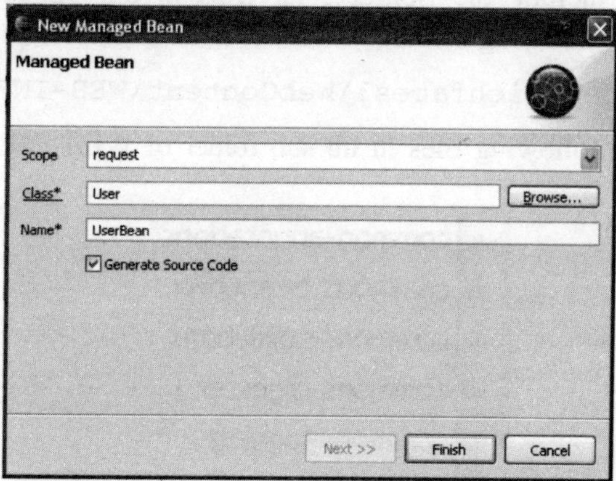

Figure 11.71 Dialog Box of New Managed Bean.

Enter the details of the managed bean as shown above and select Finish button. The class file User.java may appear as shown in Figure 11.72.

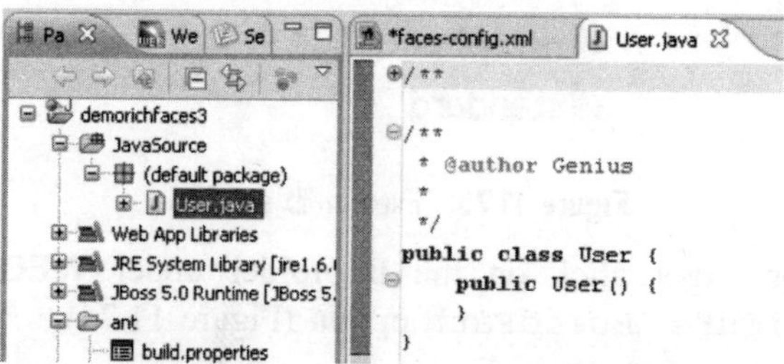

Figure 11.72 Location of User.java file.

Add an attribute: "name" of type String and also make its setter and getter methods to the User.java class file:

```
public class User {
    String name;
    public User() {
    }
    public String getName()
    {
        return name;
    }
    public void setName(String name)
    {
        this.name=name;
    }
}
```

Select `File->Save All` to save whatever is done up till now.

Now, we need to include the richface. jar files in our application. So, let us copy richfaces.jar files at the following folder:

```
C:\workspace\demorichfaces3\WebContent\WEB-INF\lib
```

So, in all, there are following files in lib sub folder of WEB-INF (Figure 11.73).

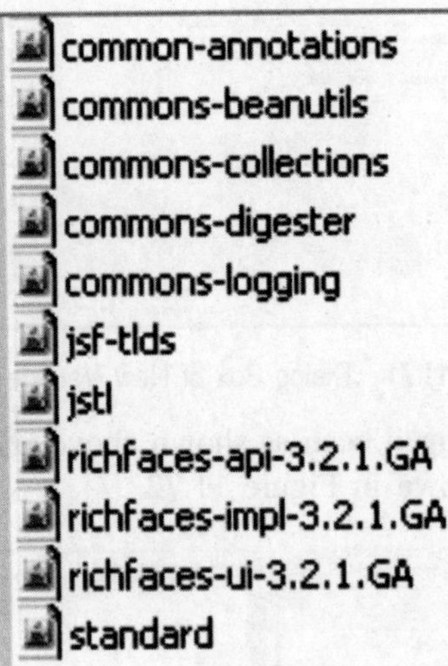

Figure 11.73 Files in lib sub folder.

In the application, right click on the lib folder under WEB-INF node and select `BuildPath->Configure BuildPath` option (Figure 11.74).

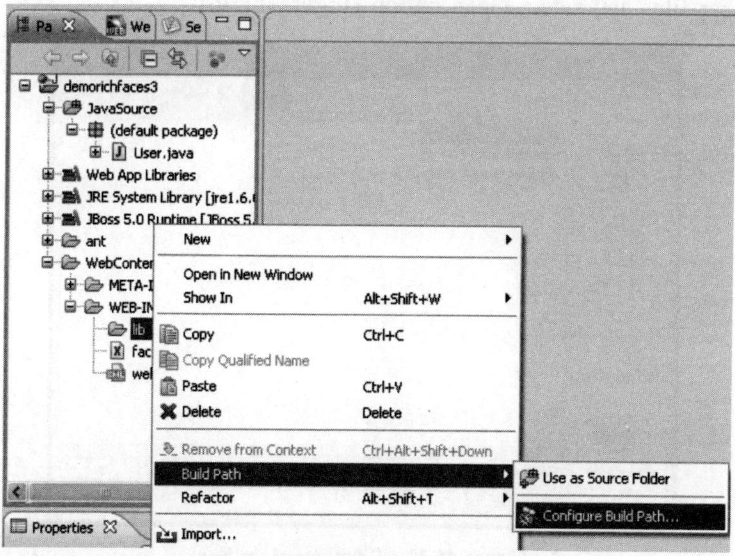

Figure 11.74   Selection of Configure BuildPath option.

Select the Libraries tab and select Add JAR button (Figure 11.75).

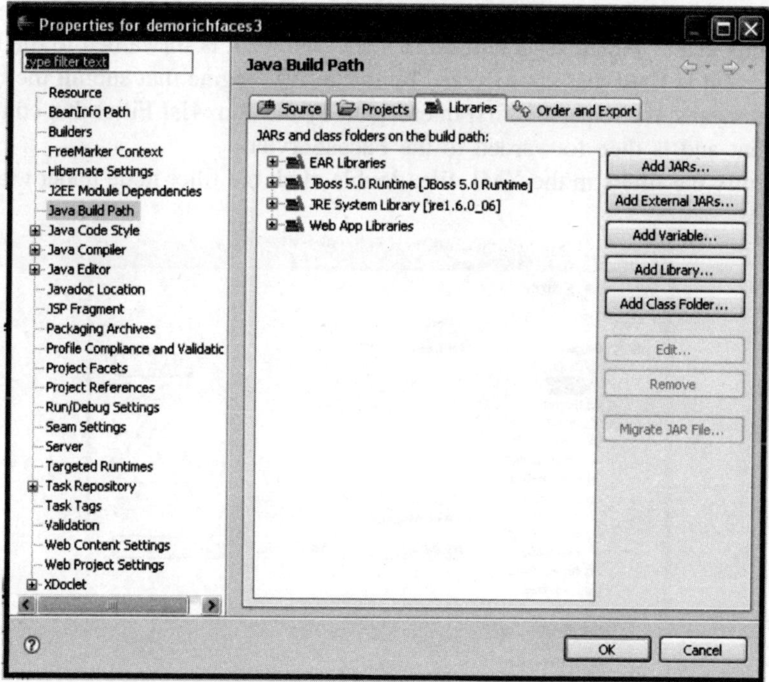

Figure 11.75   Selection of Add Jar button.

Select the jar files and select Open button (Figure 11.76).

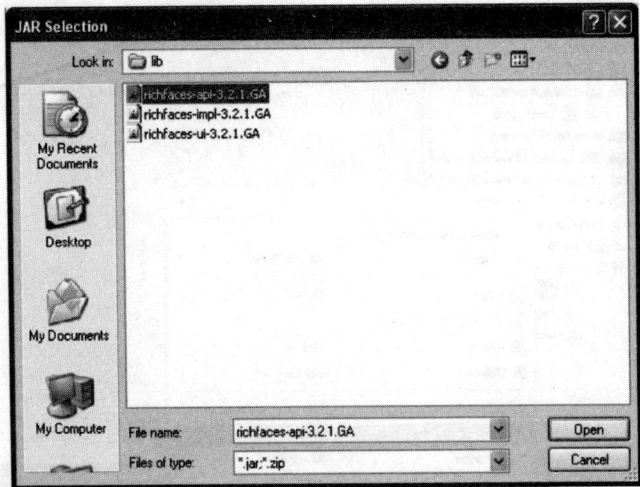

Figure 11.76 Selection of jar files.

To apply AJAX to our application, we need to write filter clause in the `web.xml` file.

Reason of using filter clause

The filter clause is for providing the Filter Servlet which is meant for adding the Ajax capability to the JSF components. Whenever a request is made, before it is forwarded to the FacesServlet, a Java Script event is fired that is processed by the AJAX engine that submit the request to the Ajax4Jsf. That means, the request is first intercepted by the Ajax4Jsf Filter that converts the data to XML Format and is then forwarded to the FacesServlet.

So, to specify the filters in the XML file, double click the filter node under `web.xml` node (Figure 11.77).

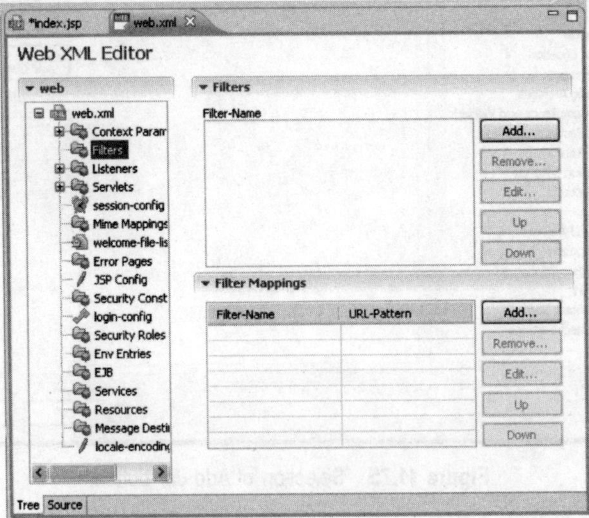

Figure 11.77 Screen of web XML Editor.

Select Add button and specify the Filter name as ajax4jsf and the Display name as Ajax4jsfFilter as shown in Figure 11.78.

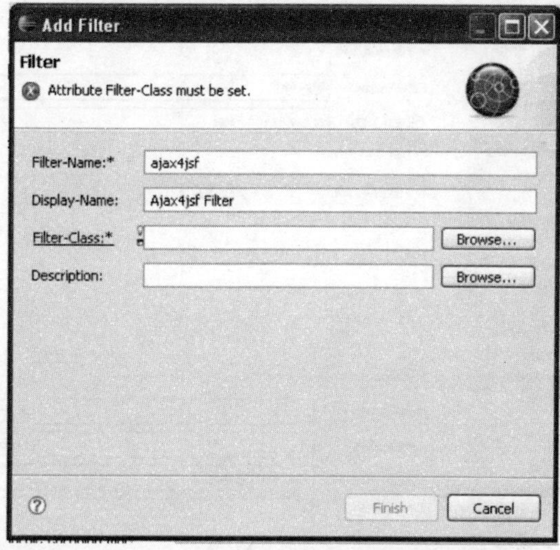

Figure 11.78　Specification of Filter name and Display name.

To specify the Filter class, select the browse button and select its type that is org.ajax4jsf as shown in Figure 11.79.

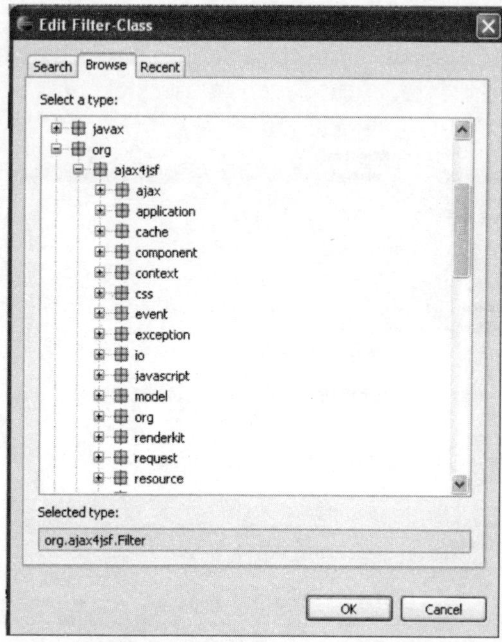

Figure 11.79　Specification of Filter class.

After selecting the node ajax4jsf under org node, select OK button (Figure 11.80).

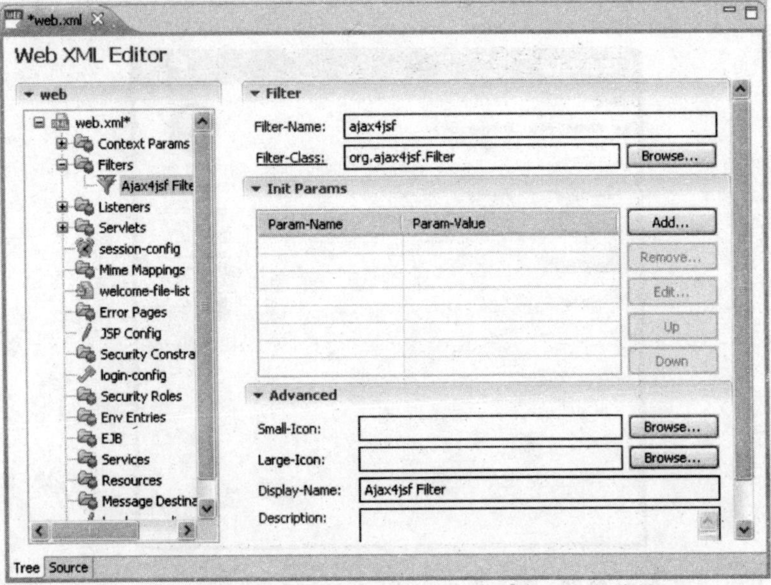

Figure 11.80   Selection of node ajax4jsf.

Save the web.xml file and again select the filters node, we get following screen to define filter mappings (Figure 11.81).

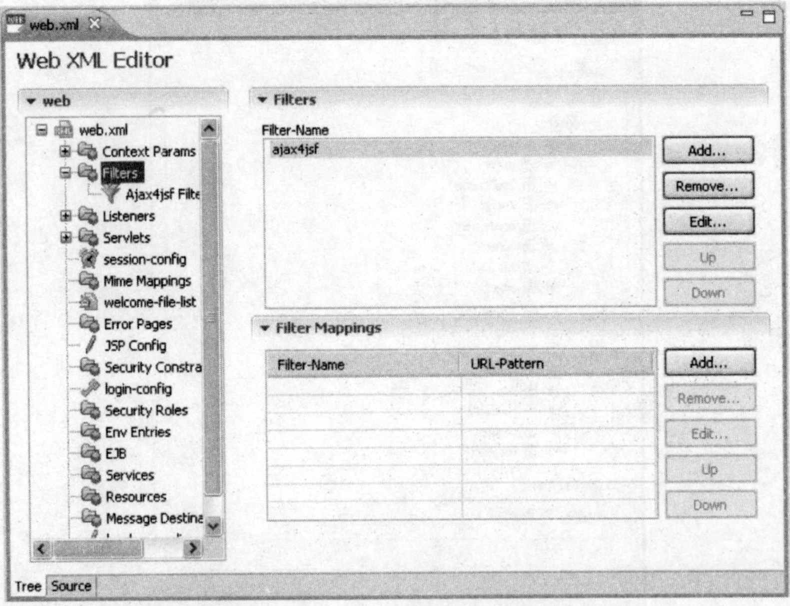

Figure 11.81   Screen for filter mappings.

Select Add button to specify the filter mapping. Specify the filter name as ajax4jsf and servlet name as: FacesServlet (Figure 11.82).

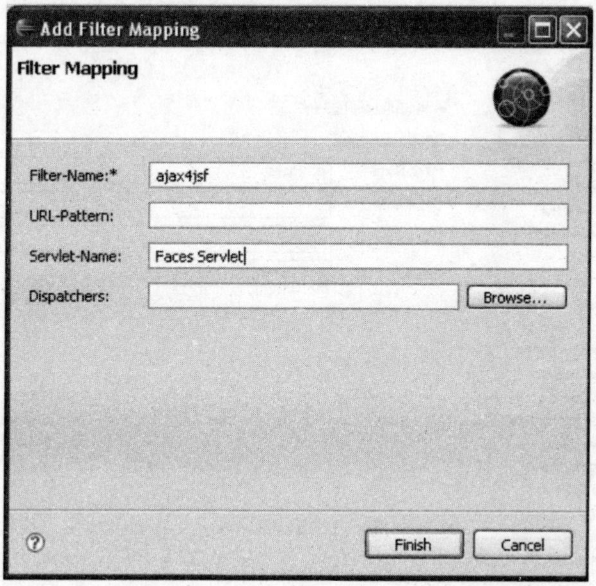

Figure 11.82   Specification of filter name and servlet name.

Also select the Browse button to specify the Dispatchers. We select FORWARD, INCLUDE and REQUEST dispatchers (Figure 11.83).

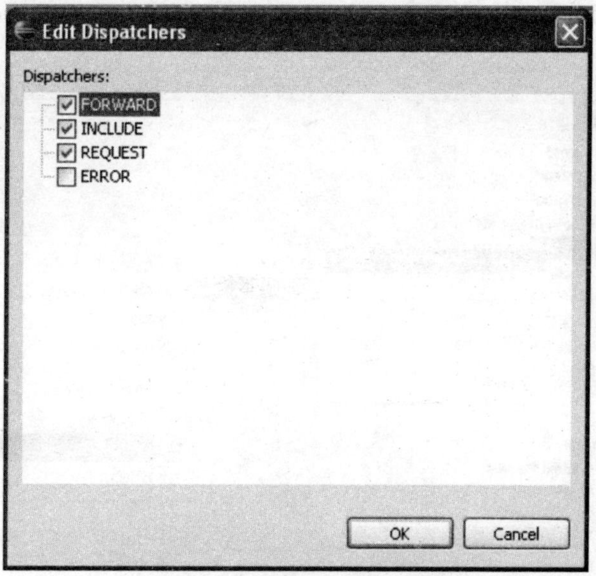

Figure 11.83   Selection of dispatchers.

Select OK followed by Finish button. Similarly, set the filter mapping for the richfaces too as shown in Figure 11.84.

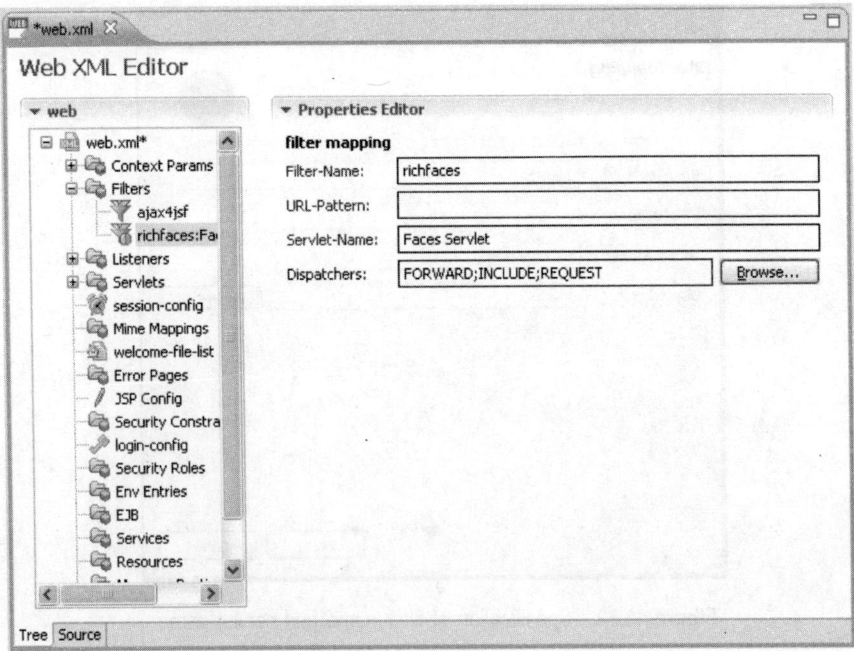

Figure 11.84 Filter mapping for the richfaces.

Save the web.xml file. Now, we will add the file index.jsp to our application. Right click on the WEB-INF node and select New->File->JSP option (Figure 11.85).

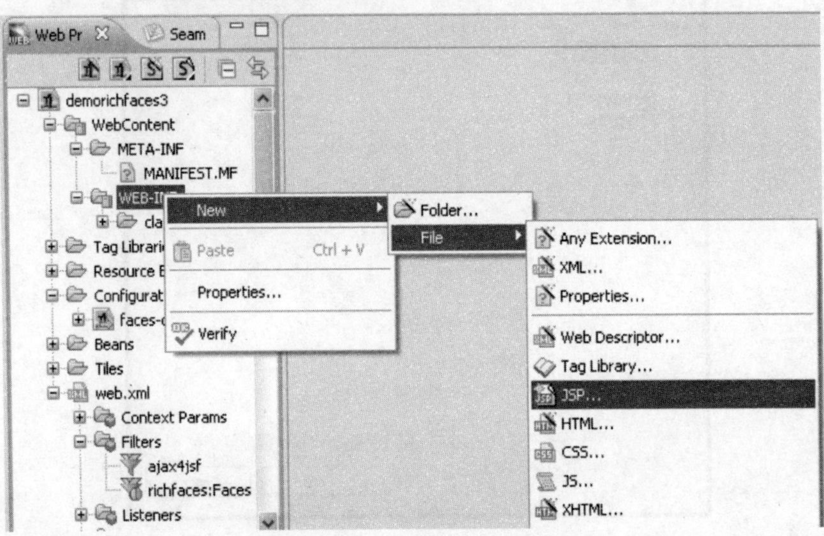

Figure 11.85 Selectiong of JSP option.

Specify the Name as `index.jsp` and the Template as: JSFBasePage (Figure 11.86).

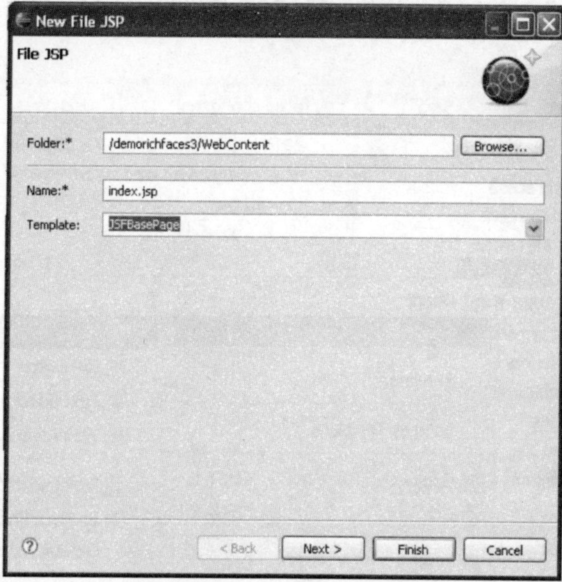

Figure 11.86   Select the names.

Select Next button and select the tag libraries. Select the four Taglibs:

`JBoss Ajax4jsf`, `JBoss RichFaces`, `JSF Core`, `JSF HTML` as shown in Figure 11.87.

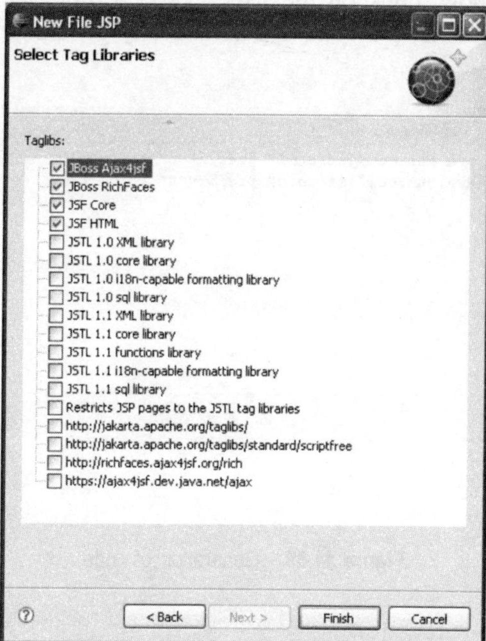

Figure 11.87   Selection of the tag libraries.

Open the `index.jsp` file with JSP Editor. So right click the `index.jsp` file and select `Open With->JBoss Tools JSP Editor` (Figure 11.88).

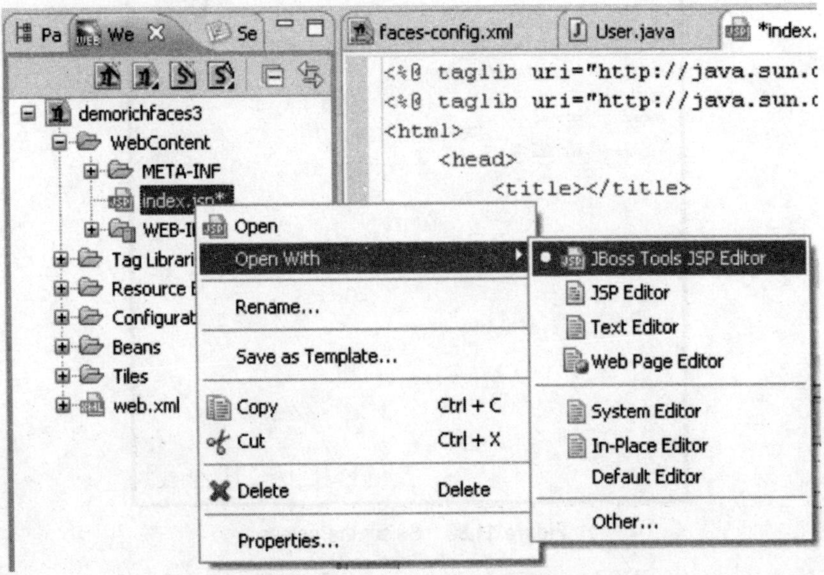

Figure 11.88   Selection of JBoss Tools JSP Editor.

From the Palette window, click on the JSF HTML section and drag and drop the form component on the canvas. Note, the code is automatically generated (Figure 11.89).

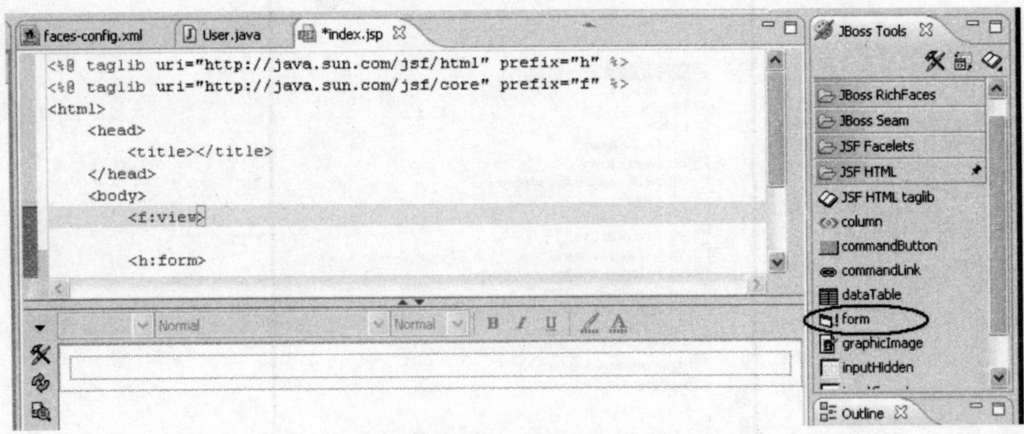

Figure 11.89   Generation of code.

Don't specify any value in any attribute. Just select Finish button (Figure 11.90):

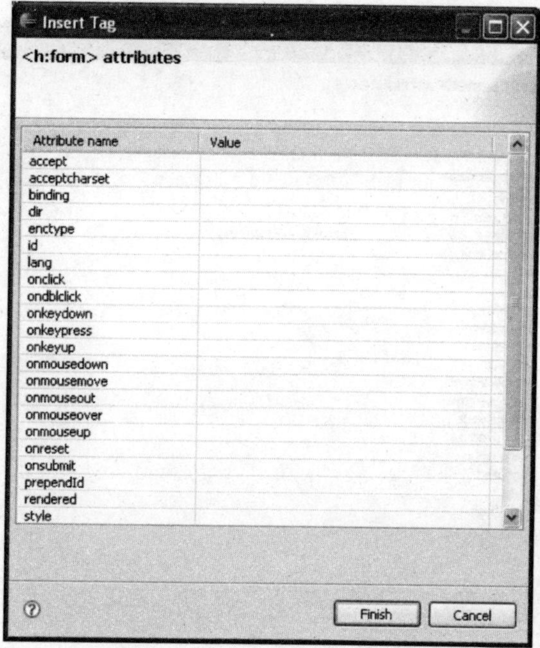

Figure 11.90 Select Finish button.

From the JBoss RichFaces Palette, drag and drop the panel component on the canvas (Figure 11.91).

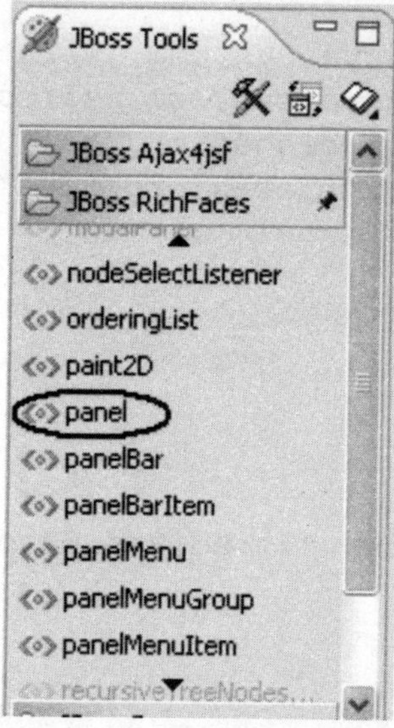

Figure 11.91 Drag & drop panel component.

In the header attribute of the rich panel component, specify the text: "Immediate Response" (Figure 11.92).

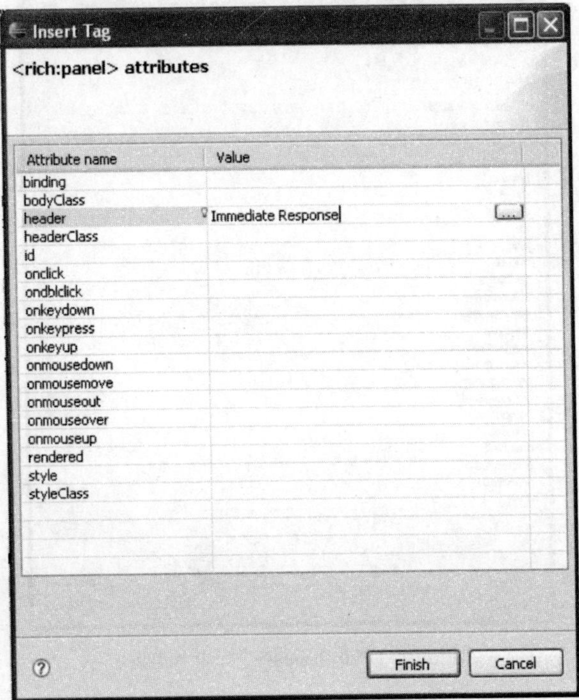

Figure 11.92 Specification of Immediate Response.

Select Finish button. The overall code of the `index.jsp` file may appear as follows:

```
<%@ taglib uri="http://java.sun.com/jsf/html" prefix="h" %>
<%@ taglib uri="http://java.sun.com/jsf/core" prefix="f" %>
<%@ taglib uri="http://richfaces.org/a4j" prefix="a4j" %>
<%@ taglib uri="http://richfaces.org/rich" prefix="rich" %>
<html>
    <head>
        <title></title>
    </head>
    <body>
        <f:view>
        <h:form>
        <rich:panel header="Immediate Response">
        </rich:panel>
        </h:form>
        </f:view>
    </body>
</html>
```

Drag and drop InputText component from the JSF HTML section of the Palette in the `<h:form>` tag (Figure 11.93).

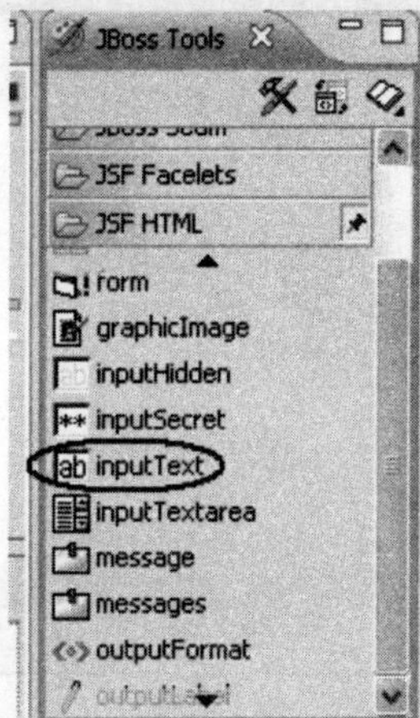

Figure 11.93 Drag & drop InputText component.

Attach the "name" attribute of the managed bean: UserBean to this InputText component (so that the name entered by the user can be assigned to the "name" attribute of the managed bean). So select the button in the value attribute of the InputText control (Figure 11.94).

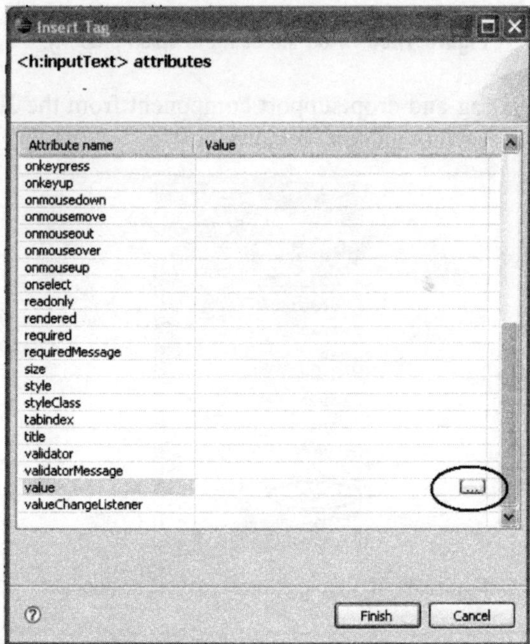

Figure 11.94 Select the button in the value attribute.

Select the name attribute of the UserBean (our managed bean) (Figure 11.95).

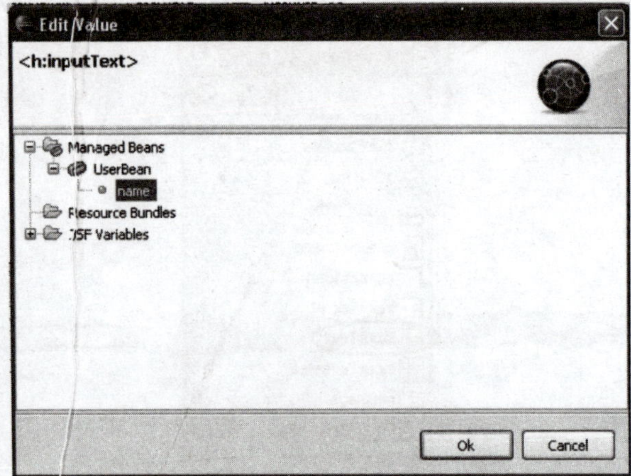

Figure 11.95   Selection of name attribute.

Select OK button. We get the following string added in the value property (Figure 11.96).

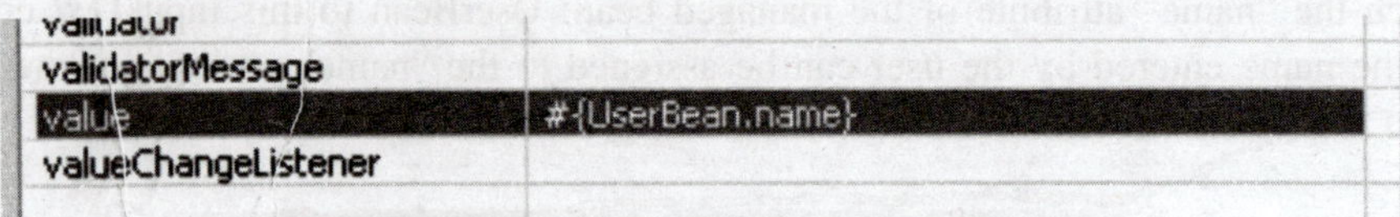

Figure 11.96   Add the string to value property.

Select Finish button. Drag and drop support component from the JBoss Ajax4jsf section of the Palette after the InputText component (Figure 11.97).

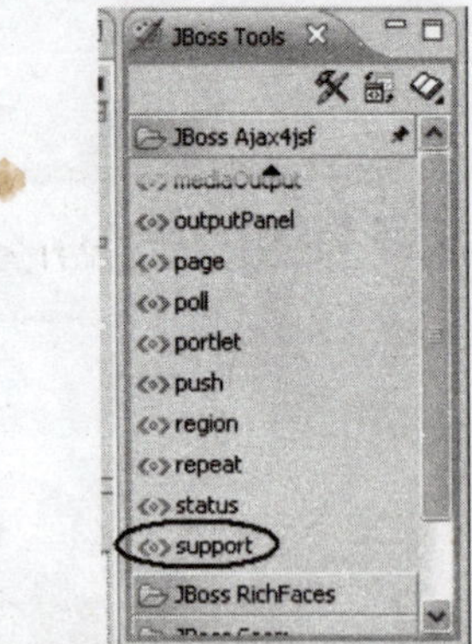

Figure 11.97   Drag & drop support component.

Set is event attribute value to "onkeyup" and reRender value to "info" so that it is fired when the key is released and will display the contents of the component whose id is "info". We will set the id of the outputText component to "id" in order to display the response (Figure 11.98).

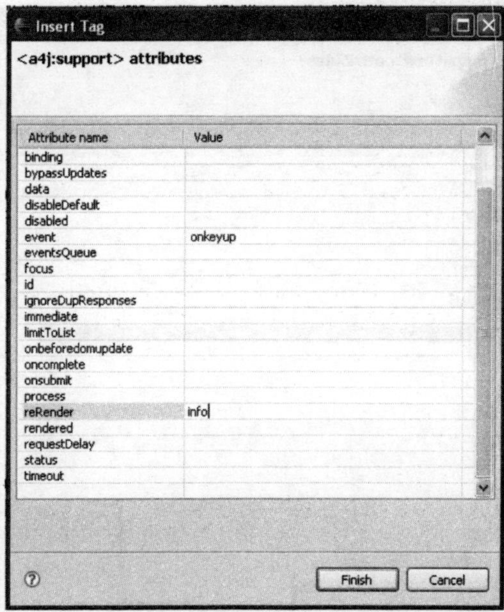

Figure 11.98   Selecting the id property.

Drag and drop the outputText component from the JSF HTML section of the Palette (Figure 11.99).

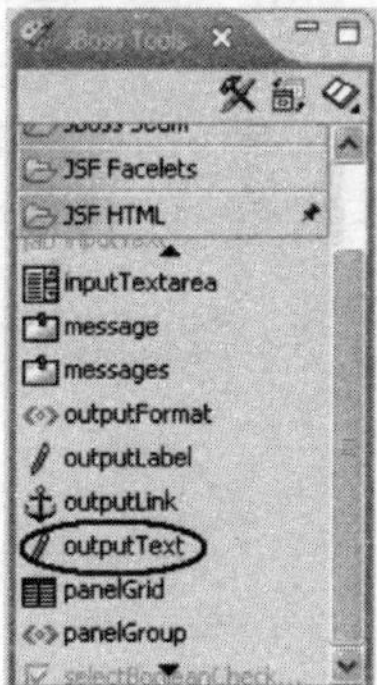

Figure 11.99   Drag & drop the outputText component.

Set the value attribute of the outputText component to "Welcome" so that it displays the text: "Welcome" while running the application. Again drag and drop another outputText component from the JSF HTML section of the Palette after the earlier outputText component.

Set the attribute: value of outputText component to the "name" attribute of the managed bean: UserBean so that the name entered by the user in the InputText component can be displayed via this outputText component (immediately as the key of any character is released). That is, as any character is typed in the inputText box, it will be displayed in the outputText component.

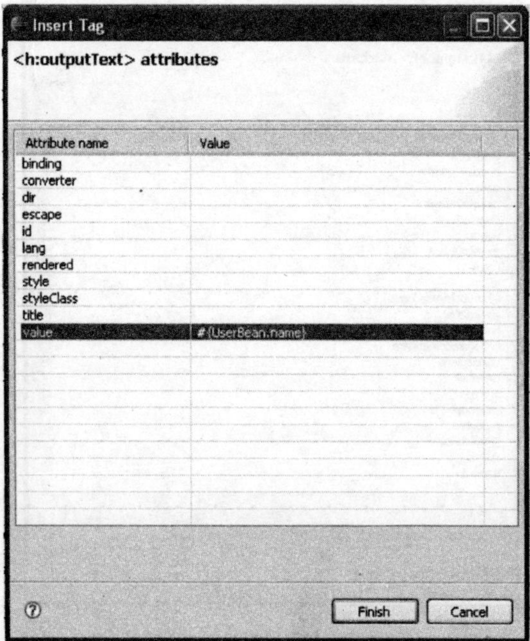

Figure 11.100 Setting the value attribute of outputText control.

The overall coding of the index.jsp file may appear as follows:

```
<%@ taglib uri="http://java.sun.com/jsf/html" prefix="h" %>
<%@ taglib uri="http://java.sun.com/jsf/core" prefix="f" %>
<%@ taglib uri="http://richfaces.org/a4j" prefix="a4j" %>
<%@ taglib uri="http://richfaces.org/rich' prefix="rich" %>
<html>
    <head>
        <title></title>
    </head>
    <body>
        <f:view>
        <h:form>
            <rich:panel header="Immediate Response">
            <h:outputText value="Enter Your Name "/>
            <h:inputText value="#{UserBean.name}" >
                <a4j:support event="onkeyup"
                  reRender="info"/>
                </h:inputText><br>
                <h:outputText value="Welcome "/>
                <h:outputText value="#{UserBean.name}"
                  id="info"/>
            </rich:panel>
```

```
        </h:form>
        </f:view>
    </body>
</html>
```

Above code reveals that user is asked to enter his name and via support component, we assure that while user is entering his name character by character, the moment any key is pressed and released, an event "onkeyup" is fired which re-renders (redisplays) the component whose id is "info", i.e., the outputText component will display the text typed in the inputText component. The design canvas may appear as shown in Figure 11.101.

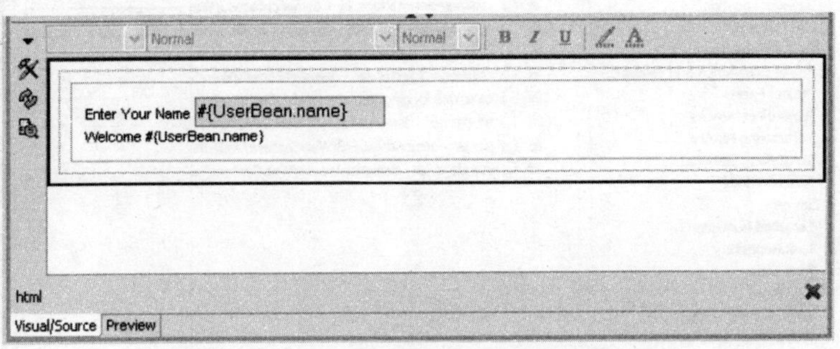

Figure 11.101 Appearence of design canvas.

We confirm that the jar files of richfaces and ajax4jsf are attached to our application. For that, right click the lib node under WEB-INF node and select Build Path->Use as Source Folder:

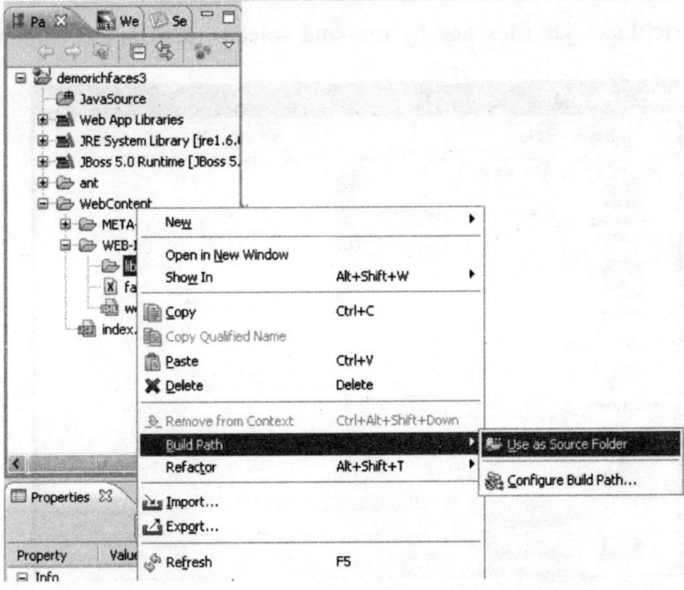

Figure 11.102 Selection of Use as source folder.

Select the Libraries tag and select Add JAR button (Figure 11.103).

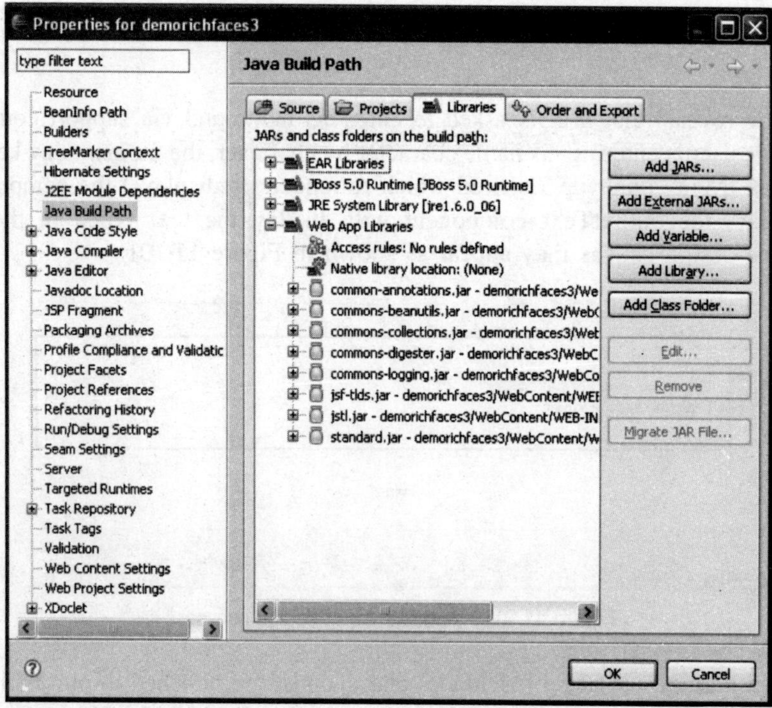

Figure 11.103   Selection of Add Jar button.

Select all the richfaces jar files one by one and select Open button (Figure 11.104).

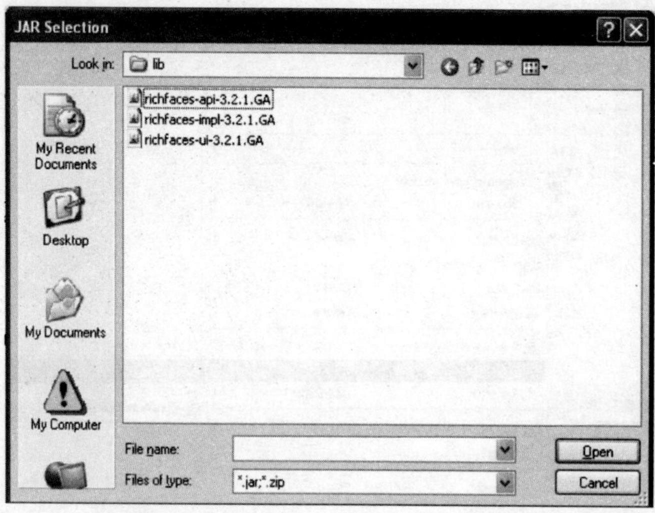

Figure 11.104   Select the files and open them.

Also select the ajax4jsf jar files and select the Open button (Figure 11.105).

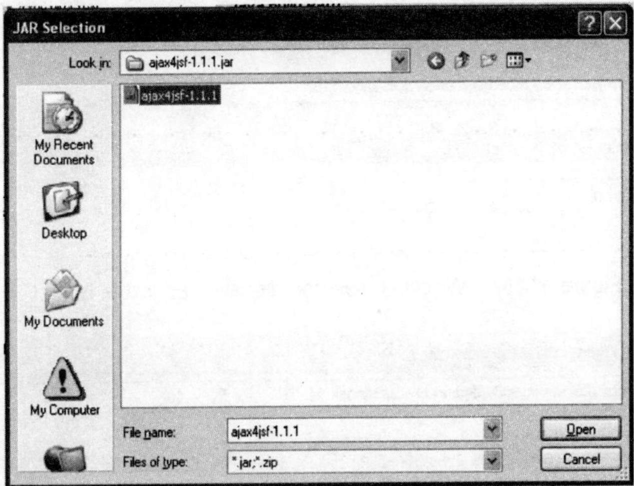

Figure 11.105   Selection of ajax4jsf jar files.

Select OK button (Figure 11.106).

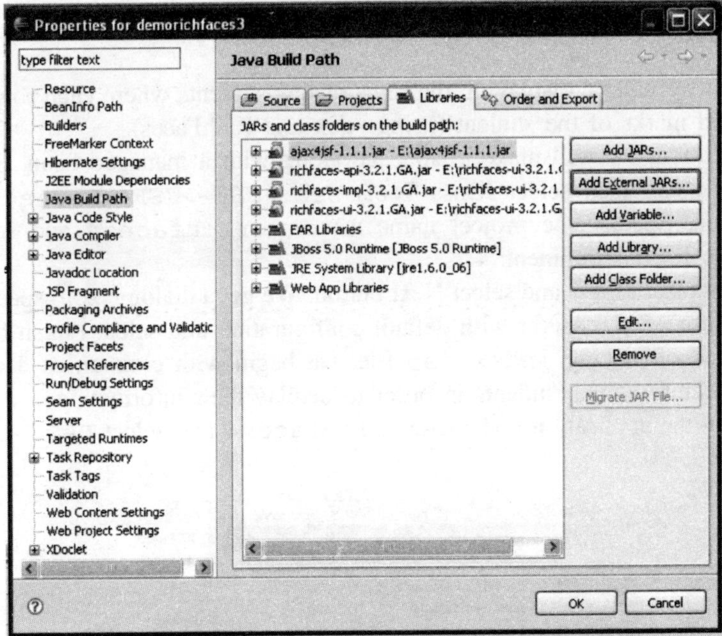

Figure 11.106   Selection of OK button.

Let us run the application now. To run the application, select the `index.jsp` file in Project Explorer window and select Run button. We get screen to specify the user name. We get the name displayed along with the welcome message as we type it in the input text component (Figure 11.107).

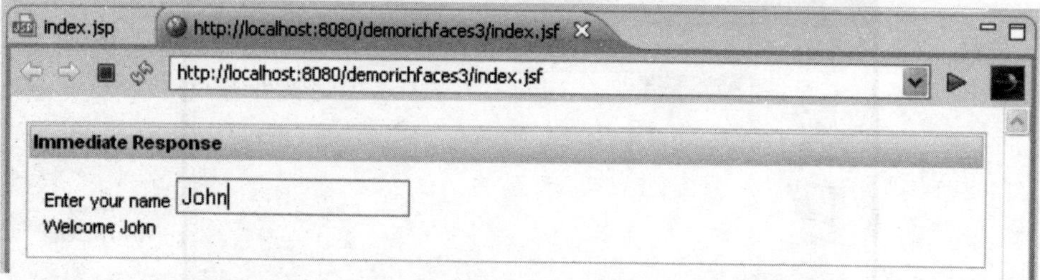

Figure 11.107   Welcome message displayed as text is typed.

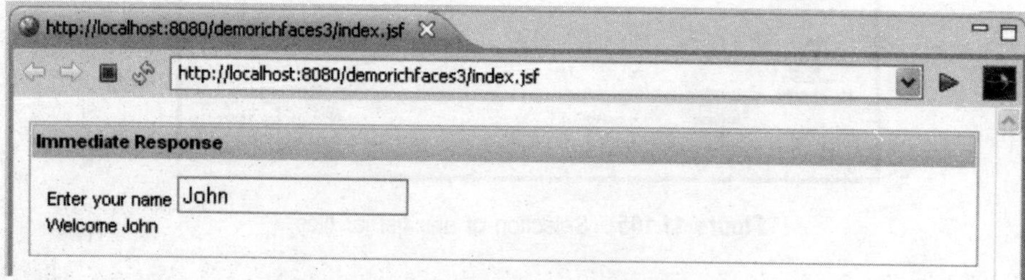

Figure 11.108   Welcome message displayed.

Fourth Application

In this application we will be displaying the rows of few students where each row displays roll number, name and marks of the student (using Ajax and RichFaces).

In this application, we will make a jsp page along with a managed bean. Select `File->New->Project` and then select JBoss Tools `Web->JSF->JSF  Project` option and select Next button. Specify the project name as: `demorichfaces4` and select JSF 1.2 implementation as JSF environment:

Leave the Template as it is and select Next button. We get a dialog box to specify the server details. Select JBoss AS 5.0 server with default configuration and select Finish button. In this application, instead of making `index.jsp` file, we begin with creation of a class file that represents the structure of the students in order to display their information

Right click on the application node: `demorichfaces4` and select `New->Class` option (Figure 11.109).

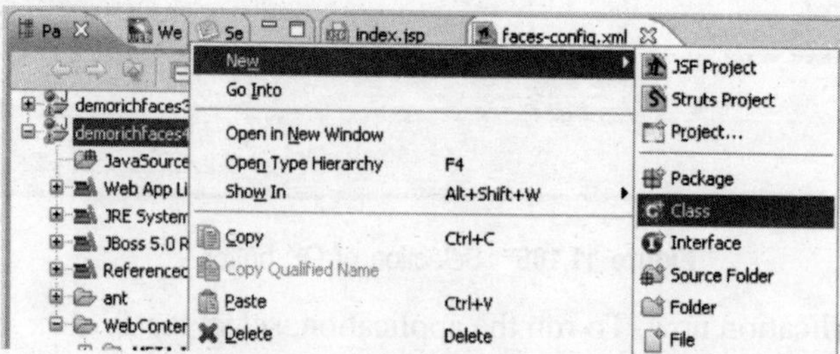

Figure 11.109   Selection of Class option.

Specify the location to place the class file and also its name. We specify the class file name as: Client (Figure 11.110).

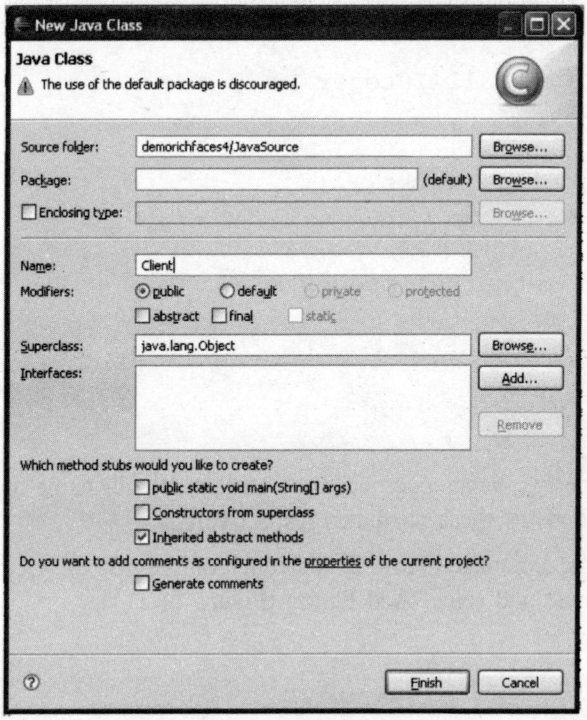

Figure 11.110 Specification of location.

Select Finish button. We get a class file: `Client.java` opened in the editor window. Enter the following code in it:

```
public class Client {
    String name;
    Integer roll, marks;

    Client(Integer r, String n, Integer m)
    {
        this.roll=r;
        this.name=n;
        this.marks=m;
    }
    public String getName() {
        return name;
    }
```

```java
public void setName(String n) {
    name = n;
}
public Integer getRoll() {
    return roll;
}
public void setRoll(Integer r) {
    roll = r;
}
public Integer getMarks() {
    return marks;
}
public void setMarks(Integer m) {
    marks = m;
}


}
```

In above class file, we have specified three attributes: roll, name and marks and also the setter and getter methods of these attributes respectively:

We will now create a managed bean. Double click on the `faces-config.xml` file, select the Managed Bean node and select Add button (Figure 11.111).

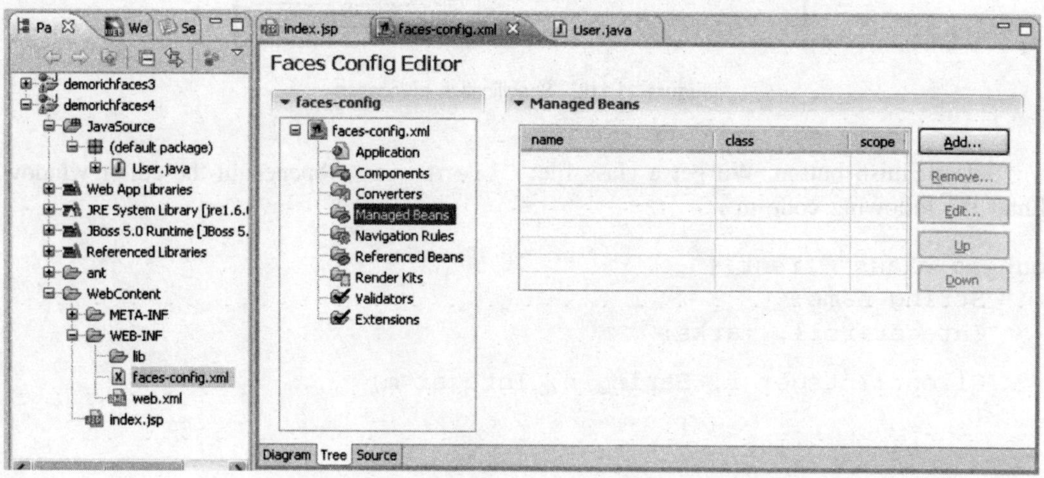

Figure 11.111   Steps for creation of Managed Bean.

Set the scope of the managed bean as "request", the class file name as "School" and the managed bean name (by which it will be referred in the program) as SchoolBean (Figure 11.112).

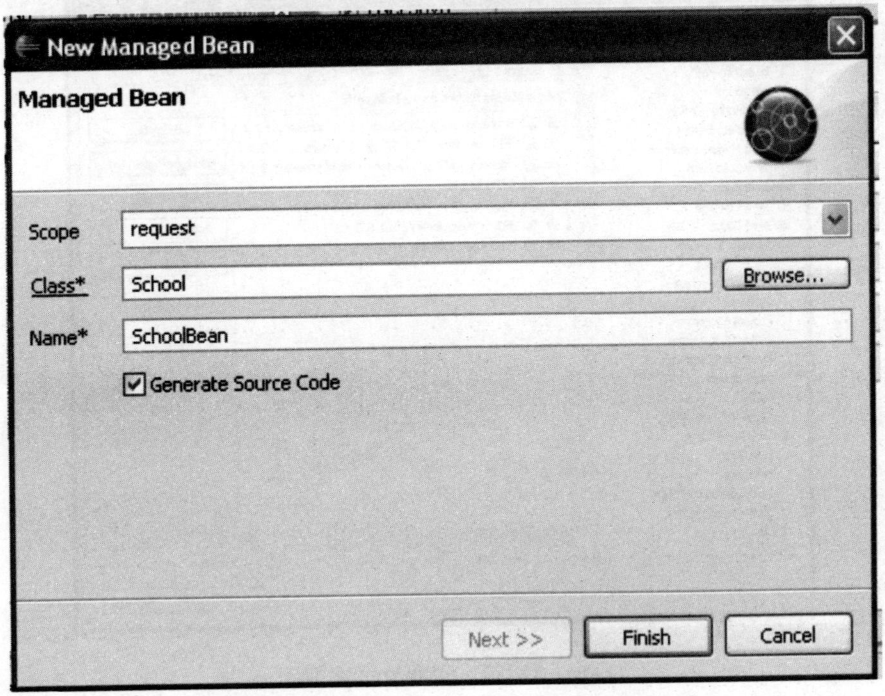

Figure 11.112 Setting the scope, class & name.

Select Finish button and then save the `faces-config.xml` file.

In the managed bean class file: `School.java`, type the following code:

```
public class School {
    public School() {
    }
    private Client[] studentlist={
        new Client(101, "Johny",85),
        new Client(102, "Peter",95)};

        public Client[] getStudentlist()
        {
            return studentlist;
        }
}
```

We can see in above code that the managed bean has an array of Client class by name studentlist that contains the information (roll, name and marks) of two students.

Add the jar files of RichFaces and ajax4jsf in this application as we did in the third application (Figure 11.113).

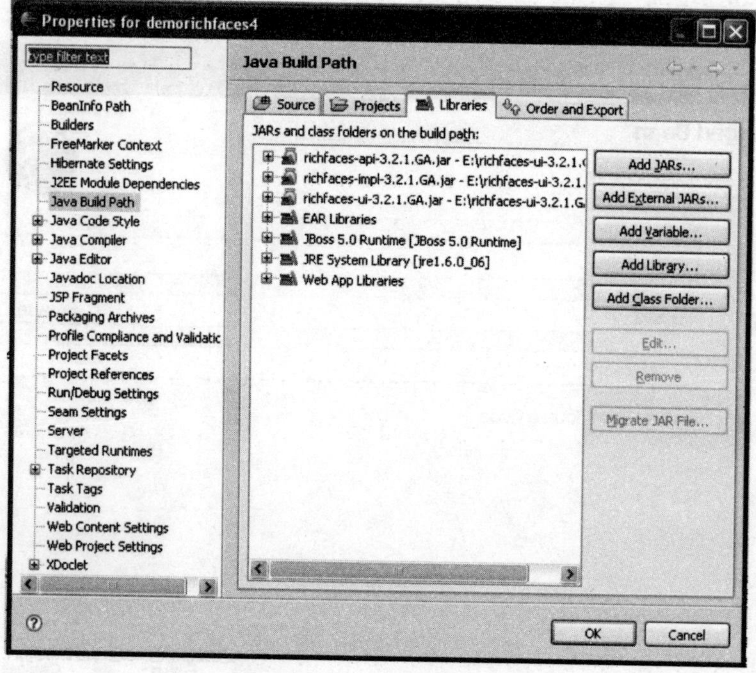

Figure 11.113   Addition of jar files.

Also set the filter mappings (Figure 11.114) of the RichFaces and `ajax4jsf` as we did in the third application:

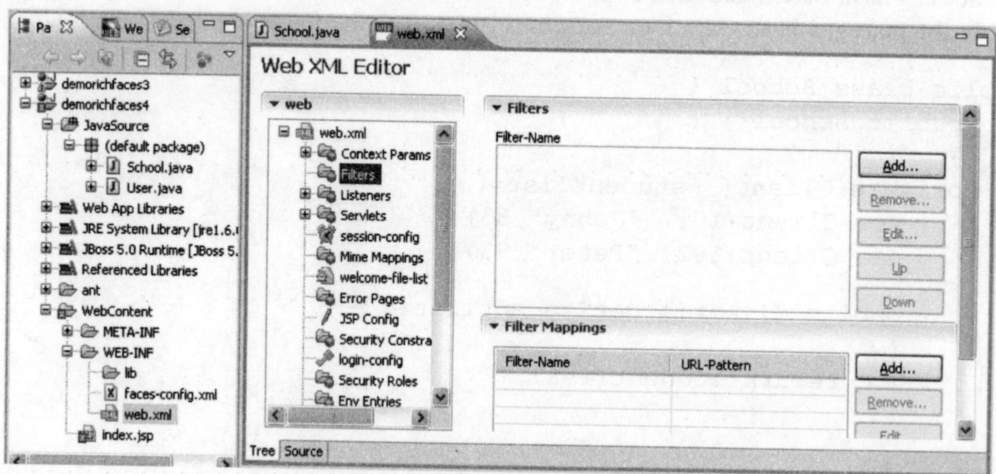

Figure 11.114   Setting the filter mappings.

Now let us add the file `index.jsp` to our application. Right click the node: WebContent and select the option: New->JSP File (Figure 11.115).

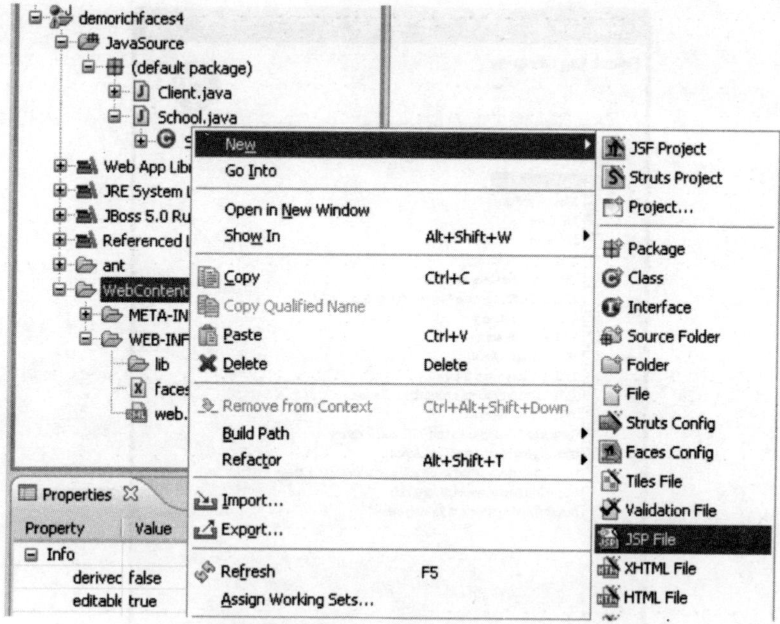

Figure 11.115   Selection of JSP file.

Specify the file name as `index.jsp` and the Template as: JSFBasePage as shown in Figure 11.116.

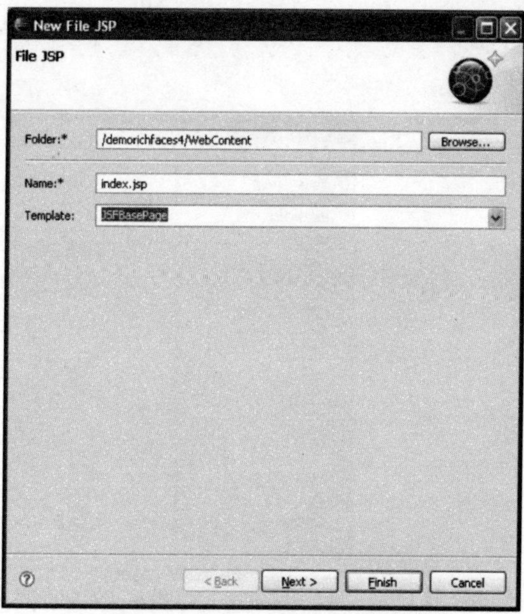

Figure 11.115   Selection of JSP file.

Select Next button and specify the tag libraries. We select the following Taglibs: JBoss `Ajax4jsf`, `JBoss RichFaces`, `JSF Core` and `JSF HTML` as shown in Figure 11.117.

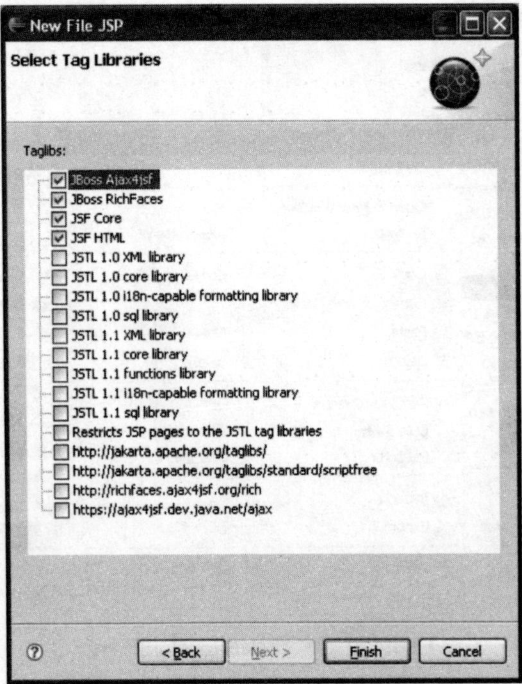

Figure 11.117   Specification of tag libraries.

Select Finish button.

In the `index.jsp` page, drag and drop the repeat component from the JBoss Ajax4jsf palette (Figure 11.118).

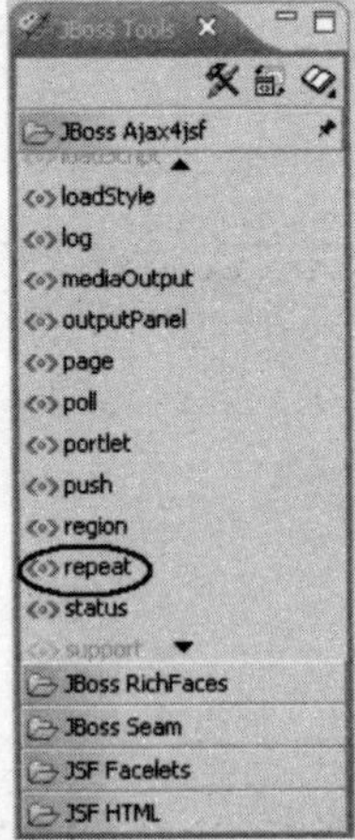

Figure 11.118   Drag and drop the repeat component.

Set the id attribute of the repeater component to "repeater", var attribute to "student" and the value attribute to studentlist of the SchoolBean (managed bean) so as to display the students information via this component (Figure 11.119).

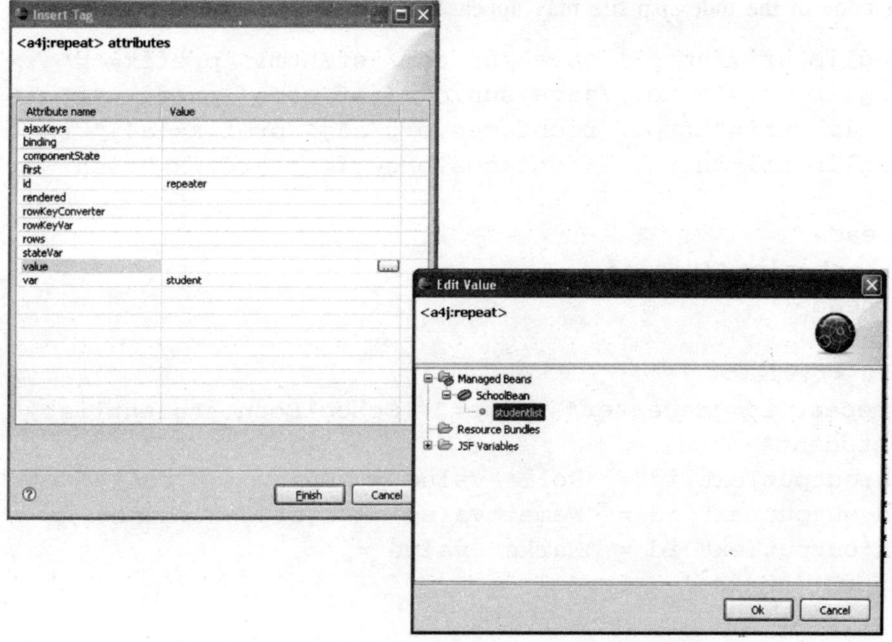

Figure 11.119   Setting the attributes of the repeater component.

Select OK button and our design canvas screen may appear as shown in Figure 11.120.

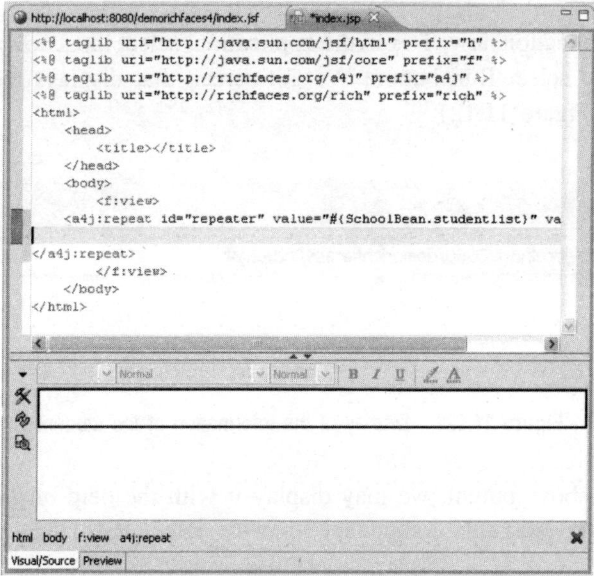

Figure 11.120   Appearance of canvas screen.

Drag and drop, three outputText control and set each to display one item of the student, i.e., one outputText control will display roll, other will display name and the third one will display marks of the student.

The code of the index.jsp file may appear as:

```
<%@ taglib uri="http://java.sun.com/jsf/html" prefix="h" %>
<%@ taglib uri="http://java.sun.com/jsf/core" prefix="f" %>
<%@ taglib uri="http://richfaces.org/a4j" prefix="a4j" %>
<%@ taglib uri="http://richfaces.org/rich" prefix="rich" %>
<html>
    <head>
        <title></title>
    </head>
    <body>
        <f:view>
<a4j:repeat id="repeater" value="#{SchoolBean.studentlist}"
var="student">
    <h:outputText id = "Roll" value = "#{student.roll}"/>
    <h:outputText id = "Name" value = "#{student.name}"/>
    <h:outputText id = "Marks" value =
"#{student.marks}"/><br>
</a4j:repeat>
        </f:view>
    </body>
</html>
```

Let us run the application now. To run the application, select the `index.jsp` file in Project Explorer window and select Run button. We get screen that displays the information of the student as shown in Figure 11.121.

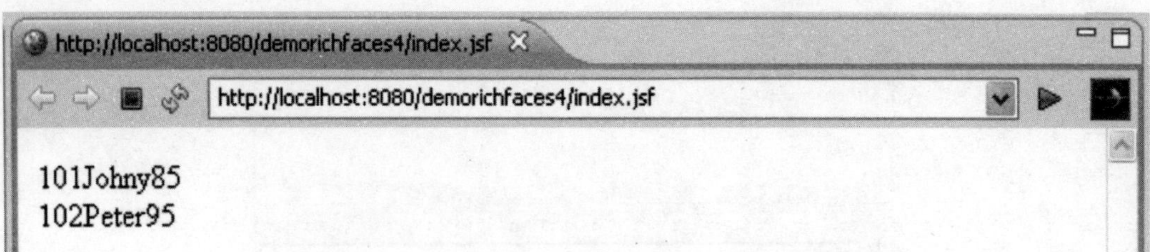

Figure 11.121   Display of the information of the student.

To organize the above output, we may display it with the help of data table component.

Drag and drop the dataTable component from the JBoss RichFaces section of the Palette (Figure 11.122).

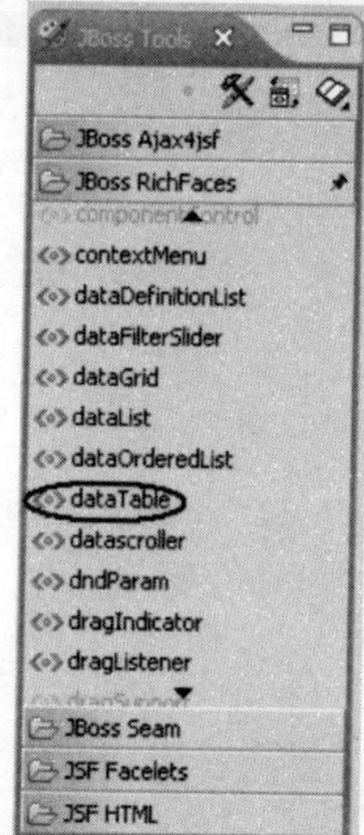

Figure 11.122   Drag & drop the dataTable component.

Set the value property of the dataTable component to display the "studentlist" attribute of the managed bean: SchoolBean (that contains the array of the students) (Figure 11.123) and also set three column attributes: `<h:column>` to display roll, name and marks of the student respectively (Figure 11.124).

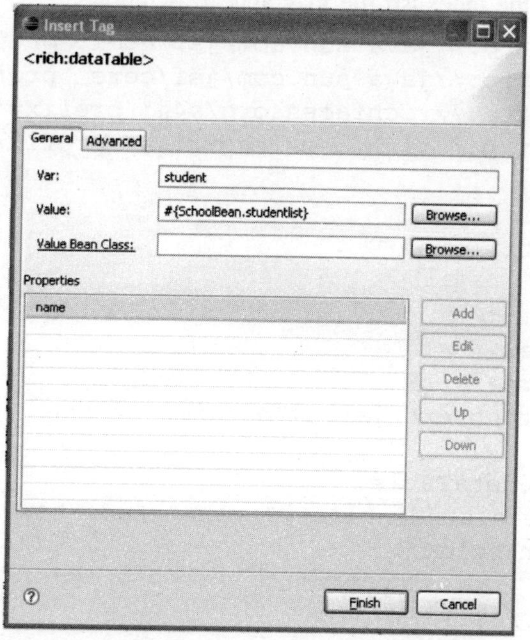

Figure 11.123   Setting the properties and attributes.

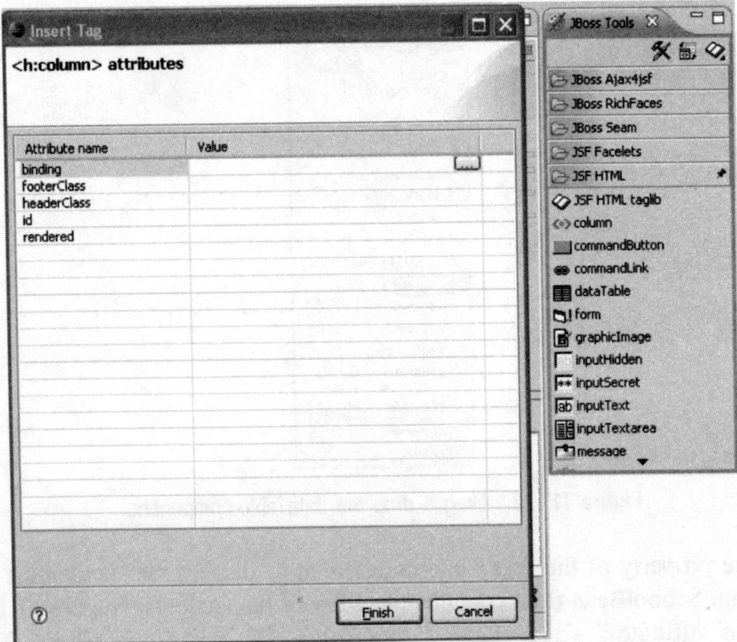

Figure 11.124 Setting the column attributes.

The overall code of the index.jsp file may appear as follows:

```
<%@ taglib uri="http://java.sun.com/jsf/html" prefix="h" %>
<%@ taglib uri="http://java.sun.com/jsf/core" prefix="f" %>
<%@ taglib uri="http://richfaces.org/a4j" prefix="a4j" %>
<%@ taglib uri="http://richfaces.org/rich" prefix="rich" %>
<html>
    <head>
        <title></title>
    </head>
    <body>
            <f:view>
            <h:form>
            <h:outputText value="Details of the
Clients are " />
            <rich:dataTable
value="#{SchoolBean.studentlist}" var="student">
                <h:column>
                    <h:outputText
value="#{student.roll}"/>
                </h:column>
                <h:column>
                    <h:outputText
```

```
value="#{student.name}"/>
                </h:column>
                <h:column>
                    <h:outputText
value="#{student.marks}"/>
                </h:column>
            </rich:dataTable>
        </h:form>
    </f:view>
        </body>
</html>
```

Now, if we run the application, the output appears to be organized as shown in Figure 11.125.

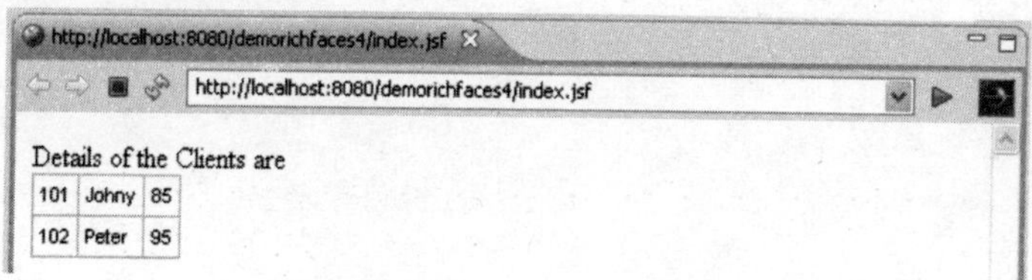

Figure 11.125   Output displayed.

REVIEW QUESTIONS

11.1 Write an application that will ask the user to enter his name and password. If the password entered is "God" then greet the user with a welcome message else display that he is an unauthorized person.

11.2 Write an application that displays different flavours of the ice creams along with their prices in a tabular form.

Index